D1593008

The Stirling Bomber

The silhouette of a Stirling bomber

THE
STIRLING
BOMBER

Michael J. F. Bowyer

FABER AND FABER
London · Boston

First published in 1980
by Faber and Faber Limited
3 Queen Square London WC1N 3AU
Printed in Great Britain by
BAS Printers Limited
Over Wallop, Hants
All rights reserved

© *Michael J. F. Bowyer 1980*

British Library Cataloguing in Publication Data

Bowyer, Michael J F
The Stirling bomber.
1. World War, 1939–1945—Aerial operations,
British   2. Stirling (Bomber)
I. Title
940.54′49′41   D786

ISBN 0-571-11101-7

Contents

	List of Illustrations	*page*	9
	Abbreviations and Terms		11
	Preface		15
	Prologue: Just Remembering		19
1	A Project Defined		21
2	Tribulations and Trials		30
3	Into Service		37
4	Let Battle Commence		48
5	Daylight Interlude		63
6	Increasing Momentum		67
7	A Super Stirling		82
8	The 1942 Offensive		87
9	Enter the Mk. III		109
10	The 1943 Offensive and Finale		117
11	Escape from Denmark		141
12	A New Role		147
13	Preparing for the Invasion		150
14	Adventure over Arnhem		159
15	The Last Rounds		169
16	Passengers and Freight		179
	Key to Camouflage Colours		184

Appendices

1	Stirling Airframe Serial Numbers, Associated Mark Numbers and Engine Marks	185
2	Summary of Stirling Squadrons	188
3	Summary of Stirling Training and Miscellaneous Units	191
4	Serial Numbers of Stirlings Allocated to Squadrons	194
5	Long Service and Outstanding Stirlings	216
6	Sorties Flown by Stirling Squadrons of 3 Group, 1941–4	218
	Index	221

Illustrations

Plates

A silhouette of a Stirling bomber   *frontispiece*

1	The half-scale Stirling (Short's)	page	28
2	Mk. V prototype on a test flight (Short's)		29
3	L7605, the second prototype		31
4	N3638 at Belfast (Short's)		35
5	The first Belfast-built Stirling (Short's)		42
6	N3637 of 7 Squadron (J. Buchan)		45
7	Stirling production line January 1941 (Short's)		46
8	Cockpit layout of early aircraft (Short's)		54
9	Bomb aimer's compartment (Short's)		55
10	Looking aft along the fuselage (Short's)		55
11	Stirling N3568 after crashing in Holland (via G. J. Zwanenburg)		60
12	Stirling R9147 at Waterbeach		71
13	R9295 of 149 Squadron (via T. Cushing)		71
14	Bombing-up 'D-Dog' at Oakington (RCAF)		73
15	'H-Harry' of XV Squadron by St. Paul's Cathedral (via N. J. Roberson)		73
16	Stirling R9304 in flight (IWM)		77
17	Flying Officer P. J. S. Boggis at the helm of 'MacRobert's Reply' (P. J. S. Boggis)		79
18	'MacRobert's Reply' after colliding with a Spitfire (M. Schoeman)		79
19	N3709 at Oakington (IWM/Planet News)		81
20	Stirling low over the factory airfield (via C. Gilks)		91
21	Not all homecomings were good (J. Helme)		95
22	The rough side of 'P-Peter' (F. Griggs)		96
23	Sergeant Griggs and crew examine the damage to N3751 (P. O'Hara)		97
24	Stirling III in factory finish (S. Phillips)		98
25	N3752 of 149 Squadron after crashing in Denmark (J. Helme)		101
26	The sortie record holder, N3721 (O. A. Morris)		103
27	N3711, a Mk. II trials aircraft (IWM)		111
28	Stirling III BK649		111
29	Stirling III BF509 on a maker's test flight (Short's)		116
30	Mines being loaded aboard a Stirling of 218 Squadron (O. A. Morris)		119
31	The mines arrive for a Stirling of 199 Squadron (J. L. Smith)		119
32	W7463 of 1657 Conversion Unit in flight		123
33	The Austin production line in 1943 (British Leyland)		123
34	No. 199 Squadron on parade for the Duke of Gloucester (D. Lockett)		125
35	NAAFI-break (J. L. Smith)		125
36	Trainee crew beneath a towering bomber (A. Hotchkiss)		131
37	The last Stirling to be delivered from Austin Motors (S. O. Woodward)		139
38	Chris Hanson and Donald V. Smith gaze across to Sweden (J. Helme)		146
39	Stirling IV EF503		150
40	A Stirling tows off a Horsa glider (IWM)		157

41   A Stirling IV of 299 Squadron (D. H. Hardwick)   *page* 157
42   A Stirling after crashing during the Arnhem operation (J. Visser)   167
43   'B-Beer' of 199 Squadron with *Mandrel* equipment (J. L. Smith)   173
44   'Kismet III', a Stirling of 295 Squadron (E. A. Woodger)   173
45   A Stirling of 196 Squadron at Shepherd's Grove (J. Graf)   176
46   Stirlings of 620 Squadron, in flight   178
47   Ground and aircrew members of 1588 Flight (J. Graf)   183

Diagrams

 1   Undercarriage assembly on Stirling   33
 2   Performance, Mk. I N3635 (Hercules II)   43
 3   Monthly accidents involving Stirlings   49
 4   Accidents to Stirling bombers attributable to undercarriage trouble during
       landings and take-offs   49
 5   Monthly losses on operations, Mks. I, III, IV   50
 6   Stirling Mk. I N3636   51
 7   Stirling Mk. I N3642   51
 8   Stirling Mk. I N3656   51
 9   Bases used by Stirlings in the United Kingdom   53
10   Maximum speeds, Mk. I, with and without turrets   61
11   Performance, Mk. I (Hercules XI), no dorsal turret   61
12   Speeds, first production Mk. I, with dorsal turret   62
13   Stirling Mk. I W7451   72
14   Short S.36 bomber to specification B.8/41, general arrangement   85
15   Standard camouflage pattern applied to Stirling Mks. I, III, IV   99
16   Stirling Mk. I R9250   105
17   Climb performance, Mk. III prototype   111
18   Climb performance, Mk. III second aircraft   113
19   Maximum level speeds, Mk. III   113
20   Performance, Mk. III production aircraft   114
21   Monthly production deliveries, Mk. I   114
22   Stirling Mk. III BK693   126
23   Stirling Mk. III LJ522   138
24   Monthly production deliveries, Mk. III   140
25   Performance, Mk. IV production aircraft   151
26   Performance, Mk. IV production aircraft, nose and tail turrets removed   151
27   Monthly production deliveries, Mks. IV and V   152
28   Stirling Mk. IV LJ949   156
29   Stirling Mk. III LJ543   172
30   Stirling Mk. IV PW443   177
31   Stirling Mk. V PJ989   182
32   Stirling Mk. V PJ996   183

Abbreviations and Terms

A.A.	anti-aircraft
A.&A.E.E.	Aeroplane & Armament Experimental Establishment
A.C.A.S.(T)	Assistant Chief of the Air Staff (Training)
A.F.D.U.	Air Fighting Development Unit
A.F.E.E.	Airborne Forces Experimental Establishment
A.G.L.T.	automatic gun-laying turret
a.m.p.g.	air miles per gallon
A.O.C.	Air Officer Commanding
A.P.	armour piercing (bomb)
A.S.	anti-submarine (bomb)
A.S.R.	air-sea rescue
B.bomb	anti-shipping bomb
B.D.U.	Bomber/Bombing Development Unit
Bf	Messerschmitt type number prefix
Boozer	radar fighting warning equipment
C.A.S.	Chief of the Air Staff
c.g.	centre of gravity
Circus	fighter escorted and covered daylight raid
C.R.D.	Chief of Research and Development
C.U.	Conversion Unit
D.D.O.R.	Deputy Director Operational Requirements
D/F	direction finding
D.G.R.D.	Director General Research and Development
Do	Dornier type number prefix
D.R.	dead reckoning (navigation)
D.Z.	dropping zone
'E' (category)	write-off
E.T.A.	estimated time of arrival
Flg. Off.	Flying Officer
Flt.Lt./Sgt.	Flight Lieutenant/Sergeant.
F.N.	Frazer-Nash (turret) type number prefix
F.S.	full supercharger
G.C.A.	ground controlled approach
Gee, Gee-H	radio, radar navigational aids
Grp. Capt.	Group Captain
G.P.	general purpose (bomb)
H.C.	high capacity (bomb)
H.C.U.	Heavy Conversion Unit
H2S	radar navigational aid
I.A.S.	indicated airspeed
I.E.	initial equipment (of squadron)

I.R.	immediate reserve (of squadron)
JG	Jagdgeschwader (fighter Gruppen)
Ju	Junkers type number prefix
L.C.	light case (bomb)
L.F.S.	Lancaster Finishing School
L.Z.	landing zone
Mae West	life jacket
Mandrel	diversionary sortie using jammer to confuse enemy radar
M.C.	medium capacity (bomb)
Me	Messerschmitt (but correct type number prefix is Bf)
MG	German machine gun
MGFF	German cannon
M.S.	maximum supercharger
M.U.	Maintenance Unit
NJG	Nachtjagdgeschwader (night fighter Gruppen)
Noball	attack on a flying bomb (V-1) site
Oboe	radio navigational aid
O.T.U.	Operational Training Unit
P.F.F.	Pathfinder Force
Plt. Off.	Pilot Officer
R.A.E.	Royal Aircraft Establishment (Farnborough)
Ramrod	fighter escorted bombing operation against specific target
R.A.S.C.	Royal Army Service Corps
R.D.X.	type of explosive
Rebecca	radio navigational aid
R/T	radio telephony
R.T.O.	Resident Technical Officer
S.A.P.	semi-armour piercing (bomb)
S.A.S.	Special Air Service
satellite	airfield close to main base, used for dispersal
S.B.C.	small bomb container (for incendiaries)
S.C.I.	smoke curtain installation
Shaker	Main Force attack incorporating O.T.U. aircraft
S.O.E.	Special Operations Executive
Sqn. Ldr.	Squadron Leader
T.A.S.	true airspeed
Tinsel	radar jamming device
T.R.E.	Telecommunications Research Establishment
Trinity	radar navigational aid
U.M.T.	transport route identity prefix
V.C.A.S.	Vice-Chief of the Air Staff
Wg. Cdr.	Wing Commander
Window	metal foil dropped to give false image on enemy radar
W.O.	Warrant Officer
W/T	wireless telegraphy
'X'	with explosive charge (incendiary bomb)

Preface

There can surely be no question but that the Stirling was the most imposing-looking bomber of the Second World War. To stand by one of its giant wheels, peer down from that high cockpit, ride in the tail turret and feel the whole machine flexing—or simply gaze as a Stirling lifted its tail and somehow swung into the air—all this is unforgettable. Surprising it is that relatively little has been written about the Stirling, the most majestic of Britain's wartime bombers.

That it retains great affection from so many who flew, built or serviced the aircraft has been very apparent to me during the compilation of this tribute to a mighty aeroplane, one from a manufacturer whose hallmark was quality.

My affection for the Stirling commenced one grey day in late 1940 when I first gazed, enthralled, upon what then seemed a huge aeroplane. Thus, it has taken me nearly 40 years to get the Stirling story out of my diaries and into book form.

But this is of course more than a personal reminiscence. When I first appealed for assistance with such a book I had no idea of the likely response. In short, it has been quite overwhelming.

I began my research into official records long before many of these were placed in the Public Record Office where now many of the files charting the aeroplane's development may be read within the Air 2 and Avia 15 classes. The squadron records have long since left the Ministry of Defence, and appear in the Air 27 class. The Group and Command records, too, are now open for inspection. But most of my research was done at the Air Historical Branch where Mr. E. Haslam, Head of the Branch for many years, has afforded me much encouragement and shown great kindness. No mention of AHB would be complete without thanking Eric Turner who, on so many days, was ever ready to aid me and bring along treasured documents. I extend my thanks for being able to use, and quote from, Crown Copyright material. My thanks, also, to Mr. B. Hallowell for helping to trace wartime aircrew.

The response from one-time builders of the Stirling has been enormous. Requests through the Rochester Branch of the Royal Aeronautical Society, who persuaded the *Rochester Evening Post* to print and 'Radio Medway' to broadcast appeals, resulted in an astonishing response, and clearly those who worked for Short's in the grand old days remember the firm and its products with tremendous affection. Short's of Belfast have helped and provided some splendid photographs for which I thank Jim White.

Several local newspapers kindly carried appeals for help, among them the

Cambridge Evening News, Wiltshire Times and the *Glasgow Herald.* The Royal Aeronautical Society printed an appeal in their newspaper and the Royal Air Force Association also helped through *Air Mail*, which led me to many useful contacts.

A host of photographs was sent along, from which I have selected those which are most likely to have general appeal and are, at the same time, suitable for reproduction.

Many were very ready to recount their memories of Stirlings in action. Surprisingly, this was perhaps more true of those who served with 38 Group in the days when the going was very bad.

I was pleased indeed to have the help of Mr. J. H. Lower one-time manager at Belfast, John Bull who flew on the first Stirling flight and of course Hugh Gordon so closely associated with the aircraft over a very long period. That outstanding pilot Geoffrey Tyson sent along some comments on Stirling handling.

From the Royal Air Force side there was help from some of the commanders of Stirling Squadrons, including Group Captain Paul Harris who commanded 7 Squadron when they first equipped. Group Captain O. A. Morris donated some very fine photographs, among them shots of the most successful of all Stirlings, one that he had flown. Group Captain J. Giles of 90 Squadron recalled tactics for mining sorties.

Workers from the Sebro repair organisation had stories in abundance of its early period, not, I fear, all suitable for printing!

Of famous incidents in the Stirling's career there were again many accounts. Tim Prosser recalled the night when he was in the crew headed by Frank Griggs and with Pat O'Hara, which destroyed three enemy night fighters. Mr. I. J. Edwards related the story of the night when a Stirling crashed in Essex with grievous results, ending a sortie calling for great courage.

Over 300 photographs were submitted for use, and with about 400 to choose from the task was extremely difficult. To everyone who sent along photographs I am very grateful. If on reading this book you have within your albums any Stirling photographs I would be most pleased to see them. It seems a good idea to gather as many as possible for a museum library.

The drawings, maps and graphs are the work of Alf Alderson whose skill, doubtless, stems from his long line of artistic forebears. I am, as always, grateful for his help and delightful company.

Keith Braybrooke very kindly read the manuscript at various stages offering very helpful advice, both then and at the proof reading stage.

From Jørgen Helme I received the account of Donald Smith's escape and later the permission to use that story. My thanks go to them both, and my admiration to Chris Hanson, the Danish Resistance leader who, so bravely, masterminded Donald Smith's escape.

Gerrit Zwanenburg provided much useful information about Stirlings lost during operations, and from Lt. Col. Arie de Jong, RNethAF, came an account of the first Stirling raid. He is in a good position to recall it for he was at the receiving end.

With this welter of assistance and adding my own records it would have been possible to produce a book of vast proportions—and fearsome cost. What I have endeavoured to compile is a factual account punctuated by personal reminiscences covering a wide field.

In closing this preface I would like to thank the following who were ready to volunteer so much useful material, for which I am very grateful. I have tried to draw something from every willing contributor and take this opportunity of thanking sincerely the many who have taken the trouble to contact me. Thus, my gratitude to:

Frances J. L'Anson, Jim Baldwin, C. D. Barnes, C. R. Barrass, T. Bate, P. Bates, P. D. Beldersen AFC, G. Bladon, Sqn. Ldr. P. J. S. Boggis DFC often pilot of the famous 'MacRobert's Reply' and who helped with the story of that aircraft, E. N. Bolton, J. T. Breeze, P. C. Burbridge, P. Burke, A. A. Busby, R. Cassingham, E. F. Chandler, G. H. Chesterton, J. Chinchen, J. Chinery, J. B. Church, D. R. Clarke, P. M. Corbell, R. W. Cox, B. Craven, T. Cushing, H. A. Davenhall, C. H. Dorrington, I. A. Downie, S. Edwards, A. Fuller, Miss W. Few, P. A. Gilchrist, C. Gilks, J. Graf, D. Green, J. E. Greenfield, Grp. Capt. F. Griggs, S. E. Groves, J. J. Halley, R. A. Hammersley DFM, Michael Hardwick, P. Harris, D. H. Harwick, C. J. Hobson, E. W. Hobson, F. N. Hodson, A. A. Holland, A. Hotchkiss, A. B. R. Hudson C.Eng., MRAeS, W. Jepson, D. Kitchingham, J. H. Llewellyn, D. A. Lockett, D. C. Marks, R. May, J. Miller-Steel, R. C. Monteith, Arthur Moore, K. W. Morgan, R. W. Mortimer, D. Murray-Peden, Q.C., A. P. O'Hara, P. Pannichelli, G. Parry, J. Payne, S. Phillips, B. Philpott, P. J. Rowland, M. Schoeman, L. H. D. Scott, Grp. Capt. B. D. Sellick, Bill Slater, R. A. Sloan AFC, J. L. Smith, W. N. Sonnfinstein, S. A. Spray, Grp. Capt. C. S. G. Stanbury, D. B. Stephen, R. A. Strachan, E. S. Summers, I. Thuring, H. Todd, E. Turrell, Mrs. Phyllis Walliker, A. E. Watson, W. P. Watson, G. Webb, T. White, Florence Willsher, N. E. Winch, E. A. Woodger and S. Woodward.

Contemporary ranks and any known decorations are included where RAF personnel are concerned.

Cambridge   MICHAEL J. F. BOWYER
May, 1978

In foreign field she lay,
Soggy; shattered when she passed that way.
Mud encrusted, fragmented far—to some a mere unpleasant scar.
A fractured wing, a sorry shoe,
Among the reeds of polder new
With heavy power plants silent now since one night long ago
When fighter foe had closed in fast
To bring the Stirling down at last.
Soaring larks survey that spot
Where, October night over Zuyder Zee
Seven Stirling men fell—for you and me.

Just Remembering

I forced my path into the polder. Nijkerk church became lost to view as I strode over land once a mile from the Ijsselmeer shore. Bob Elliot's lofty form was useful; he could gaze above the rushes covering the reclaimed land.

'It's over there, Mike', came Gerry Zwanenburg's deep Dutch tones. 'Recognise it?' There was no mistaking the shapely wing embedded in the mud. 'No', Gerry said, 'I'm afraid the wing is too battered to be worth keeping. The navigation lamp holder is well preserved. Take it and treasure it.'

Oval panels over the fuel tanks made certain the identity of the machine. Ever strong—its strength its failing—what torture had it known? A propeller blade marked the buried location of a Hercules engine whose maker's plate confirmed that it was BF523 that it had taken on its final journey.

I tried to restrain a tear as footwear was retrieved. Dutch War Graves Commission officials sifted the site of the rear turret framing. Further away lay an empty small bomb container, indicating that the bomber was homeward bound when the fighter attacked.

We knew the entire crew were treasured in memory. Three had been buried in Nijkerk during 1943; now we wished to find a hallowed place for the others.

Sifting the mud, I came across a bright flash. Genuine Delftware and ancient— fallen, maybe, from the hand of a Volendamer. Moments later a huge bone was retrieved. 'Of course it's not a man's, Mike! That's from a cow.' Strange place to find a cow.

My, it was cold! And although the sun beamed down, this would surely be a cold spot for any caring soul.

Group Captain Martin Chandler, British Air Attaché, joined us, together with a television team whose previous assignment had been a Shakespearian production. What would he have made of this tragedy?

The recovery team handed me the 'Mickey Mouse' bombing computer, then I wandered back alone to the Mess hut with memories of Stirling days. So many times, as an impressionable teenager, I had thrilled to the sight of those mighty machines; and the journey home brought another incursion into nostalgia as Air Anglia's Dakota muttered its way over a sunlit sea on a magnificent evening. There was no brandy for those who made similar but much more action-packed night journeys in Stirlings.

Brief passage through Horsham St. Faith followed. A customs official regarded me with total disinterest as I impressed upon him that I really *was* importing a bomb release mechanism—exported and now imported without a licence.

Soon we were in an Aztec heading for Marshall's, passing Lakenheath and Mildenhall from where many Stirlings travelled. South lay Ridgewell where, at 30 minutes past midnight on 13 May 1943, BF523, in 90 Squadron's hands, set forth for Duisburg on its final flight.

Cambridge Airport was lit, but there was still light enough to glimpse distantly Waterbeach, as well as Oakington, the premier home of the Stirling.

We bumped back to reality as the Aztec taxied in. John Stephens, Controller at Cambridge, called to me: 'Did you see it, was it a Stirling?'

Indeed it was, probably the last I shall ever see. Although it is no longer possible to marvel at that huge, impressive form, nothing can erase thrilling memories of those grand aerial battleships drifting, nay swinging overhead as only a Stirling could.

Chapter 1

A Project Defined

'The Air Staff require a heavy bomber for world-wide use, an aircraft exploiting alternatives between long range and very heavy bomb load made possible by employing catapult launching in overloaded condition. The aircraft must possess high performance but at the same time have strong defence in all planes.

'An aircraft fulfilling these requirements will probably be large, but it should not exceed a span of 100 ft. In order to maintain maximum reliability during, and immediately after catapulting, and also to be able to retain height with one engine out of action, the aircraft should be four engined. Since it will be required to operate from bases anywhere in the world, the aircraft must possess facilities for maintenance in the open.'

Thus ran the preamble to Specification B.12/36 from which the Stirling stemmed. The requirements continued in detail: 'The speed at 15,000 ft. at maximum cruise revs. must not be less than 230 m.p.h., range 1,500 miles at 15,000 ft., after a take-off run of 500 yd. carrying normal loading including 2,000 lb. of bombs. In overload condition range, after a 700 yd. take-off, must not be less than 2,000 miles at 15,000 ft. at maximum cruise revs., with not less than 4,000 lb. of bombs. It is hoped that a range of at least 2,000 miles will be obtained when carrying the maximum possible bomb load—i.e. 14,000 lb. Overload range, after accelerated take-off and at 15,000 ft., must not be less than 3,000 miles with not less than 8,000 lb. of bombs.'

Such performance in the mid-1930s would be outstanding. Short's must have wondered if it could be achieved. Nevertheless they opted for a land based version of their magnificent Sunderland flying boat.

'Rate of climb is secondary.' (This was later amended to read 20,000 ft. in 25 minutes.) 'Service ceiling should not be less than 28,000 ft. carrying normal load with 2,000 lb. of bombs. The aircraft must be able to fly level at 10,000 ft. on any three engines with any loading.'

Such a ceiling was difficult to achieve using existing engines. Power plants must be new, untried. Power loading and wing loading would be important, for the aircraft must use a standard sized field and clear 50 ft. in 500 yd. when fully loaded. Landing run with full normal load must be 500 yd. Difficult figures to meet; some said impossible.

Crew would number six: two pilots (one acting as navigator), observer/front gunner/bomb aimer, relief radio operator, two air gunners (one amidships to monitor engine instruments, one a radio operator). A twin-gun front turret would cover the area wing tip to wing tip. A retractable belly turret might be remotely controlled. In the tail must be a four-gun turret, and access between all crew stations was needed.

A wide variety of bomb loads was specified, including 8×250 lb. G.P./S.A.P./A.S./L.C./B. or smoke curtain installation; or 4×500 lb. G.P./S.A.P./A.S.; or $1 \times 2,000$ lb. A.P. In overload condition with a 700 yd. take-off run the load could be 16×250 lb.; or 8×500 lb.; or $2 \times 2,000$ lb. Heaviest loads on take-off seemed possible only with the aid of catapult launching and totalled 14,000 lb.: 28×500 lb.; or $7 \times 2,000$ lb. Internal horizontal stowage or positioning in vertical tiers was acceptable. No high degree of manoeuvrability was specified, but a good view was needed for formation flying. Among items of equipment would be sunproof head covering at crew stations 'to obviate the need for sun helmets in the tropics'—a quixotic idea easily met.

These demands differed little from the Draft Specification of 28 April 1936 which was finally circulated to manufacturers. Upon reading the draft, Grp. Capt. R. D. Oxland, Operational Requirements Staff, thinking the aircraft unduly large, argued that performance might be met by an aircraft spanning less than 100 ft. Catapult launching could hinder performance, despite offering heavy loaded take-off weight.

Air Commodore A. W. Cunningham wondered if 3,000 mile ferry range was sufficient, pointing out the need for food, sleeping and sanitary arrangements on a 13 hour flight. He asked whether diesel fuel had been considered, pointing out that rate of climb was important to ensure the bomber reached operational height before entering enemy airspace, with as little fuel wastage as possible. He suggested heavier calibre tail guns, but the Air Staff considered four .303 in. guns sufficient. A maximum cruise speed of not less than 230 m.p.h. seemed slow, silencing would be needed to reduce fatigue.

Others were uneasy about vertical bomb stowage. It led to inaccuracy. Incendiary bombs, with which the Stirling later operated successfully, were not considered.

Further comments of 22 May 1936 pointed out that the normal loaded range of 1,500 miles was low for, with diversions, etc., action radius was 600 miles. A strong undercarriage was essential in case the aeroplane had to land in a heavily loaded state, and fuel jettisoning was suggested. Stress was laid upon noise. The Battle's Merlin engine was as noisy as nine Bulldogs. Four engines would produce a cacophony, but silencing would mean extra weight.

On 18 May 1936 the specification draft circulated at the Air Ministry, preceding the Operational Requirements conference held on 27 May. Chaired by Air Vice-Marshal C. L. Courtenay, C.B.E., D.S.O., Deputy Chief of the Air Staff, the Committee comprised Air Vice-Marshal W. R. Freeman, C.B., D.S.O., M.C., Air Commodore A. D. Cunningham, Air Commodore S. J. Goble, Air Commodore R. H. Vernay, Air Commodore A. T. Harris (later Sir Arthur), Group Captain R. D. Oxland, Wing Commander A. W. Milne, Wing Commander B. Mcentegart, Squadron Leader O. R. Gayford, Squadron Leader N. H. Bilney and Captain R. Liptrot, with Mr. W. F. Jacks as Secretary.

Air Vice-Marshal Courtenay opened the proceedings, asking whether there was need for an aircraft of the size visualised, for the Vickers B.1/35 (Warwick) had a span of 97 ft. and the new Handley-Page bomber a span of 96 ft., and their all-up weights were 25,000 lb. and 29,000 lb. respectively. One large bomber, though, was worth two smaller ones.

Group Captain Oxland, Deputy Director Operational Requirements, said the aircraft they had in mind would not be much larger than the 1/35. Normal all-up weight would be 31,200 lb.; 36,000 lb. overloaded for a 700 yd. take-off; 46,000 lb. when catapult launched. Engines would be Rolls-Royce Goshawks. Deputy Director Plans wondered whether a smaller aircraft would suffice: two small ones would be cheaper than one large one. The medium bomber envisaged had a 3,000 mile range but half the bomb load.

A point influencing the opinion of the Chairman was B.12/36's ability to carry 2,000 lb. bombs. The large number of P.13/36s would be supplemented by a number of heavy bombers. Cunningham felt that the operation of a 50,000 lb. bomber would be difficult in bad weather. Gayford considered that there should be metalled runways in addition to catapults. It would take three minutes for one catapult launch, and a long time to launch a dozen bombers. The 3,000 mile range was questioned, but it was pointed out that it was needed in case Russia became aggressive, and for overseas reinforcement.

Maintenance was discussed. One large aircraft seemed more economical than two medium ones. Yet it was possible to maintain a heavier scale of attack with the latter. Heavies would spend longer over enemy territory with more risk of interception. Cunningham suggested speed a better safeguard than defensive armament, thereby promoting the idea of the Mosquito and Vulcan. It was quickly pointed out that politicians gauged the strength of the Air Force by numbers—better to have a large number of heavies!

The morning's deliberations had little effect upon the Draft. When Milne suggested a higher speed, Captain Liptrot said that what was asked for was the best they were likely to get. Bombs of heavier weight than 500 lb. would be used against ships, special fortifications and magazines.

Liptrot estimated the overload service ceiling would be about 25,000 ft., and the landing run, using flaps, about 250 yd. at 60 m.p.h.

Remotely controlled armament was appealing. It was asked whether this could be fitted in the rear of any nacelles. But it meant that both turrets could not be brought to bear on any one target, and none under the tail. A ventral station was then approved.

The Chairman felt there was no need for a dinghy, but the pilots' seats would need armour, and soundproofing was essential, likewise a toilet.

Thus, with few amendments, the specification was sent out for tenders on 9 July 1936, to Messrs. Fairey, Westland, Hawker, Bristol, Armstrong-Whitworth, Rolls-Royce, Napier, Saro, Short, de Havilland, Blackburn, Avro, Bristol, Supermarine, Gloster, Armstrong-Siddeley, Vickers, Handley-Page and Boulton Paul.

Slight amendments to the specification followed. It could have radial or in-line engines; the track must be wide enough to prevent overturning when manoeuvring; tyre pressure must not exceed 35 p.s.i., since the machine must be able to operate from grass surfaces. The tailwheel could be retractable.

Tenders from Bristol, Armstrong-Whitworth, Short, Vickers and Supermarine were sifted late in 1936. Although the Bristol design looked reasonable, it was dropped, leaving only the Supermarine and Short designs to go ahead. They differed radically.

Supermarine's was graceful. Its fuselage cross section was too small to allow a man to stand, and maximum bomb load was less than called for. Two prototypes were ordered because of good performance. One would have Rolls-Royce Merlins, the other Bristol Hercules. Both were destroyed by bombing in 1940, by which time they had fallen behind the preferred design.

Short's worked along the lines of a landplane Sunderland. To speed the project, a span of 112 ft. was chosen. The company were relying on years of experience with large aircraft, few of them landplanes.

The Air Ministry's wingspan limitation was based partly upon hangar size, but there was more to the restriction than just that. They feared that B.12/36 might become very large and unwieldy, and require long runs. Acquiring land for new airfields was meeting opposition, and it was deemed unwise to opt for very large aircraft. Accelerated take-off also imposed weight limitations. Therefore they turned down Short's first scheme, and B.12/36 had to conform to the 100 ft. span.

Revision of the mainplanes drastically altered calculations, increased power loading and resulted in an aeroplane with increased rate of roll but longer take-off run—and that the Ministry wanted reduced. A fuselage that was long in comparison with the wings would bring trouble when taking off and landing in crosswinds.

The Short B.12/36 construction was strong, upon semi-monocoque lines. The constant section fuselage consisted of stringers passing through three main component joints, and was flush riveted. Four fuselage main sections were joined by bolts passing through, and frames reinforced internally by extrusions riveted across joints.

Wing construction was similar to the Sunderland's and had lattice braced ribs, adopted instead of tie rod torsion box bracing in the upper truss. This continued through the fuselage, with close tolerance bolted joints at root ends. Wing tips were detachable. For repair purposes, spar booms outboard of outer nacelles were later jointed. Outboard of this, a watertight wing afforded buoyancy on ditching.

Lower section spar booms fitted level with the fuselage decking, which was supported by two deep longitudinal girders to form three 42 ft. long bomb cells. Six long doors in three sections hung from the girders. Fuselage narrowness resulted in cells only 19 in. wide. These could never accommodate weapons of greater girth, as a result of fitting the strengthening girders.

Pilots sat side by side above the forward end of the bomb cells. Navigator's, radio operator's and engineer's stations were close by. Suspended above the bomb aimer's position was the nose gunner. Autopilot steering controls were fitted below him, and oxygen bottles above the spar in the fuselage. Flares and launch tubes were aft of the bomb cells, and a ventral Frazer-Nash F.N. 24 turret was chosen.

Four large fuel tanks in each wing were marked by external oval shaped access panels. Two more tanks fitted between spars and flap shrouds. Another in the wing leading edge was intended for ferry purposes. The others were later to be covered by rubber and soft latex, preventing fuel leakages caused by enemy fire.

The extremely strong airframe added to the structure weight, but meant that the bomber could absorb great punishment and survive. Short's designed the aircraft to the specification, stressing it accordingly.

Fuselage mock-ups of both selected designs were built by late 1937, by which time performance outlines for the Short B.12/36 were available, as follows:

Weight loaded lb.	Max. speed 15,000 ft. m.p.h.	Cruise speed m.p.h.	Wing area sq. ft.	Take-off run yd.	Landing run half fuel, no bombs. yd.
41,600	323	275	1,300	473	494
43,120	327	285	1,300	440	600
44,745	327	285	1,300	450	640
45,300	327	285	1,420	430	600
45,600	323	282	1,480	350	500
48,500	311	273	1,850	350	500

The length of the likely take-off and landing runs worried the Air Staff. In March 1938 they decided that the wing area of B.12/36 should not exceed 1,320 sq. ft., offering a landing run of 600 yd., and prescribed a maximum take-off weight of 45,700 lb.

By May 1938 Supermarine's design, with an all-up weight of 44,500 lb., was forecast to have a landing run of 740 yd. This increase arose partly because the intended Rolls-Royce KV 26 engines were to be replaced by more powerful, heavier ones. Reassessment of wing area led to an increase to 2,145 sq. ft. in the Short design, further increasing the structure weight. Long landing and take-off runs seemed unavoidable.

Accelerated take-off was now discarded. Tactical inflexibility, and the risk of enemy attack, were against it. Rocket assisted take-off trials were later conducted at Boscombe Down, but unsuccessfully. Rockets were carried beneath the mainplanes, and one fired spontaneously, igniting the rudder.

On 13 May 1938 Mr. Lipscombe, Short's Chief Designer, asked for another increase in take-off weight, to 60,000 lb. Without assisted take-off the undercarriage needed strengthening and tyre pressures had to be increased. Because of the increased weight, new figures were prepared for both B.12/36 designs (Table A).

The problem of landing run was far from solved, the Supermarine aircraft's ever lengthening. Further comparison of the designs was made in August 1938 (Table B). The Supermarine design now had the edge over the Short bomber, but both designs continued.

Short's considered the take-off run to be longer than was necessary. Sliding Gouge flaps could be increased in area by a second flap aft to take care of the trouble. Nevertheless they decided to test the matter by building a half-scale

Table A

Short (4 Bristol Hercules Mk. I SM)

Weight loaded lb.	Max. speed 15,000 ft. 2,000 lb. load, m.p.h.	Cruise speed 1,500 miles m.p.h.	Take-off run yd.	Landing speed m.p.h.
43,120	327	285	440	78
48,570	327	284	605	78
59,090	327	282	—	—

Supermarine (4 Merlin)

42,640	329	284	475	85
47,910	329	282	650	84
58,380	329	279	—	84

Table B

	Weight loaded lb	Range miles	Cruise speed m.p.h.
Short			
2,000	50,336	1,500	263
4,000	56,120	2,020	259
8,000	69,600	2,830	254
14,000	66,400	3,000	254
Optimum (take-off run 1,000 yd.)			
9,000	61,300	2,000	256
Supermarine			
2,000	44,790	1,500	273
4,000	50,200	2,000	270
8,000	60,300	3,000	265
13,500	58,000	2,000	266
Optimum (take-off run 1,000 yd.)			
11,500	58,000	2,000	266

	Short	Supermarine
Take-off over 50 ft. screen, yd.:	790	680
Landing over 50 ft. screen, yd.:	650	690
Max. speed at 15,000 ft., m.p.h.:	305	317
Tare weight, lb.:	34,920	29,500

plywood aerodynamic replica of the bomber. Included would be a half-scale undercarriage. Four 90 h.p. Pobjoy Niagaras would drive two bladed propellers. It was given the number S.31, but known as 'M4'. The silver monoplane was first flown by John Lankester Parker and Hugh Gordon from Rochester on 19 September 1938.

After 10 half-hour flights 'M4' flew to and from Martlesham on 21 October. It brought back bad tidings. Martlesham's pilots were impressed by handling and manoeuvrability, but considered take-off and landing too lengthy. Fearing worse with the full-sized aircraft, they made the radical suggestion that wing incidence be increased by 3°. It had been set at $3\frac{1}{2}°$ to decrease drag.

Tooling and prototype planning was advanced, and no such major change was possible. Instead, Short's produced the only possible solution: they added 3° to the ground angle by lengthening the undercarriage, thus introducing the notorious gear which later became so troublesome. The undercarriage legs were already lengthy to allow for loading and to cope with any extension of the belly turret during landing. The shortened wingspan combined with this complex undercarriage, were to cripple the design, but the otherwise long runs would be unacceptable.

The half-scale S.31 was modified, and flew with the new undercarriage on 22 November. Then it was re-engined with more powerful Niagara IVs of 115 h.p., with which it first flew on 10 January 1939. Horn balanced elevators were later fitted.

The specification for the production Short S.29 Stirling 1/P1 was finalised as similar to L7605, the second prototype. Detailed modifications for production aircraft were: more rapidly detachable outer mainplanes; no catapult provisioning; dual controls; Bristol Hercules III engines; armour to be fitted to the pilots' and radio operators' seats, oil tanks and both inboard fuel tanks. The crew would number six, one manning the midships retractable turret; the off-duty radio operator would man the rear turret. Wire cutters would be fitted to wing leading edges to cut barrage balloon cables. Self sealing was to be fitted to the tankage for 1,912 gal. also the 308 gal. leading edge tanks. The alternatives for bomb provisioning would be:

(a) 14,000 lb. S.A.P./B./L.C./G.P. load
(b) 24 × 500 lb. G.P./S.A.P./A.P.
(c) 7 × 2,000 lb.
(d) 3 SCI smoke containers.
There was to be provision for converting bomb racks from 250 lb. or 500 lb. carriers to 2,000 lb. type in a short time.

The contract now called for a take-off run of 600 yd. at normal all-up weight. Ranges were specified as:

1,500 miles at 15,000 ft., two-thirds max. cruise revs., 2,000 lb. load
2,000 miles at 15,000 ft., two-thirds max. cruise revs., 4,000 lb. load
3,000 miles at 15,000 ft., two-thirds max. cruise revs. after 30 mins. at max. power
Maximum range 3,000 miles

Short's original tender quoted a normal load of 4,600 lb. and maximum loaded weight of 56,900 lb. The figures agreed on 5 January 1939 were:

Normal loaded weight:	50,844 lb. for 1,496 miles range
Maximum loaded weights:	56,240 lb. for 2,000 miles range
	66,240 lb. for 2,912 miles range
	67,000 lb. for 2,000 miles range

A 10,000 lb. bomb load was to be carried at 62,470 lb. for 2,000 miles.

Aerodynamic trials with the S.31 ('M4') continued while work was under way on the prototype, L7600. On 14 March 1939, King George VI and Queen Elizabeth toured the Rochester works, seeing the mock-up of a possible Stirling successor, the S.34, to Specification B.1/39. This, the hoped for 'Ideal Bomber', resembled a Stirling with the desirable increased span, and dorsal and ventral turrets carrying 20 mm cannon. Like other B.1/39 designs it was rejected. Their Majesties were shown the Stirling prototype, and then went to Rochester Airport, where Harold Piper flew 'M4'. The little aeroplane flew around in such grand style that the Queen asked for, and was duly given, a repeat performance.

A larger tailplane was soon fitted to 'M4' and it was used to investigate behaviour under abnormal conditions. Weighing 5,700 lb., it had a top speed of 180 m.p.h., and handled like a fighter. In years to come, Hugh Gordon and Bob Gilmour sometimes used it to engage in mock combat with American Thunderbolts.

1.   The half-scale Stirling.

2.   Mk. V prototype on a test flight over the Medway.

Early in the war 'M4' was lent to the R.A.E. for turret tests in their 24 ft. wind tunnel, investigating a midships 20 mm cannon turret. Late in 1941 it became airworthy again for communications duty. By the end of 1942 it was worn out. Its end came at Stradishall. Squadron Leader E. J. Moreton was taking off in bad weather when 'M4' turned over, and was damaged beyond repair.

Design definition was over by 1939. Earlier decisions were to have far-reaching consequences, none more so than the shortening of the wingspan, which was possibly unnecessary. But the bomber was desperately needed, and by 1939 construction was under way.

Chapter 2

Tribulations and Trials

Prototype building commenced late in 1938. By January 1939 alarm was expressed, for the weight had risen by 9,200 lb. The major item was a structure weight increase of 5,700 lb. Barrage cutters and de-icers would add 1,800 lb., extra flaps 300 lb. The likely normal loaded weight would be 53,000 lb. Worry centred on the slender margin between the new loaded and maximum permissible take-off weights.

The Air Ministry estimated a limiting weight of 63,000 lb., needing a 1,000 yd. run to clear 50 ft.—way beyond the specification limit. It could mean a maximum bomb load of 7,000 lb. for 2,000 miles, a mere 1,000 lb. for 3,000 miles—and tyre pressures would be about 43.5 p.s.i.

'In view of the disappointing load carrying capacity to be anticipated from this type', commented N. E. Rowe, 'it may be necessary to review commitments on the Stirling.' Detailed investigation followed, and new figures suggested a range of 1,490 miles at 52,954 lb. take-off weight; 1,980 miles at 58,350 lb. At the maximum loaded weight of 69,100 lb., range would be 1,980 miles. With a 10,000 lb. bomb load, at 64,580 lb., range would also be 1,980 miles.

Such deliberations were unknown to Short's workers, who viewed the aircraft as prestigious. Proud they were, especially of their flying-boats. However, at the factory, Gregg Webb recalls, 'concern was felt about the configuration of the main undercarriage with new type oleo legs'.

One of Short's craftsmen was D. C. Marks. He 'started work as a boy of 14 in 1938 at the seaplane works—still there, but now C.A.V. Ltd. There was a road through the centre, works being divided into "Shops", running to No. 18 during the war, fronting the River Medway for a mile or so. The first Stirling was started in No. 1 Shop.'

On his first day at Short's he reported to red-haired Mr. Shepard. 'In the Shop the fuselage was being assembled. It was the biggest I had ever seen, being put together with a series of large rings of Z-section following the fuselage lines. Each ring had been made by hand in smaller Dural sections. All was riveted together to make one ring, which included in its shape the bomb floor and doors. Work on the "Night Bomber" was to the extent of building the fuselage.

'Early 1939 No. 1 Shop moved to Rochester Airport, where the prototype was completed. Rumour had it that wingspan had been reduced to allow it out of the hangar. Excitement built. Early summer was boiling hot. The completed Stirling was outside on the grass most days. They seemed to be engine running all day.'

3. L7605, the second prototype, at Boscombe Down in 1940.

There had been a major disappointment. Bristol were unable to deliver the Hercules Mk. III, and inferior Mk. Is were fitted. 'Being on piecework', recalls Gregg Webb, 'we could not be absent from work long. I used any excuse to walk by the windows near the drawing office to watch what was happening outside.

'One day excitement mounted as the bomber moved down the field to the other side of the aerodrome. Throttles were opened for what looked like a fast taxi. It never took off; the first flight occurred at the weekend when we were not at work.'

Aboard L7600 for the maiden flight were John Lankester Parker (pilot), Squadron Leader E. J. Moreton (second pilot), George Cotton (foreman of engine installation and flight engineer) and John Bull (flight engineer), who recalls that first flight.

'It took place on Sunday 14 May 1939. The first form 1909 was issued the previous day. The aircraft taxied on that date to check brakes, etc., and a number of fast runs across the airfield were carried out. For some reason a flight was abandoned. It could have been that the wind was unfavourable, as the aerodrome at Rochester was an odd shape and was grass surfaced.

'I don't think any of us had any misgivings about the undercarriage, although it was a strange shape. This, of course, was mainly for convenience of bomb loading. Considerable trouble was experienced with the undercarriage door functioning, and a lash-up with Bungee cord to close the doors when retracted was introduced. I was instructed, prior to the first flight, to see whether the doors closed after retraction, and if not to give a hefty pull on the yards of Bungee running through the fuselage.

'Take-off appeared to be normal and the aircraft flew quite well. But it appeared that as the weight of the machine came on to the undercarriage on landing the back arch gave up the ghost, fractured, and L7600 finished up in a belly flop approximately in the middle of the airfield. I would mention that the back arch was of light alloy extrusion. On the second prototype this was changed to steel tubing.'

The 'concern . . . felt about the configuration of the main undercarriage' by Gregg Webb and the others had been fully justified. It meant delay, going back to the drawing board at a crucial time. Morale at the works had been high following the success of the Empire Boats and Sunderland, though some wise folk were concerned at the narrowness of the Stirling's bomb cells. Few realised how serious would be the reduction in span.

'The unfortunate landing produced a wave of depression, expressed forcibly by the old stagers whose opinions I had come deeply to respect', recalls Gregg Webb. ' "Short's never could make a landplane," they said.' Thereafter main pride rested in design and manufacturing craftsmanship. It took weeks for the firm to recover from this major blow. The first prototype was so badly damaged as to be fit only for scrap, and the whole project was seriously delayed. Some considered that the undercarriage should have been left alone, the long run chanced. There could be no going back now, though: the task was to make the best of the Stirling. The country needed it—and so did Short's.

The undercarriage had to be put right. It was strengthened, and the door mechanism finalised. Every care was taken with the second prototype, L7605, which made its first flight on 3 December 1939, as John Bull records.

'On this occasion the undercarriage was not retracted, deliberately, although it could have been. Apart from that the flight was normal, like the landing. Then the aircraft was grounded, enabling it to be prepared for Boscombe Down. The task had been just to prove the aerodynamics of the machine. I believe horn balanced elevators were on for the first flight, and then replaced by the normal type.

'The next flight took place on 24 December 1939, and was successful. The undercarriage retracted, doors closed satisfactorily. Flight trials continued without any incident.'

A feature of the Stirling was the use of Exactor throttle controls. Short's pilots had plenty of experience of them in the flying-boats. Exactors were to become a source of persistent complaint among RAF pilots, and John Bull recalls this feature.

'In view of the complaints about Exactor throttles when the aircraft was in service, comment seems opportune. I had considerable experience of them. They were fitted in the Empire Boats. It was my job as fitter on those to install, prime and set up throttle mixture controls. Exactors were also my province on the first Stirlings.

'When the second prototype was about ready for A. & A.E.E., John Parker was of the opinion that the four throttles had become too heavy for one-handed operation, so something had to be done about it. All the units, both transmitters and receivers, were removed and the glands eased off to bring the operating load

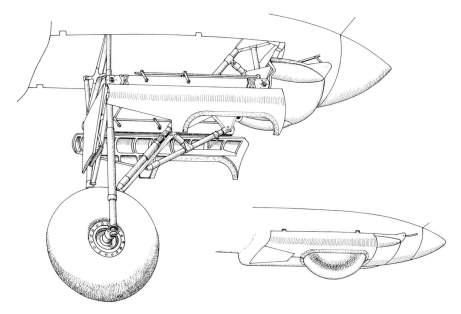

1. Undercarriage assembly on production Stirling Mk. I.

down to an acceptable poundage. When reinstalled in the aircraft it was found, when the engines were running, that the Exactors would not stay in place, but moved to "closed throttle" when the hand was removed. The modification to overcome this consisted of four serrated arcs of metal mounted on the throttle box with spring loaded detents mounted on the throttle levers, so that the throttles would stay in the desired position.

'In service, a further modification was introduced: a hinged top position to the throttle levers which, when pushed or pulled, lifted a spring loaded detent which registered with an adjustable stop for cruising power. This appeared to be the ultimate answer to Exactor controls.'

On 22 April 1940, L7605 was delivered to Boscombe Down for four months' trials, spending a brief time at Ringway for safety in August–September before returning to Short's on 2 September 1940.

Work on the first production aircraft was hastened in early 1940 to recapture lost time. The intended Hercules Mk. III engines were still unavailable, so Mk. IIs had to be fitted. On 7 May Parker flew the first production aircraft, N3635, for 25 minutes. An engine cut at take-off, caused by slow throttle movement, brought concern. Rapid throttle change met with slow response, owing to the lag in the unpressurised liquid column through which movement was translated.

After makers' checks, N3635 flew to A. & A.E.E. for performance trials. N3636 remained at Rochester for makers' flying tests. On 29 May N3637 was flown to C.F.S. Upavon for preparation of pilots' notes. On that occasion Hugh Gordon was second pilot to John Lankester Parker. They landed the machine 'uphill'—there was a pronounced slope at Upavon—but despite this it was realised that Upavon was too small for an aircraft of this size, and it was flown to Boscombe Down the following morning.

Through the summer of 1940, as the Battle of Britain raged, Stirlings were put through their paces at Boscombe Down, their actual performance revealed. It was disquieting. The initial findings were as follows:

Weight during tests: 57,400 lb.
Take-off to unstick: 640 yd.
To clear 50 ft: 1200 yd.
Service ceiling: 15,000 ft.
Speeds:

Height ft.	Max. speed m.p.h.T.A.S.	Time to height min.	Rate of climb ft. per min.
5,000	253	5.6	950
10,000	249.5	12.5	560
15,000	218	27.5	160

Stalling speed 107 m.p.h.I.A.S.
Landing speed 110 m.p.h.I.A.S.
Glide-in speed 120 m.p.h.I.A.S.

All were vital measurements, but for bombing operations, range and cruise performance details were needed. The cruise tests revealed:

Aircraft	Height ft.	Weight lb.	Cruise speed 2400 revs., weak mixture m.p.h.
N3635	10,000	57,400	184
N3636	10,000	48,000	194
N3637	10,000	45,000	195
N3644	10,500	53,000	200

Above 10,000 ft. performance deteriorated. The original specification had called for a cruising speed of 230 m.p.h. at 15,000 ft. for a range of 1,500 miles carrying a 2,000 lb. bomb load. Overload take-off run was to be 700 yd. for a 2,000 mile range at 15,000 ft. with 4,000 lb. load, and 14,000 lb. was to be carried for 2,000 miles. Maximum range was to be 3,000 miles. How far short of these figures the Stirling fell is all too clear.

Some improvement in cruise performance was obtained with compensation for position error, suggesting a cruising speed of 232 m.p.h. at 10,000 ft. at 54,000 lb., the average flying weight after take-off at 57,400 lb. Full throttle maximum engine condition for economical cruise was achieved at a mere 10,000 ft. with the Hercules Mk. II, rated at 1,100/1,150 h.p. at 5,000 ft. with

4. N3638 at Belfast, July 1940. Force landed Turnhouse, 28 November 1940.

$+1\frac{1}{2}$ lb. boost, 1,375 h.p. at 2,750 revs. at 4,000 ft. These figures were close to those of the Hercules H.E.1M fitted to the prototype. Mk. III engines would have a better output at greater height, so hopes rested on engine development.

N3635 was examined in detail, and tested at 3,000 and 10,000 ft. at typical service loading of 57,400 lb. (41,160 lb. tare, 48,000 lb. on landing). The gradual weight rise during design had reduced performance. Take-off weight was restricted to 64,000 lb. This included a tankage of 1,935 gal. from a possible total of 2,293 gal., and a bomb load of only 3,500 lb.

To increase the bomb load, fuel had to be drastically reduced, so that with 1,096 gal. bomb load was 10,000 lb.; and with 584 gal. 14,000 lb. Some 200 gal. of fuel were needed for run-up and climb to 10,000 ft. It was difficult to maintain 15,000 ft., the absolute ceiling being considered as barely 14,000 ft. At 10,000 ft. the range obtainable was barely 5% more, trials with L7605 showing little difference.

Range and speed trials undertaken at Boscombe Down with the aircraft weighing 64,000 lb. at take-off and 62,500 lb. after climb to 10,000 ft. revealed these disturbing figures:

m.p.h. I.A.S.	m.p.h. T.A.S.	Revs.	a.m.p.g.
184	195	2,400	.86
161	171	2,200	1.07 (-3% lb. boost, 160 gal. per hr.)
192	207	2,400	.99 (209 gal. per hr.)

The most economical cruise at 10,000 ft. appeared to be 158 m.p.h.I.A.S./184 m.p.h.T.A.S. at 2,400 revs. using 162 gal. per hr., i.e. 1.34 a.m.p.g. Climb to 10,000 ft. took 27 minutes (145 m.p.h.I.A.S. to 5,000 ft., then 138 m.p.h.I.A.S. to 10,000 ft.), taking about 150 gal. to cover about 70 miles. Range in maximum cruise condition (2,400 revs., $-1\frac{1}{4}$ lb. boost) was 1,740 miles at 187 m.p.h.I.A.S. At 170 m.p.h.I.A.S., range was about 2,020 miles. Absolute range at 60,500 lb. with hot intakes was 2,140 miles, with cold intakes, 2,200 miles.

These depressing figures were being obtained as production came slowly under way. N3638 left Rochester on 8 June 1940 for allocation to Short & Harland, Belfast, who were already starting Stirling production. N3669 went to A. & A.E.E. in June, N3640 to 10 M.U., Hullavington, on 8 July, N3641 to 48 M.U. on 20 July, N3642 to 19 M.U. on 25 July, N3643 to 22 M.U. on 31 July and N3644 to 10 M.U. on 9 August.

By then the first Stirling squadron had been formed. The first 10 production aircraft, with Hercules Mk. IIs, and clearly unsuitable for operational use, were designated Stirling Trainers. N3644 was later re-engined with Hercules Mk. IIIs for XV Squadron. The Trainers had engines in monocoque nacelles, making engine change difficult. (Later nacelles were truncated at firewalls just ahead of the wing leading edges. Tubular steel engine mountings on the Stirling Mk. III were fitted to the firewalls, allowing the entire engine plant to be detachable.)

The inboard nacelles were slung low, to enable the 6 ft. diameter tyres and the complex undercarriage to retract into the nacelle and wing. On the first prototype the undercarriage hinged on the front spar. In subsequent aircraft a crate hung below the spar and swung forward as the wheels retracted backwards into the crate. The advantage of this arrangement was that it hardly altered the c.g. Little of the wheel protruded. Undercarriage retraction, flap operation and retraction of the twin tailwheels (chosen to permit more internal space after retraction) was electrical. The undercarriage motors were later sited in the fuselage to permit manual override if motors failed.

Production came under way as the Beaverbrook Plan for concentration only upon aircraft in service was announced. The Stirling had been delayed because of the tooling need, and time taken to build components. It was 18 October before the first Belfast built machine, N6000, flew. Now Stirlings were in squadron hands, but far from operational.

Chapter 3

Into Service

'We were expecting the aircraft. Engines were heard; they weren't a Whitley's Merlins. We hurried on to the tarmac. In the distance we glimpsed this lovely aircraft doing a circuit before landing—a beautiful sight.

'I remember so well the high cockpit, long fuselage and tall tailfin—and we were absolutely thrilled', recalls Bob May, then with 7 Squadron at Leeming.

'It circled, made a married man's landing, then taxied slowly to the hangar. We viewed it eyes goggling with amazement. It had looked impressive flying, but when it taxied to that hangar we were amazed to see that undercarriage—gaunt, like a lot of scaffolding. It was huge, much bigger than anyone would have imagined the aircraft needed. It was all tubular spars intertwined and linked. We soon found it to be a dangerous contraption. . . .

'But, to the delight and thrill of 7 Squadron, the Stirling had arrived.'

It was 2 August 1940. The Battle of Britain was approaching its climax, the Stirling was a tremendous morale booster. On 14 July Air Ministry had ordered the resuscitation of 7 Squadron in 4 Group. The range of the Stirling suggested that it was a suitable replacement for the squadron's Whitleys, which were the slowest of the bombers in service. Otherwise it was an unsuitable choice: the Group flew Merlin engined aircraft and held spares for that engine. Arrival of a Bristol engined machine upset this arrangement. Later, the Whitleys were replaced, more logically, by Halifaxes.

Personnel selection also brought problems. The only pilots with four engined experience were in Coastal Command, flying Sunderlands or, in some cases, Singapores. Some were drafted to 7 Squadron, but they were without bomber experience. This mattered little, however, for the initial task was to discover snags and work up handling techniques on the ground and in the air. The taking of crews from Coastal Command was unpopular, since training flying-boat pilots was a specialised task. But there was at least affinity with a Short aeroplane.

Other pilots came from 4 Group squadrons. Groundcrew also needed careful selection, few having experience of a large aeroplane.

On 3 August Wing Commander Paul Harris arrived to command 7 Squadron. They were informed that they would receive eight Stirlings when production permitted. Production was very slow. Despite the Beaverbrook order, Short's continued to build the aircraft singly, applying their craftsmen's skill to produce strong, superbly built machines.

'There weren't many of us on the Squadron at this time', recalls Bob May. 'We hadn't much equipment, but we were tremendously intent upon our tasks. The Stirling meant a break from the monotony of cleaning hangar floors! Now we had something to work upon, a sort of great status symbol. Fighter Command held the headlines and we felt our turn would come. We had the first four engined bomber in the R.A.F., and we were very proud of it. We worked on our one aeroplane whenever we could, for as long as we could. We were supposed to do a daily inspection—we sometimes did 12. Just to get the trestles around the engines was quite a performance. People somehow liked to do this. We used to put covers on the engines, although we kept the aeroplane in the hangar whilst learning all we could about it. It was all very exciting. We knew little about its past.'

The few aircrew shared the machine with the groundcrew, each claiming their priorities. Simple handling came first, then it was time to arm the turrets.

At Short & Harland in Belfast, Stirling production commenced in June 1940. Mr. J. H. Lower had, in October 1936, been appointed by Short's (who held 51 % capital, the remainder being put up by Harland & Wolff) as Works Manager. The company locally recruited workers skilled in all branches of engineering, relying upon them for tooling, and for building Bristol Bombays, Blenheim components, and then Handley-Page Herefords. Nearly 30 Stirlings were in various stages of construction when, late on 14 August 1940, German bombers visited the works.

About 15 Heinkel He 111s of KGr. 100, based at Vannes, Brittany, delivered a sharp attack which damaged the final assembly shop, reducing N6025-28 to scrap and splintering others. But this was only a foretaste of the next day.

Sydney Groves joined Short's at Rochester Airport in May 1939 as a time recorder. Transferred to the night shift, he had been at work on 12 July when distant crumps were heard. The enemy was getting nearer. 'In daylight', he recalls, 'we found a string of small bomb craters, coming from the direction of the Davis Estate and finishing just short of the hangars. One bomb landed in the road close to the duckpond of the farm across the way—a bomb fell in the later big raid in exactly the same place.'

The next attempt, by Ju 87 Stukas on 13 August, was narrowly averted when R.A.F. fighters drove off the dive bombers.

Thursday 15 August 1940 brought a massive onslaught against Britain, the Germans mounting a maximum effort. Soon after dawn a Junkers Ju 88 reconnoitred the Rochester area. Around 2 p.m., over 80 Dornier Do 17Zs of KG 3 began taking off from Antwerp, led by Chamier-Glisczinski. Over 100 Messerschmitt Bf 109s of JG 51, JG 52 and JG 54, took up defensive positions around the bombers, which crossed in over Deal at 15.30 hrs. Meanwhile, a formation of about 60 BF 109s sped in at Dover, splitting into two groups to protect the flanks of the bombers. Hurricanes of 111 and 151 Squadrons, and a dozen Spitfires of 64 Squadron patrolling between Manston and Hawkinge, were vectored to intercept. Although they were joined by Hurricanes of 1, 17 and 32 Squadrons, their total strength was insufficient to breach the fighter screen whose top cover, in particular, engaged them, driving them off. Over Faversham the Dornier force split into two formations, leaving Stab. KG/3, I and II/KG 3 to make the attack on Rochester Airport.

'It was about 3.30 in the afternoon when we received an alert and cleared the factory', recalls D. C. Marks. 'Within minutes the whole air shook in rapid concussion and deafened us in our shelter, for all the bombs came down together. Our chargehand went to the door of the shelter, looked out, and told us solemnly that our factory was burning—but it was actually only a small fire. We apprentices were sent home for the rest of the week.'

Sydney Groves had been resting ready for his night shift. He was awakened by his wife about 4.00 p.m. 'I went out to see, from my home in Strood, a huge pall of smoke over the hills in the direction of the Airport. I cycled over Rochester Bridge and along City Way, only to be stopped by another alert as I entered Arethusa Road.

'I reached the Airport gate at about 4.15 p.m. and was able to enter in my capacity as air raid warden. I joined Ron Davies (later landlord of the 'Prince of Wales', Railway St.) in a tour of inspection. Smoke and water were everywhere. The production Stirlings were a sorry sight, with their backs broken. Everywhere were signs of shrapnel riddled sections and buildings. A fire watcher's post—a large, bell-like device—was riddled with holes made by parts of oxygen bottles exploding, and a very likeable Mr. Oakley died at this post. He was the only casualty.

'We worked all through the night, and into the next day, and later held a pay parade on the tarmac outside the hangars, soldiers with fixed bayonets hovering around. Invasion seemed imminent, and large stakes were now driven in over the airfield.'

Six Stirlings, N3645 and N3647 to N3651, were destroyed in the bombing, and production halted at Rochester.

There were many stories of the strange twist of events. Mr. Bates, just released from the Army to work at Short's, placed his shoes by his sandwich case. Returning to the factory he found a piece of shrapnel had removed an eyelet from a shoe, passed through his case and bisected his sandwiches. A few unexploded bombs poked from walls: it was not a healthy place in which to tarry.

Marks returned to work the following Monday, finding the detail shop in confusion. Air raid warnings punctuated the day, everyone hastening to the shelters. There was an enormous hole in the roofless shop. 'We were very nervous, and put to work repairing splinter holes in finished parts. I remember a chargehand saying to me: "This makes us all the more determined to go on building the bomber." Craters were everywhere outside the factory.'

'Within a week dispersal orders were effected', recalls Sydney Groves. 'I was one of the first into Strood Extension. I set up office with a table, chairs and a cabinet surrounded by a screen of sacking over a framework of battens. The unfinished building needed ramps, walls and roofing. The Mainplane Section was eventually established at Strood, long articulated lorries having to negotiate the narrow streets.'

After the bombing Mr. J. H. Lower's task was to establish dispersed units for Stirling production in the Swindon and Gloucester areas. Strood Extension was the result of a Ministry requirement. Components only were built there.

'After Rochester was bombed', recalls Mr. Lower, 'M.A.P. arranged for Stirling production elsewhere. Part of the G.W.R. works at Swindon was acquired, and material salvaged from bombing sent there. Some of Philips & Powis works, South Marston, were obtained and a hangar at Sevenhampton. Production Control was established in a large house at Stratton St. Margaret.

'Some of the Gloster Aircraft Co. works, Hucclecote, was used on a short term arrangement until Rochester re-opened. There, some early Stirlings intended to be Rochester built were completed and flown at Swindon, some at Gloucester. The Drawing Office dispersed to Kidderminster.'

Ten Stirlings (Hercules Mk. II) had been Rochester built before the bombing. It was obvious that the aircraft's ceiling with these engines was insufficient for operations, yet interruptions might force operational employment. On 20 August it was decided to be essential for succeeding aircraft to have Hercules Mk. IIIs. There could be no retrospective fitment, because of the earlier special nacelles.

On 12 August N3641 reached 7 Squadron, on 29 August N3642. Two more joined in September. Bomber Command wanted a Stirling for A.F.D.U. assessment of ventral and dorsal defence. None was available, such was the pressure on 7 Squadron. When fuel consumption tests were being conducted on N3641 on 1 September, it was fired upon over the Isle of Man, but no damage was suffered.

Attempted loading of N3641 with 12 × 250 lb. G.P. bombs showed that the cables were too short for beams to be lowered to accept the weapons. The bomber took off with a small load, with results that were worrying to the squadron. The take-off run was long for Leeming, so the squadron was alerted to fell trees on the runway line if invasion came. Instead, the trees grew on.

Stirling high explosive bomb loads could be arranged in 12 ways, the main loading being 7 × 2,000 lb. A.P.; or 24 × 500 lb. G.P./S.A.P.; 8 × 500 lb. A.S.; 24 × 250 lb., released in 2 or 4 salvoes; and 5 × 1,000 lb. or 6 × 500 lb. G.P./S.A.P. Modification 266 enabled the Stirling to carry 7 × 1,900 lb. bombs.

Fuel consumption rates needed assessment before operations could commence, and on 29 September 1940 Flg. Off. T. P. A. Bradley, D.F.C., took N3640 on test. About 12.30 hrs. engine trouble developed. With a halted engine the Stirling quickly lost height, crashing into a stone wall at Hodge Branding, near Barton, south of Lancaster.

Three aircraft now remained with 7 Squadron and even with these, snags were plentiful. Undercarriage motors were burning out; the rear turret was exceptionally cold; rain seeped into the cockpit. Engine plugs brought ignition problems; and N3641 encountered tailwheel retracting mechanism troubles, which were traced to the operating motors. Brackets for gill motors came adrift; and oil leaks during plug changes were serious. Oil temperatures ran high on port motors, oil coolers needing replacing on early aircraft.

On 30 September 1940 a report summarised four weeks' 'intensive flying', during which N3638 replaced N3640. The Stirling was judged unfit for operation in the foreseeable future—a bitter blow. When ready, N6002 would fly to Hucclecote for makers' intensive trials, and be fitted with a revised cabin heating system.

Cockpit noise was intolerable for long flights. Windows were sucked out by air pressure; even when in place they made loud noises and let a strong draught in. Sliding windows were stiffened, and covers were placed over the high cockpit canopies at dispersals. The setting of undercarriage selection levers strained cables; but the greatest worry surrounded the Exactor throttle.

During the test flying at Boscombe Down the throttle controls had brought concern. The Air Ministry questioned their suitability for a four engined landplane. The problem was raised between the Air Staff and Short's on 24 August, and discussed again on 4 September. As a result Short's agreed to fit rod and chain controls on the forthcoming Cyclone engined Stirling Mk. II at an early stage. They were impossible for the Mk. I without disrupting the whole production plan.

Just how easily a throttle problem could arise was shown on 15 October. N3636 force landed at Scampton. The engines failed to respond after being throttled back, the Exactors not being able to translate fast enough. On a flying boat this mattered less; on a limited landing run it could be disastrous.

A test pilot with much experience of Stirlings was Geoffrey Tyson. His opinion remains that 'slamming open the throttles on airfields with not much more than 1,200 yd. run available and some on grass was certainly one cause of flying accidents. The Stirling had a built-in tendency to swing to starboard from slipstream effect, and if the wind was from a starboard vector as well the opening of the starboard outer throttle (and sometimes the starboard inner too) had to be staggered behind the port ones to prevent swinging. Pilots were reluctant to do this—at least, inexperienced ones—as it increased the take-off run. I think, too, that the Stirling with its stalky undercarriage and high c.g. was more prone to weathercocking than other bombers. I flew Lancasters and Halifaxes and they were certainly less prone to swinging on take-off in my view. The Stirling had a tall rudder which presented a bigger "keel surface" to a cross wind. This was an advantage, of course, with a wind from port.

'I somehow doubt whether Exactors were a contributory cause. Throttles were primed in the forward position and the first job on sitting in the seat was to prime them; it was almost a religion. And of course they were automatically reprimed on opening-up.'

A conference on 20 October 1940 at Bomber Command discussed the Stirling, particularly as to whether to operate it by day or night. Boscombe Down's report on trials with N3635 and N3637 was available. The truth about the take-off run on 64,000 lb. was at last known: it was 1,500 yd. Other tests concentrated on flying at 57,400 lb., when the service ceiling was reached after 34 minutes. Climb started at 132 m.p.h.I.A.S. to 3,000 ft., falling by 1 m.p.h. per 1,000 ft. Maximum level speed was 246 m.p.h.T.A.S. at 4,000 ft.; most economical cruise speed 165 m.p.h.I.A.S. at 10,000 ft., where fuel consumption was 175 gal. per hr. Maximum range was obtained at 160 m.p.h.I.A.S. at 3,000 ft.

At these speeds the Stirling would be unable to penetrate far on short summer nights. Some operations would have to be in daylight, and fighters might give some cover. The Commander in Chief agreed: he wanted an aircraft to bomb Germany now. 'In the immediate future we are confined to night operations', he said, 'and must arm a bomber with this in mind.'

5. N6000, the first Belfast-built Stirling.

But was the Stirling armed for night operations, particularly as it had been decided to fit pairs of beam guns, which were reckoned unnecessary at night? Should they be removed or held in abeyance? The Assistant Chief of the Air Staff pointed out that it had recently been agreed to fit a dorsal turret. The ventral F.N. periscopic sight would not be ready for six months. Beam guns seemed of little extra value to the Stirling, whose two turrets produced a field of fire that converged just beyond the wingtips. Bomber Command in early 1940 had pressed for beam guns on all bombers. It would be bad for industrial morale if they were cancelled, so it was decided that beam mountings, but not guns, would be fitted.

No. 4 Group were told to withhold judgement on the Stirling until Hercules Mk. III engined aircraft were available. If enough armour was removed, the bomber could carry another 500 lb. bomb. Representatives of 4 Group retorted that armour gave crews confidence, which was important especially if the Stirling operated in daylight.

From N3640 onwards, Stirlings could carry six mines against the Halifax's two. The Manchester carried none, but later could carry four.

Throughout October and November, 7 Squadron held three Stirlings with little hope of more, although N6000 (Hercules Mk. III), the first Belfast machine, had reached Boscombe Down for trials. No. 7 Squadron was to move to Benson to be nearer Short's production centre. When N3641 visited the station on 24 October, a tailwheel collapsed. Problems with that unit were never fully overcome. Another failure occurred in November. By then the squadron had been ordered to Oakington in 3 Group, because their aircraft had Bristol engines.

Early Stirlings had leading edge wing tanks interchangeable with leading edge mounted cable cutters. The first 30 Stirlings had tankage without cutters; likewise the first 10 from Belfast all of which had de-icers. Subsequent aircraft had cutters as well as tanks, but no de-icers.

On 11 November 1940 the A.C.A.S. Liaison Committee met. A.C.A.S.(T) reported serious Exactor trouble, feeling another system must be fitted. 'Unreliability was intolerable.' Difficulty came with synchronisation, improvements aimed at remedying hydraulic leaks being insufficient. Servicing was a major problem. Nevertheless, it was again agreed that a change to rod and chain could not be brought about easily. All Stirling Mk. Is would have to have Exactors, bad as they were said to be.

The Under Secretary of State at the Air Ministry enquired about the Stirling's poor performance with Hercules Mk. IIs. This engine was limited to a take-off boost of $1\frac{3}{4}$ lb., preventing take-off from an ordinary airfield with full tanks and a reasonable load. Hercules Mk. IIs were being replaced by Hercules Mk. II (Mod.), improving take-off and allowing a bomb load of 3,000 to 4,000 lb. for a range of 1,300 miles. Operational height remained poor. Hercules Mk. IIs had

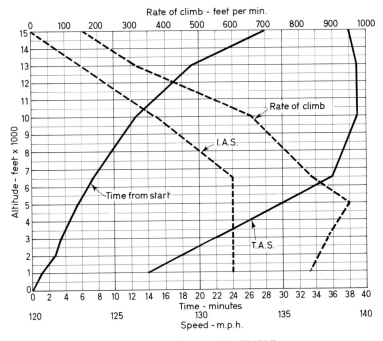

2. Performance, Mk. I N3635 (Hercules II)—57,400 lb.

single-speed superchargers rated at 5,000 ft., allowing an absolute ceiling of 14,000 ft.—an operational height of only 10,000 ft. Robert Saundby did not consider that use of a valuable aircraft on operations over enemy territory was justified until operational height could be increased by the Hercules Mk. III to a minimum of 15,000 ft. Future hopes would be pinned on the Hercules Mks. X and XI. The weights of such aircraft were compared and forecast:

	Stirling Mk. I (Hercules Mk. II)	Stirling Mk. I (Hercules Mk. III/X):
Tare, lb.	39,194	41,938½
Service load, lb.	5,761	16,388
Fuel 1354 gal., lb.	10,155	10,155
Oil 70 gal., lb.	630	630
Gross weight, lb.	55,740	69,111½
Max. service load, lb.	18,135	22,061½
Gross weight, operational lb.	64,009	?
Max. loading weight, lb.	57,000	?
Max. for take-off	64,000	?

Experience showed a need for many modifications, which were discussed at Gloucester on 25 November. They included propeller de-icers, alcohol de-icing for carburettors, rudder pedals nearer the pilot, improved emergency exit, blind flying visor, better weatherproofing, increased chord for rudder trimmer, Marston oil coolers, stronger tailwheel chassis, Hercules Mk. II (Mod.), stronger wing leading edge between nacelles, Lorenz gear for operational aircraft, W/T master aerial and D/F loop, heated windscreen, improved flare chute, and other changes.

Boscombe Down had experienced bombing up the Stirling. Stations 10, 11 and 12 could each carry a 1,900 lb. bomb, Stations 1 to 6 and 22 to 27 each a 500 or 250 lb. bomb. Nos. 1 to 6 and 22 to 27 could also each take containers as an alternative. They had done a trial loading of 7 × 2,000 lb. H.C. bombs. There was only a 2½ in. clearance between the tails of bombs on stations 4, 5, 6, and 11, and at 10, 11, 12, and 17, only ¼ in. clearance each side of the bomb at door hinge level, owing to the position of the door brackets.

The armament at this time comprised an F.N.5A twin gun nose turret, F.N.25A belly turret, F.N.4A four gun tail turret and beam guns on F.N.55A mountings. This armament applied to Mk. I series 1 aircraft, the first 80 built, still allowing for 26 troops to be carried: three in the bomb aimer's compartment, eight in the centre section, ten on the starboard side aft and two on the port side, with another on the port side ammunition shelf.

Troubles precluded much flying by 7 Squadron. During November N3644 had front turret hydraulic problems, the Exactors were troublesome, and the bomb door cables had to be repositioned. Weak tail chassis grounded N3642.

Moving to Oakington took several weeks. Rumours raced around that secret bombers were coming to the station. As the first circled the aerodrome, I stood on Midsummer Common, Cambridge. The Stirling looked huge at that time, and to me seemed a strange looking affair. Through binoculars I saw that complex undercarriage, and thought how difficult it would be to model! The arrival of the

6. Mk. I N3637 of 7 Squadron at Oakington in 1941. A.F.E.E. trials in 1942, became 3361M at 2 S.T.T. 15 September 1942. Written off 16 February 1945.

Stirlings was a tonic when things were bad. Their size suggested might was on our side.

The second forced landing came on 28 November. Pilot Officer R. W. Cox had engine trouble south of Edinburgh. He landed at Turnhouse, N3638 suffering no damage.

By 30 November squadron personnel included many who were to be well known in the early operational phase. Wg. Cdr. Paul Harris was in command, Flg. Off. L. G. Bristowe Adjutant. Other officers were Sqn. Ldr. J. M. Griffith-Jones, Flt. Lt. G. H. Smith, Flt. Lt. G. W. Bennett, Flt. Lt. A. Chambers, Flt. Lt. H. S. Browne, Flt. Lt. A. C. Ward, Flg. Off. G. B. Blacklock, Flg. Off. V. F. B. Pike, Flg. Off. E. W. Best, Flg. Off. S. G. Stock, Flg. Off. G. K. Larney, Plt. Off. R. W. Cox, Plt. Off. F. H. P. Austin, Flg. Off. B. A. R. H. Mathe, Plt. Off. D. T. Witt and Plt. Off. C. R. Barrett. In December Sqn. Ldr. P. W. Lynch-Blosse arrived to command 'B' Flight. The squadron held five aircraft—N3636, N3638, N3641, N3642 and N3644.

On 21 December N3637 arrived. All received were Trainers. It was now clear that these might have to be used operationally.

The number of corporals and airmen at Oakington soared. One arrival was Mr. R. C. Monteith, previously at Sullom Voe, in the Shetlands, who was a Sunderland electrician. When he arrived at Oakington Station he saw some aeroplanes dispersed close by. He went over to a porter and asked: 'What kind of kites are they, then?' The reply was: 'They'm be Starlins, they'm be.' He'd never heard of them before.

'I phoned the guardroom. A truck took me to the guardroom where I was asked what Section I was for. I said: "Electrical!" "What, another one?" the Corp. replied. When I reached the Section, there were between 50 and 60 electricians there. The Stirling was an "electrical wonder", and we were like bees round a honeypot, for there were so few aircraft. The station didn't need so many

7.   The Stirling production line on 31 January 1941, airframe 20 nearest,
earlier aircraft ahead.

electricians, though: the plan was to familiarise us with the aircraft. We were to
become preachers to other stations when they changed over to "Starlins".'

By January the squadron held N3641:D, N3642:E, N3636:A, N3637:B,
N3638:C, N3644:H (the first with Hercules Mk. IIIs, and which had arrived on
25 September 1940); N3643:G arrived 3 January 1941. Icing trouble with
carburettor controls manifested itself. The squadron was told not to fly in icing
conditions until modifications had been made.

Weather was atrocious, cold and snow greatly reducing flying. Serviceability
was low. In the first week of January only 21 hr. 20 min. flying was completed.
Between 7 and 13 January five aircraft were unserviceable. On five days when two
were serviceable only 7 hr. 35 min. flying was possible.

On 16 January King George VI and Queen Elizabeth visited Oakington,
inspecting N3652. N3644 was flown. Next day Plt. Off. R. W. Cox left for St.
Athan to collect N6003 (Hercules Mk. X), 7 Squadron's first operational Stirling.
It reached Oakington on 22 January, replacing N3637 in the intensive flying
programme.

Among the Stirling crew was an entirely new member: the flight engineer. He
monitored engine performance and generally assisted the captain. The Air
Ministry asked that sergeants be posted for special training, but it was impossible
to find qualified men. The Squadron began training aircraftsmen.

Experience after six months' flying was depressing. A summary of each week's flying was ordered. That for 27 January showed just how low serviceability was. N3641, awaiting an undercarriage motor, had not flown. N3642 had done only 1 hr. 45 min. before the starboard undercarriage motor went unserviceable. Undercarriage motors were being changed on N3638, which had logged 2 hr. 35 min. N3636 was grounded awaiting spares. N3644 had managed 2 hr. 35 min. and was awaiting repair of a contact breaker. N6003, upon which high hopes had been pinned, had in all flown only 3 hr. 10 min. (1 hr. 10 min. on the Squadron) and now was grounded, awaiting the fitting of a Graviner fire extinguisher and modifications to the rudder balance.

Boscombe Down investigated tailwheel lowering problems. Keys and worm drive shafts had sheared under loads: the design was insufficiently sturdy. The emergency gear only dealt with mechanical malfunction.

Sunday 27 January was sunny, 7 Squadron managing some flying. I visited Oakington; it was a mass of sightseers, who were rewarded with views of a Stirling with yellow undersurfaces. Dispersed near Oakington station were two of the huge machines. Someone said they looked like huge dragonflies, which was an apt description. The crowd, enjoying a close look, were discussing the Stirling's misfortunes—so much for security.

Times had been hard, but soon the unready bombers were ordered into action, which boosted morale. One can, however, imagine the feelings of the crews.

Chapter 4

Let Battle Commence

Lord Beaverbrook was keen to get Stirlings to Berlin, Churchill and Bomber Command sharing his desire. Wing Commander Harris visited Beaverbrook, explaining why his Stirlings could not go. He also called on Air Chief Marshal Sir Charles Portal, explaining that he would be lucky to get three or four Stirlings away, and even more fortunate if one returned. Losses would be due to technical malfunction. A Berlin raid would be a failure.

Sir Charles Portal replied: 'It is not a good thing to be associated with failure.' He was accurately summing up the situation. The Stirling was far from ready for operations.

Weather remained bad and serviceability poor, and the heavy aircraft became bogged in Oakington's mud. Senior authorities did not curb their impatience for action. On 2 February a Stirling was ordered for mining, but snow put paid to this idea. The pressure for operations increased. Cross country flights were made as far as Cape Wrath and Portreath, and on the 6th another crew stood by for mining. It snowed again: prayers were being answered. Next day three crews stood by for a Boulogne raid, foiled again, as was an Antwerp venture on the 8th. Then came the first undercarriage failure at Oakington.

The 9th was a dull day, but Flg. Off. R. W. Cox managed some flying. On return he was unable to lower an undercarriage leg. For hours N6003 droned around, the crew desperately trying to find a cure. But 4 hrs. 50 min. later, after jettisoning all they could, and with fuel low, Cox lined up 'V-Victor' for a wheels-up landing, which had not been attempted before. Cox achieved an immaculate belly landing on the mud, skidding 165 yd. before coming to rest. Little damage was caused, but fumes from an exploding accumulator engulfed the crew, who climbed out hastily to cheers from onlookers.

Railway sleepers were brought and, with the aid of inflatable bags and a large crane, the aircraft was lifted. The undercarriage was manually wound down, and it was found that it was the temperamental motors that had caused the failure.

The weather briefly improved, and on 10 February Hanover was raided by 3 Group's Wellingtons. Another 14, flown by 'freshmen' were ordered to Rotterdam, and with them went 3 Stirling Trainers.

At 19.00 hrs. the engines of N3641 'D-Dog' burst into life. From its dispersal near Oakington Station, it began to taxi across the rough surface. In the captain's seat was Flt. Lt. G. Howard-Smith, with Flt. Lt. G. B. Blacklock as second pilot. At 19.05 hrs. its take-off run began: the Stirling had been made operational. It must have been with very mixed feelings that the crew climbed out over the Fens.

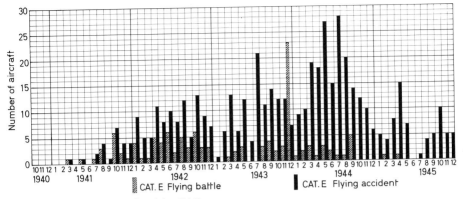

3. Monthly accidents involving Stirlings.

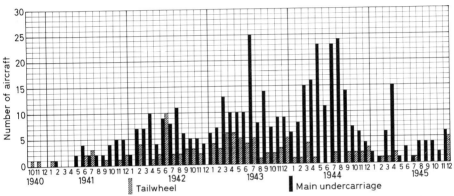

4. Accidents to Stirling bombers attributable to undercarriage trouble during landings and take-offs.

Half hour later it was the turn of N3644 'H-Henry', flown by Sqn. Ldr. P. W. Lynch-Blosse; and at 20.00 hrs. Acting Sqn. Ldr. J. M. Griffith-Jones in N3642 'E-Easy' began his flight. Each Stirling carried 16×500 lb. G.P. bombs with which to blast oil storage tanks near Rotterdam.

Wellingtons opened the attack. At the receiving end was Lt. Col. Arie de Jong, now Director of Public Relations, Royal Netherlands Air Force, who recorded in his diary that 'defending searchlights were switched on at 20.07, around the Hook of Holland'. What the Germans would have made of a teenager keeping such a diary one scarcely dare imagine! Ten minutes later, Arie recorded that the air raid sirens wailed in Rotterdam, and at 20.32 hrs. the first bombs fell on a Shell refinery south of Vlaardingen. Tanks were hit, fires raged. Thirteen minutes later another bomber arrived, its flares illuminating the scene. Soon there were two oil fires at the Pakhuismeesteren Depot, 1 mile south west of Vlaardingen. At 20.57 hrs. a very heavy salvo fell, perhaps from N3641.

Ground observers claimed to see five aircraft in the bright moonlight, three of which turned in for another attack. Heavy flak opened up on them. Further flares illuminated the area at 21.35 hrs., as anti-aircraft guns blazed away and searchlights swept the sky. Two minutes later another heavy bomb load crashed

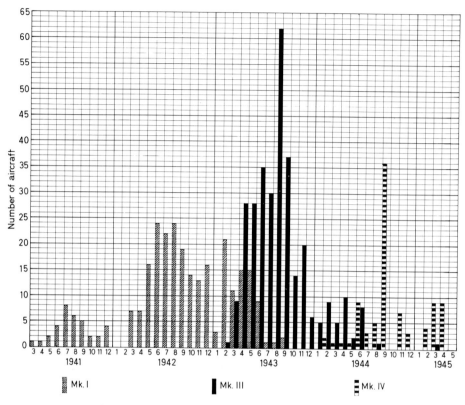

5.   Monthly losses on operations, Mks. I, III, IV.

down, possibly from the second Stirling. Bombing continued from 21.40 hrs. and at 22.40 hrs. a final heavy salvo was released.

All three Stirlings made a safe return to Oakington, although N3641 and N3644 each had a bomb hang-up. The most disappointed person at Oakington must have been Wg. Cdr. Harris, sickness having prevented him from taking part. He returned to duty the next morning, but then bad weather halted operations.

Unserviceability remained high. N3641 was grounded awaiting electric motors, and N3642 managed only 55 min. flying. N3638 flew 3 hr. 50 min. before brake trouble halted flying. N3636 was awaiting spares, N3644 had magneto trouble. N6003 was grounded with intercom. problems.

In the second week of February 28 hr. was accomplished. N3641 had tailwheel retraction problems, after 10 hr. 10 min. flying N3642 had a burnt out under-carriage motor, and N3638 had a jammed undercarriage. N3636 flew for 30 min., and N6003 was still under repair. By 17 February N3641 had managed another 2 hr. 5 min., but needed a gill motor and a new tyre. N3636 was awaiting under turret removal. N3644 needed an electric motor, and Short's were busy on N6003.

6. Stirling Mk. I N3636 (Trainer). After Short's trials delivered to 10 M.U. Hullavington 3.9.40. To 7 Squadron 24.9.40, retaining yellow undersurfaces. Used as 'MG:A', resprayed with black undersurfaces, used for training. Grounded 28.10.41 as 3056M at Oakington. (For key to camouflage colours see page 184)

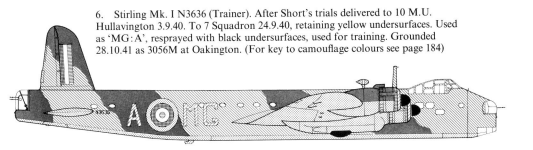

7. Stirling Mk. I N3642. Delivered to 19 M.U. 25.7.40; to 7 Squadron 29.8.40; became 'MG:E' early 1941 for intensive flying. On first Stirling raid 10.2.41. Flew 6 operational sorties. To XV Squadron 16.4.41 for training, to 1651 C.U. 6.10.41. Grounded 4.42 as 3012M. Used at No. 4 School of Technical Training. Written off at 78 M.U. 19.8.44. (For key to camouflage colours see page 184)

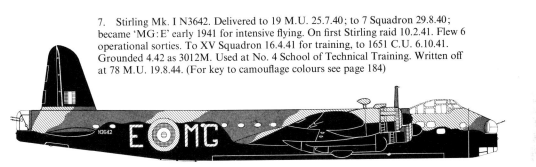

8. Stirling Mk. I N3656. Delivered to 10 M.U. 2.41, to Wyton 27.4.41. Became 'LS:H' of XV Squadron 2.5.41, flew 15 sorties. Damaged on day raid 21.7.41. Crash landed Honington returning from Berlin 12/13.8.41, struck off charge 30.8.41. (For key to camouflage colours see page 184)

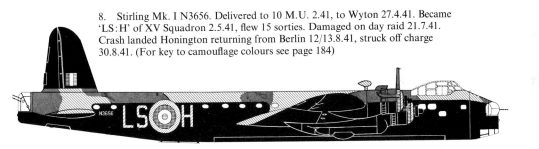

Meanwhile, glimpses of the Stirlings heightened my interest: something special in R.A.F. history was being closely enacted. On 15 February I took another look. Close to Oakington village N3641 'D-Dog' was on dispersal. Nearby was a gate through which personnel passed to the village. Amazingly, it was unguarded.

I cautiously made my way to 'D-Dog'. It seemed gigantic. As I stood alongside the 6-foot mainwheel I felt dwarfed. N3641 was incredibly shabby, thick black paint now extending up the fuselage sides. Mud encrusted the aircraft. I duly noted the serial number and was about to proceed to 'K-King' when a young pilot officer asked me what I thought I was doing. I answered honestly: 'Having a close look.'

He must have concluded I was harmless, showed me more of the aircraft and told me that the pilot sat 22 ft. above the ground. I could see just what an amazing structure the undercarriage was. 'This part folds up into the crate halfway up, then the whole thing is hauled into the nacelle', I was told.

Thanking my unexpected host, I cycled home—to fit a more accurate undercarriage on to my model, as well as streamlined spinners and a black coating halfway up the fuselage.

I remain amazed that an onlooker could wander around a secret bomber. Little wonder that the Luftwaffe had already lit the scene with flares. Maybe someone more sinister than I had looked around a Stirling.

Later that day Flt. Lt. C. E. Bennett and crew boarded N3641. Sterkrade's oil refinery was the target for 3 Group, which also detailed 14 Wellingtons for Boulogne. With them was Wg. Cdr. Harris in N3642. Bennett dropped 16×500 lb. bombs across the docks. Twenty minutes later Harris made an east to west run, claiming another six hits on Docks 4 and 5.

Crews of 7 Squadron were reporting various speeds with their aircraft. On 20 February a further report was issued by A. & A.E.E. Tests with L7605, N3635 and N3643 (Hercules Mk. II powered) indicated that 2.4 minutes were needed to reach 2,000 ft at 249.5 m.p.h.; and 15,000 ft. at 218 m.p.h. Brief tests using N6008 (Hercules Mk. X) at 50,000 lb. gave a speed of 200 m.p.h., showing no improvement. It was currently flying duration cruise flights.

The third Stirling operation, on 24 February, was the first in which Stirlings were part of the Main Force. The target for them and 33 Wellingtons was a Hipper Class cruiser in Brest. Bennett (N3636) was away first, his bombs straddling No. 8 Dock. Three crews set off around 18.00 hrs. for the five hour flight. Again the load was 15×500 lb. G.P. bombs, Flt. Lt. G. B. Blacklock flying N3642 and Lynch-Blosse N3652.

Enemy awareness of Oakington's importance was evident when a Dornier Do 17Z dropped two bombs, putting the airfield out of action. The station was further put into a state of alarm when Lynch-Blosse went missing in N3652. The weather had been particularly bad, and he had encountered a snow storm over Wiltshire, where he jettisoned his load. But Group H.Q. had misunderstood a signal, for Lynch-Blosse had landed safely at Boscombe Down.

February 25 was cloudy. During the lunch hour a Do 17Z of KG 2 bombed Oakington, machine gunning N3652 as it raced over low.

Captain Harold Balfour, Secretary of State, arrived on 1 March to see the Stirlings. Three crews stood by and the visitor learned first hand about the intensive flying programme, in which N6004 had now replaced N6003. At dusk Wg. Cdr. Harris and Flt. Lt. Best left for Brest, but bad weather thwarted the operation, and Harris landed at Newmarket with bombs aboard. Luckily the surface there was firm.

Electric motor and switch trouble continued into March. On the 3rd three Stirlings, each taking $4 \times 2,000$ lb. bombs, headed for Brest. Two certainly bombed the target, but Flt. Lt. V. F. B. Pike jettisoned his bombs at sea. Sgt. L. McCarthy bombed, but from N3653 and Sqn. Ldr. Griffith-Jones and crew no more was heard. They had come down in the sea, and all but one perished. After this, more snow halted operations.

The A.O.C. 3 Group, worried over undercarriage malfunction in N6003,

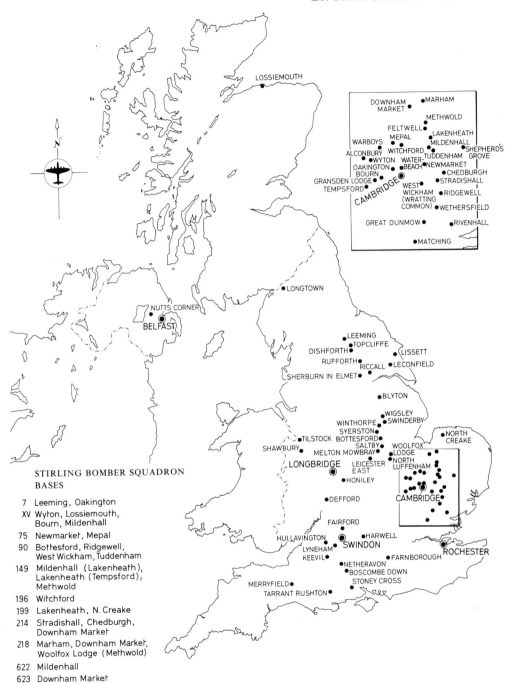

STIRLING BOMBER SQUADRON
BASES

7	Leeming, Oakington
XV	Wyton, Lossiemouth, Bourn, Mildenhall
75	Newmarket, Mepal
90	Bottesford, Ridgewell, West Wickham, Tuddenham
149	Mildenhall (Lakenheath), Lakenheath (Tempsford), Methwold
196	Witchford
199	Lakenheath, N. Creake
214	Stradishall, Chedburgh, Downham Market
218	Marham, Downham Market, Woolfox Lodge (Methwold)
622	Mildenhall
623	Downham Market

9. Bases used by Stirlings in the United Kingdom.

ordered that no more N6 . . . aircraft were to be accepted before undercarriage gear boxes were modified. Following handling trials, N6001 went to Sealand, and then a ferry pilot took it to Short's modification depot, now at Wyton. Its undercarriage failed to lower, and another wheels-up landing occurred. When N6006 left Wyton on 13 March, Flg. Off. Blacklock arrived over Oakington only to find that his undercarriage had to be lowered by hand, a laborious business.

During early Stirling development little thought had been given to beam attacks. At last a mock-up of Modification 215 for two pairs of beam guns was installed in N3644 at Oakington. It proved acceptable and a number of aircraft were thus fitted, until a dorsal turret replaced the feature. Cutting the hatches and fitting guns took place at Wyton. An unlucky moment occurred when one of the team responsible accidentally fired a gun, spraying the works team, who were resting, and bringing no mean panic.

Since December 1940 N6008 had been on trial at Boscombe Down with modified Exactor throttle controls. The report was encouraging. The Establishment recommended easier access to the controls in nacelles, since maintenance often needed to be undertaken, and it was a lengthy business. The draught problem in the Stirling was still unbearable, though, and the machine's heating system remained unacceptable.

By mid March Oakington's muddy surface was so bad that aircraft were

8.   Cockpit layout of early Hercules II powered aircraft.

9. Bomb aimer's compartment in an early Mk. I.

10. Looking aft along the fuselage. The ventral turret may be seen retracted in this early Mk. I.

getting bogged—dangerous for a heavy aircraft whose undercarriage was troublesome. On 16 March 'A' Flight was ordered to Newmarket Heath, where the long run on grass was sited on a dry chalk base. Stirling control was switched to Stradishall.

With ground personnel the move was unpopular. Their quarters were established in the racecourse grandstand. For many 'other ranks' this meant sleeping in cold, atrocious conditions. Arthur Moore, one of them, remembers that 'the rats in these one time stables seemed very interested in the newcomers'.

But before the move took place, Lynch-Blosse took the Stirling on its first raid directed against Germany. He left Oakington on 17 March in N3652 taking, for the first time, a mixed load of $5 \times 1,000$ lb. and 8×500 lb. G.P. bombs. Some 20 Wellingtons of 3 Group also took part. A 500 lb. bomb hung up in a wing cell, but otherwise it was an uneventful sortie.

Stirlings were now delivering sizeable loads, despite their dangerously low ceiling. Squadron Leader A. F. Robertson unloaded 22×500 lb. G.P.s on Rotterdam, but it was mainly Channel ports that were attacked during the work-up phase.

For the Stirling's manoeuvrability A. & A.E.E. pilots had nothing but praise, and admired its strong structure. Shortening the span had brought about this good manoeuvrability factor. Aileron control was very effective, but the rudder proved sluggish during the early part of a take-off run.

A technique had been worked out for handling the temperamental throttle controls. Before starting engines, each throttle lever would be moved to a priming position slightly beyond full throttle setting, held for a few seconds against the Exactor spring then brought back to 'closed' very slowly. Each engine was started with the throttle set $1\frac{1}{2}$ in. forward of 'closed'. When the engine fired off the starter magneto, each engine was switched on without moving throttle levers. As the aircraft moved forward, propellers were set to coarse pitch then slowly returned to fine.

For take-off, flaps were first set to 40% of total travel and elevators trimmed. Brakes were fully applied and airscrew controls reprimed, usually by the second pilot. Gills were closed, brakes released, and the throttles opened as quickly as possible, leaving one lever in the halfway position so that if the machine swung to the right, as it tended to, this could slowly be opened to counteract the swing. The tail was raised as soon as possible, and at 100 m.p.h.I.A.S. the Stirling would be lifted off and gills opened when the aircraft was airborne. Climb-away was at 135 m.p.h.I.A.S., and climb at 57,000 lb. was still possible on three engines.

Landing technique was first partly to extend flaps at 140 m.p.h.I.A.S. and retrim the machine then to hold about 130 m.p.h.I.A.S. until ready to land. On approach the undercarriage was lowered, flaps fully extended and the glide angle held at 120 m.p.h.I.A.S. A three point landing could be made by using elevator control, and hard braking was possible without the tail lifting.

Operations continued. On 23 March 1941 Sqn. Ldr. A. F. Robertson set off for Rotterdam. On return, for reasons unknown, N3643 hit high tension cables at Halewood Common, Leiston, the crew unaware they were so low. The deepest penetration so far came on 27 March. Flt. Lt. E. V. Best in N3652 joined 40

Wellingtons for a 3 hr. 45 min. flight to Cologne. The load of $5 \times 1,000$ lb. and 6×500 lb. G.P.s was dropped from 14,000 ft. Temperamental bomb doors had to be wound shut by hand.

No. 7 Squadron had moved to Newmarket the previous day. From 5 April, after one ineffective operation, the personnel of 'B' Flight returned to Oakington, proceeding daily to Newmarket by road.

Inevitably Bomber Command, encouraged by the Prime Minister, ordered Stirlings to Berlin. On 9 April three crews left Newmarket for the 'Big City'. It was too soon for such an operation. Apart from the distance involved, it meant penetration of flak and searchlight belts at relatively low altitude. With meagre radio aids, and the possibility of weather deterioration, it was exceptionally risky. Flying Officer J. F. Sach had propeller trouble, turned back from the Dutch coast and jettisoned his load. Blacklock aborted with engine trouble. Near Lingen N6005 was shot about when a Bf 110 attacked. The crew bombed Emden from 16,000 ft. Berlin had probably escaped attack, but from Flt. Lt. V. F. B. Pike and crew nothing was heard apart from a faint call for instructions. N6011 was shot down near Lingen by Feldwebel Scherling of 7/NJG 1, making the Luftwaffe's 98th night kill, and was destroyed.

Production now totalled 33 Stirlings, sufficient for a second squadron. Flt. Lt. Best took N3644 to XV Squadron, Wyton, on 11 April, and 'B' Flight 7 Squadron returned to Oakington, which had now dried out.

Wg. Cdr. Harris's task of working up 7 Squadron was complete, and his place was taken by Wg. Cdr. H. R. Graham. Next night, 14 April, three crews made an attack on the *Scharnhorst* and *Gneisenau* at Brest. Kiel and Emden were targets the following night. Then, on the 17th, came another try for Berlin. Flt. Lt. Williams dropped his $5 \times 1,000$ lb. and 7×500 lb. bombs across the centre of the city, the first bombs certain to have fallen there from a Stirling.

Lord Trenchard visited Oakington on 18 April and, on the 20th, 75 'other ranks' left for Wyton and 7 Squadron's strength reverted to normal. Wg. Cdr. Graham took N3655 to Hatfield, demonstrating the aircraft to VIPs. Also in the flying display was that 'wonder bomber', the Mosquito—the antithesis of the Stirling.

Next evening Flt. Lt. Cruikshank set off for Cologne, but failed to locate it. He jettisoned his bombs but, on homing to Marham, he crashed at Stanbourne 'Q' site. An enemy intruder had latched on to N6009, its bombs narrowly missing the crashed Stirling.

Thoughts were being directed towards the 1941 summer bombing offensive. At Bomber Command on 9 April a meeting discussed possible daylight employment of the Stirling.

The short hours of darkness made speed and defensive armament essential. The Stirling performed reasonably well on both counts, and planning went ahead.

On 26 April Sir Archibald Sinclair visited Oakington to acquire first-hand knowledge of the squadron's operations. He enquired about range and general capability with an eye to summer operations.

Future production of the Stirling was brighter, for a third source was now in being. Austin Motors had built Fairey Battles at Birmingham while they were preparing to switch to the Stirling late 1940. Bombing of Birmingham impeded progress, however, and it was not until March 1941 that the first Austin Stirling was completed.

Austin Motors was a separate Stirling production unit set up by M. A. P. Short's initially passed on 'know-how' to Austin's, but new jigging methods were introduced at Longbridge. Austin's were more geared to production line methods, and their tooling allowed for faster building than at Short's. It was a widely held opinion that the workmanship on Short machines was superior to that of Austin's, but that the airframe was heavier. Short's were also building Sunderlands, and officialdom exhorted them to build both at faster rates despite their capacity being already fully utilised.

Eager to assess the merits of the Austin aircraft, Boscombe Down conducted a brief analysis of W7426, the first flown, which was tested at 53,390 lb. Controls seemed heavier, the ailerons in particular feeling uncomfortably heavy at high speed. Elevator and aileron controls seemed slacker, but stability was normal. With flaps and undercarriage down the aircraft dropped the starboard wing, rectification only coming after a dive. But generally the performance was as good as that of parent firm aircraft. About 30 of the first Austin machines were powered by Hercules Mk. Xs, which were also power plants for a batch beginning with N6005 at Belfast.

On 27 April it was decided to begin daylight operations. At 11.30 hrs. Sqn. Ldr. Lynch-Blosse left Newmarket on the first cloud cover day raid, but he ran out of cloud and aborted. Next day Flg. Off. Witt set forth in N6010 and, using cloud cover, managed a lunchtime raid on the centre of Emden unloading 18 × 500 lb. bombs. He then flew across the town at 2,000 ft. machine gunning the docks.

Meanwhile at Wyton, XV Squadron had converted from Wellingtons in remarkably quick time under the leadership of Wg. Cdr. H. R. Dale, ably assisted by Sqn. Ldrs. Menaul and Morris. The squadron first operated on 30 April, ambitiously against Berlin. Flt. Lt. Raymond penetrated to the city, but 10/10 cloud obscured it. He came home via Kiel, where bombs fell on a searchlight concentration. Dale in N3654 was unlucky. His engine oil temperature rose dramatically and low engine revs. occurred in a port engine, so he bombed searchlights near Hamburg. Squadron Leader Morris had such a high rate of fuel consumption that he turned off track and bombed Kiel (the main target for 3 Group) from 16,000 ft. Sqn. Ldr. Menaul encountered engine trouble and was forced to turn back off Borkum.

Nine Stirlings had operated, the highest number yet—but not without loss, for N6014 of 7 Squadron crashed at Wenhaston, Suffolk on return, probably owing to fuel shortage. The starboard wing hit a hedge, the aircraft swung and its lowered undercarriage collapsed.

There was, at this time, a spate of engine troubles due in part to fuel pump failures. Sqn. Ldr. W. T. C. Seale, taking off from Oakington on 8 May, had two engines cut out for this reason; N6019 slithered to a halt without damage. But 7 Squadron was more sobered on 2/3 May. Three crews had been to Hamburg, accompanied by Wellingtons. As Flt. Lt. Cruikshank circled Oakington preparatory to landing, a marauding Ju 88C came upon the Stirling. With the crew fatigued after their operation, and inadequate ground control, the Stirling circled low. The German fired as the Stirling's undercarriage was lowered. N6012 was soon ablaze, and on approach hit trees near Dry Drayton. The crew died.

Day raids were now mixed with night attacks. On 5 May 7 Squadron's incendiaries fell for the first time, from N3655, on Mannheim. On 6 May Lynch-Blosse bombed a convoy in daylight, with uncertain results. The usual load at this time was $5 \times 1,000$ lb. H.E.

At Wyton, XV Squadron were getting into their stride. They had first dropped incendiaries on 2 May, on Rotterdam. Plt. Off. Campbell set off for Berlin on 8 May, but again engine trouble occurred. Another crew placed their bombs on Berlin, but on approach the starboard inner engine failed and boost on the port inner fell alarmingly. N6013 lost height fast. After 'bombs away', searchlights picked up the aircraft at 11,000 ft. The pilot corkscrewed to 7,000 ft. amid intense, accurate flak. Soon the gyrocompass and artificial horizon were out of use; but the bomber returned on three engines, the pilot relying on his airspeed indicator and turn and bank indicator.

On 10 May XV Squadron sent two more crews to Berlin. Raymond managed to pinpoint Steinhunder Lake and, despite cloud topping 12,000 ft., bombed from 18,000 ft. Flak was intense, and N6018 was hit in many places. Then the port inner motor burst into flames. About 20 miles north of Dummer Lake, searchlights held the aircraft and a single engined fighter attacked, firing from 200 yd. on the starboard quarter. The rear gunner fired, possibly damaging the fighter. Raymond dived, released a flare which attracted searchlights and a fighter, which possibly believed it to be a burning bomber. Raymond hastily made for home.

At 00.04 hrs. on 11 May, Freya F 42 radar at Medenblik, Holland, on the west side of the Ijsselmeer, picked up an incoming bomber. It was N3654 of XV Squadron, flown by Wg. Cdr. Dale; he had already been contacted by Oblt. Prinz zur Lippe of 4.NJG/1. F 42 held his Bf 110 on course, with the bomber flying on a reciprocal track about 5 km north. The fighter was then put on to a collision course. As soon as the bomber came into view, zur Lippe placed himself slightly below the Stirling out of range of the tail gunner. The rear gunner did not see the fighter until it delivered its second attack, when a series of fast S turns were made. After a fifth assault the Stirling turned for the west, by which time it was over the Ijsselmeer. Three thick fuel trails streamed from wing tanks. In the face of return fire, two more assaults were made. As zur Lippe came in for his eighth attack the port inner engine was ablaze; he took up position alongside the bomber, from which the bombs were being jettisoned near the F 42 installation. N3654 was now quite low, but the crew baled out as the port outer engine burst into flames. Left to its fate, the Stirling slipped into a vertical dive, broke up in the air and disintegrated upon impact. The Germans were unable to identify the wreckage. The Bf 110D–O had required 561 rounds of MG 17 and 53 of MG FF to bring down the first Stirling to fall in Holland.

German fliers assessed that the bomber cruised at 200 m.p.h. and had well

11.   Stirling N3568 'E-Easy' of XV Squadron crashed near Hengelo, Holland, at 04.05 hrs. on 8 September 1941, the first Stirling to fall reasonably intact into enemy hands. One of the crew was Richard Pape who recounted his story in *Boldness be My Friend.*

protected fuel tanks from which fire had spread slowly. They reckoned the Stirling just able to fly on two engines; and that the attacking position that had been used, below the rear turret, was outside its field of fire. Had a successful belly turret been fitted the story might have been different. Instead, the retractable 'dustbin' turret on early Stirlings had been removed because it persistently lowered itself particularly over rough ground when taxiing.

Wg. Cdr. Dale's place was taken by Wg. Cdr. P. B. Ogilvie. About this time Sqn. Ldr. R. D. Speare took over 'A' Flight of 7 Squadron from Sqn. Ldr. Lynch-Blosse.

Both squadrons again headed for Berlin on 2 June. They took off before darkness fell, relying upon cloud cover on their outward flight. Flg. Off. Mitchell and crew of 7 Squadron were missing, but Sgt. Needham of XV Squadron, making slow progress, bombed Kiel. Quiet on arrival, it was soon covered by searchlight glare. Then a fighter was vectored on to him, but was shaken off.

The arrival of N3663 at Oakington on 6 June marked an important advance for the Stirling. This was the first to enter squadron service fitted with Hercules Mk. XIs and a dorsal turret. The 81st and subsequent bomber Stirlings—from N3662 and N6066 on—all had dorsal turrets, though slow delivery rates meant that few would see service for some weeks. By 6 June only 47 Stirlings had been accepted by the R.A.F.

The Hercules Mk. XI developed 1,315 h.p. max. power at sea level, 1,460 h.p. max. power at 9,500 ft. On normal climb at 2,500 revs. the power outputs were 1,315 h.p. at 2,000 ft. and 1,185 h.p. at 12,750 ft. Cruise power was 1,020 h.p. at 7,500 ft. and 920 h.p. at 17,750 ft. on 2,500 revs. For take-off at 2,900 revs. the

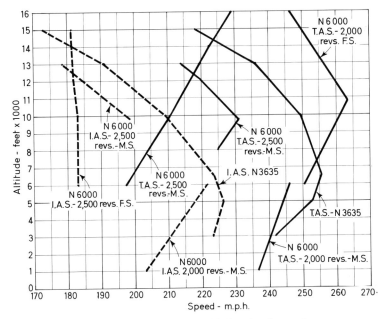

10. Maximum speeds, Mk. I N6000, with dorsal and ventral turrets—70,000 lb.; N3635, without turrets.

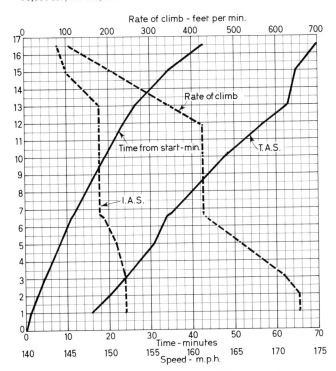

11. Performance, Mk. I N6000 (Hercules XI), no dorsal turret—70,000 lb.

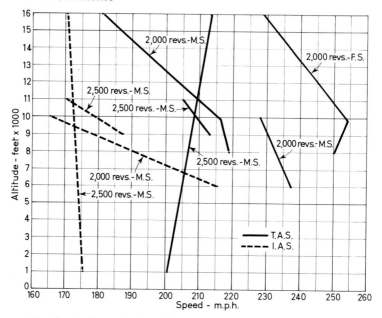

12.   Speeds, first production Mk. I N3662 (Hercules XI), with dorsal turret—70,000 lb.

output was 1,590 h.p., a considerable all-round improvement in engine performance.

Modification 312 introduced the dorsal turret in place of beam and ventral guns, representing the third stage in Stirling armament. The Stirling Mk. I Series i had an F.N.5A nose turret, F.N.25A ventral and F.N.4A rear turret. The Mk. I series ii had F.N.55A beam mountings, replacing the F.N.25A. The new Series iii, still able to accommodate 26 troops for reinforcement purposes, had an F.N.5A in the nose, F.N.7A (later F.N.50A) dorsal and, later, provision for F.N.64A ventral turret and an F.N.20A (Modification 216) in the rear position. This latter turret differed from the earlier one by having servo feed. Additional turrets pushed the c.g. further aft.

The curiously shaped F.N.7A, first introduced on the Blackburn Botha, had also been fitted to the Avro Manchester. There, it had brought severe vibration to the central fin; indeed some had disintegrated, so urgent tests had to be carried out on N3662. They showed some vibration of the fin during turret rotation, but the turret had little effect upon speed. Urgent comparison was undertaken with the F.N.50A. That turret vibrated badly, and further modification was needed; whereas the aerodynamics of the F.N.7A were satisfactory. No coaming was yet fitted at the base of the turret.

The Mk. I series iii was in short supply for some time, although on 12 June 7 Squadron sent off its 100th Stirling sortie, N3663 being among the seven that went to Hüls. Three Stirlings of 7 Squadron had so far been lost on operations, and four in accidents. By the end of June 1941 7 Squadron had despatched 135 night sorties and XV Squadron, for the loss of three aircraft, had sent out 70. But now the emphasis was about to change to daylight operations.

Chapter 5

Daylight Interlude

The Air Staff hoped that new bomber types would undertake daylight raids in the summer of 1941. The brief hours of darkness meant that such raids seemed a necessity.

On 9 June the Blenheims of 2 Group were still trying to halt German ships supplying occupation forces in France. Wg. Cdr. Graham and Flt. Lt. R. W. Cox set off to bring added weight to the campaign, and German fighters were quick to respond. Two Bf 109s, one of which was shot down, attacked Cox's aircraft; then another two went after N6020, Graham's machine, which was hit in many places.

Next day Flt. Lt. G. Blacklock in N6022 and Sqn. Ldr. W. T. C. Searle in N6003 set out for Emden. Cloud cover ran out, and they turned back. North West of Vlieland, Blacklock, then at 7,000 ft. was attacked by three Bf 109s. He dived to sea level and then into cloud, one enemy fighter having fired on him. Sgt. A. J. Graham, the rear gunner, engaged the enemy, first on the port side then on the starboard. Two more double stern attacks were delivered. During the second the enemy aircraft approached from astern to 150 yd., breaking off to port. Using the Stirling's excellent manoeuvrability, Blacklock quickly turned to starboard, giving Graham another chance to fire, which sent one Bf 109 into the sea. Then, to Graham's dismay, two rear gunsights went out of action. Through eight more attacks he directed his pilot to avoid enemy fire before the stoppage was cleared. The final attack came from the starboard bow, allowing Sgt. E. V. Ashton a long burst which finally discouraged the foe. The crew had survived an 18 minute attack.

Six Stirlings, three from each squadron, were despatched to attack Emden on 28 June. Plt. Off. Campbell's aircraft, N3656:H of XV Squadron, was damaged by fighter fire, but it was 7 Squadron who bore the brunt of the defender's wrath.

Sqn. Ldr. D. Speare (N6020) found no target, but his companions, Flt. Lt. Collins (N6007) and Flg. Off. G. B. Blacklock (N3663) were set upon by three 109s for a three minute fight. Collins closed up on Blacklock, and they finished the engagement at sea level. Five minutes later half a dozen yellow nosed 109s attacked from astern and beam. One closed to 25 yd., facing fire from the mid-upper gunner and retreated, smoking. Another attacked from ahead, sharply swerving to port as the nose gunner fired. Collins again closed on to his colleague, but his outer starboard engine was now out of use. His airspeed had fallen and he was unable to retain formation. Blacklock circled to afford protection while his crew tried to contact Collins's crew by Aldis lamp. They feared that some of these were injured, maybe dead. It was to no avail; N6007 struck the water nose first, then its tail broke off by the fuselage door. The rear part sank vertically into the water.

Blacklock set course for home, but the ordeal was not over. At 17.40 hrs. off Southwold, a couple of Hurricanes dived in to attack from starboard, one opening fire from 600 yd. The bomber crew flashed the colour of the day, whereupon the Hurricanes sheered off.

The next running battle for 7 Squadron came on 4 July. Plt. Off. D. T. Witt, Sgt. B. Madgwick and Flg. Off. J. Kinnane set out to bomb Borkum's seaplane base. Messerschmitt Bf 109s soon shot down Kinnane's aircraft. Witt was attacked four times by Bf 109Fs, but his gunner, Flg. Off. J. L. A. Mills, though wounded, drove them off. He then left his turret, but another attack developed. He courageously returned to his turret and shot down a Bf 109 despite his wounds.

Saturday 5 July saw Stirlings introduced to *Circus* operations. Squadron Leader Menaul left Flt. Lt. Gilmour and Flg. Off. Thompson to bomb the Fives-Lille steel works. Their escort was met at 10,000 ft. over Southend, where Kenley and Northolt Wings took up station, Hornchurch Wing giving escort cover and Biggin Hill and Tangmere Wings target support. With 312 Squadron close, the Stirlings made landfall at Dunkirk, meeting flak near Gravelines, over Roubaix and in the target area. Flying Officer Marsh met his fighter escort over West Malling and dropped 18×500 lb. bombs on Abbeville without resistance.

The others made a dummy run, then placed $15 \times 1,000$ lb. and 30×500 lb. bombs around the target from 12,000 ft. Moments before, Bf 109s had dived from 25,000 ft., and they passed through the bomber formation. 312 Squadron raced into action, claiming a Bf 109 trying to attack the bombers' stern.

Spitfires of the Target Support force closed in over Dunkirk as the enemy, by diving at the bombers, tried to draw off the fighters towards Lille. No. 616 Squadron drove them off, and 610 Squadron covered the withdrawal.

Early on 6 July Wg. Cdr. Graham, Cox and Witt set off for Le Trait's shipyards; but bombing was poor. In the afternoon XV Squadron despatched two formations led by Sqn. Ldrs. Menaul and Piper to Fives-Lille. They rendezvoused with the Hornchurch Wing over Manston at 13,000 ft., reached Lille at 14.28 hrs. and bombed from 14,000 ft., dropping $24 \times 1,000$ lb. and 56×500 lb. bombs, two or three sticks falling in adjacent marshalling yards. Flak was heavy, and again fighters broke through to the Stirlings. Sgt. Ward, Flt. Lt. Gilmour's front gunner in the second vic, damaged a Bf 109. The Stirling was also damaged before the fighter broke off, hotly pursued by Hurricanes of 71 and 306 Squadrons from the close escort. At the time of attack the bombers were half a mile apart, so the rear of the forward formation was unprotected, allowing three Bf 109s to close, one of which was shot down. No. 71 Squadron was continuously engaged back to the coast, and 242 Squadron attacked Bf 109s pestering the withdrawing bombers.

Both Stirling squadrons again operated on 7 July. Plt. Off. Stokes attacked Hazebrouck, but the bombs fell wide. A Bf 109 was shot down and three claimed as probables, without British loss. Menaul, Gilmour and Thompson went for the

Kuhlman chemical works at Chocques. The load of $15 \times 1,000$ lb. and 42×500 lb. H.E. burst on a cooling tower and ammonia works. Four crews of 7 Squadron went for the aircraft factory at Meaulte-Albert, where $21 \times 1,000$ lb., 30×500 lb. H.E. and 360×4 lb. incendiaries burst around the works. No enemy reaction was encountered by the bombers, but the escort claimed two Bf 109s and two Spitfires were lost.

Early on 8 July three Stirlings left Oakington for a chemical works north-east of Lens and the power station at Mazingarbe. Rendezvous was over Rye, but the Stirlings were diverted from entry over Boulogne by heavy flak. Two bombed Lens, where hits were claimed on coking ovens and a gasometer. Enemy fighters penetrated to Witt's aircraft. Plt. Off. Morley was miserably unlucky, for anti-aircraft guns opened up on him as he recrossed the English coast. N6034 caught fire and crashed.

The same day Sqn. Ldr. Piper, Needham and Campbell went for the Kuhlman works at Lille, and Lille power station. Heavy flak forced violent evasive action, and photographs showed that the attack had failed. All three bombers were hit by flak, and one was attacked by three red nosed Bf 109s. Fighter action cost the R.A.F. seven pilots.

Bombs from XV Squadron missed Mazingarbe on 9 July. Haze over France caused the secondary target at Lebuisière to be chosen. Bf 109s concentrated on the bombers, which claimed a fighter.

Rendezvous took place over Rye at noon on 10 July, Flg. Off. Witt leading three 7 Squadron aircraft. Near Boulogne, Flg. Off. Frazer ran into a salvo of about five shells which scored direct hits. His N6012 was blown to pieces, but some of the crew baled out. The remaining Stirlings bombed buildings and rail sidings. Rolfe's aircraft came under fighter attack, hits being scored on his tail unit. Return fire from the beam gun entered the enemy's engine.

Nos. 7 and XV Squadrons operated again on 11 July. Wg. Cdr. Graham led Flt. Sgt. A. Yardley and Plt. Off. K. O. Blunden at Yainville power station and submarine building yards at Le Trait. It was an uneventful operation. Then 7 Squadron resumed night operations.

During the afternoon XV Squadron tried again for Fives-Lille, but owing to thundery conditions the trio missed their target, bombing Hazebrouck marshalling yards instead.

On 12 July *Circus* 46 was directed against the ship lift at Arques. All three Stirlings were hit by flak, and their bombs overshot.

Then, for three days, XV Squadron stood by, but the weather was unsuitable. Several times the Stirlings took off, only to be thwarted by cloud. The suspense of operations was endured to no purpose; even worse was the jettisoning of thousands of gallons of fuel prior to landing.

July 19 brought another tragedy over the French coast. Sqn. Ldr. T. W. Piper set off, leading three aircraft, to bomb a factory near Lille. The formation met 10/10 cloud over the primary target and had to turn about for the last resort, Dunkirk docks, where the enemy gunners were waiting for the Stirlings and placed accurately predicted shots around them. The leader's aircraft was hit, and his port inner caught fire. Flames pierced the port wing and pieces began to fall away. Piper ordered all aircraft to release bombs, then his aircraft curled away to port. Two of the crew baled out; then, after straightening out, N6018:C zoomed into a vertical dive from 1,500 ft., spiralling into the ground.

Dense cloud resulted in an abortive operation against Hazebrouck on 20 July. Early next day three crews left for the accumulator factory at Lille. Visibility was poor, and bombs were jettisoned in Barrow Deep. Flak had been heavy around Dunkirk. Sgt. H. Taunton was forced to put down at Manston after his starboard inner had been put out of action. He had lost height to 7,000 ft. over Merville when two Bf 109s sneaked up, fired on him and caused his starboard outer to stop too. Escorted by Hornchurch's Spitfires, he lined up on Manston. He was unable to make the customary left-handed circuit, so he turned right. On his second attempt he brought off an extremely difficult landing safely.

The final *Circus* was a failure, poor weather preventing rendezvous. Clouds towered to 23,000 ft. and the operation was abandoned, the 'fourth consecutive failure—a colossal waste of effort, fuel and bombs', in XV Squadron's opinion. Stirling *Circuses* ended. They had not much roused the enemy, although his gunners had scored some spectacular successes. Fighter losses were quite high, and postwar research indicated that the British claims were highly inflated.

This was not the end of Stirling day raids, in spite of what had been intended. On 23 July events developed with speed and ferocity. A reconnaissance flight over Brest revealed that *Scharnhorst* had slipped her moorings, and it was immediately decided to attack her with 2,000 lb. A.P. bombs. Her move caused surprise and suspicion, for a large scale day raid on Brest had been planned for the morrow. Had there been a leak—was it pure coincidence?

Scharnhorst sailed south. At first it was believed she had gone to La Rochelle, but later information showed that the battle cruiser was at La Pallice.

At 17.45 Sqn. Ldr. R. W. Cox in N6037, Flt. Lt. G. B. Blacklock in N6035 and Flg. Off. Witt in W7434 became airborne. After skilful navigation by Flg. Off. Walker, La Pallice was found and the ship attacked from 15,000 ft., each aircraft using $3 \times 2,000$ lb. A.P. bombs. Flg. Off. G. Walker's bombs straddled the ship, which was hit by a 2,000 lb. bomb. The other bombs missed her. As 7 Squadron turned away from the target, six Bf 109s attacked. Sgt. Cappell, in Cox's machine, claimed two. 'Well done 7 Squadron', signalled the A.O.C., 'on a first class effort.'

XV's trio was less fortunate. Plt. Off Needham could not raise his under-carriage and was forced to jettison his fuel and land with bombs still aboard. Sgt. Jones pressed on, and came across a ship at a jetty on an island. He had found Fromontine, not La Pallice. Flg. Off. Campbell was believed to have bombed the target, but with what success was unknown, since he ditched 50 miles from Milford Haven.

Chapter 6

Increasing Momentum

After their arrival at Brest, *Scharnhorst* and *Gneisenau* attracted much bombing, but by July 1941 sinking of Allied shipping had temporarily declined. Bomber Command was free for redeployment against German industry.

Overcoming the Ruhr haze seemed an insurmountable problem. Only moonlight brought in worthwhile results. By August 1941 the Telecommunications Research Establishment had evolved *Gee*, which was thought to be usable as a blind bombing aid, but it was soon found to be insufficiently accurate. Not until early 1942 was *Gee* fitted into Stirlings.

When 3 Group's Wellingtons began dropping 4,000 lb. 'cookies', the Stirling was outclassed. The longitudinal stiffeners in the bomb bay precluded bombs of greater girth than that of the 2,000 lb. A.P. weapon. Otherwise, however, the Stirling's bomb capacity was not as poor as often presented, for to Ruhr targets it could haul a 10,000 lb. load. By 1942 it was clear that the most effective raids had been those when a high proportion of incendiary bombs were used. Stirlings could carry these in plenty.

For the present there were only two Stirling squadrons. Production remained slow, the first Austin-built aircraft coming along in June 1941. By the close of July only 48 Stirlings had reached the R.A.F. That month eight were lost during operations, 16 so far. Another three had been written off owing to battle damage, five in accidents. Sorties totalled only 292. The picture was far from bright.

A new bombing directive of 9 July ordered moon period attacks on nine railway centres to cut the Ruhr and Rhineland off from the Russian front. Nearby civilian population centres would be raided on dark nights. The average strength of the force sent out was 60, very few of them Stirlings.

It was hoped that serviceability and performance would improve now that Hercules Mk. XI engined aircraft were entering service. N6029, the first from Belfast, joined XV Squadron on 15 June and W7432, the first Austin example, on 4 July.

On 14 July six crews of 7 Squadron set off carrying 30 × 1,000 lb. and 33 × 500 lb. H.E. bombs and 42 × 250 lb. S.B.C.s of incendiaries to Hanover. Flg. Off. Witt found his fuel consumption high. He nursed the aircraft to England, where the crew baled out, and landed the Stirling at Newton Slotman.

For the others, the return journey became an alarming experience as the weather deteriorated. Only one landed at Oakington. From N6033, unable to land before fuel ran out, the crew baled out, believing that the aircraft could crash in open country. Instead it crashed in the centre of Northampton—much to the disgust of the Chief Constable, who remarked: 'I can't have this.' Flt. Lt. D. A. J. Sanders in N6036 ran out of fuel and overshot Bircham Newton. Sqn. Ldr. Speare landed safely at Waterbeach; but Flg. Off. K. O. Blunden, who put down at Honington, damaged his tailwheel doors.

July ended spectacularly for 7 Squadron. Five crews set out for Cologne, four attacking the city. On return Wg. Cdr. Graham, flying at 10,000 ft., entered an electrical storm 30 miles E.S.E. of Bexhill. The temperature was $-4°C$. Severe glazed ice formed, there was a blinding flash and the Stirling began to fall out of control. The instruments went out of use, and the autopilot was switched off. At 4,000 ft. control was regained, although both D.R. and P.4 compasses remained out of use. The crew reached base with the aid of dead reckoning, map readings and Q.D.M.s, for the compass had a 70° error and the aircraft retained a lot of induced magnetism after the lightning strike. Flg. Off. C. I. Rolfe in N6029 encountered similar trouble when his machine was struck and the radio burnt out. He landed at Martlesham.

On 2 August 3 Group detailed 49 aircraft to attack Hamburg while five Stirlings, along with seven Wellington Mk. IIs carrying 4,000 lb. bombs, participated in the first of a series of small-scale raids on Berlin. From that night's operations Flg. Off. C. I. Rolfe and crew were missing in N3663, the squadron's first Hercules Mk. XI Stirling. It had first operated on 12 June against Hüls, carrying $5 \times 1,000$ lb. G.P., 12×500 lb. G.P. and 240×4 lb. incendiaries, the sortie, however, being abortive. It was used to bomb Ostend on 16 June, Kiel on three nights, for a Bremen day raid on 28 June and, in the hands of Wg. Cdr. Graham, in a Bremerhaven raid on 29 June, when a Bf 110 engaged the Stirling off Texel. The fighter was claimed as a probable. The bomber was extensively damaged and did not operate again until 30 July, when Cologne was the target.

The night of 14/15 August was a bad one for XV Squadron, who at the time were operating from Alconbury, since runway building was under way at Wyton. Four crews were briefed, one for Hanover and three for Magdeburg. Sqn. Ldr. J. F. Foulsham had difficulty raising the undercarriage so set course for the Wash to jettison the load. Almost immediately the port inner engine lost power and, unable to maintain height, he crashed near Ramsey. Pilot Officer Gould swung badly as he took off from Alconbury, and the undercarriage collapsed. Only two of 7 Squadron's crews reached Magdeburg. Plt. Off. W. N. Crebbin (N6042) short of fuel, made a forced landing at Graveley, where the aircraft crashed on the runway. At Oakington both Wg. Cdr. Graham and Witt overshot on return. Then an intruder placed a 250 kg. bomb on Barrack Block 'E', but this caused no casualties.

Duisburg was target for both Stirling squadrons on 28/29 August 1941. Seven crews of 7 Squadron set off, five claiming to attack the target area. Flt. Lt. D. J. H. Lay was attacked by a Bf 110. Shots blew out perspex from the rear turret and the gunner, Sgt. Macree, was severely wounded. When the Stirling began to perform an Immelmann turn and fall out of control, Macree baled out. By united effort Flt. Lt. Lay and Sgt. Tourville regained control. N3666 was now tail heavy, with trim tabs out of action. Notwithstanding, they located an alternative target, dropped $5 \times 1,000$ lb. and 8×500 lb. G.P.s, then came home at 135 m.p.h.I.A.S.—the fastest speed they could achieve—and made for Newmarket's long grass runway. The undercarriage was wound down by hand, but as they touched down the port gear failed; luckily there were no further casualties. Robinson, wounded, had kept to his station throughout the operation. It was a splendid effort by the entire crew.

Attempts were made to rationalise the Stirling modification programme. Some 450 gal. additional tankage was considered, for 1,945 gallons gave a still air range of 1,800 miles, whereas the aircraft was designed for 2,000 miles and an 8,000 lb. load. Current operational range, 1,300 miles with 6,000 lb. bomb load, was less than that of the Halifax. But the Stirling could carry a heavier load for a short range, so it was decided not to alter the tankage.

Operationally the event of the month was the first Stirling raid on Italy. Oakington sent seven aircraft, XV Squadron six, to bomb the Royal Arsenal, Turin. This involved a long, hazardous mission in the face of exacting weather conditions. Threading a way through the mountains or flying over the peaks was impossible: the ceiling of the Stirling would not permit this. Even the western route across Lake Geneva meant passing close to the Mont Blanc Massif, not a happy thought in darkness. Yet, with all this to conquer, the first journey to Italy on 10 September proved surprisingly successful.

All the 7 Squadron crews reached Turin, no mean achievement. Wg. Cdr. H. R. Graham's bombs burst across the town centre, Sqn. Ldr. Speare's too. Bayley's incendiaries caused three fires, and more were started by Flt. Lt. Lay and Flt. Lt. D. A. J. Sanders. Bombs from Ellis-Brown's aircraft burst north of the railway station. All returned safely after dropping $30 \times 1,000$ lb. H.E. and 120×50 lb. incendiaries.

Wyton's crews were less fortunate: only three reached Turin. This night Wyton's new satellite, Warboys, opened.

In mid September a Wyton Stirling arrived at A.F.D.U. Duxford for tactical fighting trials. They found it more manoeuvrable than they expected. 'When all the turrets are manned', read their report, 'there is extremely good all-round view.' The arc of fire from the three turrets covered the hemisphere above the aircraft. Beam attack could easily be countered now. Attack from below was against a blind spot, although some Stirlings had a gun poking through the emergency rear exit.

A second Italian raid, to Genoa, came on 28 September, only XV Squadron taking part. Group required 49 Wellingtons and six Stirlings, but eventually only two Stirlings and 45 Wellingtons took part. Cloud was 8/10 at the target, which both Stirlings reached, but strong winds brought anxiety over fuel states. Plt. Off. Jones landed at Thorney Island with fuel tanks almost dry.

On 3 October 7 Squadron sent nine crews to Brest. Cloud was thick, and they brought their bombs back. No. 7 Squadron was now operating from Bourn and Oakington, and to the former Sqn. Ldr. D. I. McCleod was returning in N6085 when, upon reaching the satellite, he was caught by a marauding Ju 88C. Six times it attacked as McCleod tried to evade. Finally N6085 was shot down in flames. Since it was near the end of the sortie, the rear gunner had left his turret for landing. Two of the crew luckily escaped by parachute, the bomber being at only 700 ft. when they baled out. Sgt. S. G. Matkin, on seeing the action, put his Stirling in a position for his gunners to engage, and they claimed to damage the Ju 88. The same aircraft, apparently, then directed its attention to Oakington, where the flarepath was lit. Night flying was in progress when bombs began to fall too close to the intrepid Wg. Cdr. Graham for comfort. Four night fighters were vectored on to the enemy aircraft, but it escaped.

Graham always showed tremendous qualities of leadership, and courage of the type often associated with a fighter pilot. A high flying Ju 88 had made some daylight reconnaissance flights over Oakington, and this, it seems, much annoyed Graham. He announced that he was going to take up a Stirling and shoot down the Junkers, but even in very light condition such an altitude was more than a Stirling could achieve.

About 60 aircraft were now in hand, and it was at last possible to expand the Stirling force. A unit was needed to give flying training to new crews. Accordingly 'C' Flight, 7 Squadron, under Flt. Lt. P. R. Crompton, was removed on 5 October to form the cadre of a new unit initially known as No. 26 Conversion Flight, and soon based at Waterbeach.

On 2 January 1942 the Flight became part of newly forming No. 1651 Conversion Unit, which provided more Stirling crews for Bomber Command than any other training unit. Much of the course at '1651' was devoted to learning how to handle an aircraft whose flying qualities could be tricky, particularly during take-off and landing. Bombing and gunnery were practised by crews teaming up prior to joining squadrons.

A new directive was issued in October making U-boat building yards priority targets. Bremen came under attack on 20 October, when 64 aircraft of 3 Group were detailed, whilst others went to Antwerp. No. XV Squadron despatched nine crews. Five bombed Bremen, but as Sgt. DeVille crossed East Anglia on his return his starboard outer engine failed and he ordered the crew to bale out, the aircraft crashing north of Feltwell. Such incidents to returning crews were not unusual.

On 22 October six crews of XV Squadron left for a sunset attack on Brest and the capital ships there. Proceeding in open formation, they approached from the seaward side to achieve maximum surprise. Flak hotly engaged them, and no ships were damaged.

One of the longest flights yet came on 28/29 October. Five crews of 7 Squadron and five of XV Squadron made for the Skoda works at Pilsen. Wind at bases was from the north-west, and the weathermen forecast cloud breaks over southern Germany. They were proved wrong, and there were violent wind changes north of Pilsen. Leaflets only were dropped in the target area, and bombs released around Frankfurt and Nuremberg.

Since the start of the war 149 Squadron had been operating Wellingtons, achieving public fame in the films *The Lion has Wings* and *Target for Tonight*. With two Stirling squadrons operational, and the conversion unit forming, it was now possible to equip a third squadron, and No. 149 was chosen. On 12 October N6093 and W7448 arrived at Mildenhall. By the end of October 149 had eight

12.   After serving 7 Squadron, R9147 joined 1651 Conversion Unit, Waterbeach, on 23 January 1943 and served until August 1944.

13.   R9295 of 149 Squadron crashed at Holywell Row, Suffolk, on 11 March 1942 and was burnt out.

aircraft, and conversion flying was under way.

Re-equipment proceeded through November. On the 26th N6099: OJ-C ventured to Ostend. Next day two air-sea rescue sorties were flown. On 30 November N6099 went to Bremerhaven with five of the squadron's Wellingtons.

The night of 7/8 November was marked by a new record for the number of Stirlings despatched. Making use of a long, dark night, 3 Group detailed 74 aircraft for Berlin, 8 for Mannheim, 22 for Ostend and 11 for Ruhr targets. Four crews were unable to take off, and 10 made early returns. It was hardly a successful night. No. 7 Squadron despatched 13 crews, the most yet; and XV Squadron sent 10, seven of these to Berlin. Weather was bad and only five of XV Squadron reached the city. Group lost 22 aircraft, two of them 7 Squadron Stirlings.

Another sobering day for 7 Squadron was 18 November. Eight crews were briefed for a cloud cover daylight raid on Brest. On take-off O'Brien had an engine fire. He tried to force land, and in doing so hit a telegraph pole and careered into a wall at Willingham, his second pilot being killed. The other crews found Brest cloud clad. One crew bombed through a brief cloud break, two on estimated positions. The remainder brought their loads back, and W7446 overshot on landing and was written off.

Poor accuracy in the Brest raids hastened the development of a radio bombing aid TR3098, code-name *Trinity*, which was later developed into *Oboe*. Trial installations were being made at Boscombe Down in N6090 of 7 Squadron, and 80 Wing fitting *Trinity* in Stirlings of both squadrons. At Rochester on 21 November a conference was held to discuss the fitting of TR1154/55 (*Gee*) in Stirlings. N3639 was first to have this (Modification 436), and N3681, just off the production line was set aside for trials at Short's.

A day raid was attempted by Wg. Cdr. Graham and Sgt. Taylor on 24 November. After attacking shipping south of Borkum, they were engaged by eight Bf 109Es, up to three attacking at any one time, giving up combat only at extreme range. One fighter had pressed home a frontal attack, the Stirling's gunner getting in some good firing. The mid-upper gunner managed some hits from a mere 150 ft., the rear gunner watching the fighter dive away smoking. Sgt. Taylor was attacked from three directions simultaneously, his upper and rear gunners being in action for 25 minutes. They claimed two fighters and one damaged. Stirling W7449 was liberally peppered in wings, fuselage and tailplane. If testimony was required as to the ability of the Stirling to absorb tremendous punishment and survive, it was surely here.

Both 7 and XV Squadrons each despatched two crews to the Ruhr for cloud cover attacks on 9 December. Absence of cloud forced XV Squadron to turn about, whereas 7 Squadron's duo had their target changed to a maritime one. Flt. Lt. Crebbin left in W7451:D at noon with Flg. Off. R. Ellis-Brown in W7440.

13.   Stirling Mk. I W7451. Delivered to 149 Squadron 26.10.41, became 'MG:D' of 7 Squadron 8.11.41. To 7 Conversion Flight. Overshot Oakington 15.5.42; repaired at Sebro. To 218 Conversion Flight 14.8.42; 1657 C.U. 2.10.42. On 4.2.43 spectacularly landed wheels-down in a field at Saville Row, 3 miles S. of King's Lynn. Written off 23.3.43. (For key to camouflage colours see page 184)

14. Bombing-up 'D-Dog' of 7 Squadron at Oakington. W7451 later served with 218 Conversion Flight and with 1657 Conversion Unit.

15. The famous Stirling N3669 'H-Harry' of XV Squadron on display outside St. Paul's Cathedral.

They came across a tanker, accompanied by two flak ships in line astern 5 miles off the Hook. As they turned for the run-up flak commenced, and Crebbin's aircraft was hit, the navigator, Sgt. H. C. Cotton being wounded. Ellis-Brown's Stirling was then hit, and its port undercarriage later collapsed on landing. Crebbin's tailwheel failed to lower, and he landed on the rear fuselage.

December's operations were almost all directed against Brest. That of 7 December was historic: for the first time Bomber Command employed *Trinity*. The apparatus did not work well, but Sqn. Ldr. B. D. Sellick bombed without seeing results and Sqn. Ldr. Swales dropped a 2,000 lb. bomb under guidance. Both 7 and XV Squadrons tried *Trinity* at Brest on 11 and 12 December, when 7 Squadron sent four aircraft, N6032: T, N6194: G, N3668: B and N3669: U; and XV Squadron used N3673: D and W7443: J.

Since it was clear that *Scharnhorst*, *Gneisenau* and *Prinz Eugen* must soon leave Brest, a heavy day raid using Stirlings, Halifaxes and Manchesters was mounted on 18 December, led by Wg. Cdr. H. R. Graham in N3669: E. Both 7 and XV Squadrons each despatched nine crews, take-off being around 09.45 hrs. The flights, in vics of three, formed up with Wg. Cdr. Ogilvie (N6093) leading XV Squadron. Rendezvous was over St. Ives, near Wyton. They then set course for Lundy Island where, it was planned, the Halifaxes would turn in behind them at 11.20 hrs. The Stirlings were a little early so they tracked out west. Then the formation turned south with 18 Halifaxes behind, after which came nine Manchesters.

Shortly after 12.30 hrs. the Stirlings began attacking from the south-east. Each vic crossed the target at one minute intervals, breaking for shallow dive bombing from 14,000 ft.

Radar cover alerted fighters before the bombing began. Wg. Cdr. H. R. Graham in N3669: E saw his $4 \times 2,000$ lb. bombs burst across the twin docks. Bf 109s were in action, and Graham's aircraft was hit both by their fire and by the intense flak. Plt. Off. G. E. Mitchell opened fire from the rear guns and claimed a Bf 109. Sqn. Ldr. W. V. Jennens in W7436: D was soon shot down, some of the crew baling out. Plt. Off. G. C. Baylie in N3668: B saw two of his bombs burst north-east of the docks. Fighters hotly engaged him, and his rear gunner, Sgt. J. M. Smith shot down a Bf 109.

As Plt. Off. G. T. Heard in N6095: K bombed, flak struck the astrodome, badly wounding Sgt. Hayward, the flight engineer. The rear gunner, Sgt. Inman, was hit in the shoulder, but kept to his post and did not report his injury until later.

W.O. N. L. Taylor's aircraft, N6089: L, suffered extensive flak damage and crash landed at Bourn. The port inner fuel tanks had been pierced, turrets put out of action, intercom damaged and a mainwheel tyre and tailwheel tyre burst.

Flt. Lt. B. Parnell in N3680 was shot down, but Plt. Off. S. G. Matkin in N6121 saw his bombs burst on the ships, although his aircraft, too, was extensively damaged. Hydraulics and undercarriage were hit, and a large portion of the rudder shot away. The port undercarriage would not lower and he crash landed at Oakington. His gunners claimed a Bf 109 and damaged another. Plt. Off. H. G. Pilling saw his bombs burst on a road at the north-west end of the docks, then his aircraft, W7454, was hit by flak in the mainplane, fuselage and rear turret, where a gunsight was put out of use.

Piloting N6086, 'MacRobert's Reply', was Sqn. Ldr. P. J. S. Boggis. 'It was a clear, crisp sunny day', he recalls, 'without a cloud in the sky. We flew into the target at about 17,000 ft. in vic formation, a long line of Stirlings, Halifaxes and Manchesters. I was leading my vic of three when we left England, but my No. 2 aborted and over the target my No. 3 was shot down, whether by flak or fighters we never knew. There was a heavy box barrage from about 12,000 ft. to 18,000 ft., and enemy fighters attacked us through this barrage; my aircraft was attacked several times, and my gunners shot down one Me 109 and claimed another. In the course of this battle we became separated from the rest of the formation. As soon as we completed the bombing run, we put our nose down and headed for the Channel.

'Once back over the sea, and down almost to sea level in case there were still fighters about—and not long since having crossed the French coast—our rear gunner suddenly reported a formation of six aircraft approaching from behind and about 2,000 ft. up. Before we had time to think the worst, someone came through with the news that these aircraft were Halifaxes—obviously returning from Brest and, like us, having lost height to gain speed. In our solitude they were a welcome sight, and when they came nearer they opened up their formation in invitation and gratefully we climbed and were enfolded in their midst. Thus we returned in grand style.' This was Boggis's last operation with XV Squadron.

By the time XV Squadron attacked the opposition was intense. Flg. Off. Vernieux in N3676:U and Plt. Off. D. A. Parkins both claimed hits on the ships, in addition to which two fighters were claimed and others damaged. Flg. Off. G. Bunce's aircraft, W7428:Z, was last seen with a wingtip on fire and diving to the sea, harried by fighters. Flt. Lt. G. G. Heathcote's aircraft, N3665:B, was also shot down. N6092 had earlier aborted, with oil covering the rear turret. N3700 of 7 Squadron also turned back.

Crews in the Halifaxes watched as the Stirlings disappeared behind a wall of flak, themselves flying in among stragglers. Being first, the Stirlings had attracted the most enemy response, and though they were the best armed of any, four were shot down, along with a Halifax and a Manchester.

Back from the raid, the squadrons received a signal from C. in C. Bomber Command: 'My warmest congratulations on a very successful and gallant action this afternoon.'

The pressure on Brest increased. On 23 December six crews of 7 Squadron made another night attack. Searchlights covered the sky, dazzling the crews, and Matkin's beam gunners tried to shoot them out. Again, no hits were confirmed on the ships.

Next day XV Squadron put up a nine aircraft formation—a very impressive sight—for bombing practice for another special day effort. *Gneisenau* had moved out of dry dock. In mid afternoon the squadron crews were told to hold three hours' readiness. They stood by throughout Christmas Day, navigators working out square search areas in case the ship slipped out during the festive season. For three days they stood by, then, at 08.00 hrs. on 30 December, were called to readiness. At 09.15 hrs. they were briefed for Operation *Veracity II*, only to find the operation cancelled at 09.45 hrs. as they were about to leave for Alconbury (from where operations were currently being mounted, runway building having begun at Wyton on 12 December). At the satellite weather was poor, visibility below 1,000 yd. Oakington's squadron had concentrated on small scale night raids using *Trinity*.

January 1942 found both squadrons making experimental raids on Brest using *Trinity*. Three modified aircraft were passed to XV Squadron on the 5th, making a total of seven, but the squadron still awaited the expected day raid for which a new bombsight had been tested. Then the tempo tailed off when poor weather interfered. On 5 January 7 Squadron were taken off operations while their aircraft were fitted with *Gee*.

At Waterbeach, No. 1651 Conversion Unit formed in January 1942. At the same time each Stirling squadron was ordered to raise a Conversion Flight, training crews to operational standard. Thus, No. 7 Conversion Flight formed at Oakington, No. XV at Alconbury, No. 149 at Lakenheath and No. 218 at Marham, where Stirlings would soon be based. Each squadron had to surrender four aircraft (2 I.E. + 2 I.R.) for the Conversion Flights, reducing squadron strength to 14 I.E. + 0 I.R.

More Stirlings were arriving with F.N. 20 rear turrets, and during January 3 Group took delivery of the first operational Stirling fitted with an F.N. 50 dorsal turret, not so cramped as the F.N. 7 but more difficult to enter.

Weather was poor in January. During some sorties crews found themselves flying between layers of cloud. It was little wonder that many of the photographs of Brest showed entry at the wrong bay along the French coast.

Although Brest was the main target at this time, other naval targets were attacked by XV Squadron in 1942, including Wilhelmshaven and Emden. Occasionally an industrial target was bombed: for example Stirlings went to Munster on 22 January. Only four crews reached it. Plt. Off. Barr, after bombing, was caught by flak and forced down to 3,000 ft. He and his crew miraculously survived no less than 15 fighter attacks.

The Commando attack on the Lofotens at the end of December 1941 convinced Hitler that the British were planning an invasion of Norway. He decided that *Tirpitz* and the capital ships in Brest must go to Norway. Reconnaissance aircraft soon located *Tirpitz* in Aasfjord 18 miles E.N.E. of Trondheim, in a narrow part of the fjord and close to land. Already attempts at camouflaging her had been seen, and the only possibility of successful bombing would be on a moonlight night. The British, of course, saw the ship as a threat to Atlantic shipping, though this was not what the Germans intended.

Orders were issued for Operation *Oiled* to take place on the first suitable night from 29/30 January. A total of 22 heavy bombers were to be used: 12 Stirlings— eight of XV Squadron and four of 149—and 10 Halifaxes.

Eventually 10 crews of XV Squadron headed for Lossiemouth on 28 January, maintaining radio silence to cover their move. Loads of 2,000 lb. A.P.s were carried in each aircraft, along with some 500 lb. A.P.s.

On 29 January 1942 eight crews were briefed to attack *Tirpitz*, taking off around

16.   R9304 of 1651 Conversion Unit photographed from an early Mk. I. Served 1651 Conversion Unit from 5 April 1942, written off after landing swing at Oakington, 28 February 1943.

03.00 hrs. on the 30th. Weather, poor at base, was expected to be excellent at the target. Eventually five crews took off.

Norwegian weather can be treacherous at any time, and changes quickly. Icing troubles increased over the North Sea, and cloud thickened to 19,000 ft. The Stirlings turned back about 100 miles from Norway in appalling weather.

They waited for a break, but it never came. One Stirling was burnt out during a refuelling operation before the detachment left for Wyton on the 7th. The last few aircraft were diverted to Peterhead for an overnight stop. Next morning they took off, one of them swinging off the runway and ploughing through a dispersal. By the time it had stopped sliding, the port undercarriage had broken off and a crushed Spitfire was rammed hard against the rear fuselage. The Stirling was N6086, probably best known of them all, 'MacRobert's Reply'.

There is a moving story behind this name. Lady MacRobert, the widow of a baronet, Sir Alexander MacRobert, who had died in 1922, had three sons. The eldest was killed flying his own aircraft before the war (not in the R.A.F. as many accounts wrongly indicate), and the other two were killed during wartime operations. Each inherited the title in turn. In memory of her gallant sons, Lady MacRobert had given money for the purchase of four Hurricane fighters and a Stirling. This created a wave of admiration and interest at the time. N6086 was chosen as the Stirling to carry the emblem of the MacRobert family and the name 'MacRobert's Reply'.

Otherwise, there was nothing special about this machine, which was assigned to XV Squadron on 15 September 1941. After acceptance checks and updating to current service standard, N6086 received the identity letters LS : F. In a ceremony at Wyton on 10 October 1941 Wg. Cdr. Ogilvie, commanding XV Squadron, formally turned N6086 over to Flg. Off. Peter Boggis. Why he was chosen for this particular honour Peter Boggis remains unsure, but he had survived 15 operational sorties to that time, and thinks that this might well have been a factor.

N6086 flew its first operational sortie on 12 October 1941, with Nuremberg as target. Two nights later, heading for the same city, icing at 12,000 ft. became so severe that Mannheim was bombed instead. On 20 October bombs and leaflets were dropped over Bremen. Then, on 24 October, Flt. Lt. Gilmour took the place of Flg. Off. Boggis for an attack on *Prinz Eugen* at Brest. The night of 28/29 October found Flg. Off. Boggis and N6086 making the long haul to Pilsen. The weather was bad and the temperature fell to $-26°C$, the poor heating system bringing terrible punishment to the crew, who bombed Frankfurt after finding Pilsen cloud clad. Crossing Nieuport on return, flak opened up, and the tail unit was damaged. This put the aircraft out of use for some weeks.

Patched up, 'MacRobert's Reply' bombed Cologne on 13 December, Flg. Off. Boggis once more at the helm. Poor weather prevented Brest from being bombed when they arrived there on 16 December; but then came delivery of $4 \times 2,000$ lb. bombs during a daylight raid, after which Flg. Off. Boggis ended his tour of operations. Three Bf 109s tried unsuccessfully to bring down the bomber. Finally came the detachment to Lossiemouth, when the take-off accident occurred.

After the incident, Sgt. Smith remained behind with 'F-Freddie'. His task was to see that the badge on the nose was carefully removed, then taken to Wyton to be transferred to another Stirling, W7531.

N6086 was dismantled and loaded on to 60 ft. 'Queen Mary' transporters which carried it on the long trek to the Sebro works at Cambridge. As the convoy passed through Aberdeen, a lot of people saw the huge aircraft on its long loader, a rare sight in those parts. Although the badge had been removed, the nose legend 'MacRobert's Reply' had unfortunately not been painted out. There being considerable local interest in the famed aircraft, many people phoned Lady MacRobert at her home at Dounside 30 miles away to tell her of what they had seen, which must surely have distressed her.

When the fuselage reached Madingley Works, word spread fast from the guardroom. Within minutes the work force streamed from the workshops. 'It *mustn't* be our "MacRobert's Reply" ' was the general sentiment. And as the wreckage passed slowly, many wept. Mrs. Phyllis Walliker among them remembers: 'Yes, I cried, and I thought of the young men who might have been in her at the time. We were all very distressed—the machine was a in a terrible mess.'

In fact N6086 was repaired, and gave useful service at 1651 Conversion Unit, Waterbeach. Nevertheless, as originally intended, a replacement, W7531, carried on the name and spirit of 'MacRobert's Reply' with XV Squadron. The legend, like that brave family, seemed bitterly ill-fated. Sqn. Ldr. J. C. Hall took off in W7531 on 17 May 1942 to drop mines in the Baltic. At 02.10 hrs., as he passed

17. Flying Officer P. J. S. Boggis at the helm of 'MacRobert's Reply'.

18. N6086 'MacRobert's Reply' at Peterhead after colliding with a Spitfire.

over the Little Belt Bridge, flak opened up and the bomber was brought down at Galsklint, near Middelfart. Three mines were found in the wreckage, a fourth having exploded. One member of the crew, Sgt. D. J. Jeffs, was taken prisoner, but the others, including two of the crew of the original 'MacRobert's Reply', were killed. Seven were buried in Odense Cemetery. One crew member, Sgt. Ronald Maycock, had no known grave and is commemorated on the Air Force Memorial at Runnymede. There was, unusually, a crew of nine on this occasion.

Stirlings were not noted for long operational service. Up till this time, W7429 had been the most successful, with 22 sorties to its credit, followed by W7436 with 20, W7428 with 19 and N3669 with 18. The last of these subsequently almost became the outright record holder.

W7429 was initially delivered to 19 M.U. on 20 April 1941 and became LS:J in early June 1941. Its first sortie was to Kiel on 23 June, in the hands of Sqn. Ldr. Boggis, who retained it for several more sorties. It took part in raids on Berlin, Karlsruhe, Cuxhaven and, flown by Plt. Off. Jones, reached Turin on 10 September. On 28/29 October it set out for Nuremberg but, because of bad weather, bombs were dropped on Frankfurt. Returning over Rotterdam the Stirling ran into heavy flak which damaged both port engines so badly that it had to land on the starboard engines only. Not surprisingly, on touching down at Warboys the undercarriage collapsed, and although W7429 was taken to Sebro for repair, this proved impossible and it was written off 15 February 1942. W7428 and W7436 were both lost during the Brest day raid on 18 December.

No. 149 Squadron's baptism came on 10 January. Four crews took off at 04.15 hrs. One attacked Brest, returning with a badly holed fuel tank, which emptied itself. Another machine, hit by flak, had to force land at Weston Zoyland with a seriously wounded rear gunner.

On 28 January four crews of 149 Squadron were ordered to Lossiemouth for Operation *Oiled*. Next day two of them were detailed for a raid on the *Tirpitz*. They failed to find the ship, W7462 'T-Tommy' crashing on landing and being written off.

Long-felt fears that the 'S & G' would slip out of Brest reached fever pitch early in February. Daily alerts for Operation *Fuller* plagued the three Stirling squadrons. When the executive order for *Fuller* came it caught them all unawares, bursting at 11.00 hrs. on 12 February. By then the three warships had completed most of their passage through the Channel, screened by atrocious weather. When the Stirlings reached them it was dusk. No. 7 Squadron sent two crews, Plt. Off. S. G. Matkin in R9300 and W. O. W. Nicholls in R9297. Their loads, $14 \times 1,000$ lb. G.P., were brought back. Matkin's crew saw nothing, but Nicholls caught a glimpse of the flotilla through a cloud break at 800 ft., only to lose them soon after. The four crews of XV Squadron and two of 149 fared no better.

A *Scuttle* daylight raid on the Rhineland came for XV Squadron on 17 January 1942, and Osnabruck was bombed. Before February ended they had been to Kiel and to Kristiansund to bolster the Norwegian pretence. No. 149 Squadron mounted raids on Lista airfield in Norway, and on Mannheim, but the main preoccupation was on preparing the squadrons for their part in the offensive being planned.

There was worry about the effect operational wastage would have if current trends continued. In February Stirlings flew only 39 operational night sorties, yet two aircraft were written off and 13 damaged. Write-off was thus 5% of operational effort and 33% suffered damage. Many Stirlings were awaiting repair, and damage at this rate clearly would prevent further squadrons equipping with Stirlings as planned for March. It was therefore imperative that plans be made to extend Sebro (the Short Bros. Repair Organisation) if squadron

19.   N3709 at Oakington. Missing 26 March 1942, came down at Genringen, Holland.

expansion was to come about.

Little increase could be made to the Sebro civilian labour force in an area where engineering skill was difficult to recruit. Instead, it was expanded by drafting Service personnel to the works, and working parties did their best on R.A.F. stations. It was estimated, though, that it would take eight weeks to repair the 13 damaged aircraft.

On 27 February the A.C.A.S. discussed with V.C.A.S. an often mentioned Stirling failing: the hydraulic pipelines to the mid-upper and tail turrets were very easily shot through during beam attacks. This vulnerability weighed considerably on the minds of crews, and led to an urgent review of the positioning of these pipes. It was pointed out, however, that most night attacks were delivered from astern.

Bomber Command was ready for a new sustained offensive at the start of March 1942, but there were still only three Stirling squadrons. Total production amounted to 210 Stirlings, of which 20 had been written off through battle damage and 40 in flying accidents. Another 35 had been lost in action, giving a loss rate of about 4.8% per operation below the figure normally judged as 'acceptable'. It was slow production that caused the shortage: the R.A.F. and other official bodies issued numerous exhortations for it to be speeded, but the quality of the finished product was such that it just took time to build. Too much time, some said.

Chapter 7

A Super Stirling

Even before the Stirling commenced operations Short's were eager to redesign the bomber. Arthur Gouge and several Short's representatives, the Director of Technical Development, Director and Deputy Director of Operational Requirements, Director of Armament, Resident Technical Officer, Stedman Williot and the Overseer, Wg. Cdr. Hutton, met on 9 July 1941 to consider a 'Stirling Mk. III'. Short's had in mind a 'Super Stirling' utilising Bristol Centaurus engines, a landplane version of the giant Shetland flying-boat.

Apart from increased wingspan and improved power to weight ratio, the new machine would carry a 'modern bomb load'. Mainplanes with $6\frac{1}{4}°$ incidence would improve take-off: the fuselage was to be cranked upwards by $3\frac{1}{2}°$ aft of the wings to achieve this. Main and tail undercarriages were to be more compact and stronger than the original Stirling's.

Another version of the Stirling was planned, powered by Hercules Mk. VIs. A circular of 29 July 1941 designated this, not the first mentioned design, as the 'Mk. III'. The new bomber needed another designation, and, as the S.36, passed into the hands of the Air Staff, who produced a draft Specification, B.8/41.

The requirement was for a Stirling powered by four Centaurus CE38Ms, carrying a heavier bomb load and suitable for world-wide operation.

A realistic weak mixture cruising speed of not less than 210 m.p.h. replaced the original 240 m.p.h.; and the range was set at 2,100 miles with maximum tankage and not less than 12,000 lb. of bombs, or 3,000 miles with auxiliary tankage. Service ceiling would be at least 23,000 ft. with normal load. The take-off run from grass was to be 1,400 yd.; the landing run (light) 1,100 yd.

Nose and tail turrets would mount .50 in. guns. Fearing a heavy dorsal turret might upset the c.g., it was planned to mount .303 in. guns here. Alternative bomb loads would be:

(a) $1 \times 8,000$ lb. H.C.$+4 \times 2,000$ lb. A.P./H.C. or $6 \times 1,000$ lb. G.P. in the fuselage
(b) $6 \times 4,000$ lb. H.C. $+6 \times 1,000$ lb. G.P. in wing cells
(c) $9 \times 2,000$ lb. A.P./H.C. $+6 \times 1,000$ lb. G.P. in wing cells
(d) $9 \times 1,900$ lb. G.P. $+6 \times 1,000$ lb. G.P.
(e) $9 \times 1,500$ lb. Type A mines
(f) $18 \times 1,000$ lb. G.P.
(g) $18 \times 1,000$ lb. S.B.C.s or equivalent

Armour plate was required on the bulkhead behind the wireless operator, and to protect the crew from belly attack. Pilots' seats would have 9 mm armour, as would vital areas of engine installations. The crew would number eight: two pilots (dual controls), a navigator/observer, four air gunners, a flight engineer with two of the gunners able to act as radio operators. Troops and paratroops could be carried, and gliders towed.

Ralph Sorley considered the specification 'attractive and well worth adopting'. The low cruising speed prescribed night operations. Four .50 in. guns in the dorsal turret might be needed for protection during moonlight attacks. Weight of fire was more important than duration, though a .303 in. turret induced less drag. Sorley suggested that some of the bomb load—say 2,000 lb.—might be sacrificed for armour. One tailwheel was preferable to two, and bigger flaps were needed to reduce landing run.

The proposed bomber was not the 'Ideal', but the A.C.A.S. felt that it was advanced enough for adoption. With 2,000 yd. runways the take-off run was acceptable. Arrester gear, he supposed, could be used to deal with landing problems. The span must not be increased. The armour needed improving, for this was a high flier. Production could not begin in under 18 months, service before another 30 months. Night fighters would have improved then, and protection would be needed against 20 mm cannon fire.

Ralph Sorley wrote to the C.R.D. on 24 September 1941 that 'the B.8/41 looks very attractive', and the V.C.A.S. agreed that it be an Air Staff requirement. The future of the S.36 seemed assured.

Short's submitted a detailed design study on 15 July 1941 for a bomber of 80,000 lb. all-up weight, span 136 ft., wing area 2,145 sq.ft. and aspect ratio 8.62. A fuel load of 12,000 lb. offered a range of 2,100 miles at 15,000 ft. The calculated performance was as given in Table A.

These details were studied by Captain Liptrot. Maximum possible bomb stowage was for 30,000 lb. comprising $6 \times 4,000$ lb., with a further $6 \times 1,000$ lb. bombs in wing cells. Short's weight assessments seemed optimistic and, with normal operating weight and 3,000 gal. fuel and 5,000 lb. bomb load, would be nearer 105,000 lb. Drag estimates seemed optimistic, but range might be greater. These figures were extrapolated as in Table B.

The S.36 seemed a logical step in heavy bomber development; its landing run was its worst feature.

On 24 January 1942 the B.8/41 draft specification reached Short's. At the end of January the fuselage mock-up was inspected. Disappointment was expressed at the lack of originality: its appearance barely differed from that of the Stirling. The blunt nose seemed an anachronism, its .50 in. turret huge. A smaller one with $4 \times .303$ in. guns was suggested, or a power mounting for $2 \times .50$ in. guns. Short's planned, just aft of the c.g., a fully rotatable $4 \times .50$ in. dorsal turret with 35° downward fire. If it were situated further forward, there was danger of fire hitting propellers. It was, however, thought retrogressive to proceed with such a turret. The flight engineer would best be positioned ahead of the armoured bulkhead. Only two engines were armoured; but all needed protection. The belly F.N.64 turret must be periscopically sighted. Oil coolers would need to be in the wing

TABLE A

Weight, lb.: structure	36,630
fuel	22,810
crew	1,400
equipment	22,940
power plants	17,100
Total all-up weight, lb.:	103,100

Loads, range & speed:	*bombs* lb.	*fuel* gal.	*range* miles	*mean speed* m.p.h.
	12,000	3,000	2,000	221
	11,000	4,350	3,000	221

		All-up weight, lb.	
		80,000	103,000
Max. speed, 3,200 revs., m.p.h.: M.S. gear		282	275
F.S. gear		311	300
Economical cruise speed, M.S. gear, m.p.h.	6,500 ft.	243	234
	24,000 ft.	262	237
Max. ceiling, max. power for climb, 'S' gear, ft.:		29,300	23,800
Service ceiling, ft:		28,300	23,000
Max. economical cruise power ceiling, ft.		21,000	14,700

	All-up weight, lb.		
	80,000	90,000	103,000
Take-off run, yd.: to unstick	390	550	810
to clear 50 ft.	710	925	1,275

TABLE B

Max. speed, 105,000 lb. flying weight, 3,000 gal. fuel: 295 m.p.h. (Short's estimate: 300 m.p.h.)

Max. cruise speed, 15,000 ft., weak mixture: 214 m.p.h. (Short's estimate (at 12,000 ft.): 22 m.p.h.)

Max. economic cruise speed 190 m.p.h. at 15,000 ft.; range 2,220 miles

Cruise range, weak mixture: 2,000 miles (Short's estimate: 2,120 miles)

Service ceiling, normal weight: 22,500 ft. (Short's estimate: 23,000 ft.)

Service ceiling, mean weight: 27,000 ft.

Take-off run, normal weight: 1,400 to 1,500 yd.

Landing run, half fuel, no bombs: 1,100 to 1,200 yd.

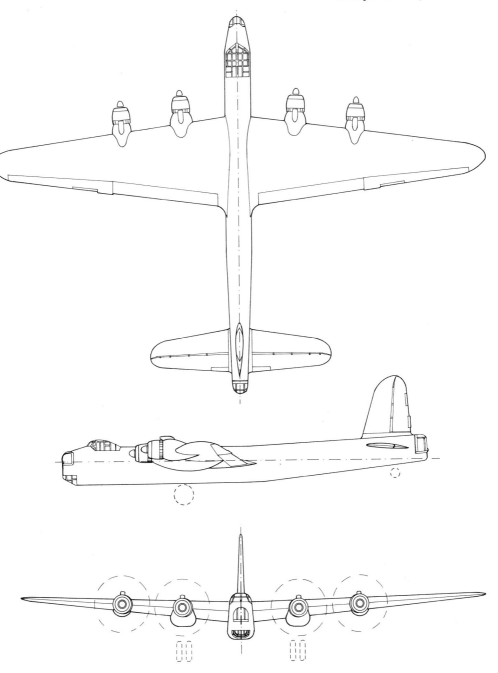

14.   Short S.36 bomber to specification B.8/41, general arrangement.

leading edges to reduce vulnerability. Dinghies were also installed in the wings to avoid a fuselage blow-out.

The R.T.O. considered the normal bomb load—only 2,000 lb. more than the Stirling's—acceptable if performance were superior. A high price was paid for .50 in. guns. The aircraft's all-up weight must not, they said, be allowed to rise.

Production was considered on 22 February 1942. Prototypes could not fly before late 1942. The increased range and bomb load would then be useful in the Far East, provided that airfields and maintenance facilities were available. The Stirling would by that time be outdated, and B.8/41 seemed a logical successor. Production assessments indicated that 24 months were needed to introduce S.36, and that 172 Stirlings would be lost for 46 B.8/41s. Monthly output would be 8, against 12 Stirlings. Production seemed unlikely before January 1944, Stirling production losses beginning about January 1943 and progressively increasing. The V.C.A.S. felt that production introduction could be retarded, allowing the greatest Stirling production losses in winter.

Clearly, B.8/41 should not be started unless production was certain. The C.R.D. favoured introducing the S.36 but production staff and Sir Henry Tizard now showed reservations. They felt that a replacement for all heavies should be the Lancaster and its derivatives. This was a turning point.

On 2 May 1942 B.8/41 was discussed with the C. in C., Bomber Command. He did not want to lose 12 real Stirlings for one possible B.8/41. He favoured 4 × .50 in. tail guns, 4 × .303 in. dorsal guns and a retractable ventral turret as preferable to .50 in. guns throughout, and felt it best to go for a 170,000 lb. bomber. He wanted an ultra-heavy bomber.

Two days later Ralph Sorley received new B.8/41 estimates from the D.G.R.D. The original bomb load expectations had not taken into account full load; it was now reduced to 12,000 lb. for 1,600 miles. With increased armour and .50 in. guns it would fall below 11,500 lb. for 1,600 miles. More alarming was the predicted ceiling of 16,000 ft. for 1,600 miles range, showing no improvement on the Stirling. Flexibility between 16,000 ft. and 20,000 ft. needed rich mixture, increasing fuel consumption and reducing range. More tankage would reduce offensive load. Additional new equipment would cut the bomb load to around 10,000 lb., leaving a practical bomb load only about 2,000 lb. above the Stirling's. There was stowage available for 24,000 lb., but for a range of only 400 miles. Further Centaurus development would probably raise fuel consumption.

It seemed best to forget B.8/41 and opt for the Hercules Mk. VI Stirling, with its likely ceiling of 19,000 ft.

On 22 May 1942 the C.A.S. decided that they should cancel B.8/41: 'it was not as promising as at first hoped'. Short's were pressed to build Avro Lancasters, but reluctant to do so. They wished to build Avro Lincolns. That order, too, was finally cancelled, like the Short S.36.

Chapter 8

The 1942 Offensive

Renault's factory at Billancourt, Paris, was chosen for the opening attack of the 1942 offensive, 29 Stirlings being despatched. On 3 March 1942 the moon was full, the night clear. In the absence of defences, the bombing of the factory, which was on an island in the Seine, was conducted from a low level. No. XV Squadron flew in at between 2,000 and 2,500 ft., claiming that every bomb hit the factory. High explosive was used because much was susceptible to blast damage. No. 7 Squadron dropped $100 \times 1,000$ lb. bombs, hitting a power station and gasometer.

Participation in a Main Force attack had been begun by Stirlings of 218 Squadron. They received their first aircraft on 16 December 1941. On 3 March N3710, flown by Flg. Off. Allen, was ill fated. As it landed with $2 \times 1,000$ lb. bombs aboard, these exploded and the aircraft burst into flames. Two of the crew died and the flight engineer was seriously injured.

This hour long attack was the first in which a flare force of 3 Group Wellingtons marked the target.

Consideration was being given to ways of improving heavy bomber capability over the next two years. Good reserve performance at 16,000 to 17,000 ft. was needed, and sufficient power for operations around 22,000 ft. Only the Lancaster—yet to prove itself—would achieve this. The Air Staff felt little could be done to improve the Stirling, and that its replacement was necessary. Careful operating techniques might improve Stirling performance. Current practice was to climb out on weak mixture, but pilots were unable to get above 16,000 ft. Would it be better to climb to operating height at full power, then cruise at that height, it was asked? Only by fitting Hercules Mk. VIs, which were rated at 17,000 ft., did improvement really seem feasible. Four-bladed propellers were considered as well.

Investigations showed that the ceiling of 16,000 ft. was not due to weak mixture climb. Bomber Command then recommended that climb still be in weak mixture in 'M.S.' gear only, changing to 'F.S.' gear in rich mix when boost had fallen to -1 lb. This avoided a painfully slow weak mix climb, but the ceiling remained as before. Service ceiling of the Hercules Mk. XI engined aircraft (starting weight 70,000 lb.) was confirmed by A. & A.E.E. as 16,500 ft., the weight having by then fallen to 67,500 lb. Further climb in rich mixture resulted in slow climb and high fuel consumption. Recommended altitude on the outward runs was not to exceed 16,000 ft., gradually reached. Also, a slower outward cruising speed than Command wished was recommended.

Essen was attacked on 8 March, a trial for *Gee* on a more distant target. A mixed Stirling and Wellington force dropped incendiaries. On the 9th Essen was the target again, 7 and 218 Squadrons dropping incendiaries, and 149 Squadron H.E.s. Next night Command tried again for Essen. It was a bad night for 149 Squadron: 'U Uncle' was missing and R9295, unable to lower its undercarriage, crashed at Holywell Row.

It was 25 March before major raids were resumed. No. 7 Squadron despatched eight Stirlings to Essen and three to St. Nazaire, out of the 27 operating. One was flown by Sqn. Ldr. Legh-Smith, whose crew lost their position, ran out of fuel and prepared to bale out over North Wales. One pulled his chute too soon and, with it billowing in the fuselage, Legh-Smith ditched N6074 off Barmouth after four of the crew had jumped. The incident provided useful information about Stirling ditching.

The most effective March raid was on Lübeck. Plt. Off. N. L. Taylor was engaged over Heligoland by a Ju 88, and claimed this as shot down. In moonlight XV Squadron dropped 250 lb. incendiaries for the first time. Huge fires burned as 218 Squadron arrived, Flt. Lt. Humphries pressing home his attack even though W7507 had been attacked over the Kiel Canal. Here, shots had first hit the starboard wing, then the fuselage. A shell entered through the cabin Perspex, exploding on the armour plate behind the pilot's head. The rear and mid-upper turrets were put out of action. Further attacks wounded the rear gunner and forced the Stirling down to 200 ft. Eventually the fighter was shaken off and the target bombed, after which an excellent flapless landing was made.

Damage at Lübeck was tremendous, incendiary attack against a combustible target being very effective. Fire bombs were something the Stirling could carry in great quantity, and the Lübeck raid led to increased incendiary loads.

March brought an even more important pointer to Stirling employment. This was the commencement of 'gardening'—mining of enemy waters. It was no easy task: mines needed to be placed from very low levels. The enemy quickly realised that strategic positioning of flak ships in shipping lanes could make mining a hazardous business. Mines had arrived at Oakington early in 1941, but not until now were any sown. It seemed more useful to send Stirlings deep into the Reich.

In March 1942, 3 Group recorded that it had 'acquired packets of seed, implements and catalogues', and was able to note that on 23 March three crews of XV Squadron (and two the following night) 'carried out the first spring sowing'. The 'gardens' were off the French coast near Groix, where on 24 March three crews of 149 Squadron planted 12 mines. From this catalyst came the intensive campaigns of 1943 and '44. Stirlings carried four mines at first, later six.

On 2 April nine Stirlings raided Poissy, and on 5 April the largest number yet despatched to one target, 29, went without loss to Cologne. Two days later Grp. Capt. C. D. Adams, Station Commander at Oakington with Grp. Capt. H. R. Graham attended a luncheon in London given by Short's Directors. Graham reported that 7 Squadron had flown 525 sorties, dropped 1,600 tons of bombs, lost 29 aircraft and suffered 199 casualties. They had claimed 34 enemy aircraft, and had been awarded a D.S.O., 12 D.F.C.s and 12 D.F.M.s. The operational loss rate of 5.6% was about normal for the period.

April's highlight was an attack, including 31 Stirlings, on Rostock, along the lines of the Lübeck raid. Sgt. Runciman was engaged by a night fighter near the target. He jettisoned his load of 4 × 2,000 lb. bombs. Doubtful of the state of the undercarriage, he ordered the crew to bale out, and four did so. Runciman then landed safely at Newmarket. One who baled out called at a farmhouse, requesting the use of a telephone to contact Oakington. Somewhat reluctantly the occupant agreed, then demanded 2d for the call. Such generosity was richly rewarded: the airman generously donated a florin to the helpful farmer.

No. XV Squadron also had an eventful night. Wg. Cdr. Macdonald in 'V-Victor' was set upon by a fighter, and his aircraft was also damaged by flak, necessitating a wheels-up landing at Alconbury.

Twenty-five Stirlings bombed Rostock on 25 April, out of 38 despatched on operations. A special raid by 218 Squadron on Pilsen was included. Among those taking part was Sgt. A. H. Hotchkiss, who vividly recalls the operation.

'The raid was to be carried out with the help of the Czech Underground movement. They would light a beacon fire near the Skoda works. I was flying in N3722, and as we reached Pilsen we could see the fire burning, and we dropped our bombs. We were the only crew to reach Pilsen. The Underground fighters began their planned sabotage, but the Germans caught and executed some, if not all, of them.

'Skoda of Pilsen was the target for a repeat operation, on 4 May. The opposition was fierce but we bombed a power house. Two crews attacked "last resort" targets at Mannheim and Mainz. Only two crews attacked Pilsen, and one other was lost. I was flying in W7469, captain Sqn. Ldr. Oldroyd. Our aircraft was shot up over the target after having been held by searchlights. We were returning over Belgium on the way home as dawn broke, when a Ju 88 located us near Brussels. Oldroyd began to weave, flying lower for protection, with the Ju 88 on our tail. The engagement came to a peak with the Stirling tightly circling a village church until the German fighter broke off combat. The Stirling's fine manoeuvrability saved us. The fighter's fire damaged our oil tanks and port undercarriage. As fuel was running low—for the tanks had been punctured—we forced landed at Manston.'

April was a busy month, the Stirling squadrons operating on 20 nights and despatching 383 sorties. A detailed summary of the Stirling's performance was prepared, since 214 Squadron was converting to them.

Unserviceability on Stirling squadrons remained high. Marham had eight aircraft damaged in four months; Mildenhall 15 in five; Wyton 35 in one year; and Oakington 38 in the same time. Mainly it was trouble with main and tail undercarriages, or flak damage beyond the unit's own capacity to repair.

Major repairs had to be carried out by Sebro, the Short Brothers Repair Organisation, which by this time was fully established. Some time earlier it had been realised that there was a need for a special organisation to back the bomber. Early in 1941 Short's had taken space in cold, draughty rooms at Trinity College Great Court, Cambridge, and established the organisation. A site was obtained on Madingley Road, just outside Cambridge, near the present Veterinary College, and by late 1941 the new factory site was active.

As mentioned earlier, one of Sebro's main problems had been the acquisition of a skilled work force. In the Cambridge area, Marshall's and Pye Radio had already recruited most of the labour. Sebro was captained by skilled workers from Rochester, and more were brought from other parts of the country. But to extend the work force further meant drafting in local labour, many of whom were without factory experience, let alone knowledge of aircraft construction and repair. They needed training at a vital time. One such person was the late Mr. S. Phillips. Although he would have preferred to serve in the Forces, he was drafted to Sebro—of which he had never heard—because he had been involved in the transport side of a local store. Like so many, he found factory work alien to his way of life, and it took months to settle in.

One of the initial problems was building up a sufficient quantity of stores. This took time, and many aircraft had to wait long for spares. Phillips recalled how on one occasion he had to travel to London just to obtain one small pump.

Sebro did not have the capability to manufacture major components at the factory, but made quite large items such as new wing ribs. A lot of the work involved fitting panels in place of those flak damaged, and parts needing replacing after accidents. Major components came from the main factories.

It would be wrong and unfair to declare Sebro inefficient. Once they were underway they proved very competent. That took time, and in 1942 the process of streamlining the organisation still had a long way to go. What impressed the local workers was the skill and devotion of Short's personnel. 'They were magnificent, with very high standards. We relied upon their skill and guidance', recalled the late Mr. Phillips. 'When the aircraft were brought in, if they were categorised "E"—write-off—all usable parts were stored for future use. Fuselages retained their identity. Mainplanes, tail units and other parts were interchangeable, aircraft often leaving with repaired wings from another machine. If a fuselage was struck off charge, the aircraft's identity was lost too. After repair the Stirlings were re-erected at Bourn airfield and test flown.'

Personal war memories are often of the least expected. All Sebro's workers seem to recall vividly 'Sebro custard'! 'The food was never very good', recalls Phyllis Walliker, 'and I never see custard without thinking of that bright yellow stuff at Sebro—it was awful!'

Repair needs and high unserviceability militated against the Stirling going overseas. Also, engine cylinder temperatures were high when taxiing and taking off, and extra tropical cooling would thus have been essential. The increased high temperature take-off run would have been about 1,680 yd., precluding Indian service at this stage.

By May 1942 R.A.F. criticism of Sebro was extensive, if rather unfair. One officer noted: 'On my recent tour of squadrons I collected nothing but complaints.' The truth was not as bad as might be imagined, as these 1941 figures show in the Table opposite.

The mining campaign had continued in earnest, 78 sorties being flown in May. Bomb door modifications now allowed six mines to be carried, and by April 1942 a further modification permitted the carriage of 7 × 1,500 lb. Type A Mk. V mines. They were laid from 200 ft.

The expense of the Stirling force came into question. A Parliamentary Select Committee studied specific items, and issued a report on 23 April 1942. The

20. A Stirling roars low over the factory airfield. Note the sit of the engines. The aircraft had a wingspan of 99 ft. 1 in., length of 87 ft. 3 in. in its bomber form, and a height to the top of the nose of 22 ft. 9 in. Wing area was 1,460 sq. ft. gross.

Date	Cumulative input to date	Output 9 weeks later
25.1.41	2	1
22.2.41	3	2
29.3.41	5	5
26.4.41	7	10
31.5.41	11	17
28.6.41	19	20
26.7.41	31	24
30.8.41	34	30
27.9.41	41	31
26.10.41	48	37
29.11.41	55	41
27.12.41	64	48
31.1.42	71	61
TOTALS	391	327

Some repair work was undertaken at Stirling bases.

ventral turret was designed to be lowered only when interception seemed imminent. The effect of this upon performance was very adverse, and in the early service days it was seldom extended. Crew armour and self sealing tank covers had added much weight, as had beam and dorsal defence, and the c.g. position was affected. The ventral turret was ordered to be deleted, but was retained on some aircraft for daylight operations. Indeed, the ventral turret was not finally ordered to be removed until Modification 492 of November 1941.

A general problem arose because Stirling spares for early aircraft were not interchangeable, keeping aircraft unserviceable for long periods. A succession of minor undercarriage defects were dealt with, only to be followed by others. Cures were not simple to effect, and could only be achieved by redesign, upsetting production rates which were already considered low.

Late in April 1942 Bomber Command representatives were sent to each squadron to collect information on aircraft states. No. 218 Squadron, had, by April 1942, been flying Stirlings for about two months. The average serviceability of its 18 aircraft had been 75% with 75% servicing personnel on strength, but this high figure was due mainly to the use of new aircraft. Ice guards were breaking on air intakes; and the hydraulics for turrets were troublesome, as were the undercarriage 'up' locks. Fuel contents gauges were inaccurate; there were problems with the Exactor throttle; flak damage repair was not readily available; ignition leads were burning out; and there were primary pipe fractures. Similar complaints were reported by each squadron. No. 149 Squadron, with 95% of the normal strength of servicing personnel, reported only 50% serviceability, owing to frequent posting of personnel. No. XV Squadron had an average of 14 aircraft out of its I.E./I.R. of 18, and an average of 10% above the normal full strength of groundcrew establishment. Even so, they were maintaining only 50% serviceability. This unit recorded many mechanical failures with undercarriage and tailwheel chassis. No. 7 Squadron, with 25% above prescribed groundcrew strength, maintained 60% serviceability. Such low rates were attributable to few aircraft in service; with the Wellington it was around 75 to 80%.

One complaint concerned the F.N.20 turret. An untrue rumour attributed losses on the April Lancaster raid on Augsburg to the turret. It was widely known that on one Stirling the turret would not rotate during violent manoeuvres, and the rumour makers highlighted this single fact.

On 12 nights in May squadrons operated: five times mining, and the rest bombing Warnemünde, Mannheim and Gennevilliers. Then came final preparations for Operation *Millennium*.

Air Chief Marshal Arthur Harris, C. in C. Bomber Command, wanted raids utilising the whole of Bomber Command, proposing forces of 1,000 aircraft against one target. The greatest number so far employed had been 228, and the average front line available strength 350. In the closing days of May 1942 Bomber Command achieved a state of readiness hitherto unattained to attack Hamburg or Cologne, the choice of target dependent upon the weather.

The first 15 minutes of the attack would be directed against the city centre, carried out by *Gee* aircraft of 1 and 3 Groups. A final 15 minutes would be given to heavies of 4 and 5 Groups, with O.T.U. aircraft and others comprising the bulk of the intervening wave. Orders were for mixed bomb loads, including some of the new explosive 4 lb. incendiaries. Fire bombs were to form two thirds of the Stirling loads.

On 27 and 28 May thundery conditions and cloud over the Continent precluded large scale raids, but at midday on the 30th the C. in C. ordered *Millennium*. The weather at bomber bases seemed likely to remain good throughout the night. Over Germany thundery conditions would persist, though the Rhineland was expected to be clearer. Therefore Cologne was chosen.

Returns show that 1,046 bombers operated, 338 of them the new heavy bombers and Manchesters. The remainder were mainly Wellingtons, with some Whitleys and Hampdens. The five Stirling squadrons despatched 80 aircraft.

Leading the Stirlings was Wg. Cdr. Macdonald of XV Squadron, who took off in W7516 at 22.34 hrs. and was first over the city, closely followed by Sqn. Ldr. Gilmour in N3707. Arriving at about 00.45 hrs., they found the city clear, moonlight revealing streets and railways. Macdonald's crew placed $12 \times 90 \times 4$ lb. incendiaries and $12 \times 8 \times 30$ lb. incendiaries (the load prescribed for XV Squadron) across the centre of Cologne, lighting a beacon for those following. Two of XV's contingent, Flg. Off. Phillips, in W7536, and Flt. Sgt. McMilland, had Exactor trouble and turned back, but the remainder reached Cologne in clear sky and bright moonlight. There was icing en route, but the cloud thinned over Holland. Fighters attacked, and Sgt. Melville's crew drove off a Bf 110; but it was the vast number of bombers that overcame defences as the attack unfolded.

No. 7 Squadron, operating at between 12,000 and 15,000 ft., carried mixed loads. With them were Stirlings of 101 Conversion Flight. There had been proposals that 101 Squadron should have Stirlings, but shortage of aircraft prevented this. Seven Oakington Stirlings carried loads of $4 \times 2,000$ lb. bombs and one 1,000 lb. G.P., the others each taking $2,160 \times 4$ lb. incendiaries, the bomb load totalling 122,760 lb. All did not go as planned, for 'S-Sugar's' bombs had to be jettisoned in the Wash, and Sgt. Templeman's aircraft was attacked by a fighter. During its second pass the crew jettisoned their load live 20 miles north-east of Antwerp. The remainder of 7 Squadron attacked without loss.

No. 149 Squadron's 17 aircraft were plagued by engine troubles. Bombs from N6083 were jettisoned near Tilburg; and N6079, like N6080, returned early with engine trouble. The crew of R9296 were forced to jettison their bombs when the aircraft entered a spiral dive as a result of slow climb. Only 12 were left to bomb Cologne, dropping 103,680 lb. of bombs.

No. 214 Squadron flew its first Stirling sorties on 18 May, mining 'Rosemary' (the areas in these 'gardening' operations were called after plants). Since then they had bombed St. Nazaire, Mannheim and Gennevilliers. For the Cologne raid they despatched 13 aircraft and delivered 84,560 lb. of bombs.

The greatest honour of the night fell upon 218 Squadron. They carried the most senior officer taking part, Air Vice-Marshal J. E. A. Baldwin, C.B., C.B.E., D.S.O., A.O.C. 3 Group, flying in R9313 'Q-Queenie' with Wg. Cdr. Hodder, D.F.C. The A.O.C. was able to see the attack unfold, a rare event for a senior officer. As the crew, one of 19 from 218 Squadron, ran in, they could see fires already burning. The squadron attacked between 13,000 and 17,000 ft. and dropped 145,280 lb. of bombs, but lost Sgt. Davis and crew.

Operating for the first time was 1651 Conversion Unit, which despatched eight Stirlings. One returned after a few minutes, but the others attacked. W7465, shot up over the target, landed at Coltishall with fuel remaining for only 5 minutes' flying.

The total weight of bombs dropped was 1,455 tons. According to German records 486 people were killed in Cologne and 5,027 injured. Some 59,100 people were left homeless; 18,432 buildings were destroyed, and 9,156 heavily damaged. Another 31,000 buildings received some damage. There were 12,000 fires—2,500 classified as major fires. In all 40 bombers—3.8% of the force—were missing, and 116 damaged, of which 12 had to be written off. Of the participating Stirlings, two were lost, though others were damaged by flak, which also accounted for the bulk of losses of all types. The Stirling loss rate of 2.5% was low.

With the bomber force marshalled, Harris decided to strike again. The weather on 1/2 June was far from ideal, but Essen—the home of Krupp—was attacked; this was because there was the least likelihood of low cloud in that area. Thus, 956 aircraft (347 from O.T.U.s) took off, only to find thin cloud covering Essen. The attack pattern was as for the Cologne raid, 77 Stirlings being in the opening phase, including seven from 1651 Conversion Unit. Although the bombers were aided on tracking by *Gee*, cloudy conditions upset the operation. The bombing spread well from the target areas. The defences were saturated as before, and 31 bombers (3.8%) were lost, including one Stirling.

This time 7 Squadron's complement was 18 aircraft, taking loads either of $2,160 \times 4$ lb. incendiaries or of $4 \times 2,000$ lb. H.C. and $1 \times 1,000$ lb. G.P. bombs. Plt. Off. Runciman's aircraft was hit by flak. Group Captain Massey was second pilot to Flt. Lt. N. E. Winch in N3750, which failed to return.

The night was eventful for XV Squadron. They had detailed 12 crews but W. O. Cowlrick could not start his engines. Wg. Cdr. Macdonald had trouble with his bomb release gear, and Sqn. Ldr. Gilmour could not identify the target and brought his bombs back. The other nine found widely scattered fires and bombed by the aid of Rhine pinpoints and *Gee*. On their return in R9318, Flt. Sgt. MacMillan's crew claimed a fighter. Over Antwerp, Flt. Lt. Parkin's rear gunner was wounded by shrapnel, and W7513 had to crash land at base. Only N3728 took $4 \times 1,900$ lb. and 1×500 lb. G.P. bombs; the rest had incendiaries.

Of 149 Squadron's 15 aircraft, one had engine trouble; but the others dropped their incendiaries. No. 214 Squadron sent out 10 crews, and 218 Squadron 15.

The showing of the Stirlings on the *Millennium* raids was encouraging. The crews drew satisfaction from having attacked above the height of the Wellingtons. 'My memory of the Cologne raid was peering through the aft escape hatch upon thousands of twinkling lights, the burning incendiaries', recalls Sgt. A. H. Hotchkiss. 'I felt safer in the Stirling than I had in 99 Squadron's Wellingtons because it had four engines. There were many of us who felt the same way.'

In the post-war analyses of the bomber offensive one aspect is often overlooked. It was a tremendous morale booster for the battered British to know that the enemy was suffering too. In the case of the Cologne raid, hundreds were in the streets watching the Stirlings, whose engine notes took a long time to die away to the east. Memorable indeed.

Repairing Stirlings damaged by flak on operations was a major task. Each constructor was responsible for the on-site repair of aircraft built by them. There was no common effort. Austin and Short & Harland sent works parties to repair machines they had made; but Short's used Sebro, helped out by Service personnel doing minor repairs on site.

On 5 June 1942 the Airframe and Modification Committee met to discuss

21. Not all homecomings were good. Here 'LS:R'—W7513—is seen on her nose at Wyton after the Essen '1,000 bomber' raid of 1/2 June 1942. The aircraft was shot up over Antwerp.

Modification 549, a new, improved form of undercarriage retraction gear with a redesigned gearbox sited in the fuselage. This affected component interchangeability, for the old wing unit would not fit the new fuselage. But already Short's were building the new undercarriage gear, and had stopped producing the earlier type.

June 1942 was a busy month for the squadrons, with Main Force operations on 13 nights of fair weather. Apart from the 'Thousand Plan' raid, and the Bremen operation of 25 June when 72 Stirlings operated, the busiest nights were the 5/6th, when Essen was again raided (19 out of 25 Stirlings attacked); 6/7th, again on Emden (19 operated); 22/23rd, on Emden (27 out of 38 attacked); 27/28th, on Bremen (26 were despatched); and 29/30th, on Bremen (44 Stirlings operated and four were lost). On that night R9330:OJ-R crashed on take-off, and MG:S ditched 50 miles off Cromer.

The night of 5/6 was eventful for 149 Squadron, eight of whose aircraft bombed Essen. Two crews were missing, and Flt. Sgt. Whitney was forced into the sea off Belgium after colliding with a Wellington which severed the fuselage, killing the rear gunner. Next afternoon they were rescued by an A.S.R. launch.

Although 1,000 bomber raids were impossible to sustain for ever, another was mounted on 25 June, target Bremen. This ended the series, 1,006 aircraft (272 from training units, 102 from Coastal Command) meeting cloudy conditions over the target. The leading Stirlings bombed with the aid of *Gee*, and the Focke-Wulf works were seriously damaged. Three Stirlings were lost. A Bf 110 attacked and seriously damaged N6079 of 149 Squadron when over the sea, and 1,800 × 4 lb. incendiaries had to be jettisoned. Throughout the engagement great coolness was shown by Sgt. J. Barrett, the rear gunner, who had to attend to faulty guns. Enemy fire stopped the port outer engine, and flaps and ailerons were damaged; but the Stirling brought the crew home. One of 214 Squadron's aircraft was attacked by fighters in the target area, initially by a Bf 109, which was claimed as destroyed. A Bf 110 then opened fire, wounding the front gunner and engineer and damaging the aircraft, as a result of which the port outer propeller fell off. Nevertheless, the aircraft limped into Coltishall.

22.   The rough side of 'P-Peter'. The inboard propeller had been shot away over Holland, and the outer engine was burnt.

The night of 27 June 1942 brought to 214 Squadron one of the most memorable Stirling sorties of the war. Nine crews set out from Stradishall to bomb Bremen. One aircraft, N3751 'P-Peter', was hit by flak over the target, the starboard engine being put out of action. After they had left the target, a fighter crept up from below and raked the Stirling, killing Sgt. Sewell, the rear gunner. Then a Ju 88 attacked from the port beam, causing extensive damage and injuring Sgt. Wildey in the arm. Again it attacked, but this time the mid-upper gunner shot it down. The rest of the story is told by Sgt. Tom Prosser, the engineer.

'Sgt. Watson was now out of the front turret aiding Sgt. Wildey, for whom we all did our best. Then came a shout that two fighters were coming in on head-on attack. Watson rushed to his turret, only to find it jammed. He couldn't get in, so Sgt. O'Hara, the navigator, held his legs to steady him as he leaned into the turret to fire his two guns. We were tremendously excited when he got one of the fighters even though he couldn't swing the jammed turret. The other fighter attacked again and the mid-upper gunner, Flt. Sgt. Waddicar, shot it down. Both his guns had jammed but he had cleared one. Another fighter attacked; Waddicar returned the fire and drove it off.

' "P-Peter" went down out of control, and Sgt. Griggs pulled it out as the tail portion went under the sea. Sgt. O'Hara brought us home by the stars, his skill guiding us to Stradishall. The port inner and starboard outer engines had been damaged but I managed to keep them working until Stradishall was reached. It was impossible to circle, we could only go straight in and try to put the Stirling down safely. Then the other two engines cut due to damage and fuel loss. We could not lower the undercarriage, damaged by enemy action. It was the skill of

23. A near one. Sergeant Griggs points out, to (*left* to *right*) Sergeants Waddicar, Watson and O'Hara, a bullet hole in N3751. On 27/28 June 1942, this crew were responsible for destroying 3 night fighters.

Sgt. Griggs that brought off a belly landing. The plane went over the boundary before coming to a halt.'

There were operations on 15 nights in July 1942. A *Shaker* attack on Wilhelmshaven on 8 July included 113 aircraft of 3 Group; but only 34 of these were Stirlings, indicating the extent to which Wellingtons still formed the backbone of the Group. During this month 3 Group received the first F.N.64 belly turret planned to be fitted in Stirlings. Several aircraft had been delivered with provision for it; but fitting problems were many, and the plan lapsed. The F.N.20s were still troublesome, jamming in rotation at high speed. Modifications were in hand to cure this.

On 16 July 31 Stirlings comprised the force for a specialised dusk attack on the Lübecker Flenderwerke AG at Herrenwyk, $4\frac{1}{2}$ miles N.E. of Lübeck and sited on the River Trave. Building was here being undertaken of 500 ton U-boats and

24. Smart factory finish adorns EF427, a standard Mk. III used by XV Squadron.

floating docks. Experienced crews were chosen, their orders being to fly in loose vics of three until 7°E was reached after which, if cloud was a minimum of 8/10, they would proceed individually to the target. Each aircraft was loaded with 6 × 1,000 lb. G.P. R.D.X. filled bombs and 2,100 gal. of fuel. All six squadrons were detailed for this attack, codenamed Operation *Pandemonium*. Take-off was made shortly before 19.00 hrs. for the daylight crossing of the North Sea and Denmark.

The attack was far from successful, Sgt. D. R. Barrett in W7524 of XV Squadron being brought down by flak five miles south east of Esbjerg before crossing Denmark, and Flg. Off. King of XV Squadron running out of cloud cover and abandoning at Haddersley. Only seven of the Stirlings finally attacked, at heights ranging between 600 and 5,000 ft. When 'H-Harry' of 214 Squadron broke cloud over Denmark, Sgt. Flemming met intense flak which killed his front gunner. Bombs had to be jettisoned from the damaged and unstable aircraft, which limped home. Three crews of XV Squadron bombed, Flt. Lt. Barr and Plt. Off. Shoemaker from 900 to 500 ft. respectively. One of the three crews from 149 Squadron claimed hits on submarine slips, and that there were fires in some of the sheds. One of these crews formated on two Stirlings of 218 Squadron and between them they shot out three searchlights; but an aircraft of 149 Squadron came home peppered with flak holes. The crew of W7475 of 218 Squadron were lucky to survive an attack by no less than five fighters; they then bombed a 'last resort' target on Fynn Island. Two Stirlings were missing.

A second dusk attack, Operation *Bedlam*, was attempted on 19 July, with the Stettiner Vulkan and Oderwerke U-boat yards as targets. Cloud cover ran out, and Vegesack was bombed instead.

Particularly strong was 3 Group's part in the Hamburg raid of 28 July. The 166 aircraft despatched included 72 Stirlings, the largest number so far except on 1,000 bomber raids; five Stirlings were lost out of 25 aircraft missing in 3 Group. Only 40% found the target. Shortly after take-off, Wellington X3668:SR-G of 101 Squadron collided with Stirling N6075:SR-W of 101 Conversion Flight,

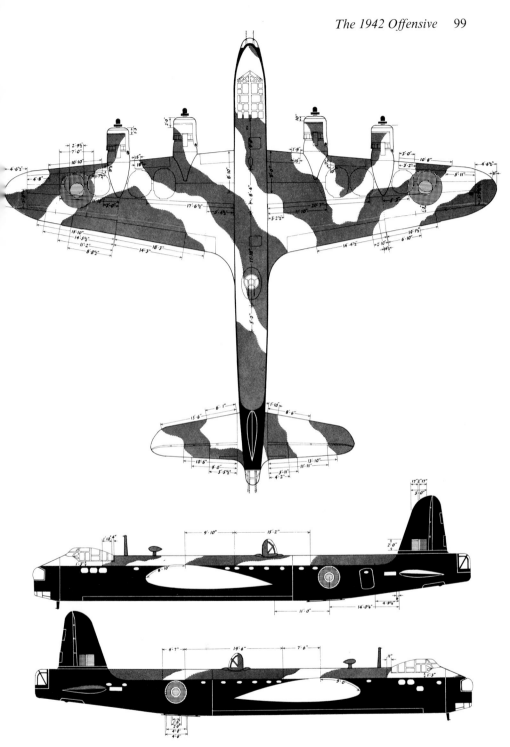

15. Standard camouflage pattern applied to Stirling Mks. I, III, V.
Shaded area green; solid area black.

operating under 7 Squadron and carrying $4 \times 2,000$ lb. H.C. and $1 \times 1,000$ lb. G.P. bombs. Its tailplane was ripped off. Outstanding airmanship by Flt. Lt. Butterfield and crew held N6075 long enough for them to bale out, but the Wellington crew were killed.

Stirlings of 1651 Conversion Unit had previously flown 34 sorties, mainly dropping leaflets. On 28 July nine crews took off from Waterbeach. Heavy icing caused three to turn back; two more did so with mechanical troubles. The shock came when the other four did not return, one of the highest loss rates endured by any Stirling unit.

On 7 August the F.N.50 turret was approved for operational use, replacing the F.N.7. Some Stirlings emerged from repair at Sebro with the newer turret, but the F.N.7 remained in use until 1944.

Although 3 Group's Stirlings operated on 15 nights in August, effort was less than in July. Mining by 29 on 10th proved the largest. During two raids on Mainz on succeeding nights 28 Stirlings participated. As can be seen from Diagram 16, losses incurred in summer were high because of greater effort in better weather.

Success of the leading flare and incendiary force of 3 Group prompted the formation of the Pathfinder Force, which until 1943 remained part of 3 Group. It began to form in August 1942, bringing re-arrangement of squadrons, which inevitably reduced operational effort.

On 12 August XV Squadron arrived at Bourn from Wyton. Bourn was a muddy, windy satellite of Oakington, ultimately to play a vital role in the bomber offensive.

The senior Stirling squadron, No. 7, switched to the marker role, flying their last Stirling bomber operations prior to transfer against Osnabruck on 17 August. For the next 10 months flare dropping by Stirlings supporting flare force leaders would be undertaken, and also bombing and mining. There was no immediate improvement in bombing accuracy when the P.F.F. formed, but it pointed a way to future success.

In the six months ending 30 September 1942, 3 Group despatched 7,096 sorties, 2,637 by Stirlings, making it the most active Group of Bomber Command at that time. The next highest total was 4,674, achieved by 5 Group, which was increasingly flying the efficient Lancaster. The Path Finder Stirling squadron flew 65 sorties in September, compared with 110 by No. 149, the 'top sortie' squadron in the Group that month. On 10 nights the Stirlings laid mines, 71 % successfully, during 85 sorties, a modified mine being used.

September opened with a concentrated attack against Saarbrücken, 36 Stirlings taking part from the five squadrons. Next night, 25 operated against Karlsruhe; and on the 4th, 36 against Bremen. The biggest night attacks, each by 38 Stirlings, came against Frankfurt, on the 6th and Düsseldorf, on the 10th; and by 43 Stirlings against Bremen, on the 13th, when they were operating on a very dark night. Thereafter the weather worsened. After a small scale raid on Munich by 18 Stirlings on the 19th, only minelaying was carried out up to the close of the month, 421 sorties having been flown for the loss of 12 aircraft.

'Gardening' was no easy option. W7579, sent to the 'Daffodil' area on 14

25. A considerable mining effort was made in waters around Denmark, and losses as a result were quite heavy. N3752 'OJ-O' of 149 Squadron crashed on the night of 17/18 May 1942 at Risegaards Mark, Denmark. Possibly there was some altimeter trouble. The crew became prisoners of war.

August, crashed into the sea off Nymindegab, Denmark. On 18 September R9351 of XV Squadron took off in extremely poor weather—10/10 cloud and driving rain—and was brought down at Korsor-Nyborg, Denmark. Plt. Off. J. M. Steel was rescued by a ferry, but his colleagues perished. Another 11 Stirlings laid mines off the Frisians; and three placed them in the 'Undergrowth' and 'Yew Tree' regions off Frederikshavn and Laeso, when one aircraft was lost. Three put 12 mines into the 'Verbena' area of Copenhagen, and two more went to the 'Broccoli' and 'Asparagus' areas off the Great Belt, from which R9351 was missing. Some 341 mines were laid by 115 aircraft, of which 45 were eventually missing, a loss rate of 39.13% which highlighted the cost of 'gardening'.

Added to this, many aircraft were damaged. On 9 September for instance, BF326 was engaged by flak at the French coast, one of six of 214 Squadron mining 'Deodar'. Mines had to be jettisoned after flak hit the fuselage centre, starboard inner engine, No. 6 fuel tank and the tailplane.

The Düsseldorf raid of 10 September, when 1651 Conversion Unit and O.T.U.s supplemented the Main Force, resulted in one of the most heroic deeds of the Stirling days. For Flying Officer J. Trench and crew in W7564 'T-Tommy' of 7 Squadron, that night would be one to remember. The story can only be told by one of the crew, in this instance Sgt. I. J. Edwards, the wireless operator.

'We had done the trip a few times before, and with some scorn it was called the "Milk Run to Happy Valley"—and to the target it had been easy. We were at about 14,000 ft. when we were coned by searchlights. Strategy was then for A.A. fire to fill the top of the cone, and it was very effective. The Stirling was very manoeuvrable, our skipper a very sound pilot. His normal method of escape was a stall turn, at which he was very expert. After quite a few, this time, we came out at about 4,000 ft., and were happy with our luck. The engineer, Sgt. Mallett, soon stopped the joy with news of the oil pressure on the port inner.

'The next move was to feather the prop. But we had too little pressure for this, and it had to be allowed to windmill until the engine seized up and we lost the prop. We, like others, had lost a prop. before, and were not too worried. The whole operation would not take too long. As it had happened on my side, the engineer awaited my running commentary. The port props. were the worst, for they went up and over when metal melted and fell away. Once the red and white hot bearings started coming out it would go—and did. The snag in this case was that our prop. had not conformed to pattern. The whole arc was slightly behind the outboard in the Stirling, and there was a little overlap. In going off it had fouled the outer prop. The next sensation was of someone out at the wing tip shaking it. Vibration was considerable and the order to "bale out" was given.

'Before this was under way there was a loud crack to port. It was then quiet, and we could see the whole power plant had left the bulkhead; so it was a case of a very low ride home. We threw out all movable objects, and were down to 150 ft. over the Dutch coast. I can remember a rowing boat tied to a jetty in a river mouth. When you looked from the pilot's seat through the bomb aimer's window and saw phosphorescent wave tops, you really were low. We had ditched all ammunition magazines. (The rear turret was served from large magazines forward of the door, and there was quite a lot of ammunition.)

'We were aiming for Martlesham Heath, and it was obvious we would have to do a wheels-up landing. We climbed to cross the coast, almost touching a haystack with our starboard wingtip.

'The rest was very fast. The engineer, one of the best in the squadron, had worked the fuel to the last drop and his power timing was perfect. We almost got the middle of Weeley village, but saw it before it was too late, and in a cloud of dust we hit the ground.

'Then it was that real tragedy struck. Crash drill, which we had done many times, was perfect. The crew were aft of the mainspar except the navigator, who was on the bed. The aft escape hatch and astrodome were off and everybody got out. Our captain and myself were knocked unconscious, but the navigator, Plt. Off. C. L. Selman, dragged the pilot clear. I came to and gave him a push up, and also had to disconnect the oxygen and R/T lines to his helmet. Then the three of us just sat on top of the cockpit glasshouse.

'The fire started rather slowly, but was enough to make us jump off and land in some bushes. After that it was run, run. We didn't know that the others also thought it was a piece of cake and had gone back in, the rear gunner telling me afterwards he went back for his peaked cap, the engineer for his tool kit and the bomb aimer for some coffee. Then the whole aircraft exploded. The rear gunner was blown out, badly burned, but the others were not so lucky. The front gunner, Sgt. F. A. Thorpe went in to try some rescue. The rear gunner, Plt. Off. W. N. Gledding, was pulled clear by the mid-upper gunner, Flt. Sgt. Jenner.

'The Home Guard rounded us up and the "local" opened up rather early that morning. Everyone was wonderful, giving us beds for the night. The rear gunner went off to Colchester Military Hospital, the other survivors to Oakington.'

Officially the incident was recorded as 'an outstanding example of courage and determination on the part of the captain and crew'.

An unusual all Stirling attack was intended for Vegesack on 23/24 September. Each of 21 aircraft carried two containers of incendiaries and the maximum 1,000 lb. G.P. load. As with *Pandemonium*, the route out was below 1,000 ft. to evade

26. The sortie record holder, N3721 'P' of 218 Squadron, in July 1942, flying over Downham Market.

detection, with a climb to 6,000 ft. just before the enemy coast. Attack, if the sky was clear, was to be followed by a fast, low return. Luck was out: there were thunderstorms and thick clouds, so the bombing was widespread.

Enlarging the Stirling force meant opening another conversion unit. Chedburgh opened to receive 214 Squadron, moved from Stradishall on 1 October. No. 1657 Conversion Unit opened at Stradishall under Wg. Cdr. B. R. Kerr, with 16 I.E. (later 32 I.E.) aircraft. The Conversion Flights were absorbed in October. On 28 September Marham passed to 2 Group. No. 218 Squadron was now at Downham Market, which was raised to full station status.

October's main effort was against northern Italy, the first raids of 1942 on these difficult targets. On both nights the weather was poor. Mining took place on 11 nights, with 80% laying success, making it the busiest month since May, and the 135 Stirling sorties constituting a record so far. Mining extended from the west coast of France to the Baltic.

Losses on mining were comparatively high. On 16 October, for instance, two out of 11 Stirlings were lost operating off France. Visibility was good, and the aircraft probably succumbed to light flak. Routes needed careful planning to avoid danger while keeping below 3,000 ft. Between March 1942 and the end of October Stirlings flew 543 mining sorties, against 3 Group's Wellingtons' 748 flights. In total 2,977 mines were laid in 44 areas. During October an all-time record of 35 sorties laying 119 mines was established by 218 Squadron.

October opened with 25 Stirlings comprising the total force for an attack on Lübeck. Next night 7 Squadron marked for a Krefeld raid, the standard load of three flares permitting bombs to be carried. Marking techniques still needed perfecting: the flares burst too high over Krefeld for accuracy. The technique on this and the Aachen raid of 5 October was for four Stirlings to go in first with strings of reconnaissance flares; after which came the illuminators; then the fire raisers; then a 10 minute attack by 3 Group; and finally the rest of Bomber Command. After approaching high, height was quickly lost on the run-in, and return made at 7,000 ft. The best attacks of the month by Stirlings were against Osnabruck on the 6th, when 31 took part and illuminating was good; and on 13th when, in good weather, the force included 29 incendiary loaded Stirlings.

On 23 October the target was Genoa, marking being by 11 Stirlings of 7 Squadron and 13 Halifaxes of 35 Squadron. Apart from a few Wellingtons of 3 Group from Marham and 50 Halifaxes of 4 Group, the 39 Stirlings of 3 Group carried the bulk of the incendiaries—two thirds of their load. Half of these were of the 30 lb. type. The length and exacting nature of the journey took a heavy toll. Of the nine crews of 214 Squadron, five made early returns. Sgt. L. T. Richards, whose aircraft was shot up over the French coast, was forced back. BF343 abandoned with engine trouble; W7614 was attacked by a fighter north-east of Paris; and W7612 had to return from the Alps, with engine trouble. R9184, flown by Plt. Off. Studd, failed to return.

Of XV Squadron's 10 crews only five bombed; and the Commanding Officer, Wg. Cdr. D. H. Lay, crash landed at Bradwell when an engine cut in the circuit. Flt. Lt. Baignot's aircraft was attacked by two fighters, the mid-upper gunner, though wounded, claiming a Ju 88. Six out of the nine crews from 149 Squadron reached Italy, but not all of their loads fell on Genoa. Only six of 7 Squadron's 11 aircraft were effective, three crews attacking Turin and one Savona. Engine failures and fuel shortages plagued the operation.

Next night Milan was chosen for a reduced effort. No. 1 Group alerted 10 Halifax crews, and 4 Group raised four. Added to these were 10 Stirlings of 7 Squadron and 10 Halifaxes of 35 Squadron. Crews relied upon *Gee* fixes; but these were only obtainable to within 200 miles of Milan, causing the most difficult part, around the western edge of the high Alps, to be flown on D.R. The forecast was of a front about halfway to the target, with cloud base down to 2,000 ft., and heavy icing up to 7,000 ft. Very strong winds from the west were expected, and the front was likely to break before the high mountains. Half the outward journey was flown at 3,000 ft. for safety before the climb across the Alps. Then they were to descend below icing level to avoid upper winds and night fighters.

It was very cloudy, the sky covered for most of the journey, the effort almost wasted. No. 7 Squadron attacked built-up areas, with flares widely scattered. Some aircraft could not climb owing to icing, and only two crews of 218 Squadron reached Milan. Italy was indeed a long, nerve racking journey.

November's wintry weather limited operations, Stirlings mining on only 7 nights. Apart from attacks on Hamburg on the 9th by 20 Stirlings, and on Stuttgart on the 27th by 27, the remainder of the effort was against Italy. The small scale Hamburg raid was a failure, high winds forcing many aircraft off track. Operation *Haphazard*, a special leaflet dropping campaign, was mounted to give the French news of the landings in North-West Africa. Over 15,000,000 leaflets were dropped over a wide area between Bordeaux and Lille when weather permitted. On every occasion upper winds were different to those forecast.

Early in the month minelaying was concentrated off the west coast of France to discourage U-boats from attacking convoys sailing to Africa. Some 84 Stirling sorties were flown, and 314 mines sown. By the end of November 1942, Stirlings had in all flown 627 mining sorties. Four Stirlings were lost during mining this month.

The main effort remained against Italian targets, Genoa being bombed three times and Turin twice by 3 Group. On the 7th, and again on the 13th and 15th, 7 Squadron marked Genoa. Some 39 Stirlings took part in the first of these Genoa raids, which was mounted on the day that Mildenhall closed for runway building. Eleven marker crews led 3, 4 and 5 Groups. There were icing problems causing fuel consumption to rise sharply and thus bringing turn-arounds.

16.   Stirling Mk. I R9250. Delivered to 75 Squadron 2.11.42, became 'AA:C'. Shot down on 8th sortie en route for Hamburg 3.2.43. (For key to camouflage colours see page 184)

Bad weather thwarted Bomber Command's effort to support the African offensives. So did a take-off accident at Bourn on the 18th, which reduced the number of available crews of XV Squadron from 11 to five. Two had taken off when the runway became blocked, and it was left to this pair only to represent 3 Group.

On 20 November 30 Stirlings set out for the Fiat works at Turin. The weather was kinder, the moon bright, visibility good. Nine crews of XV Squadron attacked, and seven of 218 Squadron. The nerve racking sensations endured during flights over such terrain would have to be experienced to be appreciated. When W7584 was nearly back to Chedburgh, two Exactor controls failed. Flt. Sgt. Corlett ordered his crew to bale out before the Stirling crashed; but he was killed.

Under Wg. Cdr. V. Mitchell, 75 Squadron flew its first Stirling sorties this night. They had a distinguished record flying Wellingtons; and now, with Stirling production rising faster and two conversion units functioning, 75 Squadron began conversion training at Oakington. Their first Stirlings came on charge at Newmarket on 16 October.

At 18.20 hrs. on 20 November, four crews of 75 Squadron, captained by Plt. Off. L. G. Trott, Flt. Sgt. J. M. Bailey, Sgt. B. A. F. Franklin and Flt. Lt. C. W. Parish, took off for the long haul to Genoa. Trouble soon overtook Franklin, whose crew jettisoned their load in the Wash. Flt. Lt. Parish had to abandon his sortie over the south of France, leaving the other two crews to make 75's first attack using Stirlings.

Marking Turin were 10 Stirlings of 7 Squadron. Plt. Off. Boylson's starboard outer transmission pipe sheared off with the constant speed unit; and Sqn. Ldr. Bribbin's aircraft had its port and centre bomb bays damaged by flak, which ignited the flares. Flg. Off. Duro's machine was also hit. His escape hatch was blown in, and the starboard elevator almost shot away.

The next Stirling foray to Turin came on 28 November, and was the biggest: 13 of 7 Squadron and 35 other bombers participated. Abortive sorties on the dark night were many. Five crews of XV Squadron set out; they had been ordered to attack from a lower level than usual. Only two reached Turin, W7585 turning back at the mountains with engine trouble. The bombs from 'T-Tommy' were jettisoned near Dijon, also because of engine trouble. Only three of 214 Squadron's seven crews attacked, and one was missing. No. 218 fared little better only three crews out of six reaching Turin.

Of the night's episodes, one would long be remembered with pride. At 18.14 hrs. Flt. Sgt. R. H. Middleton, an Australian pilot, opened the throttles of BF372:OJ-H. Within moments the heavily laden Stirling had cleared Laken-heath. Around 21.30 hrs. the bomber was running up on the Alps; fuel consumption was causing concern. On reaching Turin, Middleton turned in the darkness for his target run. On the third pass he descended to a mere 2,000 ft., into a hail of flak. A shell burst in the cockpit and a splinter tore into his face, ripping away flesh, tearing out his right eye and the flesh about it. A second splinter hit him in the chest, a third in the leg. By his side was Sgt. L. A. Hyder, who received severe leg and head wounds.

Flight Sergeant Middleton fell unconscious from his appalling wounds and the Stirling plunged down. Hyder, summoning great strength and courage, managed to level out the aircraft at 800 ft. The bombs were then dropped; and, despite the alarming fuel state, they climbed to 1,500 ft. and set course for home. Most of the windscreen had been shot away, making the flight extremely cold. The aircraft was damaged again by flak. Middleton recovered consciousness, and insisted on taking over, allowing Hyder's serious injuries to receive attention. There was little chance of reaching England, but Middleton stayed at the controls to afford the others a chance of survival.

Despite his wounds, Middleton flew over the Alps and across France; then over Boulogne, flak opened up and BF372 was hit again. On reaching the coast near Dymchurch the aircraft had fuel for only about five minutes' flying. Middleton flew along the coast and most of the crew baled out, leaving the front gunner and flight engineer to stay with their courageous captain. Within a few minutes the aircraft plunged into the Channel. Not many hours later bodies of the two crewmen who had stayed behind were recovered. Middleton, it was thought, had gone down with the aircraft.

On 1 February 1943 his body was washed ashore. It was taken to St. John's Church at Beck Row where Flt. Sgt. Middleton was laid in state. On 5 February he was buried in the churchyard, while the Band of Bomber Command played. A special salute from Fighter Command was given by Wg. Cdr. Strange. From the Headquarters of Bomber Command came the C. in C.'s representative, Group Captain H. R. Graham.

Surely there could have been no finer person to represent all those who flew in

Stirlings, or indeed in all Bomber Command. The inscription on the headstone soon read 'Flight Sergeant R. H. Middleton, V.C.' He was the first Stirling crew member to receive the highest award for bravery.

Another attempt to hit Fiat in Turin was to follow on 29 November 1942. Again treacherous weather wrapped the mountains, and it was the usual story of fast dwindling fuel and aircraft heavily encrusted with ice—so much so that two thirds of the 27 Stirlings made abortive sorties. None of 149 or 214 Squadrons' crews reached Turin. It was, however, attacked by another crew, who briefly spotted the factory from 10,000 ft., turned, lost it, found it again and ran in very low to make sure of their aim.

When the sums were worked out it was found that about 223 tons of bombs had been dropped that month, but of the courage and misery of those alpine ventures there could be no measure.

There had been one unusual attack in November. On the 3rd, using cloud cover, three crews of 218 Squadron set off from Downham for a daylight attack on rail targets at Lingen. When they reached the town, they found the cloud base at 800 ft. Each crew could make only one pass without exposure to unjustifiable hazard. As a result one load undershot; the next careered beyond the rail yards into a built-up area. The third crew, seeing accuracy virtually impossible to achieve, brought their load back.

Winter weather in December reduced that month's sorties to 199. There were two raids on Turin in hazy weather, moderately successful; and 7 Squadron marked on a third attack. Nine markers and 13 Stirling bombers were sent against Frankfurt on 2 December when a trial R/T commentary to aid accuracy was attempted. This led later to the 'Master Bomber' concept.

During mining operations 53 Stirling sorties had been flown; then the weather became too poor. The dropping level had been raised from 1,000 ft. to 6,000 ft. Mining with 1,500 lb. mines was also carried out on the 16th and 17th, bringing the month's sorties to 68. Some sinkings were directly attributable to 214 Squadron's effort.

The bad winter weather reduced Bomber Command's effort. The smaller number of aircraft made them easier targets for fighters. On the 16th Diepholtz airfield was selected for attack, and eight Stirlings took off. Three crews were from XV Squadron. Flt. Sgt. McMonagle in BF355 was three times intercepted by Bf 110s. The first was shot down; the second shaken off; and the third gave up battle. The Stirling landed, with a wounded crew member, at Coltishall. R9168 was shot down near Aalsmeer, all but one of the crew evading capture. Those in R9186 were more fortunate for, although flak set fire to incendiaries in the wing cells, they managed to reach home.

Mining operations on the 16th claimed another crew in distressing circumstances. The long grass runway at Newmarket held a serious hazard. Running along the edge was the low ridge known as the Devil's Dyke. At 22.11 hrs. Sgt. B. A. Franklin of 75 Squadron began his run in R9245 carrying mines for the Gironde Estuary, the fourth of the night's detail to take off. The starboard wheel clouted the earth rampart about 4 ft. from its summit and was carried away, tearing out the inner starboard oil tank in the process. Almost at once the engine seized, and the aircraft spun in about a mile from the Dyke. Two mines exploded, killing the crew.

Next night 15 Stirlings took off for Fallersleben. Fighter pilots easily located the force, shooting down five of the bombers. One was BF396, captained by Wg. Cdr. V. Mitchell, Commanding Officer of 75 Squadron; on this night four out of their five aircraft were missing. It was also a bad night for XV Squadron for, upon return, one of its aircraft crashed near Bourn, and another caught fire on landing. Both aircraft of 149 Squadron were also involved in crashes. Too few aircraft participating had meant that the defenders were not overwhelmed. It was moonlight, and the only hope of avoiding fighters was by flying low through the fighter belt. Although Group had ordered this to be done, the warning was unheeded. But when 27 Stirlings were despatched to Duisburg on the next raid, it was stressed that they remain in company. None was lost.

Expansion of the Stirling force continued when 75 Squadron rearmed; then on 1 December 1942, 90 Squadron reformed at Bottesford and BK644 arrived. As it taxied round the perimeter track it collided with a roller whose driver quickly jumped to safety before the vehicle crashed into the tailplane. On the 29th 90 Squadron set out by air for its operational station, Ridgewell, satellite to Stradishall. First to touch down was Flt. Sgt. Freeman in BK625. The all too frequent swing on landing overtook him, and he ended in a ditch. The remainder of the orbiting Stirling crews were evidently of the opinion that Bottesford was a safer haven and returned there, flying south the next day.

It was intended that 115 Squadron should also rearm in December, and on the 8th some crews moved to Oakington for operational conversion. Several Stirlings were flown in for them, and the unit's identity letters 'KO' were applied. But by late December it was clear that there were still insufficient aircraft to allow full conversion, and 115 Squadron reverted to operating Wellington Mk. IIIs.

During 1942 Stirling squadrons flew 3,880 sorties for the loss of 162 aircraft. The slow production rate had reduced the effort. Not until well into 1943 was a '100 Stirling' raid possible. By then the Mk. III was in use.

Chapter 9

Enter the Mk. III

When the newer Stirling was introduced, the hope was that the fitting of Hercules Mk. XI engines would improve climb and ceiling. Boscombe's tests with N6000 so fitted showed that, at 70,000 lb. and gills open, climb fell away to 430 f.p.m. at 10,000 ft. (164 m.p.h.T.A.S.), and to 110 f.p.m. at 15,000 ft. (175 m.p.h.T.A.S.). The greatest height reached was 17,000 ft., in a little under 70 min., and the change from M.S. to F.S. gear came at 13,150 ft. The take-off run had been 1,380 yd. The climb to 15,000 ft. was over 100 miles, and used 275 gal. of fuel out of 1,940 gal. carried. About 60 % of the fuel would be consumed en route to the target, weight then being 61,000 lb.; it would be 53,000 lb. on leaving the target, and 47,500 lb. on arrival at base. The return cruise could readily be made at 20,000 ft.

The fastest speed, weak mixture at 15,000 ft., was about 226 m.p.h.T.A.S. outward, fuel consumption about 1.22 gal. per mile, giving a range of about 1,740 miles in 7 hr. 45 min. The homeward speed would be 217 m.p.h.T.A.S. If outward indicated airspeed were reduced at 15,000 ft. to 155 m.p.h.I.A.S. (192 m.p.h.T.A.S.) consumption was 1.03 gal. per mile, allowing 9 hr. 30 min. flight. Maximum possible still air range at 70,000 lb. at 10,000 ft. was computed as 2,110 miles, 200 m.p.h.T.A.S., 1.07 gal. per mile outward, 1.27 on return allowing a duration of 11 hr. 15 min.

Additional new equipment—flame dampers and extra turrets—was not accounted for in these figures. Drag from the dorsal turret would cut speed by about 5 m.p.h., and range by 6 to 8 % at 15,000 ft.

N3662, first with F.N.7 and F.N.64 turrets and new equipment, began Boscombe trials in May 1941. At 70,000 lb. for take-off it could barely maintain 15,000 ft., which was no better than N6040, loaned for comparison by XV Squadron. The latter's performance seemed so poor that it was considered a rogue aircraft, but compared with N3662 it did not look so bad. The comparative results were as given in the Table on page 110.

15,000 ft. could only be maintained in summer, when 12,500 ft. was just comfortable for cruise. Unmodified Mk. Is could just hold 15,000 ft. at 66,000 lb. To cruise at heavy weights at 15,000 ft., an increase in boost to 1 p.s.i. was needed.

Unmodified N6000 was compared with N3662, now with F.N.50 dorsal and F.N.64. Full throttle speed loss on N3662 varied from 7 to 9 m.p.h. in M.S., 11 to 18 m.p.h. in F.S. Both aircraft were then brought to similar modification states, mock-up turrets being fitted to N6000, whose maximum speed then fell by about 11 m.p.h., and by 8 to 14 m.p.h. in weak mixture.

Overall speed reduction with additional features was accepted by Short's early

Height ft.	Weight lb.	Supercharger gear	Revs.	Speed	
				m.p.h.I.A.S.	m.p.h.T.A.S.
N6040					
10,000	64,200	M.S.	2,450	178	210
10,000	66,500	M.S.	2,510	177	207
11,000	66,750	F.S.	2,500	160	194
14,000	67,000	F.S.	2,500	159	194
N3662					
10,000	66,000	F.S.	2,500	186	223

in 1941, since no improvement was possible without better engines. With Hercules Mk. II/III operation altitude was a mere 10,000 ft.; with Hercules XI the usual cruise altitude was between 12,000 and 15,000 ft. on outward journeys. But now much better performance would be needed.

Bristol were bench running the Hercules Mk. VI, upon which hopes were pinned when the Cyclone powered Mk. II proved no better than the Mk. I.

The decision to re-engine with Hercules Mk. VI was taken in May 1941, when N3662 proved disappointing. It was not until the spring of 1942 that Mk. VIs reached Rochester. R9309 was then re-engined. The Mk. VI had a revised cooling layout, so 12 in. diameter oil coolers were sited below each nacelle, replacing the leading edge intakes. Thermostatically controlled shutters could close the duct exits. Extended air intakes were sited above cowlings, containing ice guards and cleaners—useful for overseas employment. Barrage cutters remained on early machines, but there was no de-icing equipment. A small blister was placed on each side of the forward fuselage for better view fore and aft. Turrets were F.N.5 nose, F.N.50 dorsal, F.N.64 ventral, F.N.20 tail.

R9309 flew in June 1942, proceeding to A. & A.E.E. on 14 July. Its performance was of particular importance now that B.8/41 had been dropped. Maximum all-up weight remained 70,000 lb. Boscombe's tests showed the rate of climb to be only 500 f.p.m. at 5,000 ft., reached after 9.3 min. at 161 m.p.h.T.A.S. This was alarming, but worse was to come. R9309 took 44.5 min. to reach 15,000 ft. (176 m.p.h.T.A.S.) where climb was a mere 90 f.p.m.

During August 1942 tests were directed to improving oil cooling. Then disaster struck. On 6 September the starboard outer engine caught fire after a cylinder fracture. The crew of six had to bale out. Burning wreckage fell on Porton Down.

Short's re-engined R9188, an ex-Cyclone machine, flying it in late September. The first production Mk. IIIs at Austin's, BK648 and BK649, were used as prototypes. BK648 passed to 19 M.U. on 1 December 1942, and to XV Squadron on 31 December for trials. BK649 went to Boscombe Down for tests early in December. There was one important respect in which these differed from Mk. Is. Wire throttle control replaced the Exactors. There were hopes that this might reduce accident rates, but these were dashed. Strong swing on take-off and landing remained, but a maintenance problem, however, was removed.

27. N3711, a Mk. II with Cyclone engines which showed little performance difference to the Mk. I. A. & A.E.E. trials May 1942, then used for Short's development work. Converted to Mk. I, and written off 30 November 1944.

28. Stirling Mk. III third aircraft BK649. After A. & A.E.E. service 8 December 1942, passed to 1660 Conversion Unit 27 March 1944 until 18 April 1944. Scrapped August 1946. Note FN64 belly turret.

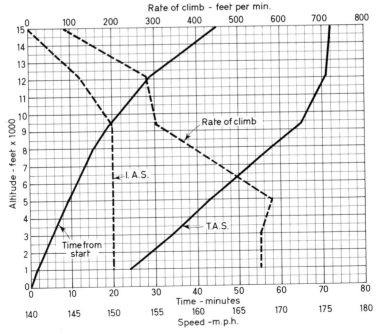

17. Climb performance, prototype Mk. III R9309 (Hercules VI)— 70,000 lb., climb 2,400 revs.

BK649 was finished, like its predecessor, as a prototype. It had none of the yellow ochre Kilfrost de-icing paste common on operational Stirlings in 1941 and '42. Its armament was as for R9309. It was first tested for climb and level flight assessment. The maximum rate of climb, gills open and in M.S. gear, was 740 f.p.m. to 5,850 ft. The height reached before supercharger change was 9,000 ft., and climb rate 400 f.p.m., which was maintained in F.S. gear to 12,800 ft. Service ceiling was 16,750 ft., and estimated absolute ceiling 18,000 ft., slightly above the fully equipped Mk. Is. Above full throttle height in F.S. gear (gills closed) the rate of climb rose by 155 f.p.m. Service ceiling became 18,500 ft., absolute ceiling 20,000 ft.—all for the outward journey. In F.S. gear (gills closed) the rate of climb rose by 155 f.p.m. Service ceiling became 18,500 ft., absolute ceiling 20,000 ft.— all for the outward journey. In F.S. gear (maximum all-up weight) the top speed was 262 m.p.h.T.A.S. at 13,000 ft. The maximum reached in M.S. was 254 m.p.h.T.A.S. at 5,800 ft., and weak mixture cruise in F.S. gear at 18,500 ft. 215 m.p.h.T.A.S. A more comfortable cruise was achieved at 16,000 ft. The maximum cruise speed (M.S.) was 228 m.p.h.T.A.S. at 12,000 ft.

Thus, the Mk. III was little better than the Mk. I, but the time to 12,800 ft. was about 12 min. less; and the operational cruise ceiling was 16,700 ft., a 2,300 ft. improvement.

The Hercules Mk. VI gave more power at high altitude, but weighed more. Figures comparing the engines are:

Engine	Dry weight lb.	Take-off power	Max power level for 5 min.	Normal climb	Max. level climb
Hercules Mk. XI	1,870	1,590 h.p. 2,900 revs.	1,315 h.p. 2,800 revs. sea level 1,460 h.p. 2,800 revs. 9,500 ft.	1,315 h.p. 2,500 revs. 2,000 ft. 1,815 h.p. 2,500 revs. 12,750 ft.	1,020 h.p. 2,500 revs. 7,500 ft. 920 h.p. 2,500 revs. 17,500 ft.
Hercules Mk. VI	1,930	1,615 h.p. 2,900 revs.	1,675 h.p. 2,900 revs. 4,500 ft. 1,445 h.p. 2,900 revs. 12,000 ft.	1,355 h.p. 2,400 revs. 4,750 ft. 1,240 h.p. 2,400 revs. 12,000 ft.	1,050 h.p. 2,400 revs. 10,250 ft. 955 h.p. 2,400 revs. 17,750 ft.

The first production Mk. III, BK650, left Austin's on 9 December. Then came the first with Hercules Mk. XVIs. They had fully automatic Hobson 132/ME carburettors with differential carburation characteristics. Performance differed little, tests showing maximum M.S. speed being reached at 11,600 ft.: 244 m.p.h.T.A.S., 192 m.p.h.I.A.S.; on F.S. gear it was 219 m.p.h.T.A.S., 177

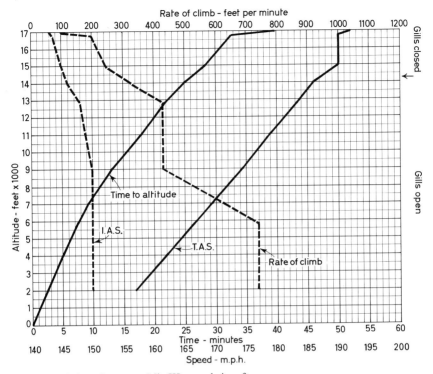

18.   Climb performance, Mk. III second aircraft.

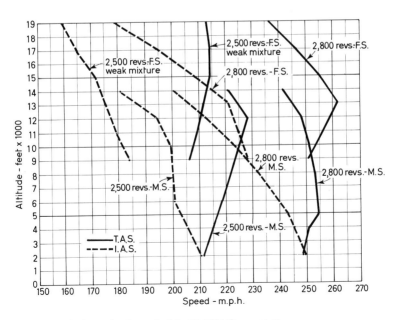

19.   Maximum level speeds, Mk. III BK649—mean at
60,000–70,000 lb.

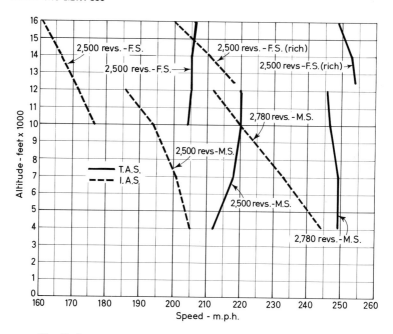

20.   Performance, Mk. III production aircraft BK761 (Hercules VI—
F.N.5A, F.N.50A, F.N.20A)—70,000 lb.

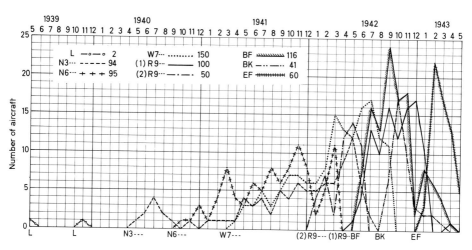

21.   Monthly production deliveries, Mk. I.

m.p.h.I.A.S. at 15,000 ft., making it a little faster than Mk. VI engined Stirlings.

Sixteen Mk. IIIs reached the R.A.F. in January 1943, going to XV Squadron. At the end of January climb performance at operational loads was explored. On 7 February the squadron despatched 15 Stirlings to Lorient, among them three Mk. IIIs: BK654:W flown by Sqn. Ldr. R. English; BK657:C, with Flt. Sgt. J. Shiells; and BK658:K with Sgt. Irwin. The bomb load of the first aircraft was 1,500 × 4 lb. and 30 × 4 lb. 'X' incendiaries; and that of the other two aircraft 2 × 500 lb. G.P., 423 × 4 lb. and 27 × 4 lb. 'X' incendiaries. All attacked Lorient, Shiells from around 16,000 ft. and the others from about 13,000 ft.

Thereafter small numbers of Mk. IIIs operated, flying to Germany (Wilhelmshaven) for the first time on 18 February 1943, when BK654, BK657 and BK667:H operated, the first returning early. Four took part in the Essen raid on 5 March. The first mining came on 27 March, and on the 29th six operated against Berlin and the first loss occurred.

Deliveries of Mk. IIIs (Hercules Mk. VI) to squadrons in the first quarter of 1943 were:

January: XV–7
February: XV–10, 90–2, 149–3, 214–3, 218–5
March: XV–6, 90–6, 149–13, 214–10, 218–8, 7–4, 75–2.

Deliveries from the second production source began with BF457 on 24 January 1943. All Mk. IIIs had an F.N.50 dorsal turret. Introduction to operations, losses and accidents to 31 March 1943 were as follows:

Squadron	First op. date	Target	Aircraft	Sorties to 31.3.43	First loss	Write-offs after flying accidents to 31.3.43
7	2.4.43	St. Nazaire	BK724:I	—	—	—
XV	7.2.43	Lorient	BF547:B	—	18.2 BF457:B	22.3 BK667:H
			BK657:C	129		
			BK685:K			
			BK654:W			
75	3.3.43	Hamburg	BF456:J	17	—	8.3 BK770
90	13.2.43	Lorient	BK693:B	22	—	—
149	28.2.43	St. Nazaire	BK696:K	32	1.3 BK692:W	—
			BK692:W			
			BK701:G			
214	16.2.43	Lorient	BK690:V	40	5.4 BK662:V	—
218	13.2.43	Lorient	BK650:L	52	29.3 BK716:J BK702:O	1.3 BK666

Total losses 1.1.43 to 31.3.43:	BF aircraft	BK aircraft	Total
January	—	—	—
February	1	—	1
March	1	6	7

The Mk. IIIs entered battle at a turning point in Bomber Command's capability. The enemy's improved defences necessitated operations on dark nights to evade fighters, at greater heights to avoid flak. The precious few extra feet that the Mk. III attained were valuable.

In January 1943 the daily average Command striking force amounted to about 500 bombers, about 330 of which were heavies, 100 being Stirlings. The backbone of Bomber Command remained the Wellington, but 3 Group had only one Wellington Mk. III squadron, and was nearly an all-heavy Group. Its efficiency had been reduced by slow Stirling production, even though the bomber could absorb tremendous punishment. It was clear that the Stirling's future was limited, for it could not accommodate large bombs now available. Strengthening of the undercarriage, which had been the cause of so much cost and trouble, was not possible. A pointer to 3 Group's future came when 115 Squadron was equipped with Lancaster Mk. IIs.

The first two months of 1943 were a period of restricted action, operations being mainly against the French west coast. Harris, in 1942, had stressed the importance of preventing the building of concrete U-boat pens there. His advice was unheeded. Now those pens were complete, impossible to destroy. Lorient and St. Nazaire were devastated, but the pens remained intact. In attacks between 1 January and 28 February, 25 Stirlings were lost.

29.   Stirling III BF509 on a maker's test flight. Used by 149 Squadron, and from February 1944 to November 1944 by 1653 Conversion Unit. Subsequently stored at Woburn Park and broken up in 1945.

Chapter 10

The 1943 Offensive and Finale

The Battle of the Ruhr commenced on 5 March 1943 when 442 aircraft set forth—only 53 of them Stirlings—to lay waste Krupp of Essen. This was the first time *Oboe* was used in a Main Force raid. Krupp's factory, often haze clad, had been costly and difficult to attack, but this time would be different.

Zero hour at Essen was 21.00 hrs. B.S.T. Mosquitoes accurately marked the factory. During the subsequent three phase attack 22 backers-up of the P.F.F., including Stirlings of 7 Squadron, placed green target indicators (flare bundles had been replaced now) over the spots where red ones had been laid. First in were 15 Halifaxes of 4 Group, then for 10 minutes came Wellingtons and Stirlings, the latter with two thirds incendiary loads. A 20 minute Lancaster onslaught rounded off the raid.

For Plt. Off. R. F. Bennett, heading one of nine crews of 75 Squadron, the operation began badly. Moments after take-off an engine seized. He had aboard a 2,000 lb. bomb, 2 × 1,000 lb. bombs and 1,740 × 4 lb. and 32 × 30 lb. incendiaries. Luckily he force landed at Newmarket, the crew unscathed.

One of 214 Squadron's 10 aircraft was coned by searchlights. The aircraft was hit by flak, and the crew jettisoned their load; this left seven other squadron crews to attack between 12,500 ft. and 15,000 ft. Loads varied, including 6 × 2,000 lb. bombs; three of 214 Squadron's aircraft carried 3 × 2,000 lb., 2 × 1,000 lb. and 1 × 500 lb. bombs. Three others were carrying 1,890 × 4 lb. incendiaries.

Only three Stirlings were lost, a rate of 3.9%—lower than expected. Analysis of Stirling participation showed:

Squadron	Despatched	Attacked primary	Early return	Crashed	Failed to return
XV	8	?	?	—	—
75	9	8	—	1	—
90	7	5	2	—	1
149	6	4	2	—	—
214	10	7	—	—	1
218	11	9	2	—	1
7 (P.F.F.)	2	2	—	—	—
TOTALS	53	35?	6?	1	3

The total loss for all types was 14 aircraft, 38 receiving major damage. About 370 attacked Essen.

Satisfied with these results, Bomber Command chose distant Nuremberg for 8 March. Unexpectedly the casualty rate did not rise; but Nuremberg lay beyond the range of *Oboe*. Few of 7 Squadron's Stirlings yet had H2S. P.F.F. flares went down at 23.12 hrs., 12 Stirlings contributing. Soon, however, the attack scattered, although heavy damage was caused; 30 of the 49 Stirling bombers attacked. Out of 335 aircraft despatched 294 claimed to attack Nuremberg. Incendiaries were dispersed, rendering them less efficient. Since no Wellingtons took part, the bomb load per aircraft roughly equalled that for Essen. Four of the seven bombers lost were Stirlings, a loss rate of 6.6%.

One of those missing was BK610:V of 7 Squadron. Over northern France, with fuel calculated as low, the captain ordered his crew to abandon aircraft. The mid-upper gunner did not receive the order, staying aboard with the pilot as the aircraft took a wayward path. Eventually Sgt. Spanton clambered from the aircraft after it alighted on a sandbank $1\frac{1}{2}$ miles off Dungeness, and later reached shore. Also missing that night was Flt. Lt. J. P. Trench and his crew, of 7 Squadron, R9270.

Munich, Stuttgart, Essen and Duisburg had all been attacked, and before March ended two attacks were mounted on Berlin, including 55 and 58 Stirlings respectively. Total losses amounted to five and one crashed, so that the loss rate was not heavy. By the end of March 18 Stirlings had been lost out of 504 despatched, an overall loss rate of 3.6%. There had been 11 nights of operations. Then bad weather halted them. Not until the last three nights of March was there a resumption, when St. Nazaire was attacked. During March 393 Stirling sorties had resulted in bombing of the target, and there had been 88 mining sorties.

Mining increased as 1943 progressed. In March 550 mines were sown by Stirlings, about 500 correctly; and Mk. XIV bomb sights were fitted in 149 Squadron's aircraft. No. 218 Squadron would have them next.

Increased Stirling production now permitted the formation of third Flights on squadrons. These would be hived off to form the nuclei of new squadrons, allowing over 100 Stirling sorties per night, a figure not reached until 23 May and meaning doubled effort within two months. The Air Staff were considering putting more Stirlings into training units, but this did not yet come about.

March saw the introduction of the Base Organisation scheme at Mildenhall where, under an Air Commodore, Mildenhall, Lakenheath and Newmarket operated as one station, able to borrow aircraft from one another as required.

An important organisation now was the Bombing Development Unit. They acquired their first Stirling in October 1942 and conducted trials, firstly, of H2S *Mk. IIG*. B.D.U. moved from Gransden in April 1943, by which time BK 594 was testing another radar aid, *Monica*, for bomber support fighters. This machine made an outstanding contribution to effective bomber operations, since it was also used to test other devices: *Oboe, Boozer, Mousetrap* and *Fishpond*. A move from Feltwell to Newmarket came on 13 September 1943, where it was then used for trials which led to high level mine delivery and the installation of ventral guns in night bombers.

30. Mines being loaded aboard Stirling EF353 of 218 Squadron at Downham Market in 1943. On its 14th sortie this aircraft crashed, while taking off, into the station's operations block.

31. The mines arrive for a Stirling of 199 Squadron.

On 1 April, 75 Squadron had formed its 'C' Flight and the offensive was sustained. In April 1943, 3 Group's Stirlings operated on 11 nights and mined on 11, Stirlings being out on 18 nights. On 4 April, 77 went to Kiel, in addition to which 7 Squadron had 14 crews on P.F.F. duty, and two more were mining, making this the busiest 1943 night so far. Using approach and departure over the sea reduced losses to two Stirlings out of 12 aircraft missing from 577 despatched, a loss rate of 2.1%—one of the lowest of this phase.

The largest number of Stirlings operated by the end of April was 84 of 3 Group with 16 of 7 Squadron, against Frankfurt on 10 April, and another 4 mining. Five were lost, two of them from 7 Squadron.

Against Stuttgart on 14 April 85 Stirlings were despatched and, working through heavily defended zones, eight were lost, a rate of 9.4%. Again 7 Squadron had the highest loss, 3 crews—attributable to them being in the marker force. Seven were lost out of 94 despatched to Mannheim on the 16th and 9 from the all-Stirling Rostock raid on the 20th.

The heaviest loss rate came, somewhat surprisingly, on 28/29 April. Nos. 75, 90, 214 and 218 Squadrons between them had 25 aircraft mining Kiel Bay. Flak ships were in the area, and six Stirlings were shot down, a rate of 24%.

Air raid warnings sounded over Denmark from between 22.40 and 23.55 hrs. as 65 bombers passed over Jutland between Hallingen and Limfjord, 20 setting course for the Skaw and Kattegat; another 20 for Langeland and the western Baltic; and 25 for the Central Belt. Marine flak units engaged some, encountering return fire from the raiders, three of which were claimed. Three Stirlings went to the Great Belt, Nyborg; seven to the Kalundborg area; 16 to Langeland Belt (one was lost); 42 to Cadet Channel (three were lost); and 22 to the Bornholm Island area. In all 227 aircraft were 'gardening' around Denmark that night, and 23 were lost. Mining was no sinecure.

The operation was, however, rewarding. At 06.00 hrs. Kreigsmarine vessels *Annakrista*, *Diana* and Sicherungsboot JK10 took over the escort of a floating dock towed by two tugs, *Holland* and *Taifun*, en route for Narvik. At 10.32 hrs. two mines exploded, one below the *Holland*, which sank in three or four minutes; only nine of the crew of 34 were rescued. *Taifun* also sprang a leak as a result of an exploding mine and sank. The floating dock stayed at Copenhagen until more tugs arrived.

At noon the Swedish ferry *Malmo*, operating between Malmo and Copenhagen, was damaged by a mine and beached near Barsebaek, Sweden. In response the Germans extended night fighter operations against minelayers and positioned more A.A. guns. There were also constant attempts by Ju 52/3m (M.S.) aircraft to locate mines and explode them from the air.

The biggest prize to fall to Bomber Command's 'gardeners' at this time was the 16,160 ton liner *Gneisenau*, sunk in the Baltic on 2 May on its way to Russia.

Analyses of effort by each Stirling squadron during bombing attacks in April showed that 218 Squadron had despatched the highest number of sorties, 127, followed by XV Squadron, whose effort of 117 was outstanding since on 14 April they vacated Bourn for 8 Group, recommencing operations from Mildenhall on the 16th. The highest success rate, 92%, was claimed by 214 Squadron, who dropped 375,000 lb. of bombs. By late April, shorter nights had reduced operational radius, but 549 sorties had been judged successful. There were 120 mining sorties. The total Stirling loss was 43.

On 10 April Flt. Sgt. Rothschild of 75 Squadron in BF455 attacked Frankfurt. Flak hit the aircraft; then fighters chased it. A prolonged track brought a low fuel state, and they had to ditch three miles off Shoreham. Sgt. E. R. Todd's radio messages raised a flight of Spitfires to provide a dawn escort before the ditching. BF455 floated for 25 minutes, giving the crew plenty of time to board the dinghy. A Walrus alighted, only to collide with the dinghy, hurling the crew into the water. All was soon well, though, and the Walrus took off with them safely on board.

April's combats included one of the 26th, when BF517, flown by Plt. Off. P. J. Buck, raided Duisburg and was attacked 30 miles north of the town. His rear gunner was killed, and the rudder and elevator damaged. All movable objects were jettisoned before the aircraft crash landed at base; two men were injured.

Although 7 Squadron should by now have had all its Stirlings equipped with H2S, and other squadrons as sets became available, it meant removing such F.N.64 ventral turrets as were fitted, and replacing them with a radome. If the enemy mounted persistent belly attacks, radomes would be replaced by turrets. If H2S was fitted the bomber force could not fulfil its secondary role of transporting paratroops, and could never have the arrester gear proposed for heavily laden aircraft. It was resolved to fit radomes to only a few Stirlings.

During March 1943 the fitting of an F.N.82 2 × .50 in. tail turret was discussed, and the effect of this and A.G.L.T. radar on trim was experimented with. Allowance was made for changes in the Stirling Mk. III with arrester gear fitted, B.12 dorsal turret, radio modifications, a Tricell flarechute and five flarechutes moved forward.

There was a shift aft of the c.g. position to 1½ in. beyond the extreme already accepted. With an F.N.64 in place it was worse, and meant reducing the rounds per gun from 2,000 to 1,000 in the F.N.82, moving the rear gunner to the rest bunk during landing, removing any arrester gear fitted and taking away the F.N.64 turret, which was already unpopular because of its c.g. alteration.

Arguments about fitting the F.N.82 droned on until early July 1943, by which time it was decided that such an interference with the Stirling when its usefulness was at its maximum was unacceptable. Installing the B.12 would have no effect on c.g., but its weight with 5,200 rounds was 550 lb. more than that of the F.N.50, which meant sacrificing bomb load and fuel. The idea was turned down.

Eight major operations including Stirlings were mounted in May 1943. On 11 nights there was mining. The first major Stirling participation came in a raid on Dortmund on 4 May, 3 Group despatching 74 Stirlings, and 7 Squadron 12. Seven were lost.

On 12 May, 72 were sent to Duisburg; but the climax came on the 23rd when 3 Group, now expanded by the addition of 'C' Flights to all squadrons, managed the magic '100 Stirling sorties', and 7 Squadron sent a further 20 to Dortmund for a total loss of six, three of them from 214 Squadron.

A total of 95 of 3 Group and 17 of 7 Squadron operated against Düsseldorf on

25 May; and the last night of the month's operations, the 29th, saw a record force sent against Wuppertal: 101 from 3 Group and 19 of 7 Squadron, plus nine minelayers—and all for the loss of eight Stirlings. During May, when 685 sorties were flown, the total loss was 43 Stirlings. In May there had been 143 successful minelaying sorties and over 700 mines had been laid.

A second Base, No. 32, had been formed in the Group. It comprised Stradishall, Ridgewell and Chedburgh. Ridgewell passed to the 4th Bomb Wing Substitution Unit, U.S.A.A.F., in May, and 90 Squadron moved to newly opened West Wickham, Cambridgeshire (later renamed West Wratting) on 31 May.

Not only had all the squadrons expanded to three Flight level, their establishment was increased by three extra aircraft and aircrews in May, the establishment for Stirling squadrons now being 24 I.E. + 6 I.R. with 33 crews. This expansion was made possible by increased output from conversion units, No. 1657 turning out 37 crews in April, who achieved 1,309 flying hours; and 1651 Conversion Unit 35 crews, flying 1,223 hours. A lot of training involved 'circuits and bumps', and in April 1943 1657 C.U. recorded 2,017 landings; 1651 made 2,070.

Stirling production permitted a further conversion unit intended to be formed at Mepal, Waterbeach's satellite, and established at 31 I.E. + 0 I.R. Mepal was not ready for occupation in time, so the unit formed Flights at 1651 and 1657 C.U.s No. 1665 C.U. began to form at Waterbeach in May, and used Great Ashfield for flying training.

Accident rates at conversion units were high, which was mostly attributable to pilot error on landing or taking off. A feature at Waterbeach was a ditch running along the side of the Cambridge–Ely road. Many a Stirling undercarriage caught and collapsed in this pernicious feature, which had to be retained for drainage purposes.

May 1943 brought a welter of courageous action. Early on 13 May Plt. Off. G. W. Young of 90 Squadron set off to attack Duisburg. Four times his aircraft was attacked by a fighter. Sgt. W. Davine was seriously wounded, but continued to play a very active and vital part in the action. Young nursed the damaged aircraft home. It was this night that BF523 was lost.

Also on that night, 90 Squadron despatched Plt. Off. Shippard, flying BF473, carrying 1,080 × 4 lb. incendiaries and 90 × 30 lb. incendiaries, the standard load for 90 Squadron on that raid. Shippard attacked the target from 11,000 ft., recording an I.A.S. of 190 m.p.h. On his return, 15 miles off the enemy coast, his aircraft was engaged by a fighter which scored hits on the rear and mid-upper turrets. The aircraft was generally badly shot up and kept falling into a nose-up attitude. Only considerable force would keep it level, and Shippard managed this by clasping the control column between his knees. By the time he reached Stradishall one of the main wheels was vibrating badly, but nevertheless he landed safely.

Night fighters did not have it all their own way. On 13 May Sgt. J. R. Mitchell of 75 Squadron was flying BK619. He was engaged by a Bf110 which attacked from below and astern, and opened fire at 400 yd. The mid-upper gunner replied as the fighter passed below the Stirling. Then the rear gunner managed a burst at

32.   W7463 of 1657 Conversion Unit. After serving with 149 then XV Squadron and XV Squadron Conversion Flight, joined 1657 Conversion Unit 8 February 1943. Written off after belly landing at Woodbridge 5 July 1944.

33.   Production line for the Mk. III at Austin Longbridge. EH883, nearest, served with 149 Squadron; EH884, ahead, with 218 Squadron.

300 yd. which put the fighter on to its back, and soon it was blazing on the ground.

Crews were at their weariest when the time came to land—and landing a Stirling needed much concentration. Sgt. T. J. Nichols of 218 Squadron was ordered to land at Chedburgh, but his aircraft at the last moment got into difficulty, and crashed, and five of the crew were killed. Sgt. W. C. Carney in BF480 joined the circuit at Downham Market. As he touched down the aircraft swung badly, careering into the operations block and killing two crewmen from another Stirling.

June began quietly. During the first half of the month Stirlings flew only one bombing operation, on the 11th, when Düsseldorf was target for 98 Stirlings bombing, and 21 in the P.F.F. In the second half of the month they carried out six raids.

First came one against Montluçon and Le Creusot, when 103 Stirlings operated without loss. On 21 June 96 bombers and 19 P.F.F. aircraft raided Krefeld and lost nine of their number. Next night the biggest force of the month, 98 bombers, 5 P.F.F. aircraft and 15 minelayers, operated with Mülheim as the main target. It cost another nine Stirlings. On the 24th 88 bombers, 10 P.F.F. aircraft and 4 minelayers operated, with Elberfeld and Wuppertal as the main target. This time 10 Stirlings were lost. Against Gelsenkirchen on the 25th and Cologne on the 28th the Stirling forces numbered over 70 aircraft, and the loss was 10. By the end of June 42 Stirlings had been lost, losses again peaking in the summer, partly owing to the greater number of aircraft operating.

Further changes in 3 Group had taken place. No. 1665 Conversion Unit left Waterbeach on 7 June, consolidating at Woolfox Lodge. Mepal, now a Sub-station, was still devoid of Stirlings, while better weather kept 75 Squadron at Newmarket for operations. No. 199 Squadron arrived at Lakenheath from Ingham on 20 June. They brought the Wellington, in its Mk. X form, back to 3 Group. No. 199 Squadron flew only two Wellington operations from Lakenheath, the last a mining operation on 13 June. Thereafter they worked up with Stirlings.

An entirely new Stirling squadron had been formed: this was 620, at the Sub-Station, Chedburgh, under Wg. Cdr. D. H. Lee. The first operation, against the Schneider works at Le Creusot, was flown on 19 June. Eight crews attacked in good visibility, although smoke spoilt aim. Attacking at between 6,000 and 11,000 ft., 620's Stirlings dropped 36 H.E. bombs and 1,944 incendiaries. The squadron next operated against Krefeld on 21 June. Sgt. P. O'Connell, flying BK724, met a Bf109 over the target, and Sgt. C. Doig fired a 30-second burst, driving off the fighter. O'Connell's adventures for the month were not over. On the 24th his aircraft was hit by flak, forcing it so low that Flt. Lt. Weston poured fire into searchlights from 700 ft. Two of the crew had superficial wounds, and O'Connell crashed at Chedburgh.

Stirlings sometimes flew daylight A.S.R. sorties. An eventful one was flown on 13 June by Sgt. J. M. Steel, in BK781 of 90 Squadron. The crew spotted a dinghy and six men, and circled until a relief Stirling arrived. A Walrus alighted close to the dinghy, and the occupants scrambled aboard. The second Stirling left as the Walrus made frantic attempts to get aloft. Smoke flares from the Stirling gave the

34. No. 199 Squadron parade before their Stirlings for an inspection by the Duke of Gloucester at Lakenheath in 1944.

35. NAAFI-break for the ground crews of 199 Squadron preparing their Stirling for operations.

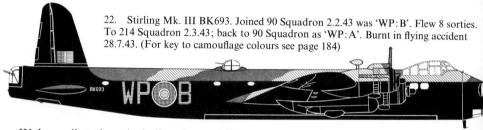
22. Stirling Mk. III BK693. Joined 90 Squadron 2.2.43 was 'WP:B'. Flew 8 sorties. To 214 Squadron 2.3.43; back to 90 Squadron as 'WP:A'. Burnt in flying accident 28.7.43. (For key to camouflage colours see page 184)

Walrus pilot the wind direction, while a second Walrus circled. An A.S.R. launch eventually arrived and took the rescued men aboard.

An amazing event occurred during a Ruhr attack by 75 Squadron on 19 June. Flt. Lt. J. Joll was flying EH880 when it received a direct flak hit which burst inside the port mainplane, severing a petrol cock, oil pipe and control cables. Oil flooded into the fuselage. The flight engineer, Sgt. G. Falloon, could not ascertain the fracture point without entering the wing. With the aircraft still under fire in the target area, he used his axe to cut a 2 ft. square hole out of the fuselage metal. He then crawled into the wing, turned off the fuel pumps and investigated the oil leak. While in the wing, he inspected the mainwheel tyre. All was well, so he crawled back to report. In this way, showing complete disregard for his safety, he enabled the aircraft to make a safe landing at Newmarket.

During July, Stirlings participated in seven major attacks, four of them against Ruhr targets, and mined on nine nights. Sorties totalled 1,026, with 90.7% bombing of primary targets during 5,040 hr. flying. The weight of bombs dropped totalled 1,466.21 tons. There were 103 mining sorties, and 199 Squadron flew its first Stirling operation, six crews mining on 30 July. In the four Ruhr raids, 3 Group despatched 75 Stirlings to Cologne, losing seven; 56 to Aachen, losing 1; 103 to Essen, losing 6; and 76 to Remscheid, which cost 8 aircraft.

The main event of the month was the switch on three nights to the horrific bombing of Hamburg. No city has ever received such prolonged torture by bombing. The second city of the Reich, it had over 3,000 industrial units, and 45% of U-boat production was concentrated there.

Bomber Command's Stirling force was near its peak strength, but German defences were improving rapidly. *Window*, metal foil designed to prevent radar tracking, was used for the first time on these raids.

The bombers kept well out over the sea, crossing out over Cromer and flying the course 54°45′N/07.00 E—53°55′N/09.45°E—Hamburg—53 15N/10°E—54°30′N/06.00E—Cromer—bases. The plan was for the first wave to comprise 117 aircraft, the second 18 Lancasters of 115 Squadron, 72 Halifaxes of 4 Group and 27 Lancasters of 5 Group. Then would come 114 Stirlings of 3 Group, leaving others to attack as ordered, the force comprising:

1 Group: 121 Lancasters, 39 Wellingtons; 6 Wellingtons mining
3 Group: 114 Stirlings, 18 Lancasters
4 Group: 160 Halifaxes, 16 Wellingtons
5 Group: 140 Lancasters
6 Group: 50 Halifaxes, 21 Wellingtons
8 Group: 114 heavies (various types), 13 Mosquitoes for a follow-up raid.

Bomb load was the usual one third H.E. and two thirds incendiaries, of which the latter were 12% 30 lb. and 15% 4 lb. 'X'. The Stirlings were to bomb from between 12,000 and 15,000 ft.

Late on 24 July 791 bombers took off: 347 Lancasters, 246 Halifaxes, 125 Stirlings (10 from 7 Squadron) and 73 Wellingtons. They took the ordered route, turning in from the north west for landfall on the north bank of the Elbe, which showed up well on H2S. On 01.02 hrs. P.F.F. marked, and the onslaught commenced. For 48 minutes bombs rained on Hamburg, bringing destruction and fire the like of which had not previously been known. It was a new kind of catastrophe. The savage blitz which the Luftwaffe had inflicted upon the British was more than avenged.

Window fluttered freely at the head of the bomber force, reducing losses to a mere 1.5%, since it completely confused the defenders. There was no cloud and only slight haze, and H2S worked well. There was some incendiary creep towards the north west. Only 12 bombers were lost, three of them Stirlings.

Within the force were 21 Stirlings of 75 Squadron, including EH935, flown by Flg. Off. G. Turner. He was avoiding searchlights when a Ju 88 approached head-on and careered into his starboard wingtip, knocking off a 4 ft. piece and rendering the aileron useless. The Ju 88 turned over and fell to earth. Control was difficult: the unbalanced aircraft was kept on an even keel only by combined strength of the pilot and the bomb aimer. After a three hour flight Turner made a perfect landing at Mepal.

On the night of the 25th the heaviest raid yet delivered on Essen took place, with 103 Stirlings in the force. Then a light, *Oboe* directed attack was made on Remscheid. But still no town in Germany had suffered as Hamburg: on the 25th and 26th from the Americans—and on 27 July Bomber Command struck again.

This time 787 aircraft, including 116 Stirlings, ran in from Denmark, between Lübeck and the Elbe, attacking for 43 minutes and leaving smoke and heat haze rising to 20,000 ft. It was mainly the south-east of the city that was savaged, 722 crews claiming to bomb. Devoid of individual instructions, night fighters and guns were merely guided towards the bomber stream, taking their chance and destroying 17 bombers (including one Stirling), and damaging another 49.

From Mepal 20 Stirlings were despatched. A Ju 88 engaged Flt. Sgt. E. J. Roberts. As it approached from port all the bomber's guns opened up. The fighter quickly broke away to port, but not before its shots had blown off a bomb door and pierced fuel lines. Nevertheless, Roberts brought his charge home.

In the streets of Hamburg conditions were horrific. Fires had raised the temperature to 1,000°C, and the uprush of hot air had a suction effect, raising a fierce wind which swept flames through the city. Trees were torn up, and people lifted off their feet into the blaze. Those who took to the shelters suffered carbon monoxide poisoning on a vast scale. Six districts of the city were destroyed.

And still the bombs came. On 29 July, 777 aircraft set off in favourable weather, and 699 crews claimed to attack. In the force were 118 Stirlings of which four were missing; total losses of all types were 30.

German fighter pilots, stung to desperation, did their best. A Ju 88 attacked Sgt. Hartstein's aircraft with cannon, and Flg. Off. G. Duncan's mid-upper gunner drove off another. Flt. Sgt. Wilkinson's crew accounted for a third. All these were members of 75 Squadron; others had similar tales to tell. It was 'the best raid so far', they said.

The final agony came on 2 August. This time the bombers also suffered, for the weather had turned sour. Icing and storms were so severe that only about half the force of 740 aircraft bombed; but this included many of the 104 Stirling bombers and six of the P.F.F. also got through. The defences destroyed 30 bombers, and damaged another 51.

In Hamburg about 61 % of all accommodation was destroyed: 40,385 houses and 275,000 flats. In addition, 2,632 shops, 24 hospitals, 277 schools, 58 churches and 83 banks were wiped out. Casualties amounted to 41,800 killed and 37,439 injured, of whom many later died. Göbbels wrote in his diary that it was 'a catastrophe the like of which staggers the imagination'. Yet, within days—and despite the loss of one third of the population—life somehow resurged among the ruination and recovery was astonishing. The devastation brought another response: a rapid increase in the strength of German defences.

At this time much reliance was placed upon H2S as the prime navigational aid, but its fitment precluded the installation of ventral guns. With the enemy rapidly improving night defences, such guns would be a worthwhile asset. Only Lancaster Mk. IIs mounted a ventral F.N.64 turret. B.D.U. was asked to look into a simpler idea for ventral defence, as were the stations.

In mid July B.D.U. installed a .50 in. gun in the aft escape hatch of a Stirling, consisting of a gun on a simple mounting behind a triangular protecting windscreen. Command examined this on 20 July, then approved it for aircraft not carrying H2S, and for all future production heavies. In addition to the mounting, some provision for downward search was needed, trials continuing into the autumn of 1943.

It was surprising that so few aircraft were struck by falling bombs. But for Stirlings, operating below the Lancasters, the risk was greater, and 149 Squadron's aircraft, seemed prone to this misfortune. Plt. Off. G. W. Macdonald in EH894 was over Aachen on 13 July when several incendiaries struck the aircraft and severed some fuel leads. His aircraft also suffered flak damage and, short of fuel and flying on three engines, he force landed at Tangmere.

Although the Stirling was making a strong contribution to the 1943 offensive, particularly with heavy incendiary loads, it was clear that it was unsuitable for further development. On 30 July 1943 a meeting discussed the future direction of Stirling employment. Four roles were considered: transport, special duties, general and meteorological reconnaissance. On 6 August a further meeting was held at Cuxton. It was agreed that, for the present, production of the Stirling bomber by Short's and Austin's would remain unaltered; the bomber would not be phased out of 3 Group until mid 1944—and only when Lancaster production fulfilled all needs.

It was now possible to hive off 'C' Flights from XV and 218 Squadrons. On 10 August 1943, these became the nuclei of 622 Squadron at Mildenhall and 623 at Downham Market, each with 16 I.E. + 4 I.R. aircraft. Thus the seven aircraft of XV's 'C' Flight became 'A' Flight of 622 Squadron, and since crews were already fully operational, it was possible for this and 623 Squadron to operate on the nights of their formation, against Nuremberg. No. 623 Squadron had a more complex formation. As well as receiving crews and aircraft from No. 218, it also took over personnel from No. 3 L.F.S. and from 1653 Conversion Unit, which disbanded. More effort was simultaneously to be put into beginning the conversion of 3 Group squadrons to Lancasters. No. 214 Squadron would move from Chedburgh to replace 623, some of whose aircraft would be switched to Wigsley under the 3 Group 'Ladder Plan'. The rest of 623's charge, and others allotted, would be passed to 214 Squadron. Consequently, 623's operations remained on a small scale.

Stirlings of 3 Group operated on nine major bombing raids in August, and mined on nine nights. On 12 August, 112 Stirlings were sent to Turin; 3 were lost.

At Downham Market 13 crews of 218 Squadron were briefed, and take-off began around 21.30 hrs. At 21.35 hrs. it was the turn of EF452, piloted by Flt. Sgt. Arthur Louis Aaron, D.F.M. Even with the Mk. III's improved operation height, flights over Alpine areas remained dangerous, and the circuitous route around the western side was favoured.

Aaron had made a safe transit of this region and was running in towards Turin when his aircraft was raked by gunfire. Official sources are adamant that the firing came from a night fighter; yet fighters were few in Italy at the time, and there have been unauthorised claims that the fire came from another Stirling. Aaron was severely wounded by the firing, three of the four engines hit and the pilot's windscreen shattered. Two turrets were put out of action, and the elevator cables damaged.

Aaron was terribly wounded in the face, one lung was perforated and his right arm was broken. As he fell over the control column the flight engineer gained control of the battered machine. He set course for the south-east in the belief that, rather than risk the Alps, they might be able to reach North Africa. Only three engines were functioning. Aaron had been carried to the rest bunk and treated with morphia. He rallied, and, as captain, insisted on returning to the cockpit, where he was lifted into his seat. His feet were placed upon the rudder pedals, and twice he tried to take over; but he was too weak. By now the bomb aimer was controlling the aircraft, with Aaron at his side. Together, they managed to coax the aircraft along until it was crossing the Mediterranean; but after five hours' flying, fuel was low. Then miraculously, the lights of Bône came into view. Aaron summoned his remaining strength to assist the bomb aimer make a wheels-up landing. Four times they tried, and on the fifth attempt succeeded, with Aaron then on the point of collapse. Nine hours later he died. For his supreme courage he was posthumously awarded the Victoria Cross.

Had he lain on the bunk to conserve his strength, he might despite his terrible wounds have survived. Instead, he gave his life for his comrades, saving them all except one other. His award citation spoke of 'an example of devotion to duty which has seldom been equalled and never surpassed'.

Four nights later the Stirlings went again to Turin, 113 of them. This was the last time they were called upon to make that long journey.

By August 1943 the British were aware that secret work was going on at Peenemünde, the rocket and jet experimental station on the Baltic Coast. On 17 August the famous raid on the establishment was carried out, involving a long flight through well defended areas. Losses seemed likely to be heavy. Nevertheless the objective was worth maximum effort, including skilled crews from 3 Group.

Eventually 593 aircraft set off: 113 from 1 Group; 143 Halifaxes from 4 Group; 51 Halifaxes and nine Lancasters from 6 Group; 21 Halifaxes and 69 Lancasters from 8 Group; 107 Lancasters from 5 Group; and 60 Stirlings and 12 Lancasters of 115 Squadron from 3 Group. Eight Mosquitoes of 8 Group provided a diversionary attack on Berlin.

Among the Stirling force were 15 crews of 90 Squadron. Pathfinders of 7 Squadron now flew Lancasters exclusively; they had used them alongside Stirlings since 24 July.

Surprisingly, only two Stirlings were lost on the Peenemünde raid: one from XV Squadron, the other from 620 Squadron. The load dropped by the 48 attacking aircraft was $10 \times 2,000$ lb., $49 \times 1,000$ lb., 58×500 lb., $1,800 \times 30$ lb., $12,980 \times 4$ lb. incendiaries and 450×4 lb. 'X' incendiaries. All 15 aircraft of 90 Squadron attacked with a load of $4 \times 1,000$ lb. G.P., 44×500 lb. M.C. and $3,240 \times 4$ lb. incendiaries.

The Stirling crews met neither searchlights nor flak at the commencement of the attack, but flak started as the raid developed. Several fighters arrived in the target area, and EE896, on its run-in encountered a Ju 88 400 yd. astern. The fighter fired a four-second burst, to which the rear gunner replied, and so the Ju 88 corkscrewed away to starboard. EF426 was also fired upon.

Both crews of 149 Squadron also found good visibility and made D.R. runs from Rüden aiming on the green target indicators. As they bombed they saw two large explosions at 00.28 hrs. The force was protected by *Tinsel, Window* and *Boozer* aids.

On 23 August the 10 Stirling squadrons between them despatched 124 aircraft to Berlin, part of the force of 727 bombers operating. The attack opened the campaign that became known as the Battle of Berlin. Visibility was excellent, and the moon was rising over the city. The raid cost 16 Stirling crews, close to a 13% loss—the highest yet on a Main Force operation.

One Stirling, BK816 of 622 Squadron, was attacked three times by fighters. The port elevator was shot away, the port inner engine set ablaze and the rear turret hydraulics severed. The injured pilot was removed from his seat and the navigator managed to get the aircraft under control. The port outer engine was accidentally feathered and the task of restarting it was tried by the bomb aimer. Between them the crew brought the aircraft home on three engines, flying dangerously low at 4,000 ft., as the navigator gave the pilot first aid. Then the bomb aimer and flight engineer managed to get the damaged engine working again once they were over the sea. The bomb aimer was at the controls, and achieved an almost impossible feat, a perfect landing. Only 75 gal. of fuel remained in the tanks. It was a superb effort by the crew.

Flt. Sgt. O. H. White of 75 Squadron and crew, in EF435, also had a

36. Yes, they were large aeroplanes. A trainee crew at 1651 Conversion Unit late 1941, Sergeant A. Hotchkiss third from the right.

memorable sortie. As they approached Berlin the aircraft was coned by searchlights and repeatedly hit by heavy flak, which caused serious damage to the port mainplane. They continued to the target, although still coned. Then they were attacked by a Ju 88, which scored hits on the rear fuselage, killing the rear gunner, Sgt. J. Poole. The aircraft was then forced into an uncontrollable dive and the captain warned the crew to get ready to bale out. In the middle of the trouble the intercom failed and the navigator, air bomber and radio operator abandoned the aircraft, since they were no longer able to contact the captain. White then jettisoned his bombs in a dive, managing to regain control at 6,000 ft. The captain and remaining crew members took stock of the damage and decided to attempt the long haul home. Without flaps, and with the undercarriage up because the electrical leads had been shot away, they crash landed at Mepal. Despite the performance failings of the Stirling, such episodes as this proved its ability to absorb tremendous punishment and survive.

The Berlin raid on 23 August cost Bomber Command 57 aircraft, in addition to the write-off of EF435. Out of the 124 Stirlings despatched 81 attacked, dropping $6 \times 2,000$ lb. H.C., $63 \times 1,000$ lb. and 944×500 lb. H.E., $23,045 \times 30$ lb. and $27,660 \times 4$ lb. incendiaries and 60×4 lb. 'X' incendiaries. Photographs later showed that 3 Group had placed 52% of its bombs within three miles of the aiming point, the most accurate bombing being credited to 1 Group, followed by

No. 5. As always it was impossible to assess the accuracy of the incendiaries. An additional 40 aircraft were making mining sorties, 32 of them effectively.

The Nuremberg raid of the 27th claimed 11 of the 104 Stirlings despatched, 85 of which were credited with attacking the target. About 54% of the bombs fell within three miles of the aiming point, and again 3 Group was placed third for bombing accuracy. München-Gladbach was bombed on the 30th by 94 out of the 107 Stirlings despatched, six of which were missing. Then came another heavy raid on Berlin in which 106 Stirlings took part, 66 attacked the city and 16 were lost. The raid was not very successful, most bombs falling S.S.W. of the aiming point. There was an unacceptably high loss rate of 15.1%. No. 75 Squadron lost three crews out of 20 sent, the largest fielded by any squadron in the Group that night.

Losses on the two Berlin raids convinced Bomber Command that the days of the Stirling were numbered, at least against distant heavily defended targets; but for the immediate future operations had to continue. The effect of August's operations may be seen from this tabulation of Stirlings on strength:

Date	I.E.	Actual strength	Aircraft fit for operations
1.8.43	136	126	90
4.8.43	160	127	120
15.8.43	160	160	111
24.8.43	160	160	108
31.8.43	144	144	115

By way of comparison, on 15 July 416 Lancasters and 272 Halifaxes were on I.E., 399 Lancasters and 263 Halifaxes on operational strength. The total strength of Bomber Command on 31 July was 936 I.E., 916 actual strength and 773 aircraft operationally fit.

In September bad weather set in. Only seven major raids were carried out by Stirlings. The following table summarises September bombing raids:

Date	Target	No. despatched	Losses
5.9.43	Mannheim	110	8
8.9.43	Boulogne area	109	—
15.9.43	Montluçon	120	1
16.9.43	Modane	128	1
22.9.43	Hanover	137	4
23.9.43	Mannheim	117	5
27.9.43	Hanover	114	11

During the month, when just under 1,000 tons of bombs were dropped, 131 mining sorties were flown.

Final approval was given to the .50 in. under gun mounting in the aft escape hatch behind a plastic shield; this had originated in XV Squadron. Ideally, another crewman would be needed to handle this gun. A trial installation in EF466 was completed at Rochester in August 1943. Plans were that 200 sets should be available by the end of October 1943.

Only one Stirling of 75 Squadron had the mounting by January 1944, but two small working parties from Short's were installing guns at Lakenheath on aircraft of 149 and 199 Squadrons. By that time many Stirlings had been withdrawn. These guns were eventually a feature of 90, 214 and 218 Squadrons as well as these two. By February 1944 they were also being fitted into aircraft at Stradishall and some other conversion units.

On 8 September a proposal was discussed whereby all bombers would have H2S radomes fitted except those with ability to carry 8,000 lb. bombs. The Stirling had an advantage in that the long fuselage would allow both the radome and the .50 in. ventral gun to be fitted. Yet again, most Stirlings were withdrawn before radomes were fitted.

A third Base in 3 Group opened in September, with Headquarters at Waterbeach controlling Mepal and Witchford. At Mepal 513 Squadron formed on 15 September under Wg. Cdr. G. E. Harrison, whose place at 149 Squadron was taken by Act. Wg. Cdr. C. R. B. Wigfall. The first crews for 513 Squadron came from 75 Squadron. It was 21 October before they received any aircraft, which also came from 75 Squadron. Before the Squadron was ready for operations 3 Group was changing over to Lancasters, and 513 Squadron was dissolved, personnel being posted to 1653 Conversion Unit forming at Chedburgh in December 1943.

In the first week of September a tactical feint invasion was mounted against the Pas de Calais. It should have brought the Luftwaffe to battle, but it failed to do so. Operation *Starkey* came on 8 September, when 109 Stirlings set off for Boulogne. As BK809 'T-Tommy' rolled at Mepal, engine trouble struck. The bomber careered off the runway, hit a petrol bowser and crashed into two houses close to the perimeter track. It burst into flames and there was a tremendous explosion as the bombs went off. Three of the crew, a W.A.A.F. officer, a sergeant, and two civilians were killed, and others were injured. The raid itself was straightforward, although a Ju 88 engaged Plt. Off. Wallis in EE966 of 623 Squadron.

Bad weather set in again, and it was 15 September before another raid was mounted, against the Dunlop rubber factory at Montluçon.

It was imperative to cut off supplies to German forces in Italy. This was done by attacking railway communications. Seven rail routes were used between Italy and northern Europe. The Mont Cenis route was allotted to 3 Group for a moonlight attack. Modane, the most vulnerable point, consisted of an international railway station and goods yard. Maximum strength was ordered for a difficult target.

The run-in was from Lake Bourget, turning point on many Italian raids. Modane was 3,467 ft. above mean sea level, and within five miles of ground rising to 11,257 ft. The attack went in around 12,000 to 14,000 ft. Regardless of wind, it was made on an easterly heading along the valley, the aiming point halfway between two targets, bomb aiming to allow half the bombs to overshoot, half to undershoot. Loads were 80% H.E., mainly, 1,000 lb. bombs, and 20% mixed incendiaries.

Bombing was concentrated at the E.N.E. end of the aiming point and negligible damage done to the yards. Several rail tracks to the Mont Cenis Tunnel were, however, cut. There had been a gap after marking before the Stirlings arrived. When new target indicators fell they did so away from the aiming point just as the bulk of the bombers arrived.

Despite the large force of Stirlings sent to Hanover on 22 September, this raid was disappointing. A repeat attack was mounted on the 27th. On the bombing run EE509 was attacked by a Bf 110. Return fire from the Stirling entered the fighter's wing. The bomber was again attacked, but survived. 'V-Victor' of 90 Squadron was also intercepted, bullets raking the fuselage and wounding the rear gunner in the foot. Return fire was poured out towards the fighter, and after the third burst it dived away trailing smoke. The night's drama was not yet ended for 90 Squadron, since Sqn. Ldr. M. I. Freeman in EE952 crashed near Bartlow.

For Geoff Parry the return from Hanover after the 22 September raid was something he would not forget. 'It was my sixteenth op., and it ended in a peculiar way. Waiting to land, we heard the rear gunner say: "Some silly so-and-so is going round the wrong way." A few seconds later control warned of bandits, and all lights were put out. After milling round for a while in the darkness, control told the first aircraft to land and switched on the flarepath. No. 1 made his approach to land. Following down the runway at low level, and clearly silhouetted in the flarepath lights, was a Ju 88. He dropped a stick of bombs along Chedburgh's runway.

'Control now had a large number of aircraft short of petrol and with no home base. Diversions were made to stations all over East Anglia. We in "C-Charlie" were sent to Newmarket, where they hadn't lit the flarepath when we arrived. On the final approach, wheels and flaps down, the two starboard engines cut dead and the other two faltered. By a miracle the flight engineer found a few gallons of fuel in the two rarely used wingtip tanks. The engines re-started, we landed; but before we were off the flarepath all four engines stopped. All the other aircraft found a safe haven too.'

The Stirling force was at its peak strength in October. Bomber Command mounted attacks on five cities in the first eight days and the Stirlings operated three times. Then came a lull lasting to the end of the month. Severe weather halted the offensive. The pattern for October was bombing on the 3/4th, 4/5th and 8/9th, with mining on three nights at the start of the month. Stirlings mined between the 17th and 28th, one being lost during 228 sorties. Mining proved an all-time record, with 850 mines correctly planted out of a total of 906.

The most successful bombing raid was on the 4th, the first well placed on Frankfurt. Of 73 Stirlings despatched, three were lost. On the 8th 97 Stirlings raided Bremen during a diversion for a Hanover attack, and two were lost.

Against Kassel on 3 October, 115 Stirlings were despatched and five lost. A feint was made towards Hanover, the Main Force flying to within 40 miles of that city before veering towards Kassel. The enemy fighters took 15 minutes to react to the course alteration, concentrating their attack on the sides of the stream, which was inadequately cloaked by *Window*.

During October, 94 of the mining sorties were to the Baltic, 79 successfully, and only one aircraft, EH960, was lost there. The Baltic offered the best return, recent traffic having increased there fourfold. October's effort caused the damage or sinking of at least 20 ships.

Innovation came to 214 Squadron on 7 October, when they flew a mission dropping supplies to the French Resistance. Hitherto such had been the job of 138 and 161 Squadrons. Now Stirlings of 3 Group commenced such flights under the control of Tempsford's experts.

Poor autumn weather with fog reduced the effort of the Stirling force at its peak size, as drastic plans were unfolded to reduce its strength. Not until 18 November did the weather permit a Stirling raid, when 89 out of 114 aircraft were despatched to Ludwigshafen and nine lost. Between them they delivered 79 × 2,000 lb. H.C., 57,420 × 4 lb. and 2,368 × 4 lb. 'X' incendiaries. Stirlings and Halifaxes made the attack, leaving Lancasters to raid Berlin. That night 884 Bomber Command aircraft were despatched. The crew of 'C-Charlie' of 214 Squadron shot down a FW 190 over Mainz; 'L' of 214 Squadron was engaged over Mannheim by three FW 190s, one of which was destroyed; and 'A' of 75 Squadron was attacked by a fighter.

Next night 74 out of 86 Stirlings attacked Leverkusen; only one was lost. With them were 98 Halifaxes of 4 Group and 67 of 6 Group, plus the marker force. Cloud gathered along the route, resulting in poor target marking. Flak was intense but ineffective, and few fighters showed up.

It was probably unknown to the crews taking part, but the operation of 22/23 November was to have a niche in history. It was the last time that Stirlings participated in a long distance Main Force attack. The target, significantly, was Berlin, for which the original call for a Stirling attack had been forcibly made in January 1941. Of 764 bombers despatched, of which about 640 attacked, only 50 were Stirlings. The decline in operational strength was abrupt.

It was a very effective operation, the P.F.F. markers being clustered closely over about a square mile. Berlin was, nevertheless, a difficult target. Only 28 Stirling crews claimed to attack it. Of 25 aircraft lost that night four were Stirlings, a loss rate of 8%—not particularly high. Stirling crews delivered 5 × 2,000 lb. H.C., 1 × 500 lb. G.P., 644 × 30 lb., 91,714 × 4 lb. and 1,806 × 4 lb. 'X' incendiaries. It was a satisfactory finale for the Stirling as a front line bomber.

The end of the Stirling force had begun when 196 and 620 Squadrons were transferred to 93 Group in mid November pending their switch to 38 Group and a transport role, in keeping with decisions made in July 1943. It had been decided that Lancasters would replace Stirlings in 3 Group. By the end of December XV and 622 Squadrons would have Lancaster Mk. Is and IIIs and, to compensate for the loss of 196 and 620 Squadrons, No. 514 would become fully operational with Lancaster Mk. IIs.

The historian of 3 Group wrote at this time: 'While enthusiastic admirers of the "Queen of the Air" will probably object to the definition of metamorphosis (i.e. a change of form from a chrysalis to a winged insect), Lancaster fans will no doubt endorse the result of this change in character. Those who regard the Stirling as an old and trusted friend will view the new equipment with a mixture of satisfaction and regret.'

And the Stirling was trusted. Those who had previously flown in Wellingtons had regarded it as a massive advance. Massive indeed, for coming face to face with a Stirling for the first time was unforgettable. It was a much larger aeroplane than the Lancaster, and no Lancaster was ever so well built. Nor could it match the manoeuvrability of the Stirling; but the Lancaster, though not all that much faster, could cruise higher, which afforded additional protection and tactical flexibility. More important, the Lancaster could accommodate larger weapons and was superior from an operational point of view. Crews found it easier to master.

If the Stirling's wingspan had not been altered, if the bomb bay had been differently designed, if engines had been developed to give more power—but history is littered with misfortune.

The Lancaster was a second generation four engined bomber, whereas the Stirling embodied ideas of the 1930s. 'Cookies' were then undreamed of, and complex operational planning left the Stirling on the sidelines. The Stirling is best compared with the Halifax, which in some respects it bettered. Unlike this, however, the Stirling was unsuited to development. The time had come for retirement.

Re-equipment of 3 Group took place over a long phase. As the last to form, 513 and 623 Squadrons (the latter ceasing to be operational on 6 December) would disband first, providing aircraft for a conversion unit controlled by 5 Group. Two squadrons, 196 and 620, transferred to 38 Group and 1665 Conversion Unit at Woolfox Lodge, would now supply crews for transport duties. While these changes took place, Stirling bomber squadrons would maintain full operational programmes, mainly mining and special duty sorties.

A major shake-up of 3 Group took place as 1651 Conversion Unit moved to 31 Base, Wratting Common, making way for 514 Squadron, and 90 Squadron moved to Tuddenham to await Lancasters. Some of the retired Stirlings would go to the new 1653 Conversion Unit which formed at Chedburgh under Wg. Cdr. Crompton on 21 November. This was the third conversion unit in 31 Base, now entirely administering training units. Also on 21 November, 513 Squadron was due to disband and commence passing its aircraft to 1660 Conversion Unit, Swinderby. Indicating future Stirling employment, 214 Squadron flew 15 supply drops in November.

The sudden decline in 3 Group's Stirling strength can be seen from these figures in the following Table.

On 16 December 20 aircraft were flown in perfect weather against two V-1 sites near Abbeville, and another on the 22nd when, however, low cloud prevented effective bombing. These small targets were too small for saturation bombing, although four more Stirling raids were tried in January 1944.

Another 24 special duty drops were flown by 214 Squadron in December, and nine by 218 Squadron. Stirlings flew about half the total Bomber Command

Date	I.E. Strength	Actual strength	Operationally fit
17.11.43	184	179	194
18.11.43	168	179	186
22.11.43	152	159	133
25.11.43	152	138	125
Total Bomber Command strength:			
25.11.43	1,072	989	857

mining effort in 1943, and completed 113 mining sorties in December, 77%
effectively, when 534 mines were sown.

The accident rate in the Stirling force had gradually decreased in 1943. When
operations were at their peak in August the rate was 1 per 455 hr. flown,
compared with 1 per 170 hr. in August 1942. But the wintry weather of December
1943 took its toll. The accident rate was bad, 36 aircraft being damaged or
destroyed in 3 Group—the worst in Bomber Command. This was generally due
to swinging on take-off and landing.

By the end of the year comparison of the Lancaster Mk. II and Stirling Mk. III
was made, showing:

Date & Squadron	Sorties	Effective %	Op. hr.	Tonnage delivered
10.43				
90	65	93.8	320.44	84.45
75	65	89.2	332.27	89.73
115 (Lancaster)	60	81.7	267.05	191.88
12.43				
90	56	85.7	320	93.71
75	69	92.7	360.43	101.07
115 (Lancaster)	62	83.9	312.55	184.25
514 (Lancaster)	43	90.7	246.03	70.02

Improved Stirling performance was achieved by attention to detail. Many
small modifications were now ordered: smooth paint to add about 6 m.p.h.;
removal of the D/F loop; sealing around the front turret; removal of the
starboard pilot head; and careful fitting of cowlings and bomb doors. A fairing
mounting two hand held guns replacing the nose turret was not proceeded with.
The hope was that three Stirling squadrons would be re-equipped in February,
and three in March. There was a counter-proposal: disband all six squadrons and
reform them with Lancasters; but this was not proceeded with. Instead the six
squadrons would gradually re-equip, two being held some time for mining
operations.

On 1 January 1943 there had been six Stirling squadrons in 3 Group, and one with Wellingtons. January 1 1944 again found six Stirling squadrons in the Group, and four with Lancasters; but whereas on 1 January 1943 operational strength was 31 Stirlings and 11 Wellingtons fit for operations, in 1944 there were still 100 Stirlings on squadrons, for some had three Flights, and there were 52 Lancasters.

Mining took place on 10 nights in January 1944, 191 aircraft making sorties, mainly to Kiel Bay and off the French west coast. February's operations were almost all mining apart from a few for S.O.E. by 149 Squadron. From 4 February, 199 Squadron was given the exclusive task of dropping *Window* on Main Force raids. Mining continued in the same areas and additionally off the Frisians, in the Seine Bay, off Le Havre and the mouth of the Adour.

For the first fortnight of March 1944 the three operational squadrons, Nos. 75, 90 and 149, flew S.O.E. sorties; then they resumed mining. The latter was punctuated five times by raids on railway installations at Amiens, Laon, Aulnoye and Courtrai.

The start of April found them again flying for S.O.E. to France, as well as mining. On 10 April Lancasters began to be operated by 75 Squadron, and after five more mining operations the Stirlings were withdrawn, the last leaving on 26 April. While 149 Squadron flew leaflet-dropping missions to explain to the French the reason for heavy night bombing raids on railway installations, 218 Squadron took part in three heavy raids on Chambley and bombed the depot at Volvorde. Four nights of S.O.E. operations by 90 and 149 Squadrons rounded off April.

May 1944 found only three Stirling bomber squadrons operational: Nos. 90, 149 and 218. No. 199 Squadron moved to North Creake and into 100 Group. Apart from one raid by 218 Squadron, again on Chambley, the entire month's effort amounted to 148 aircraft used on mining sorties, and 140 on S.O.E. sorties. Apart from one mining operation on the 19th, 218 Squadron had withdrawn from operations on 2 May to train for a specialised role in the forthcoming invasion. No. 149 Squadron moved from Lakenheath to Methwold on 12 May so that runway extensions could be built at Lakenheath.

Mining continued in June, then on 5/6 June 1944 came the D-Day landings.

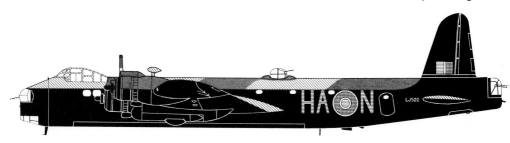

23.   Stirling Mk. III LJ522. Delivered to 19 M.U. 13.1.44. To 218 Squadron 3.4.44, became 'HA:A'. Flew 15 sorties. To 149 Squadron 27.7.44, became 'OJ:N', flew 7 sorties. To 1657 C.U. 25.8.44; 6 M.U. 7.12.44, struck off charge 19.7.45. Note ventral gun position. (For key to camouflage colours see page 184)

37. The end of the line: LK619, the last Stirling delivered from Austin Motors. Used by 1332 Conversion Unit January–May 1945. Mr. Alington, the work's test pilot, cousin to the one-time headmaster of Eton, is indicated by the cross.

Led by Sqn. Ldr. J. Overton, 218 Squadron took up position off Boulogne during the night, six special *Window* droppers orbiting at precise stations and gradually advancing so that the metal foil strips presented a radar image similar to that of a moving convoy of ships. This feint continued as the real invasion stormed ashore in Normandy.

In an arc from 50°42′N/00.23′E to 51°04′N/02°33′W, eight pairs of Stirlings of 199 Squadron, flying at 18,000 ft., jammed enemy coastal radar to cover the attacks by heavy bombers on Normandy, and set up their *Mandrel* screen to protect them.

Another seven Stirlings of 149 Squadron, led by Wg. Cdr. M. E. Pickford in EF140:M, left around midnight to drop dummy paratroopers and various pyrotechnics to simulate an airborne landing near Yvetot in North-West France. Two of these Stirlings were shot down.

Mining operations were resumed, and on 15 June, 30 Stirlings made a night raid on communications targets at Lens. On the 17th, 19 Stirlings, with 6 Lancasters of 90 Squadron, were sent unsuccessfully to bomb a rail cutting south of Montdidier. This operation concluded 90 Squadron's Stirling operations. Mining operations were carried out on a further five nights in June; then, on the 24th, 28 Stirlings made a night raid on V-weapons targets at Rousseauville and Rimeux.

With only two squadrons left, mining continued in July 1944; then, with Allied air power supreme, they began daylight *Ramrod* operations, firstly on the evening of 17 July when as part of *Ramrod 1099*, 28 Stirlings with 20 Halifaxes and strong fighter cover attacked Mont Candon V-site.

To ease maintenance problems, 218 Squadron began to move to Methwold as daylight operations continued. On the evening of 27 July, 24 Stirlings of the two squadrons bombed more *Noball* targets at Les Landes and Les Lanvielles-et-

Neuss. Next day 21 Stirlings bombed Wimereux-Capelle and Fromental, and on the 29th 16 were despatched to the Fôret-de-Nieppes, all daylight raids.

On 2 August, during *Ramrod 1152*, Mont Candon was again attacked with 500 lb. bombs; 218 Squadron had flown its last Stirling sorties. For these attacks crews had been aided by *Gee-H* radar, and dropped their bombs under the leadership of those at the head of each vic. Within a week 218 Squadron was operating Lancasters. Only 149 Squadron kept their Stirlings.

Four more operations were flown in August, the last mining sorties having been flown to the Brest area by 218 Squadron on 23 July. On the night of 12/13 August, 149 Squadron bombed Falaise. Then came a series of air-sea rescue sorties; and on the 25th, six Lancasters arrived at Methwold for 149 Squadron. By 29 August they had received their full complement.

The end of the Stirling's role as a bomber was close. In September, Bomber Command was making life unbearable for the Germans remaining in Le Havre, and unloading huge tonnages upon the port in daylight. On 5 September five crews of 149 Squadron operated against this target; on the 6th another two went. At 05.05 hrs. on the morning of 8 September four Stirlings of 149 Squadron, LJ632:P, LJ481:U, LK401:G and LK396:M, took off from Methwold carrying between them 22 × 500 lb. bombs for Le Havre. Around 09.25 hrs. they were circling Methwold for final approach. It fell to Flg. Off. J. J. McKee (R.A.A.F.) to make the last touch-down of the Stirling bomber in Bomber Command hands at 09.31 hrs.

But endings are often only a prelude to a new start, and so it was for the Stirling, for within days, in the hands of 38 Group, the Stirlings were again fighting for their lives.

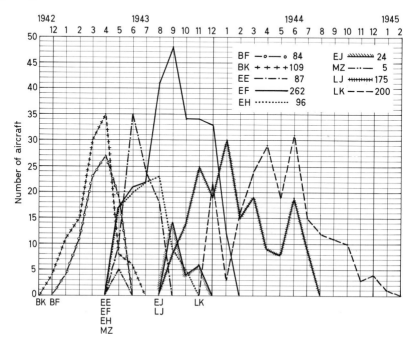

24.   Monthly production deliveries, Mk. III.

Chapter 11

Escape from Denmark

Many escapes by wartime R.A.F. aircrew from Europe took place in Holland and France. But a fair proportion of Stirling operations were made around Denmark. It is therefore apt that the following events took place there. The story is told in the words of Sgt. Donald V. Smith, a Canadian flight engineer of 7 Squadron.

'It was 20 April 1943. We were detailed to attack Stettin. After a hearty meal of fried eggs, chips, tea, bread and butter with jam—quite a good meal, considering that the war had been going on for three years—we clambered aboard R9261:MG-M just as the sun was setting.

'By 21.00 hrs. we were climbing across the North Sea. The sky was full of aircraft and a sharp look-out had to be maintained. As we crossed the Danish coast night fighters could be seen leaving their airfields and coming up to attack. Ground defences opened up, and we saw two aircraft shot down on our starboard side.

'We were pathfinders on this trip. Besides markers we carried several general purpose bombs to make up full load. Nearing Stettin about 50 searchlights turned on. A couple picked us out. By skilful management our skipper soon weaved out of their beams.

'Just as we were about to run in our starboard inner engine packed up, probably hit by flak. I told the skipper, Flt. Lt. C. W. Parish. He immediately feathered it and turned away from the target. As we made our second run-in on three engines our bombsight failed, so we had no alternative but to turn back. Dropping markers at random would hinder the raid.

'We saw an airfield, and the bomb aimer asked the skipper if he could drop our can of anti-personnel bombs on it. We flew low, and we could see hangars and barracks, upon which we dropped the bombs. Searchlights picked us up, and the skipper was forced to dive low out to sea to get away.

'By the time we reached the island of Zealand he had managed to get the aircraft to 6,500 ft. The moon was full and it was cloudless. It was more like a daylight raid.

'Just as we crossed the Bay of Korsor two Me 110s appeared, one not more than 50 ft. from our port wing tip—you could see the pilot. The one on the port side attacked, scoring a few hits. Sergeant Lees, our rear gunner, replied. Then from starboard came the No. 2. He fired, setting our port mainplane on fire. Our aircraft went out of control. A calm voice came over the intercom: "Sorry boys, you are going to have to jump." Time was 02.00 hrs.

'As the aircraft was going straight down, it was almost impossible to climb back to the escape hatch. We were hit again below the mid-upper turret. This ripped up the floor and I was able to see it as a ladder to make my way to the exit. I believe the upper gunner, Sgt. Farley, and the wireless operator, Sgt. L. Krulicki, were killed in this attack. As I reached for the static cord to fasten on to Lony's parachute, my chute pulled out of the shoulder catches and I was pulled free of the aircraft. As I fell, the chute fell right back into my arms. I pulled the cord and in no time was floating down. The plane hit the ground within a few seconds and exploded. What happened to Flt. Lt. Parish, Sqn. Ldr. W. A. Blake (the second pilot), Plt. Off. E. R. Vance (the navigator) and the bomb aimer, Flt. Sgt. J. S. Marshall, I do not know, but they were found dead in the aircraft.

'I landed a few fields south of the plane. It was a freshly ploughed field and I landed fairly softly beside a water hole. I threw my parachute and Mae West into some bushes, and started out in a south-easterly direction. Soon I was knee deep in a swampy area. I came to a lane and two German scout cars almost had me in their headlights. I kept up a steady walk and run till 5.30 a.m. By this time I was dead tired and the sun was rising. I made my way to a clump of trees and some water, covered myself with dead branches and slept for an hour or so.

'As I peeped out of my hiding place I noticed a man not 10 yards away sowing grain. I ducked out of sight till noon, and stripped off my Canadian badges, stripes and wing. At noon I made my way to a deserted farmhouse, where I hid, keeping an eye open for the best way to go.

'Around 5.30 in the evening, while it was still light, I mustered enough courage to chance it. Suddenly a German plane swept over low, as if on a search. I walked across fields and up river beds until around 9.30 p.m., then was at a loss as to which way to go.

'Seeing a solitary farmer I approached him. He did not seem to know what I wanted until his young son and daughter came along. They knew who I was, and went for their mother. She knew what I was up to, and took me into their farmhouse. Their young son kept a look-out for Germans while she cooked three eggs, some meat, black bread and coffee made from roasted grain. I was grateful for it. Before I left they fetched a phone book and pointed out my position. I was no more than 10 km from where I wanted to go.

'After filling my water bottle I set out, using a railway track as guide. On 22 April around 1 a.m. I was too tired to go any further, so unrolled my flying suit and lay down beside some small pine trees. My sleep was broken by field mice running over me.

'Around 4.30 a.m. I started out again. My feet began to blister from wearing loose fitting flying boots. I was beginning to wonder if it was all worth while. About 7 a.m. I came to a small stream and washed and shaved, for in my escape kit I carried a razor, soap and mirror.

'After this cold wash and shave I started off again. I wrapped my feet in flying socks, easing the pain. I walked until I caught sight of the town of Soro, circled to the south and found a pile of sugar beet. I ate some and put others in my pocket for later use—thus I had sugar beet and dandelion leaves for breakfast. I walked through the bush until around 8 a.m., reaching the outskirts of Soro. At 8.30 a.m.

I came across a small farm. After resting I went to a door and knocked. A girl of 15 or 16 opened it, saying something in Danish which I couldn't understand. Her brother came, and I asked for my water bottle to be filled. He scanned the road then pulled me into the house. It was very small, of about three rooms. They sat me down at a table and I had breakfast of black synthetic coffee and rye bread.

'Within half an hour I was making my way to the outskirts of Ringsted. The sun was very hot, my feet swollen. Entering a farmyard, I found the Germans were using it as a rifle range. Running as fast as I could, I went into a pasture and a gulley. Here I slept by a manure pile, later to find that I had left my water bottle there.

'Coming across another farm, I entered the yard. A man took me into a barn and showed me where the tap was. The hired man, or son, brought me a bottle of beer and some carrots; I put some into my pocket. Starting out in a north-easterly direction I came across the small, isolated town of Hom. As I walked through, my uniform on, people kept staring at me. I later found that it was a public holiday.

'I cut through a bush and hid among some pine trees, resting my feet, then it started to rain, so I headed for a neat farmhouse. A young deer jumped up in front of me and headed into a thicket. Seeing no one about I went to the door. A middle aged woman opened it. Unable to understand English, she called her husband. He could see I was an Allied airman, and took me into the house. They gave me soap, hot water and a towel, relieving my tired feeling. I ate heartily of sandwiches made of cheese and liver roll. I had a couple of glasses of beer and left with a bottle and some sandwiches.

'It was very difficult walking now. Around 7 p.m. I came across a small stable. Inside was some spring water. I washed and shaved, still looking scruffy. I cut off the top portion of my flying boots and made a pair of shoes out of them. As I was doing this a man and woman with two small children approached. He immediately sent the woman and children away; he recognised my uniform. After trying to make him understand where I wanted to go to, he pointed at my clothes, shaking his head and indicating by marking a swastika on his arm that there were too many Gestapo around. I found that he was George Rasmussen. He led me inside the horse stable and made it clear that I was to stay here until 9.00. This I did without question. At 9.05 he appeared with a bundle under his arm. In it he had a pair of trousers, a knife, a glass mirror and other useful articles. He then took off his coat, rubber boots, and sweater, and took away my boots and flying suit.

'By pointing at his watch and shaking his head I understood it was unwise to leave before 5.00 a.m. because of curfew. I slept in the stable and arose at 4.30 a.m. As I went out on the road in the civvies he had given I was met by the same man. He took me into his house, gave me breakfast and some sandwiches. He produced a Shell road map and pointed out the way to Copenhagen. Swastikas drawn on the map showed heavily defended areas. As I was about to leave he gave me 20 kroner, all the bills he had, and about 80 ore in change. In return I gave him the 40,000 francs I had in my escape kit. He walked with me to the main road, indicating the route to take.

'It was easier travelling in civilian clothes, but the rubber boots soon made my blisters bigger. By 10.00 I realised I was on the wrong road and made my way to a small farmhouse. In the yard was an old man raking the lawn. I showed him that I wanted a drink of water. He took me in the house, where I met his wife, son and daughter. I was given a glass of milk and a cup of coffee. With their help I was soon on the right road.

'After some time I looked for a place to sleep. It had been hot; my feet so swollen I could not take off my boots. On nearing Taastrup I went to a farmhouse to try to get somewhere to sleep and some food. On the edge of the town was a house and barn surrounded by a high red brick wall.

'I knocked on the door. It seemed some dinner party was going on, with everyone in formal dress. The Sörensen family invited me to join them. After a hearty meal I was asked: "When will the British free us, where are they going to strike next?" I could not really answer, but assured them the day was drawing near. I left to their good wishes.

'As I walked through Taastrup, Germans looked suspiciously at me. There were many German transports on the road to Copenhagen, so I headed across fields. At another farmhouse two elderly men greeted me. I made signs indicating I was an Allied airman wanting somewhere to sleep. They took me to a suitable spot.

'I wandered through a small village which I presumed to be Hersted. Darkness falling, I made for a haystack. I then decided first to go to the nearby house. A middle aged woman greeted me and called her husband. With the aid of an English–Danish dictionary they informed me they had their children about and I had not to be seen. Then the husband went to phone friends—or Germans? I did not know, and by this time did not care much. I could walk no further. As it turned out he had phoned a friend, E. Marborg, the head teacher at the school. He spoke perfect English, and told me the surrounding farmers were pro-Nazi and every precaution had to be taken. I had coffee and sandwiches, then was given two blankets and taken to the hayloft in the cowshed. I was given instructions to meet him in the morning in Glostrup.

'I got up at 4.30 on the 24th and shaved by flashlight. The farmer brought coffee and sandwiches, bandaged my feet before I left and gave me all the change he had.

'I walked for an hour and met him in Glostrup, but by entering the town so early, I was continually watched by the Gestapo—perhaps my queer attire had them wondering. They did not question me, and I finally found my man. He went to the station and bought two tickets to Copenhagen. It was only a short ride, but we had hours to wait for the train and the station was filled with Germans. Finally we boarded the train for Elsinore. People stared at me but said nothing. On arriving at our destination we headed along the coast to the ferry terminus. Every half hour a ship would leave for Helsinborg, Sweden, but it was hopeless to try to get on the ferry. My escape was barred by German guards.

'My companion had no links with the Underground, suggesting I contact some fishermen. It was soon evening, and I had to find somewhere to sleep. As I walked along the beach I found a small wooden hut. A room was unlocked and I found a table, chairs and a blanket. After eating a sandwich and a Horlicks tablet I slept. In the early hours of the 25th I was awakened by a Danish police officer. Either he did not notice me, or looked the other way. It started to rain, and I walked between Elsinore and Aalasgaarde at least three times looking for a boat or help. In the late afternoon I noticed a house flying a Danish flag. I knocked at the door, and a young lady who could speak English answered. She told me they had no boat and could not help me. As I left, a young man called me back for a meal. It was my first real one for three days. After dinner I listened to the B.B.C. news with Mr. and Mrs. Folmer and then returned to the hut on the beach.

'Next day I approached an old fisherman for help. He could not speak English, but knew what I wanted. The Germans had taken his boat. All hope of escape had vanished. I had lost about 20 lb. weight and I was beginning to feel effects of undernourishment.

'Across the road I could see a man reading in a sun room. I knocked at his door and his wife, who spoke fluent English, answered. I told her my predicament and she fetched her husband. I was taken inside and doors locked—they had three children staying with them. They gave me a really good meal of roast meat and delicacies, and let me have a bath. I was shown into a bedroom, where I had a lovely rest, although I was too tired to sleep and thoughts of escape would not leave me. Suddenly the door of the Knudsens' bedroom opened, and a fat little man came running in shouting: "You will go to Sweden." He disappeared just as fast, and I lay there thanking God for his help. A gentleman came in speaking in English. I learned he had spent some time in the U.S.A., and was married to an Englishwoman. After checking my identity he told me to wait.

'Around 6 p.m. on 25 April he welcomed me to his home. In the evening a distinguished-looking man interrogated me, and said he would have my story verified by London. He also told me that if it could not be verified . . . and at this point he pulled a small revolver from his pocket. We spent a quiet evening and, before retiring, had a lovely meal.

'In the morning I had a breakfast of ham and eggs, was given some clothes and a pair of plus-four socks and shoes. On 26 April after dinner Mr. Tjoern, the distinguished-looking gentleman, again called and took me by taxi to the next town, then by train and taxi to Hellerup. He kept close to me, making sure we were not followed. We walked the last few blocks to his flat at Fristdedt 3, and I met his English wife. I stayed for two days, and was taken on a tour of Copenhagen.

'On the night of the 27th, when Mr. Tjoern returned from work, he informed me I would be going right away. We went by taxi to Skodsberg. Our boat was not ready, so we slept the night there and walked on the beach by day. Chris Hanson (who made the final escape possible), Lars Tjoern and I had a few Danish beers.

'When darkness came we were escorted across the road to the beach. Members of the Danish Resistance had assembled a collapsible kayak and carried it across the main road with us. During the day we had been taken to the downtown office and given a coloured light with which we were to signal if a patrol boat came near, the colour being the code for that night.

'At 11 p.m. we got into our kayak, and with a good swig of Danish schnapps, off we went. On the way a searchlight picked us up, and a patrol boat came after us. The water was quite rough, so we kept our heads flat on the gunwale and the boat passed by. At 3 a.m. on 1 May we landed just south of Helsingborg.

'The Swedes had left a portion of their beach free of barbed wire so escapees could land safely. We walked inland, circling a small village to keep away from patrols. Around 9 a.m. we went to the British Consulate. We were taken to the home of the Consul, where we were welcomed by his Danish wife. We gave ourselves up at the police station and the police were wonderful to us. After two days I was allowed to go free, having to report once daily at 11 a.m. I stayed at the Savoy Hotel, where I had the pleasure of meeting the Swedish Crown Prince and Princess, the Prince later becoming H.M. King Gustav IV. I stayed at the Savoy until 5 May 1943, when I left Stockholm—after a farewell party with the police.'

One cannot but marvel at the courage of so many Danes who, under the noses of the Germans, were prepared to help Donald Smith. Years later, under the guidance of Jorgen Helme, Donald Smith revisited Denmark to greet some of those who made his escape possible, and in particular the courageous Chris Hanson. Of Donald Smith's tenacity one surely cannot speak too highly: it was in the best spirit of 7 Squadron, premier Stirling squadron, and surely of the Royal Air Force ... or perhaps *he* would prefer, of the Royal Canadian Air Force.

38.   Chris Hanson (*left*) and Donald V. Smith view the sea-crossing to Sweden, many years after they conspired to free the Canadian airman.

Chapter 12

A New Role

The wartime history of British military transport aircraft is a sorry one, but one in which the Stirling was the hero. For all their vast territorial control, the British had long relied upon a handful of antique Valentias and a few Bombays to provide air supply of men and materials. Parsimonious expenditure on transport aircraft development was to cost the country dearly in the decades ahead, paralleling current ineptitude on the part of politicians where defence is concerned.

German success with airborne forces brought rapid demands from the Prime Minister for British equivalents. Hurried and none too well conceived plans for a glider force were produced. When the gliders became available, there were no aeroplanes suitable to tow them into action—other than the Albemarle, which had been foisted upon the Air Staff against its wishes by its civilian counterpart.

Attempts were made in May 1941 to engineer a transport out of the Wellingtons. It was quite unsuitable, and when glider towing, its structure stretched. Instead, the airborne forces had to accept the outdated Whitley as tug and paratroop carrier. Looking enviously at the capacious fuselages of the new four engined bombers, they began to exert pressure for them, few as they were in number, to be used by airborne forces—much to the alarm of Bomber Command.

Full details of the transport aircraft position were demanded by the Prime Minister in July 1941. It became clear that the only hope of expansion rested with American supplies. In September 1941 the Stirling was considered for paratrooping, but rejected because of paratroop exit problems.

Mid January 1942 saw the emergence of a Lancaster freighter to serve as an inter-Dominion ferry, paratroop carrier and, in an astonishingly outdated concept, as a bomber transport with turrets and a 15,000 lb. bomb load, a latter day Valentia.

The main emphasis so far had been on finding a paratrooping aircraft. It was easier to train paratroopers than produce a glider force. The Americans could provide Lodestars and C-47s (DC-3s), but they had no aircraft suitable to tow the large Horsa and Hamilcar gliders.

On 29 January 1942 the Stirling was cleared—on paper—to tow three Hotspur training gliders in train, or one Horsa. There was also hope that it might tow a Hamilcar tank carrying glider. Provision could be made for glider towing equipment, and this was introduced on production lines from 31 March 1942.

During August 1942 choice for a glider tug fell upon the Albemarle, the 100th and later examples being suitably completed. Although it could take off with a Horsa fully loaded, the Albemarle's two engines quickly heated, bringing some alarm to the crews.

Soon after, the apparent lack of development potential in the Stirling caused a second look to be taken at its future employment. It could already carry 26 troops, which was encouraging.

The importance of finding a glider tug had been emphasised on 12 May 1942, when 2,345 Horsas and 140 Hamilcars were on order. Even more alarming, the Army was expressing a need for 3,500 Horsas and 360 Hamilcars, necessary, they argued, for two operations against the Continent. This required a pool of about 500 tugs and a similar force of paratroop aircraft, even if paratroops descended from Horsas.

Stirling N3702 had actually towed 3 Hotspurs at A.F.E.E. in May, but these were only training gliders. When the initial layout for the new 38 Wing, Airborne Forces, emerged in July 1942 it depended almost entirely upon the Whitley, with which 38 Wing was equipped when it was formed in the autumn.

Paratroop drops were tried from a Lancaster in January 1943, but every such machine was needed for Bomber Command—and so were the Halifaxes.

Between February and May 1943 A.F.E.E. looked further at N3702. Its bomb bay readily accommodated panniers, 24 Mk. III or 21 Mk. I and three Mk. IIIs, and no problems arose. Indeed it seemed ideally suited to the task.

Even more important were trials assessing the ability of Stirling BK645 to tow a loaded Horsa, in particular its climb and level performance. Conducted in April 1943, they showed no snags with the tug at 54,300 lb. and Horsa 15,250 lb., its normal loaded weight. This permitted the tug 1,160 gal. fuel and 70 gal. oil and a crew of five. During the trial, all turrets were left in place, and so the signs were good for an unarmed Stirling tug. Unstick was achieved at 950 yd. at 90 m.p.h.I.A.S. and climb-away at 110 m.p.h.I.A.S. after a run of 2,040 yd. to clear 50 ft. The combination took 26.2 min. to reach 8,000 ft., 16.2 min. to 6,000 ft. At 8,000 ft. climb fell away to 150 f.p.m. The Stirling did not have overheating problems; it was an answer to the glider tug worry.

Thus a new employment for the Stirling was in mind when a committee examining its future role met on 30 July 1943 at the period of the Stirling's most extensive service with Bomber Command. Short's, who had already been asked to prepare schemes for Stirling transports, produced plans for the Stirling 'A', a conversion of existing Mk. IIIs into transports; the Stirling 'B', or Mk. IV, a fully redesigned Mk. III with some or all turrets deleted, and for use as a glider tug or paratroop carrier; and the Stirling 'C', or Mk. V, with a fully redesigned fuselage for passenger and freight work, to include a large freight door aft. Some soundproofing would be fitted in the fuselage, and a swinging nose installed to permit freight loading. The Stirling 'C' offered Short's a postwar civil aircraft.

They were asked how long it would take to get the first two schemes into operation at Rochester and Belfast, with some conversion at R.A.F. maintenance units. All unnecessary equipment would be removed, including the nose and dorsal turrets. Provision would be made for bulky equipment and troops;

paratroops would clear via the rear exit door in the floor. Aero engines and perhaps jeeps might be lashed to the belly, since there was such good ground clearance. The future for the Mk. IV looked bright, and events proved it to be an excellent machine.

Some proposed modifications to Stirling bombers were cancelled, including fitting of H2S radomes. Short's could then proceed with all speed on the stripped transport, the Mk. IV, and work upon the fully fledged derivative, the Mk. V.

There were soon misgivings. Air Ministry were uncertain about going ahead with the Mk. V, but the Mk. IV flew in August 1943, which strengthened its case. A month later they wondered whether Short & Harland should build the Avro York rather than the Mk. V. In October 1943 it seemed there would be ample Stirling Mk. IVs for the foreseeable future, and in any case stripped Lancasters and Halifaxes from Bomber Command could be made into troop transports.

On 20 October 1943 the decision to drop the Stirling Mk. V seemed final, in view of Short's incapacity to cope with the design work on this variant as well as the much wanted Lancaster Mk. IV (later named Lincoln) which it was intended that Short's should build.

Yet to have perhaps 575 Stirling Mk. IVs by June 1945, instead of some of the much superior Mk. V, seemed a pity. Short's were pinning hopes on being able to develop a civil version of the Mk. V, and so finally it was decided to give it a reprieve, and production orders were placed. All would be built at Belfast.

And so the die was cast for converting large numbers of Stirling Mk. IIIs into Mk. IVs to be used as glider tugs and troop carriers, while allowing the Mk. V to go forward as a passenger and freight aircraft for the Middle East and India runs.

Chapter 13

Preparing for the Invasion

The first two Stirlings converted from Mk. III bombers to Mk. IV transports emerged rapidly in August 1943. EF506 came on charge 26 August, and EF503 on the 28th. The former, after initial trials at Rochester, was sent to A.F.E.E. on 18 October for four months on acceptance trials and operational clearance. EF503 went to A.&A.E.E. for handling trials before returning to Rochester late in February 1944.

39.   Stirling IV EF503, another development aircraft used for A.&A.E.E. and maker's trials before being passed to 1651 Conversion Unit, where it served July–November 1944.

The latter was devoid of all turrets, those in the nose and tail being replaced by plastic fairings. Lower all-up weight and crew reduction to five conferred an increase of 1,100 ft. in service ceiling and 3,000 ft. in cruise ceiling. At weak mixture power an extra 12 to 15 m.p.h. was achieved. A take-off weight of 70,000 lb. was still possible, which meant a sizeable drop load. At that weight service ceiling was 19,100 ft., gills closed and at 2,400 revs. Maximum weak mix cruise speed was 235 m.p.h.T.A.S. in M.S. gear at 11,800 ft.

Range trials on EF503 conducted early in 1944 at a take-off weight of 66,000 lb. (for paratrooping use, take-off weight was usually 58,000 lb.) showed maximum still air range as follows:

58,000 lb. (paratrooper), 1,640 gal. fuel: 1,980 miles at 2,000 ft.

57,900 lb. (transport/glider tug), 2,245 gal. fuel: 2,360 miles at 10,000 ft.

Attempts were made to cool the engines by fitting fans and spinners. Some production aircraft had these features for improved cooling overseas. They brought no significant change to engine temperatures, as tests on BK651 revealed. Flared propeller blades were tested on BK649 in October and November 1943, but these had little effect on cooling either. Cooling was always a matter of concern with glider tugs. After plans to equip 3 Group with Lancasters were agreed,

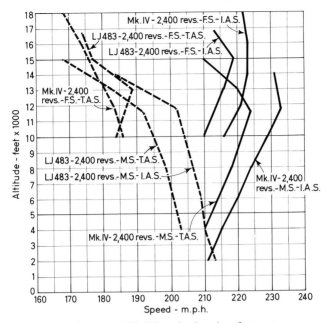

25. Performance, Mk. IV production aircraft, turrets removed, faired over—70,000 lb., level speeds; LJ483 (Hercules XVI)—70,000 lb., level speeds.

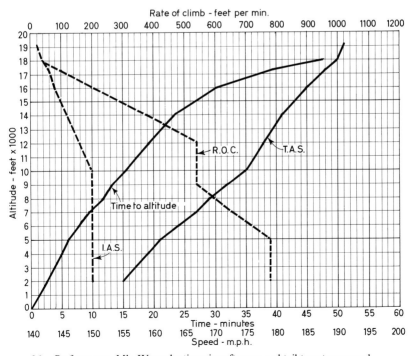

26. Performance, Mk. IV production aircraft, nose and tail turrets removed, faired over—70,000 lb., gills open, 2,400 revs.

production switched to the Mk. IV. Bombers were still required by squadrons and conversion units; it was unacceptable to halt their production. By the end of October 1943, 6 Stirling Mk. IIIs had been delivered to 23 M.U., Aldergrove, where turrets were removed and they were converted to full Mk. IV standard. Generally, only the nose and dorsal turrets were removed. Another eight aircraft for conversion arrived in November, 21 in December and five in January 1944. The first Mk. IVs were then ready for delivery. A switch to completing Stirlings as Mk. IVs began in December 1943 with EF317 to 323 inclusive at Belfast.

The total number of aircraft converted from Mk. III to Mk. IV was 120. Mk. IIIs converted after completion to Mk. IV numbered 190. Another four were completed as Mk. IVs for trials, and seven were converted on the production line.

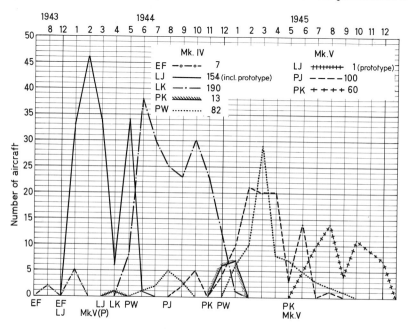

27.   Monthly production deliveries, Mks. IV and V. Graph does not include Mk. III conversions to Mk. IV

Probably it was EF318, which left 19 M.U. St. Athan for 299 Squadron at Stoney Cross on 2 January 1944, that was first to join a squadron. No. 299 Squadron had reformed there on 4 November 1943 with Ventura glider tugs. On 29 December 1943, 21 crews went for Stirling conversion training at Woolfox Lodge.

Second to equip was 190 Squadron reformed at Leicester East on 5 January 1944 with the usual strength of 16 I.E. + 4 I.R. They had to train crews, and received their first six aircraft on 21 January 1944, training beginning in February. To reinforce the transport force, 196 and 620 Squadrons had left Bomber Command in November 1943. No. 620's first Mk. IV was received at Tarrant Rushton on 30 January 1944.

John Payne, flying with 620 Squadron at the time, recalls the events of that period: 'Round about October 1943 a large bunch of slightly bewildered aircrew were posted to Leicester East, an awful quagmire on a hill above Cadby, a suburb of Leicester.

'Primitive accommodation we in 38 Group were to endure until the end of the war—that is, those of us who survived the longest unbroken wartime tours of operational flying.

'We were intrigued to discover that we were now to be engaged in "Special Duties"—something we had only previously associated with a mysterious group of ace pilots who did hairy things like landing Lysanders in fields in France under the noses of the Jerries.

'But we had no aircraft, so the burning question during the subsequent weeks of inactivity was: "*WHAT* are we going to fly?" We had star studded dreams that at least we would get Lancasters, but more likely some extra special type so far unveiled.

'Imagine the near mutiny which took place when something like 600 aircrew, representing an almost equal number of Commonwealth countries, were told we would be getting . . . shudder . . . Stirlings! The C.O. gained a slightly better hearing when he said: "Ah, but wait till you see *THIS* mark, the IV."

'We waited with growing impatience until the day when a strange and gleaming Stirling appeared, fresh from Short's. We piled into any vehicle, even rode two to a bike, to get to the airfield. It was a Stirling all right, no doubt about that "22 ft. above the ground" posture, no doubt about that enormous undercart, that tall fin. But where was the front turret, the dorsal, and what on earth was that enormous, horseshoe shaped lump of steel wrapped round the belly just below and forward of the tail? It began to look more impressive—particularly with those four Hercules XVI radials.

'The first trial flights ended with the skippers outwardly reserved but inwardly jubilant. This "ugly duckling", built like a battleship, had a T.A.S. which proved it could outpace any other four-engined type we knew of.'

Other crew members were also happy, though the general pleasure was tempered in the case of the veterans with the knowledge that they were to lose their gunners as 'surplus to establishment'.

'Then the questions began. "What is the purpose of the horseshoe?" "It is a strop guard to prevent strops, which serve to pull open paratroopers' chutes, from lashing holes in the fuselage." "So we're to carry paratroops?" "That's right." "In daylight ops?" "That's right" (and remember, all those crews were ex-Bomber Command). This information was supplanted by news that we were also going to tow gliders—and again, all Hell erupted.'

With 190 Squadron was Flg. Off. G. H. Chesterton. He had trained on Venturas at Pennfield Ridge. The day he and his crew arrived at Bournemouth, a holding station, was that of a disastrous raid by Venturas, which were soon withdrawn. A conversion course on to Bostons followed; meanwhile questions were raised as to what should be done with the Venturas. When glider towing trials were undertaken a Ventura stretched—just as Stirlings were being retired from Bomber Command. So Flg. Off. Chesterton was posted to 1665 H.C.U.

Woolfox Lodge for Stirling conversion, and on to what he felt to be his most concentrated course ever.

'Much of my training was on Stirling Mk. Is lettered OG. I felt that the Exactor controls were a fine example of a brilliant idea that went wrong. Certainly the serviceability was poor, and I vividly remember the constant priming of the throttles. One night in three hours' circuits and bumps we went through three separate aircraft, although admittedly I had just signed on a new, nervous, meticulous flight engineer. On New Year's Eve 1944 we finished our last landing in someone's chicken run amid a load of feathers. We soon had our introduction to Stirling Mk. IIIs—letters NY. These certainly seemed blissfully easy after the Mk. Is.

'I was one of the founder members of 190 Squadron. We were a cosmopolitan lot. "A" Flight had seven British captains and seven mixed Australian and New Zealand ones, and hardly a crew without a Canadian. The crews established during March were each six strong. The three of us who had started at Pennfield Ridge were joined by a bomb aimer, engineer and air gunner. In the early months a very happy family atmosphere developed, and happily—and unlike Bomber Command—we didn't lose a crew until late June: a very popular New Zealander and his crew.

'The Squadron was commanded by Wg. Cdr. Harrison and "A" Flight by Sqn. Ldr. Gilliard. They did much to engender the splendid atmosphere. This was still in the days when each captain had his own aircraft and groundcrew, another feature that led to a real spirit of unity and loyalty.'

During February the squadrons were brought up to full strength. Operations by the Mk. IV commenced on 3/4 February, when EF469 and EJ110 of 196 Squadron were despatched on night supply drops to the French Resistance. Such 'cloak and dagger' operations were undertaken by Stirling Mk. IVs on many succeeding nights. Indeed, on the night after 196 Squadron began operating, 620 Squadron despatched EF203, EF495, EF121 and LK395 from the generally used advance base, Tarrant Rushton.

Flying Officer Chesterton began his S.O.E. flying in April 1944. 'Each full moon period was the time for S.O.E. and S.A.S. operations. These operations were highly secret; indeed, each was entered in one's log book as "operations as ordered". My first trip was on 14 April 1944, when we took 24 containers south of Caen. We received the code letters necessary and made our drop. We later had an acknowledgement that the containers were received. One wonders whether they fell into the right hands.

'We operated alone on these flights, crossing the Channel as low as possible, climbed to about 10,000 ft. to cross the enemy coast, then dropped down to carry on to the D.Z. at 200 or 300 ft., almost always in bright moonlight. We were directed to Boscombe Down on return from our first trip, the static lines trailing from the empty bomb bays. Rather pompously I refused to be debriefed there, and had to wait until we flew on the next morning. Really a rather good place, of all places to withhold secret information—one of life's good moments!'

During these low level operations flak could be a great hazard. On 8/9 February Flt. Lt. Hannah of 620 Squadron (EF197) was fired upon by light flak when at 500 ft. over his D.Z. His rear gunner had the satisfaction of silencing the enemy gunners. Flg. Off. Bell, in EF121, also encountered flak which his rear gunner silenced; and Flt. Sgt. McNamara of 620 Squadron, in EF203, on the same night was attacked by concentrated light flak over Tours when at only 200 ft. His starboard inner oil cooler was shot away and the propeller was hurled against the lower side of the fuselage, making a large hole by the second pilot's seat and engineer's position. Back at Tarrant Rushton he encountered the old problem. He could not lower his undercarriage, and made a belly landing.

Both 196 and 620 Squadrons were staffed by experienced Stirling crews, whereas 299 had spent February working up, and on the 18th flew its first glider exercise. At the end of February they moved to Keevil, beginning operations on 5 April 1944.

March was busy for the Stirling Mk. IV squadrons. They took part in a number of large scale glider exercises. Indeed, 190 Squadron flew 179 glider towing flights before moving to Fairford on 25 March. On 31 March they commenced S.O.E. drops from Tarrant Rushton. No. 196 Squadron, which flew 14 S.O.E. sorties in March, took up operational residence at Keevil on 15 March; and three days later 620 Squadron, also busy on glider training, moved to Fairford.

Exercises and S.O.E. drops continued as squadrons worked up their role in the Normandy landings. On the 4th, 190 Squadron took part in a typical training mission, Exercise *Dream*. Thirteen Stirling/Horsa combinations took off at night in 18 minutes, and after $3\frac{1}{2}$ hours' flying the gliders were released.

'By the time D-Day came', recalls Flg. Off. Chesterton, 'we had done 24 glider lifts. They were a fascinating business. The tug taxied out, and within seconds the groundcrew hooked up the Horsa's towrope (nylon by this time) and a batman, rather as on a carrier, beckoned one to take up slack. Traffic lights to the left gave the signal to take off, and meanwhile the rear gunner told his pilot when the rope was fully taut. Take-off was surprisingly easy, the glider being airborne after about 200 yards. The drag directly astern limited the amount of swing, and the tug lumbered happily into the air well before the end of the runway. Cruising speed with a Horsa was about 140 knots. The gliders assumed what was called the "high tow position", but many glider pilots preferred to move down to the low position below the tug's tail as soon as practicable. There was a primitive communication cable between tug and glider, which seldom worked with satisfaction. After exercises, the tow ropes were dropped at the D.Z. on the edge of the circuit. In May the other squadron lost two aircraft in collision when rope dropping—a grim day for the whole station.'

Massed glider training flights were almost complete by the start of May, but S.O.E. flights by the four squadrons continued, over 50 being flown. By the end of the month the squadrons were at peak readiness as the invasion drew near.

Planning for the Normandy landings commenced in 1943. Stirling squadrons at Keevil and Fairford would carry paratroops of the 5th Paratroop Brigade in Phase II of Operation *Tonga*. Each Stirling carried 20 troops and their equipment.

At Keevil on 5 June, a day of gloomy weather, cloudy sky and strong winds, the station was very tense for, if the weather did not soon improve, the momentous operation would have to be called off. At 14.00 hrs. crews of 196 and 299 Squadrons were called for briefing. Despite the weather, said Air Vice-Marshal Hollinghurst, A.O.C. 38 Group, the operation would take place the following night. The aim was to drop troops of the 6th Airborne Division on D.Z. 'H', a space about $2\frac{1}{2}$ miles square on the east side of the River Orne near Oistreham. They would hold bridges crossing the Orne and Caen Canal.

28.   Stirling Mk. IV LJ949. Delivered to 6 M.U. 31.3.44. To 196 Squadron 19.5.44. Crashed at Leende during Arnhem resupply drop 23.9.44. (For key to camouflage colours see page 184)

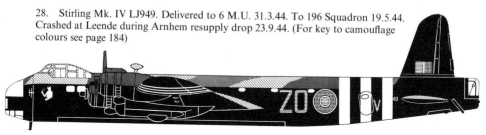

Last minute preparations as groundcrews swarmed over the 46 Stirlings would ever be memorable. The aircraft had to be lined up in correct sequence, close, diagonally facing each other and tightly packed along the edge of the active runway's end. By late evening, troops were busily engaged fitting their parachutes, aided by scores of airmen and W.A.A.F.s. They would never forget the enthusiasm of the men of the 12th Battalion, 6th Airborne, who seemed relieved that the long wait for battle was ending.

At 23.00 hrs. engines of the Stirlings burst into life. Run-up complete, the first Stirling rolled at 23.19 hrs. and the whole force was soon away at half-minute intervals. They made straight for the D.Z. Light flak streamed up from Oistreham and Cabourg, but a line of guns by the D.Z. had already been silenced by a Lancaster attack. All the crews delivered their passengers except possibly Flt. Sgt. T. Gilbert, who was shot down. Several other aircraft suffered flak damage and W. O. Ellis, bomb aimer in Flt. Lt. Taylor's aircraft, was seriously wounded. After the drop the Stirlings turned eastwards to exit over Fécamp, and made a safe return to base. Considering the importance of the night's delivery, all had gone extremely well.

Take-off in the black and white striped Stirlings—thus adorned three days earlier—was set for 23.30 hrs. on 5 June 1944 at Fairford. Cloud, 5/10 over Britain, thinned over the Continent as the transports went in low, loose formation, in moonlight and good visibility, for their $3\frac{1}{2}$-hour round trip. The two Fairford squadrons, led by No. 620, encountered light flak which shot down Sqn. Ldr. Pettit and two other crews. Four more aircraft had flak damage. Expectations of heavy losses were unfulfilled.

During the daylight hours of 6 June crews snatched their rest while groundcrews patched up the aircraft, refuelled them and made them ready for the next adventure. It came early in the evening.

At Fairford and Keevil 71 Horsa gliders were marshalled into position alongside their tugs, and shortly after 18.00 hrs. troops of 6th Airborne emplaned in the gliders. The aim was to deliver the Horsas to D.Z. 'W', the object to

40. A Stirling IV of 196 Squadron tows off a Horsa glider.

41. Photographed in June 1944, a Stirling IV of 299 Squadron used for D-Day operations. Possibly EF267, and named 'The Saint'.

reinforce paratroops dropped to seize the bridges. From Fairford 35 gliders were towed aloft, and from Keevil another 36 were equally shared by 196 and 299 Squadrons.

There was a surprising lack of enemy interference. It seemed that both sides had stopped fighting for a moment to marvel at the spectacle as Operation *Mallard* unfolded. These reinforcements, the crews learned later, arrived just in time. Many of the gliders, however, ran into 15 ft. high poles at the D.Z., causing casualties and damage.

'On the afternoon of 6 June', recalls D. H. Hardwick with 299 Squadron, 'we towed a glider full of supplies and troops to reinforce the paratroops. The sight over the Channel that afternoon was unforgettable; ships and aircraft as far as the eye could see. Each of us seemed to have a squadron of fighters as escort. Two incidents come to mind. The naval barrage balloons were supposed to be lowered to let us through as we approached; but nothing happened, so we had to press on. A fair number of balloons went up towards the moon that afternoon.'

Wg. Cdr. G. E. Harrison had led 190 Squadron from Fairford. His squadron met intense machine gun fire, which killed the bomb aimer in Sgt. Coeshott's aircraft. Six others suffered flak damage, but all 18 Stirlings released their gliders. Another 18 of 620 Squadron also took part.

Flt. Lt. F. Thoing's machine, hit by light flak, was forced to land in a French field. The crew escaped, and everyone at Fairford was delighted when they turned up a few days later.

Barely had the squadrons touched down when a number of crews left on S.O.E. and resupply missions, which were to be repeated on many nights in June and July. Sometimes these entailed container drops in Normandy. Such operations were far from easy; in three months 38 Group lost eight Stirlings, and 3 Group, assisting in the task, lost two.

During July 190 Squadron dropped 93 paratroops and operated on 11 nights, participating in small scale, very secret operations with curious code names such as *Grog*, *Percy* and *Stationer*. As many as 18 Stirlings would operate on one night. On 10 and 18 July 196 Squadron was similarly busily engaged.

An important feature of July was the addition of two more Stirling squadrons to 38 Group. No. 295 Squadron at Harwell received its first Stirling on 14 June and took on charge nine more in July, as replacements for Albemarles. Work-up was rapid after D-Day, while the Albemarles continued S.O.E. sorties. Their first Stirling sorties, by two aircraft, came on 27 July and next night LJ951 was shadowed by a Ju 88 near the French coast.

No. 570 Squadron began to convert to Stirlings on 1 July, crews converting at 1665 C.U. Tilstock. By 5 July the unit held nine Stirlings in addition to 32 Albemarles. They, too, commenced Stirling operations on 27/28 July, when the C.O., Wg. Cdr. R. J. M. Bangay, delivered 24 containers and packages to the Brest Peninsula. Next night, with enemy fighters active, LK133, flown by Plt. Off. D. Robson, was missing, but LJ622 delivered a load in the Massif Central. Then they operated in the Sens area and, on the 30th, around Dijon.

Throughout August S.O.E. activities continued, and by the end of the month 190 Squadron had dropped 216 parachutists. The squadron participated in an unusual activity on the 8th, when 10 aircraft set off with containers, but only two dropped them, on account of bad weather. Meanwhile Wg. Cdr. Harrison and Sqn. Ldr. Gilliard dropped H.E. bombs and incendiaries on a special target, an unusual activity for 38 Group. Fighters were still around, and on 9/10 August Flt. Lt. Gardiner was chased by a Ju 88. His rear gunner fired, and the Ju 88 gave up the chase.

Night drops continued until 11 September, when the squadrons began to prepare for the next momentous event, the Arnhem operation.

Chapter 14

Adventure over Arnhem

On 17 September 1944 the second airborne assault was released, landing the British 1st Airborne Division in Holland in an attempt to establish a crossing of the Rhine. To achieve this meant the capture of bridges across the Maas at Grave, the Waal at Nijmegen and the Rhine at Arnhem. The latter was the task set the 1st British Airborne, the Airborne Corps H.Q., a Polish Parachute Brigade and the 878th U.S. Aviation Engineering Battalion, who would build landing strips.

Operation *Comet* was planned at the end of August 1944. On 6 September, 38 Group Operations Order 524 was despatched to Group stations, to Fairford (190 and 620 Squadrons), Keevil (196 and 299 Squadrons) and Harwell (295 and 570 Squadrons). They held about 210 Stirling Mk. IVs, their establishments of 22 I.E. + 4 I.R. (total 156) being well exceeded because D-Day losses had been low and production was rapid. At each station the establishment stood at 100 Horsa gliders, though Keevil had 130 on dispersals.

Operation *Comet* called for landings before and just after dawn. Six gliders would be landed close to each main bridge, then 700 gliders and a large number of paratroops would follow. Two huge lifts, aided by the U.S. IXth Troop Carrier Command, would be mounted by 38 and 46 Groups. On the next day a further lift of 157 IXth T.C.C. tugs and gliders, 26 38 Group tugs and gliders and 100 aircraft of 38 Group making resupply drops would follow, all forces to be ready to operate on 8 September.

This assumed the Americans would be ready for night operations, for which the R.A.F. were trained. In the event, the Americans were unready and the scheme fell through. A new plan was devised.

Operation *Market*, drawn up 15 September, again had three bridges as its objective, but two U.S. Airborne Divisions were added. Delivery of the 'pathfinder' force of gliders, as well as resupply, at Arnhem would be achieved by 38 and 46 Groups. American C-47s would undertake all paratroop drops, and deliver airfield builders and defenders. The operation would be in daylight, despite greater vulnerability. Insufficient aircraft were available for one assault, so the operation would take place over two days, with a third available for resupply. Fair weather was essential.

Arnhem's bridge was the key to the whole operation. It had to be held, and it had to be reached by ground forces in a comparatively short time, for troops landed there would be 60 miles behind enemy lines. Enemy reaction would be likely to hold these troops within a small area around the bridge. Thus a large force must be landed to support those holding the bridge.

There was an area 4 miles north of Arnhem which was suitable for glider landings, but in a heavily defended zone, so it was rejected. South of the river lay polder ground, soft and crossed by ditches and dykes which prevented glider landings. Only to the north-west of Arnhem was there a tract of country, shielded by trees, where gliders could land in force with natural protection. The area was, however, too small for two glider lifts to be placed upon it. In any case the landing ground would have to be held for the second day's lift, tying up a large proportion of those landed, and leaving the bridge holding troops on their own for a long time. Discussion surrounded use of L.Z.s by the bridge, but finally Major-General R. E. Urquhart, D.S.O., opted for the landing of gliders north-west of Arnhem, near the present site of Oosterbeek cemetery.

Meanwhile the enemy was concentrating flak defences, in particular along routes planned for the transport aircraft. The Tactical Air Force was ordered to carry out an onslaught on these A.A. defences. Nevertheless heavy losses were expected on the first lift. To help course keeping *Eureka* beacons were set up at sea and some of the first troops to land would establish more to aid resupply forces.

The first suitable day as far as the weather was concerned appeared to be 17 September, and Operation *Market* was ordered.

'The whole of Keevil was more or less confined to camp for five days prior to 17 September', recalls E. F. Chandler. 'The only visitors at that time were food supply, coal and brewers' lorries, which usually raised a cheer when seen. Several crews, including ours, were seconded to 1st Airborne units around Grantham, to get the feel of things. As aircrew N.C.O.s, we were very well treated, whereas in an R.A.F. mess one was one out of hundreds.

'It was a beautiful day, with a few patches of low cloud. Leading the operation were 295 and 570 Squadrons, carrying between them 12 loads of pathfinding troops to be landed close by the bridges at Arnhem and Nijmegen. Shortly after 11.00 hrs. departure began at one minute intervals as Stirlings taxied on to the runway, towropes were attached, and, with a tremendous surge of power and a "green", the heavy gliders were towed off. They circled Harwell and began to head a stream in loose pairs at 2,500 ft., 175 m.p.h., and the long procession towards Hatfield was on its way. There the ever lengthening line increased as other squadrons tagged on after changing course for exit over Aldeburgh, those from Fairford having commenced take-off shortly after 10.00 hrs., and Keevil's contribution a few minutes after 11.00 hrs.

'At Keevil everything seemed to go smoothly, the only mishap coming when a towrope went taut, hurling a Fleet Air Arm fitter 15 ft. into the air. Fleet Air Arm fitters were working in 38 Group to gain radial engine experience prior to Far East service. At least one of them, from H.M.S. *Daedalus*, took part in the actual operation and, losing his life, was later buried in Oosterbeek cemetery.'

There were the inevitable early towing problems, and one glider accidentally cast off from a 190 Squadron Stirling over South Cerney, another from 295 Squadron over Melksham. The stream took about an hour to pass.

Above Aldeburgh the streams of participating transports converged to cross to West Schouwen almost without incident. Over the Dutch coast 295 Squadron lost another Horsa, but the defences were almost inactive. A host of Allied fighters covered the transport force as it made its way to s'Hertogenbosch and the final point for the run-in to the L.Z.s.

They ran up in loose formation with mixed loads. No. 190 Squadron, for instance, had six aircraft carrying 97 pathfinder troops and another 19 towing gliders, the loads of which totalled 130 troops, 17 Jeeps, seven lightweight motorcycles, a heavy motorcycle, 17 trailers, seven guns and a bicycle. No. 196 Squadron had two towropes break, one glider ditched and another cast off, whereas all 12 gliders towed by 570 Squadron were released at the L.Z.

Once the gliders had been released, towropes were dropped, then the Stirlings climbed away for home at 180 m.p.h. Incredibly despite the long haul over enemy territory, there was little hostile response. It had been silenced by the Tactical Air Force.

By mid afternoon the Stirlings were home safely, bearing a few scratches from desultory flak. The weather had remained clear. At the L.Z.s troops deplaned effectively, and were taking up ordered positions.

During the remainder of the day groundcrews worked feverishly on the tugs, and prepared some 300 more gliders for passage.

When dawn broke on the 18th, it revealed fog clad airfields, which caused some alarm. A five hour delay was enforced, and even then there were cloud patches and hazy conditions to face. Flak had been rushed to the likely approach lanes, and when the Stirlings headed into Holland things were by no means as easy as on the preceding day.

This time 190 Squadron was towing 21 Horsas carrying 92 troops, 19 Jeeps, 7×5 cwt. cars, 4×6 lb. guns, 6 Bren carriers, 21 trailers and a heavy motor cycle. 196 Squadron towed Horsas, two of which prematurely released. Containers were carried by 17 Stirlings of 295 Squadron, three more of the squadron towing Horsas. One of the latter swung off the runway on take off, but the other two reached Arnhem. Containers were dropped at L.Z. 'X', Groesbeek, near Nijmegen. All of 299 Squadron Stirlings towed Horsas, and so did 10 of 570 Squadron. Nine gliders were released, but near Over Flakkee LK121, captained by Flt. Sgt. C. W. Culling, was hit by flak and crashed. Its Horsa was cast off and landed safely, though fired upon on the way down. Another of the squadron's Stirlings, hit by flak in the same region, eventually crashed near Breda. No. 620 Squadron towed 22 gliders; one towrope broke over England.

E. F. Chandler was in a Stirling. He recounts: 'After take-off we had our glider in high position, but many glider pilots preferred the low state. It fell to the flight engineer to peer from the astrodome and signal to the glider pilot with an Aldis lamp the time for release, following instructions from the bomb aimer who was map reading. We ran in for release at 2,000 ft., but supply droppers were going in at around 1,000 ft. or less, and were drawing most of the anti-aircraft fire. This enabled most of the tug aircrew to return safely to base.'

The route taken was as on 17 September. Flak had increased considerably since the preceding day. No. 570 Squadron's 15 supply droppers proceeded in vics of three, line astern, at about 15 second intervals, and went in from s'Hertogenbosch at 1,500 ft., dropping to a mere 700 ft. and 140 m.p.h. for the drop. In the dropping zone the cloud base was between 2,000 and 3,000 ft. Flak claimed another Stirling, and damaged LK555 which crash landed at base.

No. 190 Squadron had an eventful time. Moments after take off Plt. Off. Sellers had his starboard outer engine fail, and he cast off his glider before landing. Plt. Off. Beberfeld had his towrope break just after leaving the English coast because the glider placed itself in the wrong position. Both glider and tug came down at Woodbridge and later returned to base. Over Holland Flt. Sgt. Herger was drawn into the slipstream of a Dakota. His glider rose as he put his nose down to avoid the Dakota and the towrope snapped, the glider landing near Over Flakkee. Violent slipstream effect was encountered by many combinations, and it was so serious that Flg. Off. Farren's glider landed 25 miles short of the L.Z. after the towrope broke. Unlucky too was Flg. Off. Chesterton, one of whose engines was hit by flak.

Ground aids gave a useful lead-in for the crews, who released gliders in increasing flak and small arms fire. German troops fired upon the glider troops as they attempted to unload the Horsas, about 50 of which were burnt out, but mainly after unloading. Although only three Stirlings were lost, over 30 were damaged by flak. Communications with troops on the ground were impossible, even with the Airborne Corps H.Q. at Nijmegen. Photographs showed the Arnhem Bridge still intact, and battle in progress.

Back at their bases crews reported a Stirling spewing smoke; another, hit by flak, seen to crash and explode; a third reported burning on the ground; a fourth crash landed; a fifth, hit by flak, from which one crewman baled out; and a sixth with fuel streaming from its starboard tank.

By 19 September American forces had seized the bridge at Grave; but at Nijmegen the bridge remained in German hands, and the 1st Airborne Division at Arnhem was cut off from outside contact. Any surprise element had now vanished and the enemy had large forces to give battle, as well as very heavy flak defences. The idea of dropping Poles south of Arnhem was abandoned; so was any notion of engineers building landing strips. Only resupply drops and the towing of gliders carrying heavy equipment were ordered to take place. Once again low cloud and generally poor visibility prevented take-off until around noon. This time 20 Stirlings were involved, some towing gliders. Although enemy fighter interference was prevented by the strong fighter cover, crews encountered flak and other enemy fire all along the route to Arnhem, ranging from small arms fire to 40 mm shells. Along the Waal, waterborne guns opened up.

Approaching the Dutch coast, Plt. Off. Beberfeld ran into cloud. His Horsa closed rapidly on the tug, nearly forcing it into the sea. The towrope broke, and the glider smashed into the water. Three men clambered out into a dinghy dropped from the Stirling. The 16 supply droppers of 190 Squadron carrying 384 containers and 64 panniers, ran into very heavy flak and many were damaged. Shrapnel wounded W. O. Pelater in Flg. Off. Pascoe's crew, Flt. Sgt. Coeshott was shot down, and Sqn. Ldr. Gilliard's aircraft was hit over the D.Z. by two shells, which severed his controls. He ordered his crew to bale out while they had time, but Gilliard and Flg. Off. McKewon were killed when the Stirling crashed.

All 17 aircraft of 295 Squadron carried containers. Before reaching the D.Z., two aircraft were badly damaged, one by flak, and the other by falling containers. All but three of the Squadron's aircraft returned to base badly damaged. One was shot down in flames near Bruges, all the crew being casualties. Another made a forced landing at Woodbridge with an engine out of use. No. 570 Squadron's 17 aircraft, each carrying 24 containers and two packages, followed a new route chosen for this day: Base—Bradwell-on-Sea—Ostend—Ghent Helinthal—Veghel—D.Z., coming down to 800 ft. for their drop.

Most of the Allies' Continental fighter airfields were covered by haze and mist, and general opposition had increased. Around the D.Z. 88 mm guns were in operation, but all the crews dropped their loads; after this, however, three Stirlings were brought down. One, with port engines failing, made a belly landing at Ghent. LJ647, flown by Plt. Off. E. D. Hincks, hit over the D.Z. successfully crash landed at Grave, the crew scrambling out to make a getaway to Allied lines. Less fortunate were the crew of EH897, taken prisoner after crashing behind enemy lines.

By the time 620 Squadron reached the D.Z. there were so many supply droppers in the area, some of them making second runs at very low levels attempting to ensure that supplies reached the right hands, that many of the squadron crews were crowded out and forced to fly too high for accurate dropping. Although some of the aircraft were hit by flak, they all reached home.

By the evening of Tuesday 19th losses among the Stirling crews were becoming noticeable. The total loss for the day was 10. Crew reports indicated that a Stirling had been seen to crash on D.Z. 'L'. The crew of 'X9-Y' of 299 Squadron reported seeing 'N-Nan' of their squadron fall in flames. Three of the crew baled out, but no parachutes were seen to open. Crews reported lack of fighters to silence flak positions. Heavy flak forced some crews to drop loads from as high as 4,000 ft., many containers drifting into enemy hands.

It was not only the loss of 13 Stirlings that worried 38 Group, it was also the alarming number of machines with severe flak damage. But many could be repaired, and the strong Group strength at the start of the operation was proving a blessing.

On the fourth day 38 Group operated 101 aircraft for supply drops. From Fairford 34 Stirlings of 190 and 620 Squadrons took part; from Harwell 34 of 295 and 570 Squadrons; from Keevil 33 of 196 and 299, with one crew drawn from 1665 C.U., Tilstock. Between them they managed 87 successful drops unloading 2,063 containers, 325 panniers, three packets, two kitbags and a sack load; but the cost was high, for 11 aircraft were lost. No interception by enemy fighters was reported on the 20th, but ground defences had stiffened. Once more the number of aircraft damaged caused grave concern.

Reports were filed of rocket projectiles being fired from two positions, and returning crews spoke of a number of Stirlings in various difficulties, which produced a confused picture. Containers had again to be dropped from high levels, and often fell short of the dropping point, which was as depressing to the crews as to those enduring Hell on the ground. Yet again, bunching of Stirlings converging on the D.Z. tended to squeeze aircraft out over a wide dropping area.

For E. F. Chandler the day brought an end to his part in the Arnhem affair. 'We had a load of 24 parachute containers, three in each wing cell and 18 in the bomb bay, plus several large wicker baskets carried in the fuselage, along with two R.A.S.C. Air Despatchers.

'Nearing the D.Z., we were all alerted. Most pilots and bomb aimers had some task trying to concentrate on position, with so much heavy flak around.

'At the back of the Stirling Mk. IV, near the port side entrance door, was a despatch hatch built within the depth of the bomb bay. The radio operator and flight engineer usually lifted the floor cover off, and then it looked like the inside of a galvanised bath. Through this opening, army despatchers would, after seeing the red warning light flash to green, push the supply baskets attached to static lines hitched inside the aircraft. With the hatch open, pieces of shrapnel would race into the aircraft, and the smell of cordite and exploding shells was quite pungent. Luckily none of us were hit.

'With two more baskets to release, we realised the aircraft had been hit in the port wing and engine, and was on fire. We pushed out remaining supplies before the pilot ordered: "Prepare to bale out." We grabbed fire extinguishers and I managed to direct mine into a gap where the mainplane was attached to the fuselage. Meanwhile another crew member had extinguished a small fire, flames from which were creeping along the main interbalance fuel line, which was lagged, and which connected the two sets of fuel tanks in each wing. As the smoke had cleared, I told the skipper that I thought the fire was out. He replied: "No it isn't, all the hatches have been opened, that's why the smoke has cleared." The port inner had been feathered earlier. He said: "It's quite serious." We were now heading west and climbing on three engines.

'At 5,000 ft. the pilot ordered everybody to bale out. The army despatchers were first away via the rear exit in the floor, followed by the rear gunner. The pilot, bomb aimer and navigator went from the front exit. The R.A.A.F. radio operator told me they had all gone: I rather stupidly decided I could work better with the intercom disconnected, and the skipper had left the autopilot flying the aircraft. I made my way safely to the rear exit followed by the radio operator/air gunner.' E. F. Chandler landed on the Allied side of the lines.

Flg. Off. Chesterton was flying LK431: 'F-Fox' (or 'Ferdinand' as they knew it), as he had on the first two days' operations at Arnhem. On the 17th they had taken paratroops, on the 18th a Horsa. The 20th saw them dropping supplies; on this drop he and his crew had the first indication that all was not well, and the reception was very warm. 'During all these operations', he recalls, 'the fighter cover was superb at high, medium and low levels—then came Wednesday.'

The losses of the previous day and general unserviceability, coupled with battle damage, cut 38 Group's effort to a total of 64 aircraft making resupply sorties. Only 47 crews reported success. Three sorties were abortive, but it was the loss of 11 Stirlings that made the day so disastrous.

The previous evening clear reports had been received from Arnhem. They now knew that only a handful of troops had held the Arnhem bridge, because the main body from the D.Z.s and L.Z.s outside the town had been unable to fight their way through. On the third day these strong groups had been forced back to the L.Z.s where supplies had hitherto been dropped. An urgent call for more supplies had been received, and so on the fourth day the Stirlings set forth again. Flak increased, but a lower dropping height was ordered for greater accuracy. This called for a very precise drop.

On the morning of 20 September there was again widespread fog and low stratus over central England which, by mid morning, had lifted to 1,000 ft., giving a visibility of 1 to 3 miles. Again the southern route was chosen for resupply aircraft, which set off in four waves around noon. The new supply dropping point was some 200 yd. east of the previous one, which shows the precision demanded of crews. But it was other concerns which chiefly distinguished this day.

They set forth, climbing to 2,500 ft.; most were carrying 24 containers and assortments of panniers and packages, No. 570 Squadron was led by Sqn. Ldr. Cleaver, and 299 Squadron headed the formation. As they ran up on the new dropping point, the flak was even more intense. It was soon apparent that Allied fighters were not interfering with the Germans, some of whom had 88 mm guns. Over Holland transit had been at 7,000 ft.; but nearing the dropping point 570 Squadron, in bad visibility, ran in at 1,500 ft., descending to 800 ft. at 140 m.p.h. for the drop and racing out of the area at deck level. In the face of a tremendous flak barrage almost all of the supplies overshot into enemy hands. Heavy fire seriously damaged two of 299's aircraft and Flt. Lt. R. T. Turner crash landed at Noordclyke, two of the crew being taken prisoner, the others escaping to Allied lines.

No. 295 Squadron delivered 237 containers, 34 panniers and eight packages, which were hurled from their aircraft before Plt. Off. D. M. Peel made a belly landing south of the dropping point. The crews of 620 Squadron, encountering poor visibility en route, noticed an absence of covering fighters at the rendezvous, though it had been planned to send 17 squadrons of Spitfires, three of Mustangs and one of Tempests. Then the squadron saw FW 190s closing in. Flg. Off. H. M. Mcleod, in LJ830, and Flg. Off. J. C. L. Carey, in LJ946, were shot down.

Nearby was 196 Squadron. It was apparent that although the first and second waves had flown in with some fighter support, the other two were without any to silence flak and guard them against enemy fighters. Just after dropping as the Stirlings were racing away at treetop height, in came five FW 190s. LJ810 was raked by enemy fire, so severely that all the crew except the pilot, W.O. M. Azouz, and the tail gunner, abandoned the aircraft, which was savaged by flak and fighters until it was brought down. Soon LJ843 and LJ928 had also been shot out of the sky.

Events were now unfolding fast—but there were still 10 crews of 190 Squadron waiting to make drops. As they approached the dropping point it was clear that they were in for a hard time. The flak was terrifying and there were about 10 FW 190s intent upon success. Flg. Off. Sigert dropped his load just before two FW 190s attacked. He dived to ground level and his aircraft was badly shot about, the rear gunner, Flt. Sgt. Welton, claiming one enemy fighter before they made their getaway as fast as they could. In the rapidly developing mêlée Wg. Cdr. Harrison was soon shot down. Flying Officer Beberfeld's aircraft was badly holed by flak over Elst, and its load had to be jettisoned. Six Bf 109s swarmed around them, set the Stirling on fire and, seeing it doomed, looked elsewhere for trade. The aircraft began to climb but from it only the radio operator, Flt. Lt. Munro, and the rear gunner, W. O. Morris, baled out. They sheltered in a village before making a safe getaway to Allied positions. Morris at least had the melancholy satisfaction of having driven off one of the Bf 109s on fire, in part avenging his crewmates' death.

As Flg. Off. Pascoe crossed the dropping point, intensive flak enveloped his Stirling, severing the control wires; then the port wing caught fire. Pascoe, with great effort, retained control. Then fighters attacked him starting another fire. He ditched in the River Maas near Appeltern, but all the crew were drowned save Sgt. Smith, the flight engineer, and the bomb aimer, Flt. Sgt. Orange, who managed to get into the dinghy and reach the bank.

Seven of 190 Squadron's 10 Stirlings had been shot down, and an eighth was written off. Flying Officer Farren's machine, badly hit by flak, crashed on landing, hurling Farren through the windscreen and seriously injuring him.

The total loss for the day had been 11 Stirlings, making a total of 29 brought down during Operation *Market*. On the 21st, the loss rate was 14%— almost as high as any which overtook the Stirling. It showed the vulnerability— always expected but hitherto avoided—that such a transport force might endure. Had the fighters attacked the Dakotas of 46 Group, the casualty rate would have been even higher: the Stirlings at least had a rear gunner.

On 22 September the weather was too poor for resupply. Some respite was afforded 38 Group, but not the men on the ground at Arnhem. On the 23rd the weather cleared again, and a final effort was made. Again the southern route was chosen, despite the fact that the enemy was acquainted with the run-in. It was impossible to vary it much.

The force consisted of 123 aircraft of the two Groups, 38 and 46, 73 of these being Stirlings. Between them they delivered 1,540 containers, 235 panniers and 50 packages. This time full fighter support was afforded by 18 Spitfire and 3 Mustang squadrons. Enemy fighters appeared but kept their distance, but the Stirlings still had to face flak. Resupply was timed for 16.00 hrs. It took the column, including American C-47s, $1\frac{1}{2}$ hours to cross the dropping point.

This time 190 Squadron's seven aircraft—all it could muster—all returned safely. The 14 crews of 295 Squadron unloaded 332 containers and 52 packages; one Stirling, hit over the target area, landed at Ghent with an engine out of action.

Crews of 620 Squadron could see the enemy mounting a vicious attack on troops below. Some Stirlings were damaged by flak, and Wg. Cdr. D. H. Lee, in LJ847, was shot down. No. 299 Squadron had three aircraft badly damaged and one forced down 6 miles south-west of the dropping point; the crew escaped safely. No. 196 Squadron had 13 crews operating. Flying Officer J. A. Norton met a hail of flak and, soon afterwards, his port propeller flew off; but he limped into Manston. LJ949 crash landed at Leenda; EF272, seriously shot up, made base; so did LJ502 and another, severely mauled.

Fighter support for 570 Squadron was poor, and 88 mm guns were firing fast. Flg. Off. B. S. Murphy crash landed LJ996 at Ghent; EF298 flown by Flg. Off.

42.   Losses during the Arnhem venture were very heavy. 'QS:H' is seen here burning on the ground near Oss in Holland, on 23 September 1944.

W. Baker was shot down; so was Plt. Off. W. Kirkham in LJ883, near the dropping point. Stirling 'V8-A' landed at Manston with serious flak damage; and Sqn. Ldr. R. W. F. Cleaver, in LK191, came down in Holland, although he and his crew reached Allied lines. From LJ991, which came down near Nijmegen, only the radio operator and pilot escaped, the others being killed. In all, 570 Squadron had lost four aircraft; and two others were forced to land away from base.

In the evening the 22nd Relief Column—infantry of the 43rd Division and an Armoured Squadron—found themselves contained by enemy tanks between Arnhem and Nijmegen. The head of the column by the Rhine had the assault boats to make a crossing, but had discarded them. At Arnhem the 1st Airborne Division had been so weakened that further resupply seemed pointless. But the R.A.F. did not leave the troops without aid: Dakotas of 46 Group were advanced to Belgium from where resupply continued, and indeed five Stirling crews of 620 Squadron tried to aid them on the 24th, despite poor weather.

Now 38 Group counted the cost. On the last day of resupply 63 of its aircraft had been either shot down or seriously damaged, a loss of effective strength of 56%. Details of crew casualties are confused.

The records of 38 Group suggest a loss of 159 aircrew members missing, a confirmed 21 killed and 12 seriously wounded. Later figures suggest far higher casualties, but by the end of the resupply missions, 10 crews had made their way back to Allied lines.

One compensation, however, was that the Stirling squadrons were able to rearm quite rapidly: by 30 September the squadron strengths were: 190 Squadron–33 aircraft (20 serviceable); 196–34 (20); 295–7 (6); 299–39 (32); 620–36 (22); and 570—details not known.

Those who took part in the Arnhem venture tell of their feeling of utter powerlessness to aid those on the ground. Determined as they were to help, they could not change the appalling situation. To their everlasting glory, the 1st Airborne had held the Arnhem bridge in a fantastic show of courage. The Stirling crews of 38 Group did all in their power to support their brave colleagues throughout the Arnhem adventure.

Chapter 15

The Last Rounds

It was 138 and 161 (Special Duty) Squadrons who were mainly responsible for S.O.E. operations. Their Whitleys and Halifaxes ranged widely in order that the Resistance forces in occupied countries should have arms for battle.

By mid 1944 their Halifax Mk. IIs had dwindled in numbers, but all available Mk. IIIs were required for bomber squadrons. The Stirling Mk. IV was chosen to replace the Halifaxes at Tempsford. No. 138 Squadron received their first Stirling on 11 June 1944, and flew their first operation with it on 11 August. Supply drops to France, Belgium, Denmark and Norway followed. From 8 September 161 Squadron followed, equipping their 'B' Flight with Stirlings, but leaving Hudsons in 'A' Flight for pick-up duties.

During October 161 Squadron operated to Denmark and Holland, completing eight sorties and losing Sqn. Ldr. Abecassis. No. 138 Squadron operated over the same areas. Sortie rates were lower than for many squadrons, 138 Squadron successfully completing 39 out of 44 in November and 161 Squadron 17 out of 35. The weather, and the difficulty of finding and identifying friends on the ground, made high success rates impossible. In December 161 Squadron flew 22 sorties, some being 'spoof drops' in the Ardennes. These Stirlings had long range tanks, and *Rebecca* radio responders to enable contact with those on the ground.

January 1945 was a bad weather month, and 138 Squadron managed only eight sorties. With much of Europe now in Allied hands, the drops were made to Denmark and Norway. February's weather was better, and 138 Squadron flew 83 sorties during 700 hours' flying. Loads were usually 16 containers and three packages.

There was a particularly distressing accident near Tempsford on 14 February. Flg. Off. Timperly was returning from an exercise in LK236, and on the outer circuit, when an American P-51 pilot of the U.S.A.A.F. 363rd Squadron made an unauthorised pass. He crashed into the tail of the Stirling, which came down near Potton. All were killed.

In March 1945 161 Squadron flew 35 successful sorties out of 71, losing three crews. In April they managed 47 out of 79, mainly to Norway, the final operations being on 25 April. During 307 Stirling sorties by 161 Squadron, 190 successful drops were made and six Stirlings lost. No. 138 Squadron was withdrawn from S.O.E. duty on 9 March 1945.

Four nights previously, Flt. Sgt. J. T. Breeze had been flying with that squadron. He recalls: 'Our last operation from Tempsford, on 4 March, was typical. Five days after full moon, we could look forward to a good trip. We were briefed at 10.30 hrs. From the fuel load I knew it was to be somewhere in Denmark, taking 24 containers and seven packages. We would have 1,946 gallons of fuel, and operate at 70,000 lb.

'We were none too happy on two counts. We were detailed for "Q-Queenie", not our beloved "R-Roger", LK119. Our navigator reported sick, and we were allotted one on his first operation.

'After my section briefing I went to do the usual checks on the aircraft—engine runs, etc.—then returned to the crew room about lunchtime, reporting all was well to the skipper. Our take-off time was 23.50 hrs., so we had a long wait. Full briefing was in the late afternoon, our dropping zone about 15 miles south-west of Copenhagen. The crews assembled in the crew room about 21.30 hrs., and were taken to the aircraft about 23.00 hrs.

'We took off at 23.50 hrs. and climbed to 2,000 ft., the normal height for the crossing to Denmark. We crossed the English coast at Cromer for an uneventful sea crossing. About 20 miles off the Danish coast our bomb aimer, "Jock" Kyle, went forward into the nose to prepare for map reading to the D.Z. I moved into the second pilot's seat, which I occupied until we crossed the coast on our return. We crossed the coast, on track by now, at about 50 ft. No problems, apart from a little light flak which curled lazily and fell short of the aircraft. It was a beautiful night as we crossed Jutland to the waiting reception. In such bright moonlight one could see the silhouette of the aircraft scudding across the ground. We climbed to 500 ft., the usual height for drops, static lines being used.

'The bomb aimer had done an excellent job in guiding us to the D.Z. We circled the field until we were satisfied with the reception flashing the correct letter, then dropped our load. A final circle of the field, then down to 50 ft. and home to eggs and bacon—or so we thought. We had a good flight back across Zealand and Jutland, and were dead on track as the bomb aimer called: "Coast coming up." The skipper called for 2,400 revs., which I gave him, and with the speed around 240 knots we crossed the coast over Ringkobing Fjord, where without warning we crashed. Mystery surrounds the crash, but two of the crew said they heard an explosion just before we went in. It was all rather weird: one minute we were flying, the next the feeling of diving. I remember pulling back on the second pilot's control column shouting: "Pull her, skip", realising where we were. The skipper replied: "What a silly place to land." I replied that we'd better get out. I pushed open the escape hatch in the cockpit, then we climbed out, took our helmets off, inflated our Mae Wests and dropped to the water. It was only about 3 ft. deep! The rest of the crew evacuated, the rear gunner by revolving his turret. He climbed on to the tail, and then fell into the sea. Then he realised its depth. It was all quite funny. Good job it was shallow, nobody had given a thought to the dinghy. We were close to an island, and left "NF-Q" with two of its engines on fire, walking away to captivity with only a few bruises. Remarkable aeroplane, the Stirling, a 240 m.p.h. crash and still intact. Fortunately the war was nearly at its end.'

Complex maintenance and the need for logistic support militated against using Stirlings overseas. But when Halifax Mk. IIs became in short supply, Special

Duty squadrons overseas had to re-equip. No. 148 Squadron was to receive Stirling Mk. IVs in August 1944, but conversion did not begin until November; then, from Brindisi, Italy, only one operation was flown, by LJ181:F on 5 November.

No. 624 Squadron was born as 1575 Flight at Tempsford on 28 May 1943, with four Halifaxes and two Venturas. Within days they moved to Maison Blanche in North Africa, and started to operate over Corsica and Sardinia on 13 June, flying special supply drops. On 22 September 1943 the Flight, based at Blida, became 624 Squadron.

In June 1944 the squadron were informed they would be converting to Stirlings. On 28 June Wg. Cdr. C. S. G. Standbury flew to 144 M.U. with Flt. Lt. Fairey to collect the first Stirling. Stirlings arrived in small numbers in June, and by the end of July conversion was complete. The first dropping operation was flown to France by Wg. Cdr. Standbury in LJ938 on 29 July.

During re-arming the squadron had seven accidents. First, an undercarriage unit jammed in the 'up' position. Next came take-off swings, with pilots failing to close throttles to counteract side forces, which resulted in sheared under-carriages. A pilot held the Stirling down on take-off even though he had reached 105 m.p.h., whereas the Stirling would unstick at 95 m.p.h. even at 70,000 lb. The third trouble, which resulted in two fatalities, was pilots returning short of fuel. Tanks were filled for 9 hours' flying when operations normally took about 7 hours, giving a fair safety margin. One 8 hour operation by the C.O. revealed sufficient fuel left for 2 hours' flying. Most troubles seemed attributable to pilot error but, to be fair, they had not been through conversion units in Britain.

By the end of August 624 Squadron's Stirlings had flown 72 supply dropping sorties. With the spate of accidents, it seemed unwise to extend Stirling operations. In any case Vichy France, the main dropping area was being overrun. The last operation was impressive. Ten Stirlings in formation set off in two flights to drop supplies in daylight in the Alpes de Haute Provence, where 235 containers fell. On 24 September the squadron disbanded.

On 1 May 1944 199 Squadron moved into 100 Group. Its role was to provide a *Mandrel* screen ahead of a night's bomber operations. Aircraft specially fitted out by T.R.E. commenced operations in June 1944, flying 107 sorties for the loss of only one aircraft. Prior to departure of the Main Force, Stirlings would take up positions in an arc, orbiting and producing a false picture on the enemy's radar, causing him to bring fighters into action too soon to be effective. In July 1944 the *Mandrel* screen was positioned on 17 nights, 12 for major and five for minor operations. It was often set up about 80 miles out to sea, usually off East Anglia. Main Force would pass through the screen, which could be combined with large diversionary sweeps, in which Stirlings played a major part, and *Window* drops. No. 199 Squadron could not operate in the Channel region without interfering with communications to the Allies in France. But when bomber routes were drastically switched, as they were on 18 July, it was an effective aid. The screen was also put up when bombers did not operate—a useful ruse.

In September 1944, when 199 Squadron operated on 19 nights, the squadron was reduced to 2 Flights, the third being hived off to form the nucleus of a second *Mandrel* squadron, No. 171. They operated under 199's control, but their Stirling days were brief, and on 21 October Halifax Mk. IIIs took over. An innovation at this time was gradually to move the *Mandrel* screen forward, and it was also set up over liberated territory.

On nine nights in October 199 Squadron set up the screen for large scale operations, using it when mining took place, and also during small 'spoofs'. There were 57 sorties by 199 Squadron, which also made *Window* drops.

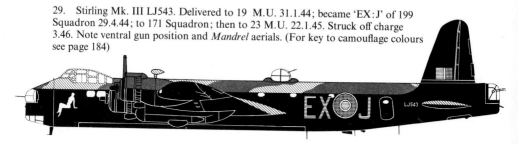

29. Stirling Mk. III LJ543. Delivered to 19 M.U. 31.1.44; became 'EX:J' of 199 Squadron 29.4.44; to 171 Squadron; then to 23 M.U. 22.1.45. Struck off charge 3.46. Note ventral gun position and *Mandrel* aerials. (For key to camouflage colours see page 184)

In January 1945, 199 Squadron operated on 12 nights, flying 89 sorties. On the 28th the screen was placed near the southern battle fronts before the squadron formed itself into a stream for *Window* dropping, and proceeded to Stuttgart with the second wave. The last *Mandrel* sorties were flown on 14 March, Sqn. Ldr. J. J. M. Button in LJ516:H bringing the Stirling's career in Bomber Command to an end.

After 'Henrietta' had landed, 199 Squadron, one of the most spirited of Stirling squadrons, recorded their sorrow at the passing of a revered friend in these words: 'Goodbye, old Stirling, goodbye, old friend,/you've never let us down from beginning to end./Whate'er it was, where'er you went,/on bombing, mining, supporting bent,/you did a grand job, the best on Earth./You're Stirling by name, you were sterling in worth.'

After Arnhem, 38 Group licked their wounds before resuming supply drops to the Resistance. If they were again to carry airborne forces into battle, they would need to operate from East Anglia. The squadrons moved into ex-U.S. 9th A.A.F. bases, 295 and 570 to Rivenhall, 196 and 299 to Wethersfield (later Shepherd's Grove) and 190 and 620 to Dunmow. Night supply drops recommenced. These were lonely missions flown at low levels. But the main task was to keep their hand in for airborne operations. Many large scale training missions were flown between November 1944 and March 1945.

Apart from supply dropping, the squadrons stood by, awaiting the next big operation and largely unemployed. For what purpose could they be used? There was no reason why the Stirling Mk. IV should not carry bombs. Crews were therefore trained off Wainfleet and Denghie Flats, bombing accuracy being aided by *Gee-H* and *Rebecca*. They were to fly night bombing operations in support of the Army and under 2 Group control.

The first operation was ordered for 21 January 1945, target Rees. No. 190 Squadron, led by Wg. Cdr. R. H. Bunker, sent four crews, each taking 21×500

43. Stirling 'B-Beer' LJ514 of 199 Squadron has a ventral gun station and an array of aerials for *Mandrel* and other equipment.

44. 'Kismet III', a Stirling of 295 Squadron. Like some others it has fully clear nose panels.

lb. M.C. bombs plus incendiaries, though the usual Stirling load on these raids was 24 × 500 lb. M.C. The Rees raid supported Allied forces in Belgium.

Cumulus towered to 11,000 ft., forcing bombing on timed runs, and crews encountered much icing. It was clear over Britain when 620 Squadron set off, but the six crews had to progress through 30 miles of cumulus after crossing the French coast, and attacked from between 7,000 and 11,000 ft. All agreed on one thing: it was a very cold night out; and a lot of coring occurred in the oil coolers.

When the Stirlings left their bases on 1 February, a strong gale was blowing which, at operational height, reached 75 m.p.h. Next night fog and low cloud at the target forced blind bombing.

As Flt. Sgt. W. R. Halford was taking off from Rivenhall on the 4th for Grevenbroich, the aircraft swung violently and crashed. The crew quickly evacuated it, getting clear before the bombs burst.

On 7 February, about 30 miles from the target, Flg. Off. D. P. J. Torens of 196 Squadron spotted a German jet fighter. Crews of 299 and 570 Squadrons also saw it, but no attack was made. The purpose of the mission had been to bomb German troops, either in billets or as they moved through three towns.

On 21 February 196 and 299 Squadrons operated, and Sqn. Ldr. Speir and Wg. Cdr. Baker failed to return. Flt. Lt. Campbell returned to Shepherd's Grove around 22.30 hrs. Unknown to him, his aircraft had been located by one of the now rare intruders over Britain, possibly an Me 410. As he lined up on finals, the German pilot opened fire, setting the Stirling ablaze. Campbell managed a good landing, and the crew—apart from the rear gunner, W. O. J. McGovern—escaped from the burning wreck to safety. The intruder then four times attacked Flt. Sgt. Payne's aircraft over Shepherd's Grove, but the only hits were those on the enemy. Payne landed safely at Foulsham.

One of those who flew these bombing operations in 1945 was I. A. Downie. Detailed for the bridge at Rees in 'I-Ivor' of 196 Squadron, he set off. 'The take-off, the first we had done with such a heavy load as 24 × 500 lb. bombs, was frightening in the extreme. After brakes were released the aircraft hardly seemed to move. I felt that its tyres were so compressed they were behaving like the wheel on a wheelbarrow being pushed through a muddy field. Everything was slower than usual, and the end of the runway was just under the nose as the needle crept to minimum speed for take-off. The controls felt much heavier than usual.

'Tension built up as we crossed into Belgium; and then we spotted flak, a single stream of tracer. The odd thing was that its arc remained unchanged, and we turned away. Had some Oberleutnant or gunner fallen asleep, his finger resting on a firing button? We shall never know, but I still wonder. Rees was completely covered in cloud, and why we dropped some bombs on a field near the Rhine is probably intriguing a few middle aged residents to this day.'

Once the brief bombing interlude was over, 38 Group resumed S.O.E. operations in earnest, particularly over Denmark. But by early March they were gearing up for the next great adventure: Operation *Varsity*, the crossing of the Rhine.

For about a month before this started, watchers in eastern England were treated to magnificent spectacles as long lines of Stirlings towed Horsas, participating in exercises with intriguing names. Gradually the numbers involved increased, and so did the length of the flights. By mid March all was set for the final glider assault.

At each of three bases 60 Horsas awaited their tugs. Tasks would be to lift the 6th Airborne Division into battle, landing them at four places to this pattern:

L.Z. 'A': 299 Sqn. + 15 Horsas; 620 Sqn. + 6 Horsas
L.Z. 'B': 196 Sqn. + 2 Horsas; 299 Sqn. + 15 Horsas; 620 Sqn. + 2 Horsas
L.Z. 'P': 190 Sqn. + 6 Horsas; 196 Sqn. + 28 Horsas; 295 Sqn. + 5 Horsas;
570 Sqn. + 30 Horsas; 620 Sqn. + 18 Horsas
L.Z. 'R': 190 Sqn. + 2 Horsas; 196 Sqn. + 14 Horsas

The effectiveness of the British part of the operation may be judged by the fact that 319 of the 320 gliders alerted set off; 207 were successfully dropped; 31 aborted; 14 were prematurely released; 7 had broken tow ropes; flak claimed 19; 9 were otherwise down; and 2 landed away from L.Z.s. Enemy fighters never came near the armada.

A summary of loads carried by the six Stirling squadrons showed that 190 Squadron lifted 318 troops; 196 Squadron 89; 295 Squadron 222; 299 Squadron 103; 570 Squadron 275; and 620 Squadron 138—added to which were the vehicles carried in the gliders.

Many of those who had served with 38 Group in early 1944 were still in their squadrons, flying the longest tours of any aircrew. It was utterly different from Arnhem: a model of efficiency, as I. A. Downie found.

'The crossing of the Rhine seemed to me the culmination of four and a half years of preparation. Rumour on the airfield was that complete plans of the Rhine crossing operation were in German hands, and that we should prepare for massive resistance. Instead, the operation was magnificent. We had a front row view—armchair comfort—feeling of being on the winning side at last.

'On the morning of 24 March, 196 Squadron seemed tuned to give its maximum performance. Every Stirling that could, flew that day. Gliders were parked on either side of the main runway, angled to preserve precious runway length. There was little wind as we boarded "E-Easy". The sun started to light the scene, the air was clear, cloud slight and high, as we sat awaiting the signal to start engines. All was in such strange contrast to the danger, destruction, disaster and death that we were to effect that day.

'I pressed the start buttons and my Hercules' whined, coughed and grumbled into life. The plane in front was only halfway down the runway when my throttles were fully open, and my bomb aimer, Lou Chevron, had clamped them tight. It seemed an age before I could feel the glider becoming airborne, but soon "wheels up" was given. We circled, cutting the corner until we were in formation, following the leaders to the south coast. It was only as we flew on that the realisation came to us of the immensity of the operation.

'Our squadron was soon joined from port and starboard by others knitting into a fast expanding stream. Altitude was low, somewhere near 1,800 ft. The stream soon stretched to the horizon. Halfway across France dots appeared on

45.   Stirling IV EF429 of 'B' Flight 196 Squadron, at Shepherd's Grove in 1945; '7T:P' also has a clear nose.

the port side—aircraft returning from the Rhine. It was an amazing sight, overshadowing all the Westerns I had seen.

'We crossed the Rhine, and map reading became more intensive as the bomb aimer and navigator kept us exactly on course, I had already worked out my tactics for getting out of what might be a tricky situation. We released the glider at 500 ft., which seemed an extremely dangerous altitude in view of ack-ack firing from small arms on the ground. I went into a climbing turn for home, viewing the continuous stream of more aircraft arriving. We were halfway back across France before we passed the end of the stream.

'Over the Channel we dropped our towrope. The Scots member of the crew felt it a great waste—surely a farmer or fisherman would have benefited from it?'

John Graf would also have memories of 24 March 1945, a beautiful day. The air was so fresh, the sky so blue. 'The stream of "matchboxes" (gliders) stretched two by two like animals heading for the Ark, ahead as far as the eye could see. We were flying Stirling Mk. IV "7T-L". It had Hercules Mk. XVIs on which fuel-air mixture regulation was achieved automatically by reference to throttle setting. At +2 p.s.i. boost economical cruising was obtained. The setting of +6 p.s.i. provided climbing conditions, or was useful for limited combat periods. Intermediate settings were prohibited since they would have brought rich mixture jets into operation, playing havoc with fuel consumption.

' "7T-L" had seen more youthful days, and towed with rather less zest than many others. At maximum cruising boost it was able to maintain station, but not altitude. I proceeded by a series of hops, which must have wearied the glider occupants. Over the intercom wired through the tow rope we wished the glider crew well, and they released on time. By then the ground was strewn with gliders. At low altitude the air seemed full of them losing height and jockeying on to their approaches to landing. Above, the air was full of tugs, now lightened of their trailing loads, banking and turning away trailing empty towropes.'

As soon as *Varsity* was over the round of S.O.E. operations was resumed, flights now being to Scandinavia. They extended through April. An interesting and little known action in which 38 Group took part was Operation *Amherst*, a paratroop invasion of north-east Holland in which 690 troops of the 2nd S.A.S. Brigade were dropped. Their purpose was to capture bridges to aid the armoured spearhead of the 2nd Canadian Division.

Within the force were eight Stirlings of 570 Squadron, each taking 15 paratroops and four containers, which were to be dropped south of Groningen from heights of between 800 and 1,500 ft., depending upon cloud conditions, or if necessary dropped after location of the D.Z. by using *Gee* fixes. All eight crews proceeded singly, flying at 2,000 to 3,000 ft. and being routed over recaptured territory. Eventually the troops jumped from 1,000 ft. through dense stratus. This was the first occasion when paratroops were dropped blind on exercises or operations by 38 Group.

30.   Stirling Mk. IV PW443 in immediate post-war markings. Delivered to 23 M.U. 9.5.45; joined 299 Squadron 12.5.45; returned to 23 M.U. 17.3.46. Crashed 5.6.47. (For key to camouflage colours see page 184)

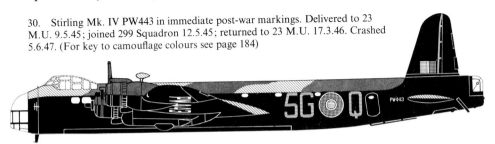

Almost to the close of hostilities, the work of contacting the Resistance continued. Then, if anything, the workload for 38 Group increased, for now the Stirlings were ferrying mail, troop supplies and petrol to forces on the Continent. On 5 May, 299 Squadron took troops in 19 Stirlings to Copenhagen, then came the carriage of others to Oslo, Stavanger and Gardermoen. Flying to Norway was sometimes hazardous, and on one flight a Stirling crashed; the 38 Group Commander was among those killed.

Repatriation of prisoners of war from German camps was soon in progress, as was the return of Canadians heading for home. On 29 May, 299 Squadron found itself carrying much needed nursing staff and blankets to Norway from East Fortune; and soon it was engaging in daily mail runs to Italy and the Middle East.

'The Stirling Mk. IV', recalls John Graf, 'carried out the transport role with some success, taking up to 24 fully armed troops, though admittedly with little comfort for them. On one occasion we brought back 39 children and 6 adults, all Jewish ex-inmates of concentration camps, from Prague to Crosby. About this time some primitive seating was installed in the rear fuselage—a row of tubular frames with canvas seats and backs along each side of the fuselage, facing inboard.

'The restricted entrance to the boxlike rear fuselage made loading difficult, and accordingly only limited cargo flying was possible. One notable exception to this had been the ferrying of jerrycans of 100 octane fuel to forward airfields. Since

46.   LK304 of 620 Squadron with 'D4-S', late 1944.

the load was concentrated in the rear fuselage, the c.g. shifted, making take-off
and landing more difficult; and the destination airfields were liberally cratered, so
that the detail was not entirely popular with the Stirling crews.'

No move of 38 Group to the Far East ever came about. Instead, its Stirlings
performed a multitude of transport tasks within and on the perimeter of Europe.
Replacement troops were flown to captured territories to relieve those who had
seen battle. Mail and newspaper runs were made to Cairo, and stores transported
to such places as Castel Benito, Libya, as well as to Italy and India. Often such
flights set off from Lyneham, and were frequently routed through St. Mawgan.

The closing months of the war saw the Halifax taking a greater part in such
operations, and two Stirling squadrons re-equipped with them soon after
hostilities in Europe ceased.

The end for the Stirling in 38 Group came in January 1946 when the squadrons
disbanded, ending an exciting period.

Chapter 16

Passengers and Freight

On the day before the Arnhem landings two Stirlings were handed over to the R.A.F. at 23 M.U., Aldergrove. They were the first two production Mk. Vs, PJ878 and PJ879. Strange they looked, with streamlined noses, shorn of turrets and unusual green-grey-blue finish. The Mk. V, outcome of plans for the 'C' Stirling, was Short's hope for the postwar airliner market. It was designed to Specification C. 18/43 for a long range transport able to carry freight and passengers on Empire routes. The prototype, LJ530, was a converted Mk. III airframe.

Mixed loads were possible. The crew numbered five, and as many as 40 passengers could, theoretically, be carried, or alternatively 20 paratroops, 12 stretchers or 14 sitting cases. Some 14 seats were usually fitted aft of the main spar.

One who flew the Mk. Vs was John Graf who recalls: 'The Stirling Mk. V had a cargo door 9 ft. 6 in. × 5 ft. 1 in. on the starboard rear side, hinged at the bottom so that it opened to form a ramp. Thus bulkier loads could be taken into the rear fuselage. An elongated nose, to which loading access was afforded by a beam block and tackle, had a hinged top. Thus balanced loading could be achieved, and the c.g. stabilised within acceptable limits. The arithmetical calculations could be quite critical.

'It was a reasonable aircraft to fly. The added weight of the nose and fuselage loading doors was offset by turret elimination. Bomb aimers, now redundant, were replaced by second pilots—often without much Stirling experience, to the consternation of all.

'The aircraft retained its hereditary characteristics: pronounced desire to swing to the right on take-off, and tricky to land; but it remained light on the controls and, when shorn of camouflage paint, it cruised along unladen, economically, at about 185 to 190 m.p.h.I.A.S.'

All 160 Mk. Vs were powered by Hercules Mk. XVIs. The absence of turrets gave the aircraft a length of 90 ft. 6¾ in. Empty weight was 43,500 lb., and the all-up weight remained 70,000 lb. In round figures the performance of the Mk. V was 280 m.p.h. maximum speed at 6,000 ft.; range up to 3,000 miles; and service ceiling 18,000 ft.

Short's prepared the S.37, commonly called the 'Silver Stirling', as the civil counterpart. It was fully furnished, sound proofed and fitted out for 30 passengers, conversion being done on PJ958. Short's hoped for an order from B.O.A.C.,but the Halifax, which B.O.A.C. ordered, quickly established itself as a transport; it had a belly pannier. Nevertheless, a dozen Stirling Mk. Vs were converted to a civil role by Airtech, Thame, in 1947. They were sold to Trans Air of Belgium, becoming 'OO-XAK' to '-XAV'. The charter company used them on routes to the Far East: Singapore, Hong Kong and Shanghai were all on its itineraries.

Stirling Mk. Vs came into R.A.F. hands late in 1944, 10 being delivered before the year was out. An effective transport force to link the U.K. with India and South-East Asia was being devised.

No. 46 Squadron, commanded by Wg. Cdr. B. A. Coventry, equipped with Mk. Vs in January and February 1945, and began training flights to Maison Blanche in North Africa on 17 February. The first route trips were flown by PJ912 and PJ913 on the 27th.

Also at Stoney Cross was 242 Squadron, under Wg. Cdr. H. Burton; they too began flying Stirling Mk. Vs in February 1945. Nearly all crews came from Bomber Command.

During March 1945, overseas training flights were continued by both squadrons, and the first flights to Mauripur were made. On 3 March 46 Squadron flew its first route service to Castel Benito. From 1 April the squadron commenced flights on alternate days, terminating at Arkonam (via Poona) or Dum Dum (via Palam).

Abruptly, and with their training largely completed, 242 Squadron was ordered to re-equip with Avro Yorks, 15 of which would replace 25 Stirlings. The York needed service evaluation on the Far East run, and afforded more comfort than the Stirling. York production rates, however, did not yet allow full re-equipment of all squadrons, and so 46 Squadron continued operations.

By the end of April 1945 three Stirlings had made the return trip to India, usually carrying 17 passengers. On 27 April new route schedules came in for the Dum Dum run, laying down arrival and departure times airline style. A freight service had already been instituted. The flights were not without moments of alarm. PJ901, flown by Flg.Off. Kczvajer, made the first run to Arkonam. On taking off from Mauripur on 9 April the old bogey of take-off swing seized the aircraft, which crashed, extensively damaging the rear fuselage.

During May 1945 21 Stirlings left Stoney Cross on scheduled flights. One encountered a lightning strike; another had its plastic nose smashed in flight by a vulture; and 12 returned within the month. Flt. Lt. Frowde was caught in a tropical hailstorm which smashed the astro hatch and cockpit Perspex, and stove in the tail leading edges. They were taking about 80 hours for the return trip without plug changes, though oil coolers needed careful control.

As soon as the war in Europe ended 4 Group was disbanded, some of its squadrons being switched at once to Transport Command. Among them were 51 and 158 Squadrons, which were earmarked for Stirling Mk. Vs.

On 19 May 1945, Wg. Cdr. Coventry flew PJ944 to Belfast for experimental stripping of paint. The result proved acceptable, and others followed. The majority of Mk. Vs in squadron hands flew in bare metal finish. It is believed that some were painted white all over, possibly at Pocklington, the Mk. V modification centre, in order to reduce cabin temperature.

Trips to India were now taking about 12 days, and flights had begun to Ratmalana. In June a lot of freight was lifted, but delays were occurring mainly because of engine trouble.

Eight Stirling Mk. Vs were delivered to 51 Squadron at the start of June, and training began. Route flights on 46 Squadron were far from eventful, though there was an occasional minor incident. Flg. Off. W. Walton took off on Freight Flight SYF41 in PJ981 on 1 June, bound for St. Thomas's Mount via El Aqir, Castel Benito, Lydda and Shaibah. He proceeded first to Elaqena, and after two days left for Castel Benito, where an engine change took five days. After leaving Shaibah, as he levelled out at 10,000 ft., an unusual noise was heard from the port side, which appeared to be due to a piece of metal. A port engine was feathered. He returned to Shaibah, and after setting out again a starboard engine gave trouble. The aircraft could not maintain height. Freight had to be jettisoned; then the starboard inner engine began to overheat and the aircraft lost height to 200 ft., but they scraped into Shaibah once more. On landing, after running 200 yd., the port undercarriage leg collapsed; but the crew escaped unscathed. On the same day 158 Squadron began training on Stirling Mk. Vs.

Freight loads were currently about 5,290 lb. By the end of June, 21 crews of 51 Squadron had converted on to Mk. Vs, and 19 aircraft were on strength.

Scheduled flights were being made to Dum Dum, St. Thomas's Mount, and Ratmalana; and shuttle flights between Cairo and Mauripur by 46 Squadron. Most flights now set out from Lyneham, and there was a lot of engine trouble on the routes.

Suddenly, all the Yorks were withdrawn from 242 Squadron and they reverted to Stirling Mk Vs. On 16 July 51 Squadron flew their first overseas training flight, to Castel Benito, and by the end of the month they were flying to India.

Both 51 and 158 Squadrons moved to Stradishall in August. Training flights to India were resumed, while 46 Squadron concentrated on runs mainly to the Middle East and North Africa; the regular service to India was maintained. Although 242 Squadron had been ordered to fly Yorks they had continued Stirling flying too and, when the Yorks were withdrawn, were still able to function fully. By August they, too, were operating scheduled flights to India, and began a service to the Azores on 19 August 1945. The squadron's training programme included 12 days of ground school and 20 hours of conversion flying, after which a 'screened' flight to India followed.

Then, to their dismay, 242 Squadron suddenly began to receive Stirling Mk. IVs, quite unsuited to route flying and with poor cargo capacity. Attempts to load the aircraft resulted in some alarming moments if the load was not well distributed, but they were able to carry passengers, albeit in discomfort. Understandably, 242 Squadron wanted Yorks back—and so did their customers.

No. 46 Squadron ran the India service without problems in October, but flights were reduced to three a week. They now had a service to Gibraltar, and from 15 October the UMT service terminated at Almaza. In October 46 Squadron flew 1,723,160 (nautical) passenger miles, 122,740 aircraft miles, and safely carried 2,705 passengers.

No. 51 Squadron commenced route flying to the Middle East on 1 October, PK115 and PJ953 also leaving for Mauripur. On the same day the squadron began to lift a large number of troops from Brussels to India, and Stirling Mk. Vs also took part in a lift of 10,000 troops from Shaibah to India to replace a similar number taken to Arkonam.

At Lyneham a bad accident occurred on 23 November. Flt. Lt. Gray arrived there late in the afternoon. He lined up for a G.C.A. landing but his aircraft careered into the control block and civilian canteen. Miraculously none of the crew was injured in the resulting fire, but two others were killed and three seriously injured.

Some crews from 242 Squadron were now switched to No. 46, which at the end of November 1945 held 30 Stirlings. Most flights were terminating in the Middle East, and more trooping took place during Exercise *Annex*. No. 158 Squadron was now lifting loads of 24 men, each with 250 lb. of equipment. On 1 November 1945, 51 and 158 Squadrons came under 48 Group as strategic mobility squadrons.

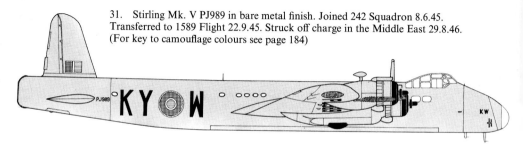

31.   Stirling Mk. V PJ989 in bare metal finish. Joined 242 Squadron 8.6.45. Transferred to 1589 Flight 22.9.45. Struck off charge in the Middle East 29.8.46. (For key to camouflage colours see page 184)

No. 242 Squadron flew its last scheduled flight to St. Thomas's Mount on 10 November, and in December moved to Merryfield to re-equip with Yorks.

On 11 November PJ980 had just taken off from Castel Benito with a heavy load when the port wing burst into flames. The aircraft crashed into a sand hill and was burnt out, with the loss of the entire crew. On the following night PJ950 also crashed taking off from Castel Benito, killing all its passengers.

Trooping using Stirling Mk. Vs ended for 51 and 158 Squadrons on 3 December 1945 as they awaited disbandment. No. 196 Squadron had a brief flirtation with the Mk. V early in 1946, but it was 46 Squadron which held them last, re-equipping in March 1946, by which time the Yorks were flying the India services.

Two other users of the Mk. V deserving mention are Nos. 1588 and 1589 Heavy Freight Flights. Their tasks were vitally important on the Indian trunk route, for they were used to carry components to stations along the line where any transport aircraft needed them. No. 1588 Flight operated between the Middle East and India, and 1589 between Britain and the Middle East. One particularly unpleasant accident befell Flg. Off. Owen in PJ947 as he took off from Lydda on 27 October 1945. The inevitable swing overtook the Stirling, which rammed itself into an Anson of the Egyptian airline Misr, SU-ACX, causing fatal casualties. These two Flights were small, each holding five Stirlings,

47. Ground and aircrew members of 1588 Heavy Freight Flight line up before a
Stirling V at Santa Cruz, Bombay, about December 1945. The Flight was the last flying
unit to operate Stirlings.

but 1588 Flight has a special place in the Stirling story, for it was the last
operational R.A.F. unit to fly them.

On 17 July 1946 a signal was sent to Santa Cruz: no more maintenance was to
be done on the Stirlings of 1588 Flight, which were to be immediately struck off
charge. Theirs were not the last Stirlings in R.A.F. hands; that distinction
probably fell to a Mk. V in storage at Polebrook.

32. Stirling Mk. V PJ996 of 1588 Flight, wearing camouflage. Joined 242
Squadron 21.6.45. To 1588 Flight 24.9.45, arriving India 11.3.46. Struck off charge
30.11.46. (For key to camouflage colours see page 184)

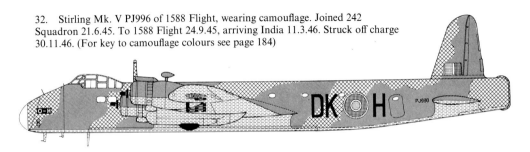

It is unlikely that a Stirling will ever again be seen intact, although the R.A.F. Museum holds parts of LK488. In Holland Stirling components have been recovered. A complete tailwheel unit was discovered some years ago, tyres inflated, and a shining Elsan from a 90 Squadron machine.

For sure, a true 'Whispering giant' will never make its way around a circuit again. Never will one have the satisfaction of seeing a Stirling outmanoeuvre a Lancaster, or give a fighter a tricky moment.

I do not think that any aeroplane that has passed my way has impressed me more by its majesty than the Stirling. Memorable, indeed, that morning when I first came face to face with N3641. Mammoth, overpowering, in a way that no other aeroplane could equal, certainly an aerial battleship, 'Queen of the Sky'.

To thrill to the sight of one of those huge aeroplanes drifting into Lakenheath, of seeing them climbing out of Oakington bound for some strange place with a then familiar name, or just to feel the exhilaration coming from watching that mighty tail lift high on take-off at Waterbeach; these are for dreams.

No talk of swing, of small bombs, of hangars too small, of irritable Exactors, can remove images of, surely, the most impressive-looking bomber of all time.

Key to Camouflage Colours and Scale
(see diagrams 6, 7, 8, 13, 16, 22, 23, 28, 29, 30, 31, 32)

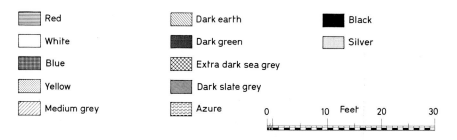

Appendix 1

Stirling Airframe Serial Numbers, Associated Mark Numbers and Engine Marks

Contract 67299/37: Short, Rochester
L7600 prototype; L7605 second prototype, became 3443M.

Contract 763825/38: Short, Rochester
N3635–3644 inclusive: 10 Stirling Trainer, Hercules II (N3644 re-engined with Hercules III; N3636 became 3056M; N3637–3361M; N3637–3013M; N3641–3010M; N3642–3012M); N3645 destroyed by bombing; N3646 Hercules III; N3647–3651 destroyed by bombing; N3652 Hercules I (?) became 3444M; N3653–3656 Hercules III; N3657 Mk. II, Cyclone; N3658–3663 (N3662 first with dorsal turret, fitted to all subsequent in the batch; N3663 et seq. Hercules XI; previous ones Hercules III); N3664–3684; N3700–3710; N3711 Mk. II, Cyclone; N3712–3729; N3750–3769 (following bombing of Rochester 15.8.40 some completed elsewhere; at South Marston N3673; 3676; 3678; 3679; 3682; 3700; 3704; 3705; 3706; 3708; 3709; 3710; 3712; 3721; 3762; and possibly others; at Hucclecote N3680; N3681; and possibly others).

Contract 774677/38: Short & Harland, Belfast
N6000 Hercules XI, became 3768M; N6001–6003 Hercules X; N6004 Hercules III; N6005 Hercules X; N6006 Hercules X, became 4165M; N6007–6019; N6020–6024 Hercules XI; N6025–6028 destroyed by bombing; N6029–6030 Hercules XI; N6031 destroyed by bombing; N6032–6049 Hercules XI (dorsal turret probably on N6032 et. seq.); N6065–6084 Hercules XI, completed at Aldergrove; N6085–6104; N6120–6129 Hercules XI.

Contracts 763825/38 (R9141–9220): Short, Rochester
Contracts 774677/38 (R9295–9358): Short & Harland, Belfast
Mk. I, Hercules XI: R9141–9170; R9184–9203; R9241–9290; R9295–9334; R9349–9358 (R9188 first with Cyclone GR-2600, then converted to Mk. III).

Contract 982939/39: Austin Motors, Birmingham
Mk. I, Hercules XI: W7426–7475 (W7432 and (?) W7455 converted to Mk. III); W7500–7589; W7610–7623.

Contract 774677/38: Short & Harland, Belfast
Mk. I, Hercules XI: to BF454; BF455 et seq. Mk. III, Hercules VI; BF309–358 (BF355 converted to Mk. III); BF372–416; BF434–454; BF455–483; (BF464 and BF468 converted to Mk. IV); BF500–534 (BF532 convered to Mk. IV); BF561–580 (BF575 converted to Mk. IV, Hercules XVI; BF580 converted to Mk. IV, Hercules VI).

Contract B982939/C36: Austin Motors, Birmingham
Mk. I, Hercules XI: BK593–628; BK644–647; then BK648–650 and remainder of batch Mk. III, Hercules VI (except BK651 Hercules XVI): BK652–667; BK686–727; BK759–784; BK798–818.

Contract 763825/38: Short, Rochester
DJ972–977 Hercules XI (replacing N3645 and N3647–3651 destroyed by bombing).

Contract 774677/38: Short & Harland, Belfast
Mk. III: EE871–918 Hercules VI (EE889 and EE900 converted to Mk. IV); EE937–975 Hercules VI (EE962 and EE966 converted to Mk. IV); EF114–163 Hercules VI (EF141 converted to Mk. IV); EF177–217 Hercules VI (EF213 and EF214 converted to Mk. IV); EF231–277 Hercules VI (converted to Mk. IV: EF234; EF237; EF241–244; EF248; EF256; EF260; EF263–265; EF267–269; EF270; EF272–277) (Hercules XVI in EF250 et seq., except EF253 and EF259 Hercules VI); EF289–323 Hercules VI (converted to Mk. IV: EF293; EF295; EF298; EF303; EF305–306; EF309; EF311; EF314; EF316–323).

Contract 763825/38: Short, Rochester and South Marston
Mk. I: EF327–369 Hercules XI; EF384–400 Hercules XI; Mk. III: EF401–412 Hercules VI (EF404 converted to Mk. IV); EF413 Mk. I, Hercules XI; Mk. III: EF425–470 Hercules VI; EF488–518 Hercules VI (converted to Mk. IV: EF429; EF435; EF441; EF470; EF506).

Contract B.982828/39: Austin Motors, Birmingham
Mk. III, Hercules VI: EH875–909 (EH897 converted to Mk. IV); EH921–961 (EH950 converted to Mk. IV); EH977–996; EJ104–127 (EJ116 converted to Mk. IV).

Contract 2008/C4(c): Short, South Marston
Mk. III: LJ440–483 Hercules VI (but Hercules XVI: LJ469; LJ474; LJ475; LJ477 et seq.) (LJ461 and LJ475 converted to Mk. IV); LJ501–544 Hercules XVI (LJ512 converted to Mk. IV prototype; LJ530 to Mk. V prototype); LJ557–596 Hercules XVI (converted to Mk. IV: LJ536; LJ566; LJ569; LJ572; LJ575, became TS266; LJ576; LJ583; LJ588; LJ590; LJ591; LJ594; LJ596); LJ611–653 Hercules XVI; LJ667–670 Hercules XVI.

Contract 2009/C4(c): Short & Harland, Belfast
Mk. IV, Hercules XVI: LJ810–851; LJ864–899; LJ913–956; LJ969–999; LK114–156; LK169–211; LK226–240; LK270–313; LK326–370 (built as Mk. IV (Special Duty): LK125; LK131; LK139; LK145; LK192; LK194; LK198; LK200; LK204; LK206–210; LK232; LK238; LK278–279; LK285; LK309; LK327; LK329; LK359 (built as Mk. IV (Tropical, Special Duty): LK151; LK172–289; LK211; LK226–231; LK233–237; LK240; LK342–343).

Contract B982939/C36(a): Austin Motors, Birmingham
Mk. III, Hercules XVI unless stated: LK398–402; LK405–427 Hercules VI; LK428 Mk IV, Hercules VI; LK429–430 Hercules VI; LK431 Mk. IV, Hercules VI; LK432–435 Hercules VI; LK436–438; LK439–440 Mk. IV; LK441–458; LK459 Hercules VI; LK460–466; LK479–485; LK486 Mk IV; LK487–497; LK498 Mk. IV; LK499 Mk. IV; LK500 Mk. IV, converted to TS262; LK501–503; LK504 Mk. IV; LK506–509; LK510 Mk. IV; LK511; LK512 Mk. IV, converted to TS264; LK513 Mk. IV; LK514–521; LK535–541; LK542–543 Mk. IV; LK544; LK545–549 Mk. IV; LK550; LK551 Mk. IV; LK552; LK553–560 Mk. IV; LK561; LK562 Mk. IV, converted to TS265; LK563–565; LK566–567 Mk. IV; LK568–572; LK573 Mk. IV; LK574–576; LK589 Mk. IV; LK590–605; LK607–624 Mk. IV.

Contract 774677/38: Short & Harland, Belfast
MZ260–264 Mk. III, Hercules VI, replacing 5 bombed at Rochester.

Contract 2009/C4(c): Short & Harland, Belfast
Mk. V unless stated: PJ878–923; PJ935–959; PJ971–999; PK115–118; PK171–186; PK225–236 Mk. IV; PK237 Mk. IV (Special Duties).

Contract 2008/C4(c): Short, South Marston
PW255–266 Mk. IV, Hercules XVI.

Contract 2009/C4(c): Short & Harland, Belfast
Mk. IV, Hercules XVI: PW384; PW385 (Special Duties); PW386–425; PW438–465; cancelled aircraft: Mk. IV: PW466–479; PW493–525; PW539–580; PW593–599; Mk. V: PW600–637.

Appendix 2

Summary of Stirling Squadrons

No. 7 (Identity letters MG)
Reformed Leeming 2.8.40; Oakington 29.10.40–8.43 (detached Newmarket 27.3.41–27.4.41; satellite Bourn 6.41–7.42). Mk. I used 2.8.40–29.8.43; first operation 10.2.41; last operation 10.8.43; Mk. III used 24.3.43–29.8.43; first operation 4.4.43; last operation 10.8.43. To Pathfinder Force 8.42; first sorties 24.8.42.

No. 7 Conversion Flight (MG)
Formed Oakington 16.1.42: first operation 30.5.42; last operation 31.7.42. To Stradishall 4.10.42. Absorbed by 1657 C.U.

No. XV (LS, 'C' Flt. DJ)
Wyton 14.3.41–13.8.42 (satellites Alconbury; Warboys). (Detached Lossiemouth 28.1.42–7.2.42.) To Bourn 13.8.42–14.4.43; Mildenhall 14.4.43–12.43. Mk. I used 14.3.41–28.12.43; first operation 30.4.41; last operation 19.5.43. Mk. III used 31.12.42–27.12.43; first operation 14.2.43; last operation 22.12.43.

No. XV Conversion Flight (LS)
Alconbury 26.1.42–4.10.42.

No. 46 (XK)
Stoney Cross 7.1.45–4.46. Mk. IV (LK555 only) used 28.11.45–9.1.46. Mk. V used 1.45–12.4.46.

No. 51 (TB)
Leconfield 6.45–20.8.45; Stradishall 20.8.45–3.46. Mk. IV used 27.11.45–16.1.46. Mk. V used 1.6.45–25.7.46.

No. 75 (AA, 'C' Flight JN)
Mildenhall 10.42–1.11.42 (detached Oakington 15.10.42–12.42 for conversion); Newmarket 1.11.42–29.6.63; Mepal 29.6.43–4.44. Mk. I: first operation 20.11.42; last operation 12.8.43. Mk. III used 13.2.43–28.4.44: first operation 1.3.43; last operation 23.4.44.

No. 90 (WP, 'C' Flight XY)
Reformed Bottesford 1.12.42; Ridgewell 29.12.42; West Wickham (renamed Wratting Common) 31.5.43; Tuddenham 13.10.43–6.44. Mk. I used 1.12.42–30.11.43: first operation 8.1.43; last operation 24/25. 6.43. Mk. III used 10.2.43–24.6.44: first operation 13.2.43; last operation 7.6.44.

No. 101 Conversion Flight (SR)
Attached Oakington 4.42–10.42. Mk. I used.

No. 115 Conversion Flight (KO)
Oakington 8.12.42–31.12.42. Mk. I used.

No. 138 (NF)
Tempsford 6.44–3.45. Mk. IV used 11.6.44–10.3.45: first operation 28.8.44; last 4.3.45.

No. 148 (—)
Brindisi 8–1.44. Mk. IV used.

No. 149 (OJ, 'C' Flight TK)
Mildenhall 11.41–4.42 (detachments, and operations, from Lakenheath during this period); Lakenheath 4.42–15.5.44 (detached Tempsford 1–2.44); Methwold 15.5.44–9.44; Mk. I used 2.11.41–5.10.43: first operation 26.11.41; last operation 29.7.43. Mk. III used 16.2.43–13.9.44: first operation 28.2.43– last operation 8.9.44.

No. 149 Conversion Flight (OJ)
Lakenheath 21.1.42–2.10.42. Participated in a few operations.

No. 158 (DK)
Lissett 6.45; Stradishall 17.8.45; disbanded 1.1.46. Mk. IV used 27.11.45–1.46. Mk. V used 29.5.45–1.46.

No. 161 (MA)
Tempsford. Mk. IV used 5.9.44–12.7.45; first operation 8.9.44; last operation 2.5.45.

No. 171 (6Y)
Reformed North Creake 8.9.44 by raising 'C' Flight, 199 Squadron to squadron status. Mk. III used 8.9.44–31.3.45 (although re-equipment with Halifax III began 10.44): first operation 15.9.44; last operation 8.10.44.

No. 190 (G5, L9)
Reformed Leicester East 5.1.44; Fairford 25.3.44; Great Dunmow 14.10.44–13.5.45. Mk. IV used 5.1.44–31.5.45: first operation 31.3.44; last operation 25.4.44.

No. 196 (ZO on bombers, ZO and 7T on transports)
Witchford 8.43; Leicester East 18.11.43; Tarrant Rushton 7.1.44; Keevil 15.3.44; Wethersfield 9.10.44; Shepherd's Grove 29.1.45–3.46. Mk. III used 22.7.43–1.44: first operation 26.8.43; last operation 10.11.43. Mk. IV used 27.1.44–3.46: first operation 3.3.44. Mk. V used 30.1.46–27.3.46.

No. 199 (EX)
Lakenheath 20.6.43, using Wellingtons. Mk. III used 5.7.43–8.3.45: first operation 30.7.43; last operation 1.12.43. To North Creake and 100 Group 1.5.44 (transferred to 100 Group 1.44). First *Mandrel* operation 4.2.44; last operation 14.3.45.

No. 214 (BU, 'C' Flight (?) PX)
Stradishall 4.42; Chedburgh 1.10.42; Downham Market 1.12.43–17.1.44. Mk. I used 5.4.42–10.2.44: first operation 18.5.42; last operation 19.11.43. Mk. III used 10.2.43–16.7.44 (most given up 1.44): first operation 16.2.43; last operation 31.12.43.

No. 214 Conversion Flight (BU)
Formed Waterbeach 10.4.42; Stradishall 4.5.42; Waterbeach 7.8.42 and absorbed by 1651 C.U.

No. 218 (HA)
Marham 12.41; Downham Market 10.7.42; Methwold 4.8.44. Mk. I used 16.12.41–18.8.43: first operation 12.2.42; last operation 25.7.43. Mk. III used 6.2.43–17.8.44: first operation 13.2.43; last operation 2.8.44.

No. 218 Conversion Flight (HA)
Formed Marham 28.2.42; Lakenheath 3.3.42; Marham 3.42; Stradishall 2.10.42 and absorbed by 1657 C.U.

No. 242 (KY)
Stoney Cross 2.45; Merryfield 9.12.45. Mk. IV used 15.2.45–1.5.46. Mk. V used 15.2.45–1.5.46. Following training flights 27.2.45–4.45 ordered to equip with Yorks, used alongside Stirlings; Yorks withdrawn 7.45; Stirlings continued to operate until 10.11.45.

No. 295 (8Z 'A' Flight 8E 'B' Flight)
Harwell 6.44; Rivenhall 7.10.44; Tarrant Rushton 12.45; disbanded 15.1.46. Mk. IV used 14.6.44–1.46: first operation 27.7.44; last front line flying 1.46.

No. 299 (5G, X9)
Formed Stoney Cross 4.11.43; Keevil 28.2.44; Wethersfield 9.10.44; Shepherd's Grove 25.1.45; disbanded 30.3.46. Mk. IV used 7.1.44–29.3.46: first operation 5.4.44; last front line flying, mail carrying, 3.46. Mk. V 15.1.45–12.3.46; 2 aircraft only.

No. 513 (?)
Formed Witchford 15.9.43, disbanded 24.12.43. Mk. III used 21.10.43–24.12.43: no operational flying.

No. 525 (—)
Lynham, one Mk. IV (LJ512) 29.5.44–27.7.44.

No. 570 (V8, E7)
Harwell 6.44; Rivenhall 7.10.44; disbanded 8.1.46. Mk. IV used 30.6.44–1.46: first operation 27.7.44; last front line flying 8.1.46.

No. 620 (QS on bombers, QS and D4 on transports)
Formed Chedburgh 17.6.43. Mk. I used 19.6.43–29.7.43, no operational flying. Mk. III used 19.6.43–2.44: first operation 19.6.43; last operation 19.11.43. To Leicester East 23.11.43; Fairford 18.3.44; Great Dunmow 17.10.44. Mk. IV used 4.2.44–9.7.45: first operation 11.2.44; last front line flying 10.6.45.

No. 622 (GI)
Mildenhall 10.8.43; formed from 'C' Flight, XV Squadron. Mk. III used 10.8.43–9.1.44; first operation 10.8.43; last operation 20.12.43.

No. 623 (IC)
Downham Market 10.8.43; formed from 'C' Flight, 218 Squadron. Mk. III used 10.8.43–10.2.44: first operation 10.8.43; last operation 4.12.43.

No. 624 (—)
Blida, North Africa 6.44; disbanded 24.9.44. Mk. IV used 7.6.44–24.9.44: first operation 29.7.44; last operation 4.9.44.

Appendix 3

Summary of Stirling Training and Miscellaneous Units

No. 1651 Conversion Unit (individual letters only to early 1943, then unit letters BS, GG, QQ, YZ)
Formed Waterbeach 2.1.42 from 26 Conversion Flight. On to 3 Flight basis 1.12.42. To Wratting Common (73 Base) 21.11.43; Woolfox Lodge 10.11.44. Converted immediately to Lancasters. Mk. I used 1.42–6.11.44; Mk. III 8.7.43–5.1.45. First operation 30.5.42; last during night diversion sweeps *circa* 8.44. Examples: W7442:B; LJ570:QQ-K; N6048:BS-P.

No. 1652 Conversion Unit
Marston Moor 12.43–2.45. Used only 1 Mk. III: LJ464.

No. 1653 Conversion Unit (A3, H4)
Reformed Chedburgh 21.11.43. To North Luffenham 12.44. Stirling phased out. Used Mk. I 21.11.43–6.11.44; Mk. III 10.12.43–7.12.44. Examples: N3702:A3-J; BK763:H4-T.

No. 1654 Conversion Unit (JF, UG)
Wigsley. Used only 1 Mk. I:BK615 10.5.44–24.5.44; Mk. III 29.11.43–18.3.45. Examples: EE899:JF-B; LK399:UG-G.

No. 1657 Conversion Unit (AK, XT)
Formed 10.42 incorporating Conversion Flights at Oakington. Immediately to Stradishall. Became 1657 (H) Conversion Unit 4.44. Stirling phased out 12.44. Shepherd's Grove used as satellite in 1944. Used Mk. I 2.10.42–17.10.44; Mk. III 18.5.43–24.2.45. Examples: N3758:XT-K; R9192:AK-B; EE881:XT-T.

No. 1659 Conversion Unit
Topcliffe. Used only 2 Mk. Is: N6049 6–12.43 and R9289 8.43.

No. 1660 Conversion Unit (TV, YW)
Swinderby. Used Mk. III 27.11.43–3.3.45; phased out 12.44–2.45. Examples EF347:TV-A; LK400.

No. 1661 Conversion Unit (GP)
Winthorpe. Used Mk. III 9.11.43–28.2.45; phased out *circa* 12.44. Examples: EF289:GP-D; LK590:GP-L.

No. 1662 Conversion Unit
Blyton. Used only 2 Mk. IIIs: EF391 8.43 and LJ463 2–3.45.

No. 1663 Conversion Unit
Rufforth, used only 1 Mk. I: W7623 6–11.43.

No. 1665 Conversion Unit (NY, OG)
Formed Waterbeach 1.5.43. To Woolfox Lodge 5.6.43; Tilstock for airborne forces training 23.1.44; later amalgamated with 1332 H.T.C.U. Stirling phased out *circa* 3.46. Used Mk. I (NY) 20.5.43–26.4.45, Mk. III (OG) 17.5.43–25.2.46, Mk. IV 20.11.44–31.3.46. Examples: EF121:OG-B; EF210:NY-P; LJ502:NY-U.

No. 1332 Heavy Transport Conversion Unit (YY)
Formed Longtown 5.9.44; Nutt's Corner 7.10.44; Riccall 25.4.45. Trained crews for Nos. 46, 242, 246, 511 Squadrons. Used Mk. IV. Examples: LJ443; LK607; PW262.

Operational & Refresher Training Unit (individual letter only)
Matching. Gave flying practice in operational roles for aircrew. Stirling IV received 3.45; towed 14 Horsas during Operation *Varsity*. Re-equipped mainly with Halifax 4.45; retained a Flight of Stirlings. To Wethersfield 15.10.45. Became 1385 H.T.S.C.U. 1.4.46, at which time it gave up Stirlings. Examples: LK366, 3.45–3.46; LK367.

Central Navigational School
Shawbury. Used only LK508 5.44–5.45 and LK589 5.44–6.44. Both made transatlantic flights.

No. 1427 Flight
Afforded flying experience on Stirlings to A.T.A. and maintenance unit crews. Formed Thruxton 12.41; to Hullavington 18.5.42 (2 Stirlings). Marham early 8.42; Stradishall 2.10.43 and absorbed by 1657 C.U.

No. 1588 Heavy Freight Flight (previously 'K' Flight)
Formed Melton Mowbray 16.9.45. Transferred to 229 Group. Drigh Road 10.45; Santa Cruz 13.10.45. Used Mk. V 22.9.45–20.5.46 on UK–India run. Disbanded 20.5.46. Example: PK178.

No. 1589 Heavy Freight Flight (previously 'J' Flight)
Formed Melton Mowbray 28.9.45, to transport spares and groundcrews to maintain any type of aircraft on trunk routes. To Cairo West 10.10.45. 4 Stirlings, supplemented by 5 Dakotas 12.45. Disbanded 30.4.46. Used Mk. V 9.45–4.46. Examples: PK147, PK149.

Air Transport Trials & Development Unit
Netheravon. Used Mk. V LJ958 only 6–10.45.

Bombing Development Unit (Individual letter only)
Reformed Gransden Lodge 21.7.42. Tested bomber aircraft and their equipment. Tested Stirling I from 10.42 (eg. Mk. VIII autopilot, Mk. IIG H_2S, rotating astrodome, Mk. IX integrating sextant, etc.). Used BK 594 23.9.42–13.2.44; EF403 23.5.43–4.7.43. To Feltwell 6.4.43; Newmarket 13.9.43. Trials of *Monica*, flame damping, *Boozer*, *Fishpond*. R9239 used for photoelectric sun compass tests, BK594 for downward search for under defence in night bombers. On 1.10.43 commenced *H2S Fishpond* and Mk. II *Oboe*, and later *Gee-H*, training. Used R9277 5.8.43–14.11.43; R9280 24.4.43–4.2.44; EE968 22.8.43–14.12.43; EF405 26.5.43–4.7.43; EF466 5.8.43–18.9.43.

Pathfinder Force Navigational Training Unit (previously Gransden Navigational Training Unit) (individual letters only)
Formed 10.4.43; to Upwood and Warboys 11–19.6.43; to Warboys 5.3.44. Used R9252 13.4.43–22.12.43; R9269 6.6.43–26.7.43; R9277 9.5.43–26.7.43; EF404 28.5.43–7.43.

Royal Aircraft Establishment
Farnborough. Used for research and trials: L7605 28.10.41–28.10.42; N3635 28.5.41–
16.8.41 (R.A.T.O. trials, written off 1.1.42); N3639 2.8.42–(struck off charge) 30.11.44;
N3728 2.4.42–7.4.42; BK615 7.1.43–21.6.43 (H_2S tests); EF434 7.7.43–24.4.44.

Signal Flying Unit
Honiley. Used LK460 13.11.44–17.1.45; PJ956 28.2.46–18.8.47.

Telecommunications Flying Unit
Defford. Fitted out Stirlings for radio warfare, e.g. 7 Sqn., 199 Sqn.

Aeroplane & Armament Experimental Establishment
Boscombe Down. Used for trials: L7605 22.4.40–19.8.40, 4.1.41–28.4.41, 10.10.41–
23.10.41; N3635 21.5.40–28.5.41; N3637 6.40–20.12.40; N3639 4.1.42–7.42; N3643
1.8.40–3.1.41; N3657 (Mk. II) 17.7.41–11.9.41, 27.7.42–31.5.43; N3662 23.5.41 (undercarriage collapsed on landing, struck off charge 23.3.42); N3678 27.1.42–8.7.42; N3702
8.3.42–11.3.43; N6000 25.10.40–11.40, 11.3.41–25.6.41; N6001 23.11.40–(missing on test
flight) 30.6.41; N6008 15.2.41–10.10.41; R9309 14.7.42–(written off) 6.9.42; BF382
2.10.42–7.11.43; BK649 8.12.42–27.3.44; BK651 21.9.43–14.3.44; EF466 18.9.43–
10.10.43; EF503 (Mk. IV) 2.9.43–21.2.44; LJ571 31.8.44–15.12.44.

Airborne Forces Experimental Establishment
Ringway, Sherburn-in-Elmet and Beaulieu. Mks. I, III, IV used mainly for equipment and
performance trials. Examples: N3702 8.3.42–11.3.43; several Mk. IV 18.10.43–28.2.44.

Appendix 4

Serial Numbers of Stirlings Allocated to Squadrons

This listing is based upon individual aircraft cards held by the Ministry of Defence. Dates are of allocation—technically of movement, although precise dates often differed. Where known, individual aircraft letter follows the serial number. The target is given for missing aircraft. The following abbreviations are used:

EFA	categorised 'E' (write-off) after flying accident
EFB	categorised 'E' (write-off) after battle damage
EGA	categorised 'E' (write-off) ground accident
FA	flying accident ⎱ (may or may not result in repaired aircraft returning to
FB	battle damage ⎰ squadron)
FTR	failed to return (precise date often not known; night of operation is given thus: 26/27.6.43 = took off on 26th)
GA	ground accident (may or may not result in repaired aircraft returning to squadron)
nr	near
RIW	repairable in works
SOC	struck off charge
S.O.E.	Special Operations Executive
uc	undercarriage

Unless otherwise stated accidents are at squadron base.

---

7 Squadron

L7605 23.10.41–28.10.41 (loan); **N3636:A** 24.9.40–22.6.41, returned 28.10.41 as 3065M; **N3637:K, G** 20.12.40–7.8.41; **N3638** 10.9.40–13.6.41; **N3640** 2.8.40–EFA 29.9.40; **N3641:D** 12.8.40–6.10.41; **N3642:E** 29.8.40–16.4.41; **N3643** 3.1.41–EFB 24.3.41, Leiston from Rotterdam; **N3644:H** 25.9.40–10.4.41; **N3652** 5.2.41–18.2.42; **N3653** 24.2.41–FTR 3/4.3.41 Brest; **N3655** 30.3.41–12.5.42; **N3663** 30.3.41–12.5.42; **N3668:B** 3.9.41–4.1.42; **N3669:H** 25.8.41–31.12.41; **N3670** 9.9.42–14.9.42; **N3672:M, U** 30.9.41–21.1.42; **N3674** 15.10.41–15.10.41; **N3677** 12.10.41–FTR 7.11.41 Berlin; **N3679:D** 24.2.42–FB 12.4.42 Newmarket, RIW; **N3680:Y** 24.11.41–FTR 18.12.41 Brest; **N3700:A** 26.11.41–16.1.42 **N3701** 22.11.41–EFA 1.12.41 Oakington; **N3705:R, F** 31.1.42–FTR 16.8.42 Düsseldorf, nr Castle Loevestein, Borkum, repaired, flown in German markings; **N3706:S** 16.1.42–FTR 30.6.42 Bremen, ditched off Cromer; **N3708:E** 26.1.42–12.8.42; **N3709:S, K** 16.1.42–26.3.42 Essen, at Gendring, Holland; **N3710:M** 5.1.42–FTR 5/6.5.42 Hamburg; **N3716:A** 18.4.42–FTR 19/20.5.42 Mannheim; **N3727:G** 29.3.42–FTR 27.4.42 mining, Holland; **N3750** 15.4.42–FTR 1/2.6.42 Essen, in North Sea; **N3754:O** 14.5.42–SOC 30.6.42; **N3760:D** 30.5.42–RIW 24.6.42; **N3764:J** 19.6.42–FTR 9.11.42 Hamburg; **N6003** 22.1.41–26.12.41; **N6004** 24.3.41–25.4.41; **N6005** 3.3.41–

23.10.41; **N6006:G** 12.3.41–13.5.42; **N6007** 27.4.41–FTR 28.6.41 Bremen, daylight, in sea; **N6009** 14.3.41–21.4.41 crashed Stanbourne 'Q' Site; **N6010** 30.3.41–FTR 10/11.5.41 Berlin; **N6011** 26.3.41–FTR 9/10.4.41 Berlin; **N6012** 29.3.41–2.5.41 shot down by intruder, Dry Drayton; **N6013** 24.3.41–FTR 1.7.41 Borkum; **N6014** 31.3.41–FA 14.5.41; **N6017** 30.6.41–FTR 10.7.41 Bethune, off Hardelot; **N6019** 25.4.41–FA 9.5.41 Oakington; **N6020** 5.5.41–FTR 25/26.8.41 Karlsruhe, lightning strike; **N6023** 29.10.41–22.12.41; **N6032:T** 3.6.41–FA 27.6.41 belly landed Oakington; **N6033** 28.6.41–EFB 15.7.41 Hanover, in Northampton; **N6035** 4.7.41–FTR 25/26.7.41 Berlin, at Georee, Holland; **N6036:Q** 30.6.41–30.5.42; **N6037** 10.7.41–FB 19.9.41; **N6039** 22.7.41–28.5.42; **N6041** 2.8.41–EFB 15.8.41 Magdeburg, overshot Oakington; **N6042** 6.8.41–FB 15.8.41 Magdeburg, landed Oakington: **N6046** 25.8.41–FTR 7/8.9.41 Berlin; **N6047** 28.8.41–uc collapsed on arrival; **N6048** 1.9.41–25.3.42; **N6049** 4.9.41–16.10.41; **N6073:Y** 25.2.42–FTR 19/20.5.42 Mannheim; **N6074:G** 27.2.42–EFB 26.3.42 in sea off Barmouth; **N6074:A** 8.3.42–25.5.42; **N6085** 10.9.41–EFB 3.10.41 Brest, shot down by intruder at Bourn; **N6087:M** 21.9.41–EFB 18.11.41 Brest, engine fire, crashed Willingham; **N6089:L** 1.10.41–31.12.41; **N6090** 30.9.41–20.11.41; **N6091** 2.10.41–FTR 7/8.11.41 Berlin, by flak at Hekelingen, Holland; **N6094** 23.10.41–14.1.42; **N6095:K** 8.11.41–FB 18.12.41 Brest, at Oakington; **N6120** 26.11.41–EFB 17.1.42 Soesterburg, crashed base; **N6121** 24.12.41–31.12.41; **R9147** 23.7.42–1.8.42 overshot Honeybourne; **R9149:S** 17.8.42–FTR 9/10.3.43 Munich; **R9150:A, O** 29.7.42–FTR 29/30.11.42 Turin; **R9154:F** 29.7.42–FTR 6/7.8.42 Duisburg; **R9156:H, S** 17.8.42–27.8.43; **R9158** 13.8.42–EFA 29.8.42 overshot Manston; **R9169:Y** 1.9.42–FTR 9/10.11.42 Hamburg; **R9199:F, T** 1.10.42–FTR 8/9.4.43 Duisburg; **R9249** 14.3.43–29.7.43; **R9252** 13.12.42–13.4.43; **R9255:Q** 21.12.42–EFA Oakington; **R9257:C, E** 14.1.43–17.7.43; **R9258:K** 2.1.43–1.8.43; **R9259:J** 17.11.42–FTR 6/7.12.42 Mannheim; **R9260:O** 21.12.42–EFA 3.8.43 landing Oakington; **R9251:M** 31.12.42–FTR 20/21.4.43 Stettin, nr Slagelse, Denmark; **R9262:A** 22.11.42–FTR 21/22.12.42 Munich; **R9263:D** 29.12.42–FTR 1.5.43 Bocholt, at Akkerwoude, Holland; **R9253:L** 22.12.42–FTR 2/3.2.43 Cologne, at Hendrik-Ido-Ambacht, nr. Rotterdam, by 1./NJG 1, Germans' first recovery of H2S; **R9266:J** 18.2.43–FTR 21/22.6.43 Krefeld; **R9267:S** 24.12.42–EFA 14.6.43 at Hatley St. George, Cambs.; **R9270:S, Q** 22.12.42–FTR 8/9.3.43 Nuremberg; **R9272:W** 29.12.42–FTR 21/22.6.43 Krefeld; **R9273** 21.12.42–RIW 3.2.43; **R9275:Y** 31.12.42–FTR 10/11.4.43 Frankfurt; **R9277:P, T** 24.12.42–9.5.43; **R9278:E** 31.12.42–FTR 14/15.4.43 Stuttgart; **R9280:E** 18.2.43–FB/RIW 2.3.43 Berlin, crashed base; **R9281:V** 2.4.43–FTR 24/25.8.43 Elberfeld, in sea; **R9283:Q** 19.3.43–25.8.43; **R9284** 5.7.43–20.8.43; **R9286:C** 21.3.43–FTR 11/12.6.43 Münster, by flak off Den Helder; **R9288** 27.3.43–1.8.43; **R9289** 19.4.43–23.8.43; **R9297:P** 30.1.42–?; **R9298** 7.2.42–27.2.42; **R9300:L** 7.2.42–16.5.42; **R9301:Q** 5.2.42–?; **R9305:R** 16.2.42–FTR 28.3.42 Lübeck; **R9306** 29.3.42–RIW 29.6.42; **R9234** 5.5.52–FTR 16.6.42 Essen; **R9238:A** 23.5.42–FTR 26/27.7.42 Hamburg; **R9331:Y** 28.5.42–EFA 14.7.42 overshot Waterbeach; **W7430** 18.5.41–FTR 2/3.6.41 Berlin; **W7433** 18.6.41–FTR 29.9.41 Stettin, in sea; **W7434** 11.7.41–FA SOC 15.8.41 landing accident; **W7435** 19.7.41–10.8.41; **W7436:D** 23.7.41–FTR 18.12.41 Brest; **W7438** 8.8.41–FTR 28/29.8.41 Duisburg; **W7440** 30.8.41–6.5.42; **W7441:J** 8.9.41–FTR 29.9.41 Stettin, by Bf 110 from Flensburg, in Little Belt; **W7442:M** 15.9.41–FA RIW uc collapsed Waterbeach 30.1.42; **W7443** 20.9.41–9.41.41; **W7444:L** 25.9.41–EFB 31.10.41 Bremen, uc collapsed base; **W7445** 29.9.41–EFB 14.10.41 Düsseldorf, crashed Detling; **W7446:S** 1.10.41–EFA 18.11.41 overshot base; **W7448:Z** 14.10.41–31.12.41; **W7449:J** 19.10.41–20.6.42; **W7451:D** 8.11.41–18.3.42; **W7454:S** 8.11.41–16.1.42; **W7466:B** 5.1.42–FTR 28/29.3.42 Lübeck; **W7467** 7.1.42–EFA 16.1.42 collision with 56 O.T.U. Hurricane, Earith; **W7468:W** 10.1.42–FA RIW 10.6.42; **W7470:U** 17.1.42–26.9.42; **W7471:J** 30.1.42–FTR 6/7.6.42 Emden, nr Holwerd, Holland; **W7472:C** 16.2.42–FTR 20/21.6.42 Emden, at sea by II/NJG 2; **W7500:B** 14.2.42–FTR 1/2.6.42 Essen, in sea; **W7501:Z** 17.2.42–FTR 28/29.3.42 Lübeck;

W7517:Z 29.3.42–5.10.42; **W7520:S** 10.4.42–FTR 19/20.5.42 Mannheim; **W7522:G, K** 3.4.42–9.12.42; **W7529:R, W** 24.4.42–2.9.43; **W7533:G** 1.5.42–FTR 28/29.7.42 Hamburg; **W7579:Y** 16.7.42–FTR 13/14.8.42 Kiel Bay; **W7616:G** 31.7.42–FTR 25.8.42 Frankfurt; **W7617:A, K** 9.8.42–FTR 11.3.43 Stuttgart; **W7620:D, L** 15.8.42–FTR 6/7.11.42 mining, 'Nectarine'; **W7629:Z** 1.9.42–FTR 6/7.9.42 Duisburg; **W7630:M** 1.9.42–FTR 10/11.9.42 Düsseldorf, to night fighter at Stramproog, Holland; **W7632:N** 6.9.42–FTR 21/22.12.42 Munich; **BF316:M** 1.7.42–EFA 29.8.42 burnt, nr Stonehenge; **BF317:D, X** 2.7.42–FTR 27/28.3.43 Berlin; **BF321:S** 8.7.42–6.10.42; **BF335:E** 6.8.42–EFA 25.8.42; **BF336:Z** 5.8.42–FTR 24/25.8.42 Frankfurt; **BF339:C, F, L** 12.8.42–28.5.43; **BF340:A** 15.8.42–3.10.42; **BF342:E** 1.9.42–3.10.42; **BF345:H** ?.9.42–16.11.42; **BF358:C** 8.9.42–FTR 22.12.42 Munich; **BF378:W** 17.9.42–30.12.42; **BF379:D** 22.9.42–FTR 11/12.12.42 Turin; **BF387: U** 1.10.42–FTR 10/11.11.42 Hamburg; **BF390:A** 1.10.42–EFB 21.10.42 British guns off Yarmouth; **BF501:N** 31.3.43–28.4.43; **BF526** 23.4.43–28.5.43; **BF532** 21.4.43–21.5.43; **BK592: M, F** 1.10.42–FTR 8/9.3.43 Nuremberg, fuel short, off Dungeness; **BK621:N** 3.11.42–29.5.43; **BK709:F** 29.3.43–FTR 14/15.4.43 Stuttgart; **BK723:E** 15.4.43–1.7.43; **BK724:I** 24.3.43–29.5.43; **BK760:X** 27.3.43–FTR 10/11.4.43 Frankfurt; **BK761** 24.3.43–28.4.43; **BK769:G** 3.4.43–FTR 14/15.4.43 Stuttgart; **BK773:T** 6.4.43–FTR 4/5.5.43 Dortmund, in Ijsselmeer, south of Einkhuisen; **BK779** 4.4.43–15.4.43; **EF361:B** 6.4.43–FTR 25/26.5.43 Dortmund; **EF363:G2** 10.4.43–23.8.43; **EF364:X** 19.4.43–FTR 29/30.7.43; **EF366: L** 6.4.43–FTR 21/22.6.43 Krefeld; **EF368:A** 13.4.43–29.8.43; **EF369:Z** 13.4.43–EFB 28.7.43 on finals Oakington; **EF384** 9.4.43–25.5.43; **EF386** 13.4.43–16.5.43; **EF387:D** 19.4.43–FTR 21/22.6.43 Krefeld, by night fighter nr Gilze Rijen; **EF388:M** 7.5.43–22.8.43; **EF390:T** 21.4.43–1.8.43; **EF392:N2** 9.3.43–FTR 25.6.43 Elberfeld; **EF393:W** 18.5.43–23.8.43; **EF401** 3.5.43–16.6.43; **EF402:Y** 18.5.43–29.8.43; **EF406:U** 30.5.43–25.8.43.

XV Squadron

N3638 13.6.41–22.6.41; **N3642** 16.4.41–6.10.41; **N3644** 10.4.41–FA 21.5.41 uc collapsed; **N3646** ?.4.41–FTR 10/11.4.41 Berlin, at Opmeer, Holland; **N3656:H** 2.5.41–EFB 13.8.41 at Honington; **N3658** 13.5.41–FTR 7/8.8.41 Essen, at Overasse, Holland, first recovered by enemy intact; **N3659:N** 6.6.41–FTR 12.8.41 Berlin; **N3660:M** 19.6.41–FA 28.9.41 overshot Warboys; **N3665:B, S** 4.7.41–FTR 18.12.41 Brest; **N3667:T** 8.8.41–EFB 12.10.41 Nuremberg, overshot base; **N3668** 4.1.42–FA 8.1.42 uc collapsed Alconbury; **N3669:H** 16.5.42–?.?.43, became 3637M; **N3670:** 7.9.41–FA 24.2.42; **N3673:D** 30.9.41–FTR 9.3.42 by flak at Apeldoorn; **N3674** 2.6.42–8.7.42; **N3675:S** 2.10.41–22.1.42; **N3676:U** 26.10.41–8.4.42; **N3682** 18.11.41–22.8.42; **N3703:G** 1.4.42–EFB 11.4.42 Essen, crashed Godmanchester; **N3704:A** 1.12.41–16.10.42; **N3707:M** 25.4.42–FA 28.8.42 belly landed; **N3728:T** 7.4.42–FTR 2/3.6.42 Essen, by II/NJG 2 in Ijsselmeer; **N3756:C** 23.5.42–EFA 12.6.42 nr Sudbury; **N3757:G** ?.5.42–FTR 29/30.6.42 Bremen; **N3758:V** 26.5.42–FA RIW 14.9.42; **N3759:Q** 30.5.42–FTR 19.9.42 mining; **N6004:F** 25.4.41–11.6.41; **N6007** 16.4.41–27.4.41; **N6015:A** 14.4.41–FTR 30.6.41 Hamburg; **N6016:G** 17.5.41–FTR 30.8.41 Hamburg; **N6018:C** 16.4.41–FTR 19.7.41 nr Dunkirk; **N6021:D** 7.5.41–FTR 15.9.41 Hamburg; **N6024:K** 22.5.41–11.6.41; **N6029:G, K** 15.6.41–FTR 25/26.7.41 Berlin; **N6030:F** 25.6.41–FTR 18.7.41 in sea; **N6038:R** 14.7.41–FTR 23.7.41 La Rochelle, in sea 50 miles from Milford Haven; **N6040:C** 27.7.41–FA 25.10.41 uc collapsed; **N6043:G** 10.8.41–EFB 14.8.41 crashed Ramsey, Hunts.; **N6044:O, E** 16.8.41–27.3.42; **N6045:U** 22.8.41–FTR 7.9.41 Brest; **N6065:D** 2.10.41–8.7.42; **N6067:E** 9.2.42–EFB 26.2.42 Wilhelmshaven, fuel short, crashed Beck Lodge Farm, Mildenhall; **N6076:D** 12.3.42–FA 15.4.42 Newmarket; **N6086:F** ('MacRobert's Reply') 15.9.41–FA RIW 19.3.42; **N6088:G, Q, X** 25.9.41–

22.1.42; **N6092** 6.10.41–5.4.42; **N6093:P, C** 15.10.41–FB 23.1.42 Münster, shot up, crash landed; **N6094** 14.1.42–EFB 25.3.42 Kiel, crashed Mildenhall; **N6097:C** 1.11.41–EFB 15.11.41 exploded taking off Wyton; **N6098:G** 1.11.41–EGA 29.1.42 burnt refuelling, Lossiemouth; **R9144:Q, R** 2.7.42–8.12.42 mining, Baltic, belly landed Newmarket; **R9151:O** 23.7.42–FA 18.8.42; **R9153:U** 31.7.42–FTR 28/29.8.42 Nuremberg; **R9168:T** 26.8.42–FTR 16/17.11.42 Turin, nr Aalsmeer, Holland, to III/NJG 1; **R9192:E** 24.9.42–RIW 29.11.43; **R9193:S** 24.9.42–5.10.43; **R9195:P** 6.11.42–RIW 18.12.42; **R9201:U** 1.10.42–FTR 6/7.11.42 mining, Gironde mouth; **R9268:R, F** 6.12.42–5.6.43; **R9274:B** 29.12.42–FTR 3/4.2.43 Hamburg, at Renkum, Holland; **R9279:J** 8.1.43–FTR 26/27.2.43 Cologne; **R9302:F** 5.2.42–5.5.42; **R9303:P** 11.2.42–5.4.42; **R9304:U** 15.2.42–5.4.42; **R9308:P** 1.4.42–FA 20.7.42 overshot Waterbeach; **R9312:C** 4.4.42–FTR 16/17.10.42 mining; **R9314** 21.4.42–12.5.42; **R9315:O** 14.4.42–17.11.42; **R9318:B, J** 24.4.42–FTR 14/15.9.42 Wilhelmshaven; **R9351:R** 3.6.42–FTR 17/18.9.42 mining, Great Belt, lost there; **R9352:T** 4.6.42–FTR 19/20.6.42 Emden; **R9353:B** 5.6.42–FA RIW 30.9.42; **W7426** 9.8.41–26.9.41; **W7427** 16.7.41–9.10.41; **W7428:F** 20.6.41–FTR 18.12.41 Brest; **W7429:J** 31.5.41–FB 29.10.41 flak damage Rotterdam, uc collapsed landing; **W7431:A** 10.7.41–EFB 21.10.41 Bremen, crashed Catsholme Farm, Methwold; **W7432** 4.7.41–20.7.41, 12.12.41–16.1.42; **W7435:W** 10.8.41–22.8.41 crashed Alconbury taking off for Magdeburg 14.8.41; **W7437:L** 30.7.41–FTR Magdeburg; **W7439:N** 22.8.41–15.12.41; **W7443:W, J** 31.12.41–21.1.42; **W7447** 16.10.41–8.12.41; **W7448:E, M** 4.1.42–27.2.42; **W7450:A** 23.10.41–FB 25.11.41 collided with Chance light landing; **W7463:B** 31.12.41–2.6.42; **W7464:H** ?.1.42–4.4.42; **W7504:A** 13.3.42–EFA 27.7.42 overshot; **W7505:V** 13.3.42–16.5.42; **W7511:T** 25.3.42–EFA 8.4.42 swung taking off; **W7513:R** 27.3.41–2.6.42; **W7514:B** 28.3.42–FTR 25/26.4.42 Rostock, crashed Kravlund, Denmark; **W7515:Q** 27.3.42–FTR 29.5.42 Gennevilliers; **W7516:S** 29.3.42–FA RIW 16.9.42; **W7518:C, U, G** 2.4.42–FTR 1/2.3.43 Berlin, crashed St. Maartensdijk, night fighter action; **W7519:O** 3.4.42–FTR 13.4.42 mining, Wangerooge; **W7523:C** 12.4.42–EFA 19.5.42 hit trees landing Graveley; **W7524:D** 12.2.42–FTR 16/17.7.42 Lübeck, in sea S.E. Esbjerg; **W7528:G** 21.4.42–FTR 8.5.42 Warnemünde; **W7531:F** 2.5.42–FTR 17.5.42 mining, Baltic, crashed at Galsklint, Denmark, to flak; **W7561:F** 21.5.42–FA RIW 9.7.42; **W7578:G** 7.7.42–FTR 25/26.7.42 Duisburg to III/NJG 1 at Horst, Holland; **W7578:A** 11.8.42–FTR 20.9.42 Munich; **W7585:T, U** 10.7.42–EFA 29.12.42 crashed approaching Bassingbourn; **W7588:J** 29.7.42–EFA 29.7.42 burnt Coltishall; **W7611:F** 24.7.42–FTR 2/3.9.42 Karlsruhe, crashed W. of the Hague; **W7624:E** 23.8.42–FTR 28.8.42 Kassel; **W7633:P** 9.9.42–FA RIW 22.11.42 Genoa, belly landed Bradwell Bay; **W7634:G** 9.9.42–FTR 1/3.10.42 Lübeck; **W7635:V** 12.9.42–FTR 8/9.12.42 mining, Baltic, in N. Sea; **BF327:D** 26.7.42–FTR 28.8.42 Kassel; **BF329:A** 28.7.42–FTR 12/13.8.42 Mainz; **BF347:J** 27.8.42–EFB 10/11.9.42 Düsseldorf, crashed West Malling; **BF350:O** 1.9.42–FA RIW 31.1.43; **BF352:U** 2.9.42–EFB 9.9.42 mining, uc collapsed Waterbeach; **BF355:F** 4.9.42–12.5.43; **BF356** 4.9.42–EFA 17.12.42 overshot Bourn; **BF376:N** 15.1.43–11.3.43; **BF378:T** 30.12.42–FTR 18/19.2.43 Wilhelmshaven in sea off Frisians; **BF380:B** 23.9.42–EFB 18.12.42 mining, undershot Bourn; **BF384** 26.9.42–E 18.11.42; **BF386:Q** 27.9.42–EFA 29.10.42, crashed, possibly after storm damage, S.W. of Downham Market; **BF411:A** 29.11.42–FTR 18/19.2.43 Wilhelmshaven; **BF412** 28.11.42–13.3.43; **BF436:E** 2.12.42–11.3.43; **BF439:D** 29.12.42–28.12.43; **BF448:T** 29.12.42–FTR 15.2.43 Cologne; **BF457:B** 24.1.43–FTR 19.2.43 Wilhelmshaven; **BF450:C, F** 11.5.43–FTR 10/11.8.43 Nuremberg; **BF465** 28.2.43–2.3.43; **BF469** 28.2.43–5.3.43; **BF470:G** 27.2.43–FTR 3/4.10.43 Kassel; **BF474:H** 15.3.43–FTR 16/17.4.43 Mannheim; **BF475:T** 4.3.43–FTR 10/11.4.43 Frankfurt; **BF476:P** 4.3.43–FTR 20.4.43 Rostock; **BF482:R** 15.5.43–FTR 24/25.5.43 Dortmund; **BF521:P** 11.5.43–10.8.43; **BF533:K** 23.4.43–11.5.43; **BF534:L** 3.4.43–FTR 26.5.43 Düsseldorf; **BF569:O, V** 25.5.43–FTR 15/16.9.43 Montluçon; **BF571:U** 13.5.43–FTR 11/12.6.43 Düsseldorf, in sea, Ameland; **BF579:B** 29.5.43–FTR 4.7.43 Cologne; **BK595:A** 25.9.43–FTR 18/19.11.42 Turin; **BK611:U** 24.12.42–FTR 25/26.5.43 Düsseldorf; **BK648:J** 31.12.42–FTR 3/4.7.43 Cologne; **BK652:V** 3.1.43–10.8.43; **BK654:W** 20.1.43–4.12.43; **BK656:A** 26.1.43–FTR 23.6.43 Mülheim, shot down by III/NJG 1 nr Deelen; **BK657:C** 25.1.43–FTR 27.4.43 shot down by fighter, Portengen, Holland; **BK658:K** 21.1.43–FTR 5.5.43 Dortmund; **BK667:H** 21.1.43–EFB 23.3.43 crashed Clyffe Pypard, from St. Nazaire; **BK691:F** 10.2.43–FTR 17.4.43 Mannheim; **BK695:O, C** 28.2.43–FTR 28/29.6.43 Cologne; **BK695:X** 28.2.43–RIW 30.4.43; **BK697:P** 28.2.43–FTR 9.3.43 Nuremberg; **BK699:E, M** 1.3.43–FTR 25/26.6.43 Gelsenkirchen, crashed Harlingen, Holland; **BK704:Z** 2.3.43–FTR 29.3.43 Berlin; **BK707:O, G** 10.9.43–FTR 18.11.43 Mannheim; **BK719:B** 22.4.43–13.12.43; **BK764:R** 9.5.43–FTR 30/31.8.43 München-Gladbach; **BK766:T** 27.5.43–10.8.43; **BK774:T, K** 17.4.43–FTR 7.9.43 mining, Frisians; **BK782:X** 13.4.43–FTR 4/5.5.43 Dortmund, shot down by fighter Midwolde, Holland; **BK805:U** 12.6.43–FTR 25/25.7.43 Hamburg; **BK814:V** 30.4.43–FTR 21/22.6.43 Krefeld; **BK818:R** 7.5.43–4.12.43; **EE907:C** 23.6.43–8.12.43; **EE908:V** 23.6.43–FTR17/18.8.43 Peenemünde; **EE910** 28.6.43–19.7.43; **EE912:U** 29.6.43–FTR 31.8.43 Berlin; **EE913** 5.7.43–19.7.43; **EE940:Y** 19.7.43–FTR 27.9.43 Hanover; **EE954:J** 19.7.43–FTR 4.10.43 Frankfurt; **EE974:O** 13.8.43–23.12.43; **EF131** 30.8.43–EFA 19.9.43 overshot Mildenhall; **EF133:U** 24.9.43–23.12.43; **EF161:Y** 27.9.43–23.12.43; **EF177:S** 8.10.43–8.12.43; **EF183:D** 29.9.43–9.1.44; **EF186:W** 18.10.43–8.12.43; **EF195** 5.10.43–EFA 15.10.43; **EF232** 26.11.43–13.12.43; **EF333:X** 16.2.43–FTR 1/2.3.43 Berlin, in sea, Ameland; **EF339:Y** 7.2.43–FA 30.7.43 belly landed; **EF345:M** 26.2.43–FTR 4/5.5.43 Dortmund; **EF347:T** 28.2.43–FTR 1/2.3.43 Berlin, crashed, Mantgum, Holland; **EF348:N** 2.3.43–FTR 23.6.43 Mülheim; **EF351:L** 27.2.43–10.8.43; **EF354:Q, C** 1.3.43–6.6.43; **EF355:A** 8.3.43–21.6.43; **EF359:B** 6.3.43–FTR 8/9.4.43 Duisburg; **EF391:M, N** 18.4.43–10.8.43; **EF399:Y** 21.5.43–6.6.43; **EF411** 31.5.43–14.6.43; **EF412** 27.5.43–14.6.43; **EF427:A** 31.5.43–FTR 30/31.7.43 Remscheid; **EF428:N** 31.5.43–FTR 30/31.7.43 Remscheid; **EF453** 5.7.43–24.7.43; **EF459:S** 3.8.43–4.10.43; **EF460:B** 19.7.43–10.12.43; **EF461** 7.8.43–14.8.43; **EF490:B** 1.8.43–10.8.43; **EF518:P** 23.9.43–8.12.43; **EH875:S** 8.5.43–FTR 23/24.8.43 Berlin; **EH879** 9.5.43–22.5.43; **EH888:Z** 25.5.43–FTR 28/29.6.43 Cologne, crashed at Heeschwijk, Holland; **EH890:U** 29.5.43–EFA 25.6.43; **EH893:J** 24.6.43–FTR 27/28.7.43 Hamburg; **EH929:F** 28.7.43–8.12.43; **EH930:A** 28.7.43–27.12.43; **EH940:H, U** 19.8.43–23.12.43; **EH941:D** 1.9.43–FTR 23.9.43 Mannheim; **EH980** 12.10.43–2.12.43; **EH985:O** 13.8.43–FTR 27/28.8.43 Nuremberg; **EH990:K** 24.8.43–FTR 4.10.43 Frankfurt; **LJ451:K** 2.10.43–13.12.43; **LJ453** 21.10.43–27.1.44; **LJ462** 21.10.43–9.11.43; **LJ464** 21.10.43–2.12.43; **MZ264: DJ-A** 24.5.43–18.8.43.

46 Squadron

PJ884 18.3.45–12.4.46; **PJ886** 5.2.46–8.3.46; **PJ888** ?.1.45–7.10.45; **PJ889** 15.2.46–21.3.46; **PJ890** 12.1.45–EGA 29.4.45 port wing burnt at 17 S.P. Tripoli; **PJ891** 12.1.45–FA 10.6.45 uc collapsed landing Shaibah; **PJ892** 16.1.45–20.12.45; **PJ893** 16.1.45–27.11.45; **PJ894** 22.1.45–20.8.45, 14.2.46–14.3.46; **PJ895** 22.1.45–21.3.46; **PJ896** 23.1.45–3.12.45; **PJ897** 2.1.45–23.9.45, 17.1.46–7.3.46; **PJ898** 2.1.45–22.12.45; **PJ899** 5.2.45–31.3.46; **PJ900** 9.2.45–4.7.45, 28.1.46–15.3.46; **PJ901** 5.2.45–EFA 9.4.45 uc collapsed landing 8. F.U. Mauripur; **PJ903** 15.2.45–28.3.46; **PJ904** ?.9.45–EFA 23.11.45 hit buildings landing Lyneham; **PJ910** 7.12.45–12.2.46; **PJ914** 31.12.45–20.3.46; **PJ916** 15.10.45–14.3.46; **PJ917** 3.12.45–29.5.45, 3.12.45–20.3.46; **PJ919** 1.3.45–12.12.45; **PJ920** 1.3.45–13.4.45; **PJ921** 1.3.45–FA 25.4.45 uc collapsed landing Mauripur; **PJ922** 31.1.46–19.3.46; **PJ923** 6.3.45–FA 6.5.45 belly landed Lyneham; 12.6.45–1.3.46; **PJ935** 6.3.45–1.3.46; **PJ936** 8.3.45–?.12.45; **PJ937** 8.3.45–4.12.45, 5.2.46–?.4.46; **PJ938** 8.3.45–

8.1.46; **PJ941** 12.12.45–25.3.46; **PJ942** 4.10.45–15.12.45; **PJ943** ?.4.45–7.10.45; **PJ944** 15.12.45–25.3.46; **PJ951** ?.8.45–17.10.45, 3.46; **PJ954** 9.2.46–20.3.46; **PJ957** 31.12.45–15.3.46; **PJ971** 12.2.46–29.3.46; **PJ973** 8.1.46–29.3.46; **PJ988** 3.12.45–1.4.46; **PJ991** 3.12.45–20.12.45; **PJ995** ?.12.45–21.3.46; **PJ997** 3.12.45–31.12.45; **PJ999** 31.12.45–8.3.46; **PK117** 28.1.46–12.4.46; **PK124** 28.1.46–22.3.46; **PK129** 31.7.45–8.2.46; **PK130** ?.7.45–EFA 31.12.45 uc collapsed taking off Lyneham; **PK135** 3.12.45–8.2.46; **PK137** 5.2.46–1.3.46; **PK141** 12.2.46–22.2.46; **PK142** 4.12.45–21.3.46; **PK152** 3.12.45–28.3.46; **PK153** 3.12.45–8.2.46; **PK155** 17.12.45–15.3.46; **PK156** 27.12.45–1.4.46; **PK158** 27.12.45–EFA 7.2.46; **PK171** 27.12.45–20.3.46; **PK173** 26.10.45–EFA 13.11.45 uc collapsed taking off from St. Thomas's Mount; **PK184** 5.2.46–25.3.46; **LK555** 28.11.45–9.1.46.

51 Squadron

PJ879 5.8.45–25.3.46; **PJ881** 2.2.46–5.4.46; **PJ883** 2.6.45–1.9.45; **PJ885** 2.6.45–30.1.46; **PJ897** ?.10.45–16.11.45; **PJ915** 2.2.46–25.3.46; **PJ916** 25.10.45–15.10.45; **PJ939** 5.8.45–7.2.46; **PJ940** 8.10.45–2.1.46; **PJ945** 27.6.45–15.1.46; **PJ953** 7.6.45–EFA 19.10.45 swung taking off from Castel Benito; **PJ955** 24.6.45–1.2.46; **PJ956** 31.5.45–14.2.46; **PJ973** 2.6.45–27.11.45; **PJ974** 1.6.45–30.1.46; **PJ980** 2.6.45–27.12.45; **PJ982** 2.2.46–21.6.46; **PJ983** 25.4.45–EGA 21.8.45 burnt out Stradishall; **PJ984** 21.2.46–4.4.46; **PJ985** 21.2.46–4.4.46; **PJ992** 8.10.45–25.7.46; **PJ998** 2.2.46–4.4.46; **PK115** 24.6.45–10.9.45; **PK119** 28.6.45–15.1.46; **PK120** 1.7.45–EFA 31.10.45 crashed Abidjan, Iran; **PK121** 1.7.45–20.2.46; **PK123** 2.2.46–21.3.46; **PK125** 8.7.45–15.1.46; **PK126** 8.7.45–30.1.46; **PK132** 5.8.45–26.3.46; **PK133** 5.8.45–12.4.46; **PK146** 2.2.46–8.4.46; **PK148** 5.10.45–8.4.46; **PK150** 11.10.45–12.10.45; **PK155** 26.10.45–27.12.45; **PK174** 2.11.45–8.4.46; **PK175** 14.11.45–9.4.46; **PK176** 17.11.45–7.4.46; **PK177** 28.11.45–EFA 31.12.45 uc collapsed Stradishall; **PK178** 15.11.45–18.12.45; **PK179** 1.12.45–8.4.46; **LJ652** 6.12.45–16.1.46; **LK144** 27.11.45–14.1.46.

75 Squadron

N3704 16.10.42–10.12.42; **N6123:Q** 15.1.43–FTR 4.3.43 mining, Frisians; **R9200:S** 23.2.43–FA 21.4.43 Jurby, Isle of Man; **R9243:C** 21.10.42–23.2.43; **R9245** 25.10.43–EFB 16.12.42 hit Devil's Dyke, Newmarket; **R9246** 31.10.42–SOC 24.11.42; **R9247** 21.10.42–FTR 17/18.12.42 Fallersleben; **R9248** 7.11.42–FTR 23/24.1.43 Lorient; **R9250:C** 2.11.42–FTR 3/4.2.43 Hamburg, crashed Elst, Holland; **R9290:Y** 28.1.43–13/14.2.43 Lorient; **W7455** 29.1.43–1.2.43; **W7469** 28.1.43–FTR 16/17.4.43 Ludwigshafen; **W7513:G** 4.3.43–FTR 28/29.4.43 mining Kiel Bay; **BF377:J** 14.4.43–25.6.43; **BF396** 23.10.42–FTR 18.12.42 Fallersleben; **BF397** 23.10.42–FA RIW 23.1.43 overshot Newmarket; **BF398:P, F** 24.10.42–EFA 17.5.43 crashed, engine trouble, Crimley Hall Farm, Talke, Staffs.; **BF399:O** 7.11.42–EFA 28.11.42 dived to avoid other aircraft, crashed at Trinity Hall Farm, Cambridge; **BF400** 30.10.42–FTR 17/18.12.42 Fallersleben; **EF412:F, Y** 13.3.43–18.6.43; **BF434:X** 13.4.43–28.7.43; **BF437:L** 24.1.43–FTR 8/9.3.43 Nuremberg; **BF443:V** 2.2.43–17.8.43; **BF451:Z** 13.2.43–FTR 16/17.4.43 Ludwigshafen; **BF455:Y** 13.2.43–EFB 10/11.4.43 in the sea off Shoreham; **BF456:J** 14.3.43–FTR 10.4.43 Frankfurt; **BF458:A** 2.5.43–FTR 30/31.7.43 Remscheid; **BF459:E** 2.5.43–FTR 23.9.43 Mannheim; **BF461:B** 2.5.43–FTR 4.11.43 mining, Baltic, shot down by NJG 3, Kallerup, Denmark; **BF465:K** 2.3.43–FTR 23/24.8.43 Berlin; **BF467:W** 15.3.43–FTR 28/29.4.43 mining, Kiel Bay, off Kappel, Denmark; **BF473** 2.9.43–14.3.44; **BF506** 6.4.43–FTR 21.4.43 Rostock; **BF513** 8.4.43–FTR 14.4.43 Stuttgart; **BF516** 11.4.43–?.4.43;

BF517 6.4.43–FA RIW 27.4.43; **BF518:E** 11.4.43–FA 31.8.43 uc damage; **BF573** 6.5.43–20.5.43; **BF575:H** 17.5.43–FA RIW, overshot Market Harborough; **BF577:M** 26.5.43–FTR 3.8.43 Hamburg; **BK602:R** 21.12.42–FTR 25/26.5.43 Düsseldorf, in the sea; **BK608:T** 21.10.42–EFB 28.11.42 undershot Stradishall; **BK609** 16.3.43–FTR 6/7.8.43 mining, Gironde; **BK615** 28.11.42–7.1.43; **BK617:D** 24.10.42–EFB 5.2.43 in sea off Cromer, burnt; **BK618** 24.10.42–FTR 2/3.12.42 Frankfurt; **BK619:X, O** 3.11.42–14.10.43; **BK620** 31.10.42–FTR 17/18.12.42 Fallersleben; **BK624:A** 15.1.43–25.6.43; **BK646:N** 10.2.43–FTR 15.6.43 mining, Gironde; **BK647** 9.2.43–FA 3.3.43 crashed taking off from Newmarket; **BK664:M** 15.3.43–EFB 17.4.43 throttle trouble, crashed into hangar; **BK695:X** 26.2.43–RIW 30.4.43, 26.9.43–17.3.44; **BK721:Z** 2.5.43–EFB 12.5.43 hit obstruction taking off from Newmarket; **BK768:L** 21.5.43–FTR 25/26.6.43 Gelsenkirchen; **BK770** 4.4.43–EFA 9.4.43 dived in nr Great Massingham, Norfolk; **BK776:B** 8.4.43–FTR 29/30.5.43 Wuppertal, shot down nr Roermond; **BK777:U** 8.4.43–3.5.43; **BK778:U** 4.4.43–4/5.11.43 mining, Baltic, crashed Berstedgaard, Fernen Belt; **BK807** 21.4.43–FTR 28/29.4.43 mining, Baltic; **BK908:T** 2.5.43–EFA 8.9.43 hit fuel bowser taking off Mepal; **BK810:G** 2.5.43–FTR 23.6.43?; **BK817** 2.5.43–FTR 11/12.6.43 Düsseldorf; **EE878:F, P** 31.5.43–FTR 31.8.43 Berlin; **EE881** 16.6.43–6.9.43; **EE886** 16.6.43–EFA 14.7.43 uc collapsed, burnt; **EE890:L** 29.6.43–FTR 24.7.43 Hamburg; **EE891:Q** 20.6.43–FTR 15/16.8.43 mining, Gironde; **EE892:F** 9.6.43–FTR 26/27.7.43 Hamburg; **EE893:N** 16.6.43–FTR 5/6.9.43 Mannheim; **EE897:G** 29.6.43–FTR 4.11.43 mining, Baltic; **EE898:D** 15.6.43–EFA 16.12.43 swung taking off; **EE915:X** 30.6.43–FTR 30/31.7.43 Remscheid; **EE918** 11.7.43–FTR 1.9.43 Berlin; **EE938:X** 16.7.43–FTR 23/24.8.43 Berlin; **EE955** 18.8.43–FTR 27/28.8.43 Nuremberg; **EE958** 11.8.43–22.10.43, 25.11.43–3.5.44; **EF130** 27.8.43–FTR 4/5.10.43 Frankfurt; **EF135** 2.9.43–FB 28.9.43 uc collapsed; **EF137:E** 2.9.43–FTR 23/24.4.44 mining, Kiel Bay, crashed Vemmenaes, Denmark; **EF142** 24.9.43–EFB 24.10.43 crashed 1½ miles from Mepal; **EF148** 15.9.43–FTR 22.11.43 Berlin; **EF152** 15.9.43–29.6.44; **EF163** 26.9.43–EFB 17.12.43, Biddington Farm, Sutton, crashed, mine hung up; **EF181** 24.9.43–25.3.44; **EF200** 21.10.43–7.11.43; **EF201** 21.10.43–4.11.43; **EF205** 21.10.43–3.11.43; **EF206** 22.10.43–4.11.43; **EF207** 23.10.43–4.5.44; **EF211** 22.10.43–3.11.43; **EF215** 1.2.44–FTR 5.3.44 S.O.E. op.; **EF217** 9.11.43–31.3.44; **EF251** 21.12.43–21.3.44; **EF254** 1.1.44–30.3.44; **EF327** 29.1.43–20.2.43; **EF332** 9.5.43–18.5.43; **EF337** 1.2.43–2.3.43; **EF340** 24.3.43–FTR 5/6.5.43 mining, Frisians; **EF398** 5.5.43–FTR 29/30.5.43 Wuppertal; **EF400** 23.5.43–30.6.43; **EF408:P** 21.5.43–FTR 22/23.6.43 Mannheim, in Ijsselmeer off Oosterland; **EF435:J** 12.6.43–24.8.43; **EF436** 12.6.43–FTR 5/6.7.43 mining, Frisians; **EF440** 8.7.43–19.7.43; **EF454:A** 16.7.43–6.4.44; **EF456** 14.7.43–26.7.43; **EF458** 19.7.43–FTR 23/24.9.43 Mannheim; **EF462** 22.7.43–24.6.44; **EF465:H** 16.7.43–26.10.43; **EF491** 16.8.43–EFB 31.8.43 Berlin, shot up; **EF501** 16.8.43–FTR 31.8.43 Berlin; **EF507:P** 27.8.43–FA RIW 1.3.44 overshot Graveley; **EF512:A** 11.9.43–FB 29.1.44; **EF513:E** 2.9.45–6.4.44; **EF514:D** 2.9.43–21.3.44; **EF515:F** 11.9.43–FTR 27.9.43 Hanover; **EH877:C** 8.5.43–FTR 27.9.43 Hanover; **EH881** 14.5.43–FTR 30.5.43 Wuppertal; **EH889:Z** 29.5.43–FTR 22.6.43 Mannheim; **EH901:O** 10.6.43–26.3.44; **EH902** 10.6.43–FTR 24/25.6.43 Wuppertal, crashed nr Bergen-op-Zoom, Holland; **EH905:R** 17.6.43–FTR 31.8.43 Berlin; **EH928:A** 6.7.43–FTR 2/3.8.43 Hamburg; **EH929** 14.7.43–28.7.43; **EH930** 20.7.43–28.7.43; **EH935:K** 8.7.43–FTR 23.9.43 Mannheim; **EH936:W** 7.7.43–FTR 23.9.43 Mannheim; **EH938** 4.7.43–FTR 30/31.8.43 München-Gladbach; **EH939:J** 17.8.43–21.3.44; **EH946** 16.7.43–26.7.43; **EH947** 15.7.43–EFB 11.4.44 crashed Icklingham, Suffolk, engine fire, with 90 Squadron; **EH948:Q** 17.7.43–FTR 24/25.2.44 mining, Kiel Bay; **EH949:P** 18.7.43–29.4.44; **EJ108:O** 4.9.43–6.4.44; **LJ441** 21.9.43–13.3.44; **LJ442** 27.9.43–FTR 19.11.43 Leverkusen; **LJ457** 19.10.43–26.3.44; **LJ462:O** 9.11.43–EFB 14.3.44; **LJ473:R** 5.11.43–EFB 5.1.44 from mining, swung landing Mepal; **LK384:X** 6.10.43–30.3.44; **LK389** 21.10.43–27.11.43.

90 Squadron

R9198 10.5.43–20.5.43; **R9256:G** 28.11.42–RIW 1.2.43; **R9271:Q** 23.2.43–FTR 6.3.43 Essen; **R9306:J** 21.1.43–EFB 17.2.43 fuel starvation, from Lorient, crashed Balborrow Hill, Blandford; **R9349:U** 29.1.43–FTR 1.3.43 St. Nazaire; **W7510** 18.2.43–10.3.43; **W7570:O** 16.11.42–?.5.43; **W7623** 20.5.43–26.5.43; **W7627:A** 16.11.42–EFA 18.3.43, swung into BK693; **BF324:H** 16.11.42–FA RIW 23.3.43 uc collapsed taking off; **BF346:G** ?.4.43–FTR 29.4.43 mining, 'Quince'; **BF376** 11.3.43–12.5.43; **BF404:A** 3.43–FA 30.5.43 belly landed Stradishall; **BF407:S** 8.2.43–16.8.43; **BF409:R** 18.11.42–EFA 5.4.43 uc collapsed Ridgewell; **BF410:E** 26.11.42–FTR 25/26.2.43 Nuremburg; **BF414:F** 28.11.42–EFA 19.5.43 tyre burst Riccall; **BF415:S** 28.11.42–FTR 3/4.2.43 Hamburg, shot down by night fighter at Montfoort/Willeskon, Holland; **BF435:X** 11.3.43–6.6.43; **BF438:D** 26.1.43–FTR 14/15.2.43 Cologne; **BF442:K** 2.3.43–FTR 20/21.4.43 Rostock; **BF449** 2.3.43–EFA 10.3.43 uc collapsed landing Ridgewell; **BF454:W** 4.3.43–EFA 14.4.43 uc collapsed landing Ridgewell; **BF460** 10.4.43–11.5.43; **BF462:P** 27.2.43–FTR 14/15.4.43 Stuttgart; **BF463:Q** 29.3.43–FTR 20/21.4.43 Rostock; **BF464:E** 23.2.43–FA 31.8.43 uc damaged taking off Wratting; **BF466** 23.2.43–26.2.43; **BF473:D** 7.3.43–13.5.43; **BF503** 5.4.43–21.6.43; **BF504:F** 4.4.43–EFA 4.7.43 overshot Wratting; **BF508:S** 31.3.43–FTR 20/21.4.43 Rostock; **BF521** 19.4.43–11.5.43; **BF523:G** 28.4.43–FTR 13.5.43 Duisburg; shot down by III/NJG 1 at Harderwijk, Holland; **BF524:N** 19.4.43–FTR 9.5.44 S.O.E. op.; **BF526:R, G** 26.5.43–2.6.44; **BF527:K** 16.4.43–9.6.43, caught fire on the ground, Cat. B; **BF529** 23.4.43–13.5.43; **BF532:W** 28.5.43–1.11.43; **BF566:T, G** 4.5.43–FTR22/23.9.43 Hanover; **BF574:F** 19.8.43–8.2.44; **BK598:N** 16.11.42–6.6.43; **BK625:D** 17.11.42–RIW 29.12.42, crash landed Ridgewell; **BK626:C** 15.11.42–FA 25.5.43 crashed Shipdham; **BK627:F** 17.11.42–FTR 19/20.2.43 Wilhelmshaven; **BK628:G** 17.11.42–18.12.42 uc collapsed, dispersal, 1 killed; FTR 24/25.6.43 Wuppertal; **BK644:T** 1.12.42–FTR 6.2.43 mining, 'Nectarine'; **BK655:B, X** 18.3.43–RIW 24.5.43, ?.8.43–FTR 8/9.10.43 Bremen; **BK661:O** 29.3.43–FTR 13.5.43 Duisburg; **BK665:D** 3.3.43–FTR 23.6.43 Mülheim; **BK693:A** 7.5.43–EFA 28.7.43; **BK718:M** 15.4.43–FTR 3/4.7.43 Cologne: **BK723:D** 1.7.43–FTR 4.10.43 Kassel; **BK725:M** 31.3.43–FTR 16/17.4.43 Mannheim; **BK755:H** 31.3.43–FTR 30/31.7.43 Remscheid; **BK780** 13.4.43–EFA 25.4.43 uc collapsed Ridgewell; **BK781:E** 9.4.43–13.7.44; **BK784:P** 14.4.43–EFB 23.5.43 hit tree, crashed Chippenham Lodge, Suffolk; **BK804:J** 9.6.43–FTR 23.6.43 Mülheim; **BK811:V** 28.4.43–6.2.44; **BK803:O** 5.5.43–FTR 25.6.43 Wuppertal; **BK814:T** 28.4.43–FTR 4/5.5.43 Dortmund; **BK816:B** 5.5.44–12.6.44; **EE873:D** 11.6.43–FTR 13/15.7.43 Aachen; **EE887:T** 5.6.43–FTR 21/22.6.43 Krefeld, by night fighter, Hoodwoud, Holland; **EE896:J, O** 13.6.43–24.6.44; **EE900:Y** 23.6.43–17.8.43; **EE904:S** 23.6.43–FTR 25/26.7.43 Essen; **EE939** 30.6.43–FA 15.7.43 belly landed Stradishall; **EE951:B** 8.7.43–FA RIW uc collapsed Wratting; **EE952:F** 8.7.43–EFB 28.9.43 Hanover, crashed approaching Wratting, at Horseheath, Cambs.; **EE129:Q** 27.8.43–FTR 5/6.9.43 Mannheim; **EF147:J** 29.9.43–FTR 6.3.44 S.O.E. op.; **EF159** 24.9.43–FTR 23/24.4.44 S.O.E. op.; **EF162:K** 24.9.43–FTR 13.4.44 S.O.E. op.; **EF179:V** 29.9.43–FTR 7/8.10.43 mining, 'Nectarine', shot down by convoy off Cromer; **EF182:V** 8.10.43–11.4.44; **EF183:Z** 9.1.44–4.6.44; **EF188:Z** 29.9.43–12.6.44; **EF191:H** 14.10.43–FTR 1/2.12.43 mining, Kattegat, west of Hemmett, Denmark; **EF193:Q** 14.10.43–31.5.44; **EF196:L** 18.10.43–24.6.44; **EF198:F** 21.10.43–EFA 26.2.44 hit trees Dinham Castle, nr Chedburgh; **EF209** 29.11.43–31.12.43; **EF212** 21.12.43–23.12.43; **EF251:P** 21.3.44–24.6.44; **EF302** 5.1.44–?1.44; **EF328** 4.2.43–EFA 9.3.43 engines cut Sudbury; **EF334:U** 27.1.43–16.8.43; **EF336** 6.2.43–4.3.43; **EF346:G** 7.3.43–30.11.43; **EF397** 16.5.43–EFA 30.5.43 crashed Stradishall on circuit; **EF426:S** 25.5.43–EFA 9.10.43 burnt; **EF431:X** 8.6.43–

25.8.43; **EF433:M** 27.6.43–FTR 28/29.1.44 mining, Kiel Bay; **EF439:H, C** 19.6.43–FTR 27/28.8.43 Nuremberg; **EF441** 23.6.43–13.7.43; **EF446:O** 27.6.43–EFA 17.9.43 overshot Wratting; **EF459** 23.12.43–20.1.44; **EF497** 20.8.43–EFA 20.10.43 crashed low flying; **EF509:X** 1.9.43–FTR 9/10.5.44 S.O.E. op.; **EF511:C** 31.8.43–EFB 26.11.43 crashed Flimpston, Suffolk; **EH876:J** 5.5.43–FTR 25/26.5.43 Düsseldorf; **EH900:Y** 9.6.43–FTR 25/26.6.43 Gelsenkirchen; **EH906:T** 18.6.43–FTR 4/5.3.44 S.O.E. op.; **EH907:O** 23.6.43–FTR 3/4.7.43 Cologne; **EH908:R** 23.6.43–EFA 5.11.43 crashed Hundon, Suffolk; **EH837:S** 10.7.43–FTR 23/24.8.43 Berlin, in Ijsselmeer off Ork; **EH939:P** 21.3.44–14.6.44; **EH944:A** 11.7.43–EFB 22/23.9.43; **EH958:O** 30.9.43–EFB 22.1.44 collided with EF138 in flight, tail damage, landed Tuddenham; **EH982:Y** 22.10.43–14.6.44; **EH989:N, P** 24.8.43–FTR 4.10.43 Frankfurt; **EH996:H** 30.8.43–FTR 18/19.11.43 Mannheim; **EJ115:K** 5.5.44–FB 8.6.44; **EJ122:E** 6.10.43–14.6.44; **LJ460:E** 5.11.43–FTR 10/11.4.44 S.O.E. op.; **LJ470:C** 5.11.43–RIW 12.5.44; **LJ506:F** 30.3.44–24.6.44; **LJ579:O** 3.3.44–EFB 23.4.44 uc collapsed; **LK380:Y** 26.9.43–EFA 9.11.43 collided with Hurricane KW800 nr Shippea Hill; **LK383:W** 13.10.43–14.6.44; **LK392:A** 17.10.43–14.6.44; **LK438:V** ?–13.4.44; **MZ262:K** 31.5.42–EFB 23.9.43 Copley Green.

138 Squadron

LJ503 20.6.44–?.7.44; **LJ932** 20.6.44–EFB 29.9.44; **LJ990:O** 11.6.44–10.3.45; **LJ993** 16.6.44–FTR 9.11.44; **LJ999:Q** 20.6.44–FTR 5/6.3.45; to D.Z. nr Copenhagen, crashed Ringköbing Fjord; **LK125:S** 20.6.44–10.3.45; **LK131** 20.6.44–EFB 1.9.44; **LK139:A** 12.7.44–10.3.45; **LK143** 15.7.44–FTR 3.12.44; **LK145** 8.7.44–10.3.45; **LK149:T** 24.7.44–FTR 23/24.2.45; **LK151** 22.7.44–FTR 27.11.44 in Little Belt, to Ju 88G of I/NJG 3; **LK192** 13.8.44–10.3.45; **LK194** 10.8.44–10.3.45; **LK198** 7.8.44–FTR 9.11.44; **LK200** 10.8.44–FTR 9.9.44; **LK204:U** 16.8.44–10.3.45; **LK206** 24.8.44–5.9.44; **LK207** 24.8.44–5.9.44; **LK208** 17.8.44–5.9.44; **LK209** 19.8.44–5.9.44; **LK210** 30.8.44–5.9.44; **LK232** 9.9.44–FA RIW 16.3.45; **LK235** 11.9.44–14.9.44 to the Middle East; **LK237** 30.9.44–9.3.45; **LK272:F** 2.10.44–FTR 26/27.2.45; **LK274:N** 29.9.44–10.3.45; **LK279** 6.10.44–FTR 10.2.45 off Fredericia, Denmark; **LK282** 29.10.44–FTR 31.12.44; **LK285:T** 7.10.44–25.3.45; **LK309** 15.1.45–9.7.45; **LK329** 1.12.44–8.3.45; **PW395** 18.2.45–6.3.45.

149 Squadron

N3638 24.11.41–3.1.42; **N3680** 27.10.41–7.11.41; **N3682;F, U** 23.11.41–23.4.42; **N3684** 15.3.42–FA 26.3.42; **N3719:S** 1.4.42–EFA 23.4.42 out of control on rough ground; **N3723:E** 8.3.42–EFB 6/7.12.42 Mannheim, flak severed rudder control, crashed nr Ascot; **N3726:G** 18.3.42–FB 6/7.4.42 Essen, fighter damage, uc collapsed landing; **N3752:C** 1.5.42–FTR 16/17.5.42 nr Risegaards, Denmark; **N3755** 14.6.42–20.8.42; **N6065:Z** 8.7.42–4.10.42; **N6068:T** 29.1.42–FTR 15/16.4.42 Dortmund; **N6079:F** 20.3.42–16.8.42; **N6080:G** 23.3.42–EFB 17.6.42 Essen, crashed nr Mildenhall; **N6081:H, G** 25.3.42–FTR 29.8.42 Nuremberg; **N6083:N** 27.3.42–EFA 24.8.42 engine fire just after take-off; **N6084:C** 27.3.42–FTR 8/9.6.42 Essen; **N6095** 24.10.41–8.11.41; **N6099:C** 2.1.42–28.3.42; **N6102:G** 18.11.41–FB 12.2.42 uc collapsed landing; **N6103:E** 23.11.41–10.5.42; **N6104** 25.11.41–11.12.41; **N6122:Q** 9.12.41–15.6.42; **N6123:F** 7.12.41–3.9.42; **N6124:R** 11.12.41–FTR 5.5.42, Stuttgart; **N6125** 13.12.41–18.1.42; **N6126:U** 14.2.42–FTR 10/11.3.42 Ruhr; **N6127:N** 15.2.42–28.3.42; **R9142:R** 27.6.42–FA 17.8.42 uc collapsed; **R9143:O** 1.7.42–6.7.43; **R9161:T** 22.6.42–FTR 29/30.7.42 Saarbrücken; **R9162:Q** 21.8.42–FTR 16/17.9.42 Essen; **R9167:N** 27.8.42–FTR 2/3.10.42 Krefeld, shot down by night fighter, Kronenburg Sevenum, Holland; **R9170:H** 31.8.42–

FTR 10/11.9.42 Düsseldorf, shot down by night fighter, Coltgensplaar; **R9200:P** 9.10.42–23.3.43; **R9202:X** 13.10.42–FTR 29.11.42 Turin; **R9203:D** 11.10.42–18.2.43; **R9242:B** 21.10.42–23.2.43; **R9253:C** 17.11.42–FTR 9.12.42 mining; **R9265:N** 1.12.42–EFA 22.12.42; **R9271:K** 20.12.42–23.2.43; **R9276:F** 29.12.42–FTR 19/20.2.43 Wilhelmshaven; **R9287** 22.1.43–4.3.43; **R9295:G** 14.2.42–EFB 11.3.42 crashed Holywell Row, burnt; **R9262:D** 13.2.42–26.3.42; **R9299** 11.2.42–19.2.42; **R9307** 29.3.42–EFA 22.4.42 uc collapsed; **R9310:P** 12.4.42–FTR 17/18.5.42 mining, Baltic, in sea off Asnaes, Denmark; **R9314:T** 12.5.42–FTR 5/6.6.42 Essen, collided with a Wellington, crashed in sea; **R9320** 29.4.42–FTR 17/18.5.42 mining, Baltic, in Ferne Belt; **R9321:R** 1.5.42–FTR 5/6.6.42 Essen; **R9327:M** 26.1.43–FTR 4/5.4.43 Kiel, at Obbekaer, Denmark; **R9329:V** 29.5.42–EFB 27.8.42 Kassel, into high ground at Dibhall, Horestry, Cornwood, Devon, shot down by British A.A. guns; **R9330:O** 24.5.42–EFA 29.6.42 crashed taking off; **R9334:G** 29.5.42–EFA 3.1.43 burnt on night training flight, Lakenheath village; **W7451** 26.10.41–8.11.41; **W7452:A** 31.10.41–EFA 9.3.42 overshot Heathfield, Ayr; **W7455:B** 9.11.41–10.2.42; **W7456** 15.11.41–EFA 22.11.41 fire, belly landed, Boxworth, Cambs.; **W7457** 18.11.41–EFA 11.2.42 uc trouble landing; **W7458** 23.11.41–EFA 28.1.42; **W7459** 25.11.41–11.12.41; **W7460** 9.12.41–23.12.41, 1.42–25.6.42; **W7461:N** 5.12.41–EFB 15.1.42 fuel short, crashed Todwick Bar; **W7462:T** 12.12.41–EFB 29.1.42 overshot, Lossiemouth; **W7463** 9.12.41–31.12.41; **W7465:V** 2.1.43–28.2.43; **W7469** 21.1.43–28.1.43; **W7508:D** 23.2.42–FTR 5/6.6.42 Essen; **W7509:U** 13.3.42–24.5.42; **W7510:B** 13.3.42–18.2.43; **W7512:A** 17.2.42–FTR 26/27.4.42 Rostock; **W7513** 21.1.43–4.3.43; **W7526:V** 28.8.42–20.9.42; **W7530** 30.4.42–8.5.42; **W7566:C** 22.6.42–FTR 16/17.11.42 mining; **W7572:R** 23.6.42–FTR 24/25.8.42 Frankfurt; **W7580:D** 2.7.42–FTR 23/24.7.42 Duisburg, shot down by I/NJG 1 at Geffen, Holland; **W7582:F, S** 2.7.42–EFA 10.11.42 fire, crashed Kingsway, Suffolk; **W7589:P** 21.7.42–EFB 18.8.42 Osnabruck, engine failure, crashed Southery, Norfolk; **W7619:A** 15.8.42–9.6.43; **W7628:B** 29.8.42–EFB 24.10.42 Genoa, crashed into houses Rye St. Cliff, Gravesend; **W7638:R** 19.9.42–FTR 14/15.2.43 Cologne, shot down by fighter, Boxmeer, Holland; **W7639:Q** 19.9.42–EFA 9.12.42 burnt; **BF310:H** 20.6.42–FTR 29/30.6.42 Bremen, shot down by II/NJG 2, Makkum, Holland; **BF311:G** 22.6.42–20.10.42; **BF312:A** 23.6.42–FTR 16/17.7.42 Lübeck; **BF320:H** 6.7.42–FTR 30.7.42 Saarbrucken; **BF325:A** 20.7.42–EFB 12/13.8.42 Mainz, attacked by Bf 110, fuel short, crashed on house at Broadstairs; **BF334:T** 4.8.42–26.8.42; **BF348:P** 28.8.42–EFB 10.10.42 mining, hit trees Gt. Cressingham, nr Bodney; **BF349:R** 28.8.42–4.3.43; **BF357:T** 6.9.42–23.2.43; **BF372:H** 11.9.42–FTR 29.11.42 Turin; **BF391:T** 5.10.42–FTR 8/9.12.42 mining; **BF392:D** 8.10.42–FTR 17.10.42 mining; **BF444:G** 13.1.43–3.3.43; **BF479:E** 13.3.43–FTR 13/14.5.43 Bochum; **BF483:C** 14.3.43–FTR 28/29.6.43 Cologne; **BF500:M** 7.4.43–FTR 14/15.4.43 Stuttgart; **BF503:U** 23.3.43–5.4.43; **BF507:S** 31.3.43–FTR 20/21.4.43 Rostock; **BF509N, B, R** 31.3.43–16.2.44; **BF510:P** 31.3.43–FTR 22.5.43 mining; **BF520:Y** 12.4.43–FA RIW 17.5.43 crashed taking off; **BF520:B** 5.5.43–FTR3/4.7.43 Cologne; **BF531:M** 21.4.43–14.6.43; **BF570:T, H** 25.5.43–17.8.43; **BF573:W** 20.5.43–21.6.43; **BF574:Y** 13.5.43–21.6.43; **BK597:F** 6.10.42–2.7.43; **BK601:N** 8.10.42–10.5.43; **BK612:E** 14.12.42–28.3.43; **BK701:G** 16.2.43–FTR 16/17.5.43 mining, Frisians; **BK703:K** 10.3.43–FTR 29.6.43 Cologne; **BK708** 14.3.43–FTR 28/29.5.43 St. Nazaire; **BK710:A** 31.3.43–FTR 25/26.5.43 Düsseldorf; **BK711:O** 12.4.43–FTR 5/6.9.43 Mannheim; **BK713:N** 15.3.43–21.6.43; **BK714:L** 15.3.43–FTR 21.4.43 Lübeck; **BK715:D** 15.3.43–EFA 31.3.43 engine fire taking off; **BK726:Z** 24.3.43–FTR 13.5.43 Bochum; **BK759:X** 24.3.43–FTR 15.4.43 Stuttgart; **BK765:P** 17.5.43–FTR 23/24.8.43 Berlin; **BK772:T** 27.3.43–6.7.43; **BK781:L** 13.7.44–17.8.44; **BK798:Q** 14.4.43–FTR 20/21.12.43 mining, Frisians; **BK799:O** 21.4.43–FTR 21/22.6.43 Krefeld; **BK806:V** 17.6.43–2.8.43; **BK812** 29.4.43–EFA 11.5.43 uc collapsed landing; **EE872:N** 26.5.43–FTR 5/6.9.43 Mannheim; **EE877:E** 14.6.43–FTR 27/28.8.43 Nuremberg; **EE879:G** 29.5.43–FTR 31.8.43 Berlin; **EE880:O** 31.5.43–

FTR 27/28.6.43 mining; **EE894** 16.6.43–FTR 24.8.43?; **EE963:N** 27.8.43–29.8.43; **EE969:E** 27.8.43–FTR 27/28.1.44 mining, Kattegat; **EF124** 17.8.43–12.9.43; **EF133** 17.8.44–13.9.44; **EF140:A** 8.9.43–FTR 25.6.44 Rousseauville; **EF185:D** 17.8.44–23.8.44; **EF188:M** 12.6.44–FTR 23/24.6.44 Brest; **EF192:F** 5.5.44–17.8.44; **EF193:D** 31.5.44–17.8.44; **EF202:L** 14.10.43–FTR 25/26.11.43 mining; **EF207:F** 14.10.43–29.8.44; **EF233:D** 17.8.44–18.9.44; **EF238:H** 1.3.44–EFB 29.4.44; **EF307:E** 30.12.43–FTR 25.2.44 mining, Kiel Bay; **EF308:R** 31.12.43–FTR 24/25.2.44 mining, Baltic; **EF327:M** 20.2.43–FA 12.3.43 uc collapsed; **EF330:P** 18.1.43–FTR 13.3.43 Essen, crashed Bergli, Holland; **EF335:E, H** 28.2.43–21.6.43; **EF336:F** 4.3.43–21.6.43; **EF337** 2.3.43–17.5.43; **EF338:Q** 16.2.43–21.6.43; **EF340:D** 16.2.43–24.3.43; **EF341** 10.2.43–17.5.43; **EF342:A** 7.2.43–17.5.43; **EF343:B** 13.2.43–FTR 4/5.5.43 Dortmund, night fighter action, Ypes-colga, Holland; **EF344:R** 16.2.43–18.7.43; **EF357:V** 14.3.43–FTR 12/13.5.43 Duisburg, shot down nr Rotterdam; **EF360:H** 14.3.43–5.10.43; **EF389:Q** 22.4.43–7.8.43; **EF395:L** 21.4.43–EFA 22.6.43 swung landing; **EF396:E** 20.5.43–28.9.43; **EF400** 30.6.43–EFA 3/4.7.43 uc collapsed; **EF438:D** 14.6.43–FTR 30/31.8.43 München-Gladbach; **EF412:F** 14.6.43–EFA 13.11.43 uc collapsed; **EF495:R** 12.8.43–FTR 27/28.9.43 Hanover; **EF502:G** 27.8.43–FTR 10/11.4.44 S.O.E. op.; **EH883:A** 20.5.43–FTR 23/24.9.43 Mannheim; **EH885:V** 17.5.43–EFA 9.6.43 uc collapsed; **EH903:L** 12.6.43–FTR 18/19.11.43 Mannheim; **EH904:K, P** 17.6.43–FB 16.12.43 Pembrey, uc collapsed; **EH909** 24.6.43–6.7.43; **EH922:O** 24.6.43–4.5.44; **EH934** 7.7.43–29.7.43; **EH943:B** 4.9.43–FTR 27/28.9.43 Hanover, crashed in sea; **EH982:S** 14.7.44–17.8.44; **EH987:P** 14.8.43–EFA 4.10.43 uc collapsed; **EH993:D** 1.9.43–FB 4.6.44 belly landed; **EJ106:O** 8.9.43–FTR 7/8.10.43 mining, Frisians, crashed 50 miles N.W. Vlieland; **EJ107:K** 4.9.43–FB 26.2.44 belly landed Coltishall; **EJ109:H, M** 8.9.43–23.9.44; **EJ115** 23.7.44–17.8.44; **EJ122:Q** 14.6.44–29.8.44; **EJ124:C** 27.1.44–FTR 15/16.3.44 Amiens; **LJ447** 17.8.44–29.8.44; **LJ472:Q** 17.8.44–14.9.44; **LJ481:U** 17.8.44–15.9.44; **LJ504:K** 1.12.43–FTR 18/19.4.44 mining, Kiel Bay; **LJ511:Q** 13.4.44–FA 7.7.44 swung taking off; **LJ522:N** 27.7.44–25.8.44; **LJ526:P** 5.1.44–FTR 23/24.4.44 mining, crashed Öster Skerninge, Denmark; **LJ568:A** 28.7.44–23.8.44; **LJ580** 29.2.44–11.3.44; **LJ582** 29.2.44–11.3.44; **LJ623:P** 27.4.44–25.8.44; **LJ632:P** 26.7.44–12.9.44; **LK382:Q** 6.10.43–FTR 9/10.4.44, S.O.E. op.; **LK385:C** 5.5.44–FTR 5/6.6.44 feint, Brest; **LK386:J** 27.11.43–EFB 24.6.44 overshot Hartford Bridge; **LK388:N, L** 9.10.43–EFA 17.7.44 uc collapsed Methwold; **LK392:O** 14.6.44–FA RIW 19.7.44 overshot, uc collapsed; **LK394:D** 22.10.43–FTR 25.6.44 Rousseauville; **LK397:K** 26.4.44–EFA 23.6.44, belly landed Methwold; **LK401:G** 17.8.44–12.9.44; **LK445:C** 30.1.44–5.5.44; **LK500:S** 29.2.44–FA RIW 24.5.44 swung taking off; **LK516** 29.3.44–11.3.44; **MZ260:C** 31.5.43–EFA 17.11.43 overshot Lakenheath.

158 Squadron

PJ881 1.8.45–2.2.46; **PJ886** 8.7.45–4.12.45; **PJ908** 1.7.45–EFA 5.8.45 uc collapsed Castel Benito; **PJ912** 27.7.45–28.1.46; **PJ914** 6.12.45–31.12.45; **PJ915** 28.6.45–2.2.46; **PJ922** 31.8.45–29.11.45; **PJ948** 24.6.45–28.7.45; **PJ950** 2.7.45–EFA 11.11.45 crashed taking off, burnt, Castel Benito; **PJ954** 29.5.45–29.11.45; **PJ957** 25.8.45–17.10.45, 15.12.45–31.12.45; **PJ976** 10.6.45–EFA 5.11.45 ground collision with Liberator KH146 (53 Sqn), Mauripur; **PJ977** 8.6.45–17.1.46; **PJ978** 10.6.45–4.12.45; **PJ982** 2.6.45–2.2.46; **PJ984** 1.6.45–17.9.45; **PJ985** 1.6.45–17.9.45; **PJ986** 2.6.45–28.1.46; **PJ998** 24.6.45–2.2.46; **PJ999** 6.12.45–31.12.45; **PK116** 27.6.45–20.12.45; **PK118** 27.6.45–EFA 28.10.45, swung taking off, burnt, Lydda; **PK123** 5.7.45–2.2.46; **PK127** 8.7.45–30.1.46; **PK128** 8.7.45–28.1.46; **PK143** 5.9.45–6.10.45; **PK145** 6.9.45–6.2.46; **PK146** 6.9.45–2.2.46; **PK147** 6.9.45–31.12.45; **PK149** 5.10.45–31.12.45; **LJ980** 27.11.45–16.1.46; **LK351** 27.11.45–16.1.46.

161 Squadron

LK119:Y 5.9.44–FTR 30/31.3.45 S.O.E. op.; **LK206** 5.9.44–10.3.45; **LK207** 5.9.44–EFA 19.10.44 broke up in flight, Potton, Beds.; **LK208** 5.9.44–EFA 21.9.44 uc collapsed Tempsford; **LK209:T** 5.9.44–FTR 22/23.3.45 S.O.E. op.; **LK210** 5.9.44–9.3.45; **LK236:Y** 11.9.44–EFA 14.2.45 unauthorised 'combat' with P-51, crashed Sandy Heath, Beds.; **LK237** 28.9.44–9.3.45; **LK238** 28.9.44–FTR 6/7.10.44 S.O.E. op., shot down by III/NJG 3 Ju 88G at Görding, Denmark; **LK278** 4.10.44–6.3.45; **LK283** 28.10.44–29.10.44; **LK285** 25.3.44–12.7.45; **LK308** 19.10.44–12.7.45; **LK312:W** 25.10.44–FTR 4/5.3.45 S.O.E. op., crashed Limfjord, Denmark; **LK329** 8.3.45–12.8.45; **PW395** 6.3.45–12.7.45; **EF345** (Mk. III) 23.11.43–9.12.43.

171 Squadron

LJ513 10.11.44–20.1.45; **LJ541:N** 17.9.44–2.10.44; **LJ543** 6.12.44–22.1.45; **LJ544** 6.12.44–22.1.45; **LJ559:R** 17.9.44–2.11.44; **LJ562** 10.11.44–23.1.45; **LJ565** 10.11.44–17.11.44; **LJ567:S** 17.9.44–10.11.44; **LJ568:H** 17.9.44–10.11.44; **LJ582** 10.11.44–31.3.45; **LJ611:E** 17.9.44–26.10.44; **LJ617:F** 17.9.44–10.11.44; **LJ649** 17.9.44–2.10.44; **LJ651** 17.9.44–2.10.44; **LJ670** 2.10.44–18.12.44; **PW256** (Mk. IV) 2.10.44–27.11.44; **PW258** (Mk. IV) 2.10.44–30.11.44; **PW259** (Mk. IV) 17.9.44–10.11.44.

190 Squadron

EF124 29.1.44–19.12.44; **EF242:Q** 11.5.44–17.5.45; **EF260** 10.2.44–FTR 21.9.44 Arnhem; **EF263** 8.5.44–FTR 19.9.44 Arnhem; **EF264** 27.4.44–20.4.45; **EF270** 6.10.44–1.2.45; **EF273:C** 27.9.44–31.5.46; **EF298** 24.2.44–23.7.44; **EF316:L** 23.4.44 20.4.45; **LJ563** 18.5.44–20.2.46; **LJ564** 14.5.44–EFA 7.7.44 overshot Keevil; **LJ816** 21.1.44–11.12.44; **LJ818:X** 28.1.44–24.2.45; **LJ822** 21.1.44–EFA 12.4.44 dived in, Kighton Farm, Hampreston, Wimbush, Dorset; **LJ823** 24.1.44–FTR 22.9.44 Arnhem; **LJ824** 26.1.44–31.5.45; **LJ825** 26.1.44–20.4.45; **LJ826** 27.1.44–17.5.45; **LJ827** 24.1.44–FTR 26.8.44 S.O.E.op.; **LJ828** 28.1.44–EFA 14.6.44 taxied into LJ829 at dispersal; **LJ829** 26.1.44–EFB 21.9.44 from Arnhem; **LJ830** 31.1.44–23.6.44; **LJ831** 26.1.44–EFB 21.9.44 from Arnhem; **LJ832:U** 27.1.44–20.4.45; **LJ833** 2.2.44–FTR 21.9.44 Arnhem; **LJ869** ?–31.3.45; **LJ881** 17.5.44–FTR 21.9.44 Arnhem; **LJ882** 2.5.44–11.5.44; **LJ889:N** 19.5.44–31.5.45; **LJ895:K** 17.5.44–24.5.45; **LJ898:M** 4.5.44–25.5.45; **LJ916** 24.5.44–FTR 21.9.44 Arnhem; **LJ927** 27.4.44–22.7.44; **LJ930:A** 21.12.44–EFA 20.4.45 caught fire low flying, crashed Woodland Lane, Berks.; **LJ933:V** 14.6.44–31.5.45; **LJ934:Y** ?.5.44–31.5.45; **LJ936:N** 21.5.44–25.4.45; **LJ937** 18.4.44–12.3.46; **LJ939** 17.5.44–FTR 19.9.44 Arnhem; **LJ943** 27.4.44–FTR 21.9.44 Arnhem; **LJ982** 11.6.44–FTR 21.9.44 Arnhem; **LK117** 18.3.45–?.4.45; **LK195** 25.9.44–FTR 6/7.11.44 S.O.E. op.; **LK196:B** 22.9.44–FA 4.5.45; **LK271:P** 28.9.44–24.5.45; **LK276:P** 28.9.44–EFA 21.11.44 belly landed Newton Field, Dunmow; **LK275:V** 28.9.44–EFB 1.1.45 emergency landed Bungay, hit tree and another aircraft after touchdown; **LK281:R** 28.9.44–17.5.45; **LK293:X** 30.9.44–17.5.45; **LK295** 7.10.44–2.45; **LK297** 7.10.44–EFA 10.5.44 control lost, bad visibility, Norway; **LK335:Q** 18.3.45–17.5.45; **LK336:W** 18.3.45–25.5.45; **LK363** 15.3.45–22.3.45– **LK431** 28.1.44–31.5.45; **LK433** 25.3.44–17.5.45; **LK498** 23.4.44–FTR 21.9.44 Arnhem; **LK513** 2.5.44–?.7.44; **LK566:G, Y** 28.9.44–5.10.44; **PW257:Z** 25.9.44–25.5.45; **PW442** 3.5.45–25.5.45; **TS265** 24.3.45–FTR 14/15.4.45 S.O.E. op.

196 Squadron

BK663:K 17.8.43–EFB 28.9.43, 1 mile S.E. Ely, approaching Witchford; **BK771:L** 19.8.43–EFA 3.2.44 collided with Halifax on take-off Tarrant Rushton; **EE874:S** 17.8.43–3.3.44; **EE957** 11.8.43–27.8.43; **EE964** 11.8.43–FTR 5/6.9.43 Mannheim; **EE972:T** 15.8.43–1.4.44; **EE973** 13.8.43–EFA 7.9.43; **EE975:G** 11.8.43–EFA 5.11.43 uc collapsed Witchford; **EF114:H** 12.8.43–FTR 16/17.9.43 Modane; **EF116:J** 14.8.43–5.11.43; **EF146** 9.9.43–5.11.43; **EF160** 23.9.43–?.11.43; **EF178:H** 23.9.43–3.2.44; **EF190** 21.10.43–1.4.44; **EF210** 22.10.43–3.2.44; **EF234** 19.4.44–FTR 9.11.44 S.O.E. op.; **EF248** 7.2.44–FTR 20.9.44 Arnhem; **EF261** 27.4.44–4.1.45; **EF272** 31.1.44–?.1.45; **EF273** 29.1.44–17.4.44; **EF274** 2.2.44–27.3.44; **EF276** 20.4.44–20.7.45; **EF292** 11.1.45–15.2.46; **EF293** 1.2.46–19.3.46; **EF309** 25.4.44–FA 19.7.44 belly landed Keevil; **EF318** 16.6.44–20.7.45; **EF429** 19.5.44–9.2.46; **EF464** 23.6.43–EFA 3.10.43 crashed approaching Coltishall; **EF468:Q** 6.8.43–21.2.44; **EF469:B** 7.8.43–FTR 6.2.44 S.O.E. op.; **EF488:W** 11.8.43–9.3.44; **EF492:X, Y** 7.8.43–1.4.44; **EF494:C** 7.8.43–EFB 9.10.43 200 yd. off coast, Hemsby Gap, Norfolk; **EF516** 8.9.43–3.3.44; **EH932:V** 11.8.43–5.2.44; **EH950** 21.7.43–19.8.43; **EH952** 2.7.43–FTR 24.8.43 A.S.R. search; **EH954:D** 8.9.43–5.12.43; **EH960:Q, X** 9.8.43–FTR 17.10.43 control problems; **EH961** 9.8.43–FTR 31.8.43 Berlin, crashed Enschede, Holland; **EH981** 15.10.43–3.2.44; **EJ110:G, M** 8.9.43–FTR 4/5.2.44 S.O.E. op.; **LJ461** 12.5.44–21.8.44; **LJ502** 12.3.44–1.2.45; **LJ583** 12.6.44–?; **LJ643** 27.9.44–FA 24.10.45; **LJ813** 29.4.44–?.5.44; **LJ834** 27.1.44–FA 16.3.44 overshot Tarrant Rushton; **LJ835** 28.1.44–?.9.44; **LJ836** 2.2.44–22.2.45; **LJ837** 30.1.44–22.2.45; **LJ838** 5.2.44–FB 6.6.44, 8.3.45–25.3.45; **LJ839** 8.2.44–EFA 28.3.44 overshot Marham, crashed into hangar; **LJ840:C** 31.1.44–EFB 21.9.44 from Arnhem; **LJ841** 31.1.44–FTR 5/6.6.44 Op. *Tonga*; **LJ842:S** 7.2.44–EFA 4.4.44 hit trees low flying, burnt, 1 mile S.W. Romsey, Hants.; **LJ845** 31.1.44–4.1.45; **LJ851** 3.2.44–FTR 20.9.44 crashed Eindhiven before D.Z.; **LJ870** 29.4.44–FA 12.11.44 tyre burst taking off Keevil, EFA 19.2.45 swung on fast landing; **LJ874** 5.4.45–23.6.45; **LJ876** 1.11.44–23.9.45; **LJ879** 10.3.46–28.3.46; **LJ888** 14.5.44–FTR 30/31.3.34 S.O.E. op.; **LJ894** 17.5.44–FTR 21.2.45 S.O.E. op.; **LJ922** 19.5.44–3.12.44; **LJ923** 7.5.44–EFA 21.4.45 swung landing; **LJ924** 25.4.44–10.6.44; **LJ925** 19.5.44–FTR 8.3.45 S.O.E. op.; **LJ926:K** 7.7.44–27.2.46 S.O.E. op.; **LJ927** 7.7.44–27.2.46; **LJ928** 29.4.44–FTR 21.9.44 Arnhem; **LJ931** 6.3.45–FA RIW 13.4.45 swung landing Shepherd's Grove; **LJ937** 18.4.44–11.1.45; **LJ944** 25.4.44–2.6.44; **LJ945** 18.4.44–FTR 21.9.44 Arnhem; **LJ947** 9.5.44–EFB 20.9.44 Arnhem, crashed nr Brussels; **LJ949** 19.5.44–FTR 23.9.44 Arnhem, crashed Leende, Holland; **LJ954** 17.5.44–FTR 20.9.44 Arnhem; **LJ977** 14.6.45–25.2.46; **LJ988** 28.5.44–FTR 20.9.44 Arnhem; **LJ998** 27.9.44–19.2.46; **LK142** 3.9.44–FTR 24/25.9.44 S.O.E. op. crashed nr Spendcourt, France; **LK146** 3.9.44–11.2.46; **LK147** 23.9.44–EFA 10.5.45, broke cloud too low, crashed nr Gardemoen, Norway; **LK193** 22.9.44–FTR 2/3.4.45 S.O.E. op., in sea off Cromer; **LK197** 25.9.44–FTR 30/31.3.45 S.O.E. op.; **LK201** 22.9.44–30.1.46; **LK205** 25.9.44–25.2.46; **LK289** 3.3.46–25.3.46; **LK295** ?.2.45–26.2.45; **LK302** 7.10.44–11.2.46; **LK305** ?–FTR 10/11.4.45 S.O.E. op., off Frisians; **LK326** 15.3.45–4.10.45; **LK341** 24.3.45–5.4.45; **LK345** 15.3.45–EFB 18.4.45 uc collapsed; **LK362** 14.3.45–27.2.46; **LK363** 14.6.45–27.2.46; **LK368** 15.3.45–30.11.45; **LK403** 12.11.43–1.4.44; **LK428** 26.2.44–?; **LK440** 25.4.44–6.6.44; **LK505** 5.5.44–22.2.45; **LK510** 23.4.44–6.1.45; **LK556** 12.6.44–EFA 14.1.46; **PJ878** 6.2.46–27.3.46; **PJ883** 7.2.46–28.3.46; **PJ885:7T–V** 30.1.46–25.3.46; **PJ887:ZO–H** 18.9.45–26.3.46; **PJ885** 1.2.46–26.3.46; **PJ959** 20.2.46–22.3.46; **PJ974:ZO–O** 30.1.46–21.3.46; **PK144:ZO–F** 6.2.46–27.3.46; **PK145** 6.2.46–25.3.46; **PK234** 10.3.46–25.3.46; **PW392** 1.3.45–27.2.46; **PW410** 31.5.45–18.2.46; **PW420:ZO–E** 3.5.45–6.3.46; **PW449:7T–K** 9.1.45–6.3.46; **PW454:ZO–N** 9.1.46–28.3.46; **PW455:7T–G** 15.12.45–28.3.46; **PW461** 15.12.45–23.2.46.

199 Squadron

BK762:C 7.7.43–30.11.43; **BK772:A** 6.7.43–28.10.43; **BK806:S** 2.8.43–FTR 28.8.43 Nuremberg; **EE910:Q** 19.7.43–EFA 22.4.44 overshot St. Athan; **EE911** 8.7.43–FTR 3.9.43; **EE913:F** 19.7.43–FTR 27/28.8.43 Nuremberg; **EE917:L** 6.7.43–FTR 30/31.8.43 Remscheid; **EE940** 11.7.43–19.7.43; **EE943:X** 5.7.43–10.4.44; **EE946:P** 5.7.43–FTR 31.8.43 Berlin, crashed Weert, Holland; **EE947:D** 5.7.43–EFB 25.9.43 undershot Lakenheath, crashed Eenwood, 2 mines exploded; **EE948:Q** 7.7.43–FA RIW 2.12.43; **EE953:E** 11.7.43–5.5.44; **EE954** 11.7.43–19.7.43; **EF118:O** 17.8.43–FTR 27/28.9.43 Hanover; **EF138:Y** 2.9.43–EFB 10.4.44 Lakenheath, crew fatigue after 9 hr flight; **EF153:D** 26.9.43–11.2.44; **EF154:V** 8.10.43–FTR 1.12.43 mining, Kattegat, to flak off Hirsholmere Is., Denmark; **EF161** 23.12.43–5.5.44; **EF192:J** 30.9.43–5.5.44; **EE270** 23.1.44–3.8.44; **EF300** 1.1.44–6.1.44; **EF301** 1.1.44–6.1.44; **EF304** 1.1.44–6.1.44; **EF450:N** 6.7.43–EFB 19.11.43 swung landing; **EF453:F** 24.7.43–FTR 4/5.11.43 mining, Kattegat; **EF455:B, W** 5.6.43–5.5.44; **EF459:X** 20.1.44–28.7.44; **EF505:K, R** 30.8.43–FTR 28.1.44 mining, crashed Is. of Römö, Denmark; **EF508:G** 29.8.43–10.5.44; **EF514** 21.3.44–12.5.44; **EH926:T** 5.7.43–7.2.44; **EH927:E** 6.7.43–FTR 23/24.8.43 Berlin; **EH930:N** 27.12.43–12.5.44; **EH934:K** 29.7.43–FTR 23/24.8.43 Berlin; **EH995:L, H** 25.8.43–29.2.44; **EJ111:P** 11.9.43–EGA 23.11.43 incendiary caught fire being unloaded, Lakenheath; **EJ115:H** 1.10.43–31.5.44; **LJ474** 2.12.43–13.12.43; **LJ510:A** 21.4.44–FB RIW 24.10.44, 13.1.45–8.3.45; **LJ513:E** 22.4.44–10.11.44; **LJ514:B** 5.5.44–24.2.45; **LJ516:H** 28.7.44–17.4.45; **LJ518:K** 29.4.44–EFB 25.9.44 hit tree, stalled in, Saxthorpe, Norfolk; **LJ520:Z** 2.5.44–24.2.45; **LJ525:R** 30.4.44–31.1.45; **LJ531:N** 29.4.44–FTR 17.6.44; **LJ536:P** 26.4.44–FTR 16.9.44; **LJ538:T** 22.5.44–21.2.45; **LJ541:K** 17.7.44–17.9.44; **LJ542:G** 30.4.44–31.1.45; **LJ543:J** 29.4.44–6.12.44; **LJ544:D** 29.4.44–6.12.44; **LJ557:Y** ?.4.44–?; **LJ559:Q** 31.8.44–17.9.44; **LJ560:H** 30.4.44–EFA 29.8.44 uc collapsed taking off; **LJ562:V** 5.5.44–10.11.44; **LJ565:Q** 14.5.44–10.11.44; **LJ567:Y** 31.8.44–17.9.44; **LJ568:L** 29.8.44–17.9.44; **LJ569:C** 22.5.44–FA 16.9.44 starboard wing torn off taking off North Creake; **LJ578:S** 29.2.44–EFB 10.9.44 uc collapsed, burnt; **LJ580:X** 11.3.44–31.1.45; **LJ582:L** 11.3.44–10.11.44; **LJ595:N** 6.7.44–22.2.45; **LJ611:A** 31.8.44–17.9.44; **LJ614:S** 30.8.44–8.3.45; **LJ617** 30.8.44–17.9.44; **LJ649:P** 30.8.44–17.9.44; **LJ651** 30.8.44–8.3.45; **LJ670** 29.9.44–2.10.44; **LK381:Z** 1.10.43–31.12.43; **LK385** 8.11.43–5.5.44; **LK387** 9.11.43–?.11.43; **PW256** 25.9.44–2.10.44; **PW258** 12.9.44–2.10.44; **PW259:V** 13.9.44–17.9.44.

214 Squadron

N3729:P 19.4.42–EFA 7.8.42 undershot; **N3751:P** 13.4.42–EFB 27/28.6.42 overshot; **N3756** 19.5.42–23.5.42; **N3762:C** 8.6.42–FTR 19/20.6.42 Osnabrück; **N3766** 5.6.42–14.7.42; **N3767** 7.7.42–FA 12.7.42 undershot; **N3768** 9.6.42–EFB 17.6.42 crashed taking off for St. Nazaire; **N3769:B** 1.5.42–1.7.42; **N6092** 5.4.42–EFA 5.5.42 swung taking off; **N6125** 30.5.42–17.12.42; **R9141:G** 26.6.42–17.8.42; **R9145:K** 29.7.42–FTR 1/2.3.43 Berlin; **R9146:S** 25.7.42–FTR 15/16.10.42 Cologne; **R9148:J** 19.7.42–13.8.42; **R9152:C** 25.7.42–30.1.43; **R9155:Q** 30.7.42–FTR 27/28.8.42 Kassel; **R9165:W** 28.8.42–SOC 11.12.42; **R9166** 23.8.42–FTR 13/14.9.42 Bremen; **R9186:F** 6.9.42–6.5.43; **R9191:O** 15.9.42–15.2.43; **R9194:N** 22.9.42–FTR 28/29.11.42 mining, 'Furze'; **R9197:V** 24.9.42–FTR 3/4.2.43 Hamburg, shot down by fighter, Bienden, Holland; **R9198:M** 30.9.42–FA RIW 8.11.42 swung taking off; **R9203:X** 18.2.43–22.10.43, became 4240M; **R9242:O** 23.2.43–FTR 14.5.43 Bochum; **R9257** 25.7.43–EFA 12.8.43 swung taking off, uc collapsed; **R9269** 26.7.43–1.8.43; **R9277** 26.7.43–5.8.43; **R9282** 2.1.43–FTR 3/4.2.43

Hamburg, shot down by fighter, Benschop, Holland; **R9283** 25.8.43–31.12.43; **R9284** 20.8.43–22.12.43; **R9285:J** 26.1.43–12.7.43; **R9288:Q** 1.8.43–EFA 8.9.43, crashed taking off; **R9316** 21.4.42–FA RIW 20.6.42; **R9317** 19.4.42–EFA 4.6.42 overshot Stradishall; **R9319:S** 28.4.42–EFA 20.6.42 heavy landing; **R9322:C** 3.5.42–EGA 3.6.42 part of bomb load fell off, burnt; **R9323:C, D, R** 3.5.42–5.8.43; **R9325** 15.5.42–EFA 31.5.42 crashed Stradishall runway; **R9326:G** 15.5.42–FTR 7/8. 6.42 mining, 'Nectarine', **R9350** 4.6.42–FTR 16/17.9.42 Essen; **R9355:O** 23.6.42–EFA 9.9.42; **R9356:U** 24.6.42–FTR 19/20.9.42 Munich; **R9358:E** 24.6.42–EFA 9.3.43 crashed nr Chedburgh after take-off; **W7449** 10.6.42–5.8.42; **W7459** 11.9.42–25.9.42; **W7526:M** 19.4.42–28.8.42; **W7527:B, O** ?.4.42–18.6.43; **W7532** 27.4.42–FA 3.5.42 undershot; **W7534:E** 10.5.42–FTR 30/31.5.42 Cologne; **W7537:H** 16.5.42–FTR 3/4.6.42 Bremen (?); **W7577:P** 5.7.42–FA 6.5.43 uc collapsed taking off; **W7584:D** 11.7.42–EFA 21.11.42 fuel short, crashed Thurlow, Suffolk; **W7610:A** 21.7.42–18.6.43; **W7537:H** 16.5.42–FTR 3/4.6.42 Bremen; **W7538** 17.5.42–RIW 26.6.42; **W7560:C** 24.6.42–FTR 26/27.7.42 Hamburg; **W7567:S** 24.6.42–FTR 23/24.7.42 Duisburg, shot down at Werkendam, Holland; **W7575:F** 19.7.42–16.11.42; **W7626** 26.8.42–EFA 5.10.42, lightning strike possible, belly landed Chedburgh; **W7627** 29.8.42–16.11.42; **W7637:W** 16.9.42–FTR 15/16.1.43 Lorient; **BF313:T** 27.6.42–FTR 3/4.7.42 Bremen; **BF314:W** 25.6.42–28.7.42; **BF326:X** 21.7.42–EFB 14.4.43 uc collapsed landing; **BF330** 29.7.42–FTR 17/18.8.42 Osnabrück, shot down in sea off Terschelling by II/NJG 2; **BF337** 13.8.42–FTR 4/5.9.42 Bremen, shot down by fighter, Staphorst, Holland; **BF341** 16.8.42–FA 18.2.43; **BF344** 19.8.42–19.5.43; **BF373** 12.9.42–30.9.42; **BF374** 15.9.42–1.10.42; **BF375** 26.4.43–18.8.43; **BF381:J, P²** 24.9.42–FTR 12/13.5.43 Duisburg; **BF404** ?.6.43–26.10.43; **BF441:N** 4.1.43–EFA 18.2.43 uc collapsed taking off Exeter; **BF444:N** 3.3.43–18.5.43; **BF445** 4.1.43–FA 26.2.43; **BF453** 13.3.43–FTR 27/28.3.43 mining, 'Nectarine'; **BF466:B** 26.2.43–19.7.43; **BF467** 17.3.43–FTR 28/29.4.43, ?; **BF469:M** 5.3.43–FTR 11/12.3.43 mining, 'Deodar'; **BF478:G** 4.4.43–FTR 23/24.5.43 Dortmund; **BF481:M** 14.3.43–6.7.43; **BF511:V** 31.3.43–19.6.43; **BF516** ?.4.43–FTR 11.8.43 Nuremberg, fuel short, ditched off Bexhill; **BF525:A** 19.4.43–4.7.43; **BF528:L** 21.4.43–FTR 23/24.5.43 Dortmund; **BF562:Q** 25.5.43–18.8.43; **BF563:J** 25.4.43–EFA 18.6.43 uc collapsed Chedburgh; **BF474:B** 20.5.43–19.8.43; **BK593:L** 21.9.42–EFA 29.11.42 burnt out, abortive take-off, Chevington, Suffolk; **BK599:R** 2.10.42–FTR 13.10.42 Kiel; **BK621** 29.5.43–8.7.43; **BK653:A** 9.4.43–FTR 17.4.43 Mannheim; **BK662:K, C** 28.2.43–5/6.3.43 FTR Essen; **BK663** 9.3.43–FA RIW 29/30.3.43 collided in flight with EF362; **BK689:E** 16.3.43–16.10.43; **BK693** 2.3.43–7.5.43; **BK707:P** 10.3.43–FA 26.5.43 overshot Chedburgh; **BK717:U** 15.3.43–FTR 4.7.43 Cologne; **BK720:Y** 28.4.43–19.6.43; **BK762** 31.3.43–7.7.43; **BK763:F** 31.3.43–FA, RIW 23.11.43; **BK767:L** 27.5.43–10.8.43; **BK771:L** 5.4.43–19.8.43; **BK800:Z** 22.4.43–19.6.43; **BK801** 18.4.43–19.6.43; **BK802** 3.6.43–?.6.43; **BK808:Q** 19.4.43–FA 19.5.43 tyre burst, Chedburgh; **DJ973:A** 3.5.42–EFB 24/25.6.42 engine trouble, crashed Stradishall; **DJ975** 4.6.42–7.10.42; **EE871** 27.5.43–18.8.43; **EE876:N** 27.5.43–18.8.43; **EE882:J** 2.6.43–FTR 3/4.7.43 mining, 'Nectarine'; **EE899:O** 16.6.43–18.8.43; **EE901:L** 20.6.43–18.8.43; **EE902:P** 19.6.43–FTR 24/25.7.43 Hamburg; **EE914** 23.7.43–FA 31.8.43 overshot Chedburgh; **EE950** 7.9.43–23.12.43; **EE956** 12.8.43–27.9.43; **EE959** 12.8.43–FTR 31.8.43 Berlin; **EE961** 23.8.43–9.3.44; **EE965** 23.9.43–10.12.43; **EE967** 5.9.43–10.12.43; **EF115** 18.9.43–10.12.43; **EF199** 15.12.43–27.1.44; **EF215** 15.12.43–1.2.44; **EF233** 20.12.43–30.1.44; **EF271** 14.10.43–30.1.44; **EF291** 15.12.43–?.4.44; **EF329:C** 14.2.43–FTR 3/4.3.43 Hamburg, in sea off Texel; **EF331:H** 28.2.43–FTR 14/15.4.43 Stuttgart; **EF332** 4.2.43–16.2.43; **EF350** 16.3.43–FA, RIW 7.5.43; **EF358:Q** 14.3.43–FA, RIW 17.4.43; **EF362** 18.3.43–EFA 30.3.43 Chedburgh, collided with BK663 during night circuit; **EF368** 29.8.43–10.2.44; **EF385** 7.8.43–22.12.43; **EF390** 1.8.43–FTR 12/13.8.43 Turin; **EF394** 18.4.43–19.6.43; **EF402** 29.8.43–19.6.43; **EF403** 29.8.43–FTR 27/28.9.43 Hanover; **EF404** ?.7.43–11.12.43; **EF405:R**

4.7.43–16.12.43; **EF407:A** 29.5.43–FTR 29/30.7.43 Hamburg; **EF409** 24.5.43–FTR 2/3.7.43 Hamburg; **EF409** 24.5.43–FTR 2/3.8.43 Hamburg; **EF444** 3.8.43–10.12.43; **EF445** 24.7.43–FTR 22.11.43 Berlin, icing trouble, crashed in sea; **EF447** 11.8.43–10.12.43; **EF463** 18.8.43–10.1.44; **EF493** 13.12.43–27.1.44; **EJ882:O** 14.5.43–FTR 23/24.6.43 Mülheim; **EH886** 21.5.43–19.6.43; **EH891** 31.5.43–19.6.43; **EH899:D, X** 5.6.43–23.8.43; **EH921:J** 26.6.43–18.8.43; **EH951** 11.8.43–10.1.44; **EH953** 22.8.43–11.1.44; **EH977** 7.9.43–23.12.43; **EH978** 11.9.43–23.12.43; **LJ477** 14.1.44–24.1.44; **LJ480** 15.12.43–30.1.44; **LJ501** 15.12.43–16.1.44; **LJ517** 14.1.44–6.2.44; **LJ521** 14.1.44–6.7.44.

218 Squadron

N3700:O 16.1.42–2.10.42; **N3708** 26.12.41–26.1.42; **N3709** 2.1.42–16.1.42; **N3721:Y** 26.1.42–EFB 3.3.42 Billancourt, bomb fell away on landing, exploded Marham; **N3713** 6.2.42–FA, RIW 13.2.42; **N3714:Q** 31.1.42–FTR 1/2.9.42 Saarbrücken; **N3715** 31.1.42–FA 27.2.42, SOC 16.3.42; **N3717:S** 6.2.42–EFB 29.8.42, crashed into Spitfire Vb of 317 Squadron and Albacore X9112 of 841 Squadron, Manston; **N3721:C, S, P** 23.4.42–1.11.43; **N3722:E** 8.3.42–7.9.42; **N3725:D** 15.3.42–EFB 15.3.42 engine trouble, spun in 1 mile E. Stoke Ferry; **N3753** 14.5.42–EFA 2.6.42 undershot Marham; **N3755:U** 18.5.42–14.9.42; **N3763:Q** 24.6.42–FTR 1/2.10.42 Lübeck; **N6070:A** 17.2.42–FTR 5.5.42 Pilsen; **N6071:G** 24.2.42–FTR 17/18.5.42 mining, Baltic, shot down nr Lyne, Denmark; **N6072:J, F** 24.2.42–FTR 7.8.42 Duisburg; **N6076** 10.3.42–12.3.42; **N6077:V** 8.3.42–FTR 28.1.43 mining; **N6078:P** 21.3.42–FTR 22/23.6.42 Emden; **N6089:L** 5.1.42–2.3.43; **N6126** 17.12.41–14.2.42; **N6127** 16.12.41–15.2.42; **N6128:T** 16.1.42–7.7.42; **N6129:X** 8.1.42–28.2.42; **R9159** 17.8.42–19.8.42; **R9184:U** 1.9.42–FTR 23/24.10.42 Genoa; **R9185:Y** 3.9.42–FTR 6/7.11.42 mining; **R9187:A** 12.9.42–FTR 23/24.9.42 mining; **R9189:K** 13.9.42–EFA 28.2.43 swung taking off Downham; **R9190:E** 16.9.42–FTR 11/12.10.42 mining, in sea off Saelgrunden Denmark; **R9196:G** 26.9.42–9.8.43; **R9203** 18.2.43–13.4.43; **R9241:L** 11.10.42–EFB 24.10.42 engine fire, broke up over Brentham, nr Colchester; **R9244:W** 15.10.42–26.9.43; **R9287** 4.3.43–26.3.43; **R9295** ?–?; **R9311:L** 6.4.42–EFA 31.5.42 hit hill just after take-off, belly landed; **R9313:Q** 7.4.42–EFA 5.5.52 shot down by British aircraft 5 miles N. Petworth, Sussex; **R9332:G** 30.5.42–EFB 31.7.42 uc collapsed, burnt Marham; **R9333:Y** 31.5.42–29.11.42, 23.1.43–FTR 5/6.3.43 Essen; **R9349** 2.6.42–FA, RIW 8.6.42; **R9354:N** 6.6.42–EFA 28.7.42; **R9357:E** 24.6.42–FTR 10/11.9.42 Düsseldorf, in sea 30 miles off Holland, engine trouble; **W7459** 18.12.41–2.1.42; **W7464:Z** 4.4.42–FTR 28/29.7.42 Hamburg; **W7469:M** 25.1.42–FA 24.6.42; **W7473:F** 11.2.42–EFA 23/24.4.42 Clinchwarton, King's Lynn, engine trouble; **W7474:K** 14.2.42–FTR 3/4.6.42 Bremen, shot down in Ijsselmeer by II/NJG 2; **W7475:H** 12.2.42–FTR 10.11.42 Hamburg; **W7502:N** 3.3.42–FTR 30/31.5.42 Cologne; **W7503:R, B** 10.3.42–FTR 25/26.6.42 Bremen, shot down by II/NJG 2 in Ijsselmeer; **W7505:P** EFA 14.3.42–?; **W7506:K** 27.2.42–FTR 26.4.42 Pilsen; **W7521:U** 12.4.42–EFB 5.5.42 Pilsen, airlock in fuel system, crashed nr Norwich; **W7530:Q** 8.5.42–FTR 20/21.6.42 Emden; **W7535:C** 13.5.42–FTR 29.5.42 Gennevilliers; **W7562:R** 27.6.42–FTR 24/25.8.42 Frankfurt; **W7568** 3.7.42–EFA 11.8.42 Brandon, engine and wiring fire, burnt; **W7573:U** 29.6.42–FTR 21.8.42 mining; **W7612:T** 25.7.42–EFA 9.11.42 undershot Tangmere; **W7613:N** 26.7.42–FTR 1/2.10.42 Lübeck; **W7614:J** 18.7.42–FTR undershot Tangmere; **W7613:N** 26.7.42–FTR 1/2.10.42 Lübeck; **W7614:J** 18.7.42–FTR 27/18.12.42 Fallersleben; **W7614:M** 29.7.42–FTR 21.8.42 mining; **W7617:V** 12.8.42–FTR 18/19.8.42 Flensburg; **W7622:B** 22.8.42–FA, RIW 5.10.42; **W7625:R** 26.8.42–30.10.42; **W7636:L** 13.9.42–EFA 3.10.42; **BF309:M** 25.6.42–FTR 28/29.7.42 Hamburg; **BF315:F** 28.6.42–FTR 28.8.42 Kassel, shot down at Elst, Holland; **BF319:C** 5.7.42–FTR 21.8.42 mining; **BF322:F** 4.9.42–EFB 5.10.42

Aachen, lightning strike, dived in nr Barton Mills; **BF338:Q** 9.8.42–FTR 21.8.42 mining; **BF343:N** 10.10.42–FTR 11/12.3.43 Stuttgart; **BF346:S** 2.9.42–?3.43; **BF349** 2.11.42–18.3.43; **BF351:C** 2.9.42–FTR 11.9.42 Düsseldorf, crashed St. Philipsland, Holland; **BF375:O** 8.10.42–26.4.43; **BF395:Z** 24.10.42–26.3.43; **BF401:N** 8.11.42–EFA 3.12.42; **BF403:R** 7.11.42–FTR 27/18.12.42 Fallersleben, naval flak, Den Helder, en route crashed in sea; **BF405:U** 2.11.42–FTR 27/28.5.43 mining, in sea 45 mile N. Leeuwarden; **BF406:Q** 18.11.42–FTR 3/4.2.43 Hamburg, shot down at Deelen, Holland; **BF408:T** 22.11.42–FTR 3/4.2.43 Hamburg; **BF413:H** 16.11.42–6.7.43; **BF416:T** 18.2.43–22.3.43; **BF440:U** 6.2.43–FA SOC 31.7.43 heavy landing Downham; **BF446:B** 15.1.43–30.7.43; **BF447:F** 7.2.43–FTR 28/29.4.43 mining; **BF450:X** 15.1.43–FTR 25/26.2.43 Nuremberg; **BF452:V** 25.2.43–25.9.43; **BF472:D** 25.3.43–FTR 27/28.9.43 Hanover; **BF480:I** 15.3.43–EFA 14.5.43 swung into Downham's watch office; **BF502:P** 23.3.43–FTR 8/9.4.43 Duisburg; **BF505:Z** 23.3.43–FTR 4/5.5.43 Dortmund, shot down at Dokkum, Holland; **BF514:X** 7.4.43–FTR 16.4.43 Mannheim; **BF515:N** 7.4.43–FTR 29.4.43 mining; **BF519:E** 14.4.43–FTR 30/31.7.43 Remscheid, crashed Numansdorp, Holland; **BF522** 5.5.43–FTR 23/24.8.43 Berlin; **BF566:H** 1.5.43–FTR 30.5.43 Wuppertal; **BF567:P** 4.5.43–FTR 24.7.43 Hamburg; **BF568:B** 5.5.43–13.8.43; **BF572:K** 7.5.43–FTR 22/23.6.43 Mülheim; **BF578:A** 20.5.43–DTR 30.7.43; **BK594:B** 30.9.42–FTR 20.4.43 Rostock; **BK606:N** 13.10.42–EFA 8.11.42 engines failed on circuit, crashed at Chiver's Farm nr Bourn; **BK607:X** 14.10.42–EFA 29.11.42; **BK650:L, T** 6.2.43–FTR 30.8.43 München-Gladbach, shot down Dorpplein Budel, Holland; **BK687:R** 7.2.43–FTR 8/9.10.43 Bremen; **BK700:L** 28.2.43–FTR 22/23.9.43 Hanover; **BK702:O** 8.3.43–FTR 30.3.43 Berlin; **BK705:K** 9.3.43–FTR 12/13.5.43 Duisburg; **B706:Y** 8.3.43–FTR 23/24.5.43 (?); **BK712:D** 13.4.43–FTR 22.6.43 Krefeld; **BK716:J** 17.3.43–FTR 30.3.43 Berlin; **BK722:G** 7.5.43–FTR 22.6.43 Krefeld; **BK727** 9.6.43–13.8.43; **BK803** 4.6.43–13.6.43; **DJ974:J** 1.5.42–FTR 27/28.6.42 Bremen; **DJ976:A** 26.9.42–FA, RIW 16.11.42; **DJ977:F** 22.4.42–FTR 19/20.5.42 Mannheim; **EE884:X, B** 31.5.43–FTR 18/19.11.43 Mannheim; **EE885:G** 2.6.43–FTR 11.8.43 Nuremberg: **EE888:H, K** 24.6.43–FTR 16/17.12.43 mining; **EE895** 30.6.43–FTR 30.7.43 (?); **EE903:Q** 7.7.43–FTR 30/31.8.43 München-Gladbach; **EE909:H** 29.6.43–13.8.43; **EE916** 29.6.43–?; **EE937:A, S** 29.6.43–FTR 27/28.9.43 Hanover; **EE944:O, H** 3.8.43–EFB 5.3.44 overshot Tempsford, sideslipped in; **EE949** 1.8.43–10.8.43; **EE966** 1.8.43–10.8.43; **EF133:A** 23.12.43–17.8.44; **EF141:H, N** 3.9.43–23.11.43, 8.1.44–11.2.44; **EF180:D** 29.9.43–FTR 22/23.11.43 Berlin; **EF181:J** 25.3.44–EFA 12.6.44 tyre burst taking off Woolfox Lodge; **EF184:L, I, V** 5.10.43–EFB 1/2.5.44 crash landed Woodbridge after attack by two Ju 88s; **EF185:L** 27.9.43–17.8.44; **EF207:F** 4.5.44–17.8.44; **EF233** 20.12.43–30.1.44; **EF249:H** 16.12.43–EFB 9.5.44 overshot, flapless landing Woolfox Lodge; **EF259:G** 23.12.44–FTR 2.5.44 Chambley; **EF291:C** ?.4.44–28.8.44; **EF299:Z** 14.1.44–EFA 13.6.44 overshot Woolfox Lodge; **EF340** 5.2.43–16.2.43; **EF352:Q** 28.2.43–18.8.43; **EF353:O** 28.2.43–FA 17.5.43 engine cut taking off, swung into crew room Downham; **EF356:O** 1.3.43–FTR 28/29.4.43 mining, Baltic, crashed Adum, Denmark; **EF365:G** 24.3.43–EFA 21.5.43 belly landed Bankhouse Farm, nr Downham; **EF367:G** 27.4.43–EFA 13/14.5.43 crashed Chedburgh; **EF410:Z** 21.5.43–27.1.44; **EF413** 31.5.43–FA 4.6.43 swung, hit gun post Downham, used again 16.10.43–29.1.43; **EF448:P** 30.6.43–FTR 27/28.8.43 Nuremberg; **EF449:J, D** 29.6.43–31.1.44; **EF462** 24.6.44–28.7.44; **EF504:P** 1.9.43–?.1.44; **EH878:I** 12.5.43–13.8.43; **EH884:H** 18.5.43–FTR 16/17.8.43 Turin; **EH887:Z** 20.5.43–FTR 25/26.5.43 Düsseldorf; **EH892:U** 3.6.43–FTR 24/25.6.43 Elberfeld; **EH898:G** 9.6.43–FTR 25/26.6.43 Gelsenkirchen, shot down at Lichtenroorde, Holland; **EH923:W, E** 30.6.43–2.2.44; **EH925** 3.7.43–13.8.43; **EH942:M** 3.9.43–FTR 22/23.4.44 Laon; **EH984:C** 14.8.43–FTR 3/4.10.43 Kassel; **EH986:X** 14.8.43–FTR 23/24.8.43 Berlin; **EH988** 18.8.43–EFA 1.9.43 engine trouble taking off Hartford Bridge; **EJ105:N** 3.9.43–EFA 22.9.43 crashed taking off for Hanover, burnt; **EJ112:Q** 12.9.43–28.7.44; **EJ125:J**

1.10.43–FTR 21/22.2.44 mining; **LJ446** 1.10.43–9.3.44; **LJ447:F** 29.9.43–17.8.44;
LJ448:D, A 29.9.43–FTR 21.4.44 Chambley; **LJ449:E** 1.10.43–17.8.44; **LJ452:S**
2.10.43–27.1.44; **LJ472:K** 28.11.43–17.8.44; **LJ481:B** 1.12.43–17.8.44; **LJ517:U** 6.2.44–
28.7.44; **LJ521:W** 16.7.44–28.7.44; **LJ522:N** 3.4.44–27.7.44; **LK396:M** 30.4.44–17.8.44;
LK401:I 10.5.44–17.8.44; **LK568:O** 14.6.44–26.7.44.

242 Squadron

PJ882 18.3.45–8.6.45; **PJ886** 18.3.45–8.6.45; **PJ889** 18.3.45–6.9.45, 27.11.45–15.2.46;
PJ897 24.10.45–?.11.45; **PJ903** 15.2.45–28.3.46; **PJ904** 15.2.45–17.6.45, 20.8.45–?;
PJ905 20.2.45–EFA 20.4.45 uc collapsed taxiing Mauripur; **PJ906** 22.2.45–17.6.45,
13.8.45–19.9.45; **PJ907** 22.2.45–12.2.46; **PJ908** 25.2.45–8.6.45; **PJ909** 25.2.45–EFA
22.3.45 swung taking off Mauripur; **PJ910** 28.2.45–21.3.45, 11.10.45–7.12.45; **PJ912**
18.2.45–8.6.45; **PJ913** 18.2.45–EFA 19.3.45 swung taking off Lydda; **PJ914** 25.2.45–
19.10.45; **PJ915** 25.2.45–8.6.45; **PJ916** 28.2.45–27.8.45; **PJ917** 28.2.45–3.12.45; **PJ918**
28.2.45–23.12.45; **PJ920** 20.10.45–22.12.45; **PJ922** 28.2.45–31.8.45; **PJ939** 8.3.45–
17.6.45; **PJ940** 15.3.45–8.10.45; **PJ941** 19.3.45–12.12.45; **PJ942** 24.3.45–30.9.45; **PJ943**
12.3.45–?.4.45; **PJ944** 12.3.45–19.10.45; **PJ946** 1.8.45–15.1.45; **PJ947** 21.6.45–4.10.45;
PJ951 21.6.45–?.7.45; **PJ979** 6.6.45–?; **PJ988** 6.6.45–3.12.45; **PJ989** 8.6.45–26.7.45;
PJ991 8.6.45–3.12.45; **PJ993** 10.6.45–19.3.46; **PJ994** 14.6.45–22.9.45; **PJ995** 14.6.45–
28.10.45; **PJ996** 21.6.45–24.9.45; **PJ997** 21.6.45–29.9.45; **PK134** 10.8.45–EFA 2.10.45
swung taking off Mauripur; **PK137** 20.8.45–3.12.45; **PK138** 20.8.34–11.2.46; **PK139**
20.8.45–1.4.46; **PK140** 20.8.45–7.3.46; **PK141** 20.8.45–8.1.46; **PK142** 14.8.45–19.10.45;
PK143 31.8.45–5.9.45; **PK152** 13.10.45–3.12.45; **PK153** 25.11.45–3.12.45; **PK154**
18.10.45–1.5.46; **PK155** 26.10.45–17.12.45; **PK156** 8.10.45–27.12.45; **PK157** 25.10.45–
20.12.45; **LJ616** 2.10.45–9.1.46; **LJ669** 23.9.45–9.10.45; **LK144** 29.9.45–7.11.45; **LK152**
23.9.45–EFA 9.10.45 hit LK118 landing Stoney Cross; **LK555** 2.10.45–28.11.45.

295 Squadron

EF274 23.9.44–EFA 18.4.45 swung landing Rivenhall; **EF293** 2.12.44–30.1.45; **EF446**
3.8.44–20.7.45; **EF470** 10.8.44–11.1.45; **LJ576** 18.8.44–25.1.46; **LJ590** 13.7.44–9.11.44;
LJ591 2.7.44–FB 20.9.44, 16.10.44–30.9.45; **LJ612** 3.8.44–10.12.44; **LJ618** 28.8.44–FTR
20.9.44 Arnhem; **LJ622** 9.11.44–24.5.45; **LJ633** 10.8.44–10.12.44; **LJ638** 1.8.44–
21.12.44; **LJ640** 25.9.44–10.12.44; **LJ652** 16.8.44–FB 19.9.44, 17.11.44–6.12.45; **LJ811**
16.3.45–5.4.45; **LJ884:8Z-L** 10.5.45–24.1.46; **LJ890** 10.12.44–15.4.45; **LJ922** 21.12.44–
21.1.45; **LJ929** 10.12.44–18.2.46; **LJ931** 13.7.44–FB 4.8.44, landing Harwell; **LJ948**
21.12.44–8.2.45; **LJ951:8E-W** 2.7.44–11.2.46; **LJ976:8E-Q** 13.7.44–25.1.46; **LJ977**
10.12.44–8.2.45; **LJ980** 14.6.44–27.11.45; **LJ986** 2.7.44–FB 25.9.44, 13.11.44–EGA
1.1.45 attacked on ground; **LJ995** 1.8.44–EFB 4.2.45 Rivenhall, swung taking off, hit tree,
exploded; **LK115** 23.8.44–FTR 21.9.44 Arnhem; **LK120** 3.8.44–FA 27.8.45 tyre burst in
flight, belly landed Woodbridge; **LK122** 10.12.44–EFA 1.6.45 landing Brussels; **LK128**
9.7.44–FB 24.9.44; **LK129** 14.8.44–EGA 13.4.45 hit by LJ616 when taxiing; **LK132**
23.8.44–FB 18.4.45 damaged landing B108; **LK134** 23.8.44–11.1.45; **LK136** 10.12.44–
1.1.46; **LK137** 28.8.44–FB 19.9.44 RIW, 30.9.44–FTR 24.3.45 S.O.E. op.; **LK140**
10.12.44–19.4.45; **LK141:8E-K** 28.8.44–FB 19.9.44, 14.10.44–9.1.46; **LK144** 10.8.44–FB
19.9.44, 11.10.44–19.4.45; **LK170** 3.9.44–FTR 19.9.44 Arnhem, crashed nr Bruges;
LK171 1.8.44–FB 19.9.44, 5.10.44–FTR 3.11.44 S.O.E. op.; **LK202** 22.9.44–10.12.44;
LK203 22.9.44–10.12.44; **LK271:8E-M** 14.6.45–25.1.46; **LK287** 30.9.44–EFA 18.7.45

swung taking off; **LK288** 30.9.44–EFA 9.3.45 taxied into tractor, Rivenhall; **LK289** 9.1.46–1.3.46; **LK290** 28.9.44–?.12.44; **LK292** 30.9.44–21.12.44; **LK300** 14.6.44–FA 21.10.45 crashed landing Istres; **LK330:8Z-A** 15.3.44–11.2.46; **LK346** 18.3.45–26.1.46; **LK351** 15.3.45–27.11.45; **LK439** 21.3.45–25.1.46; **LK513** 15.3.45–16.1.46; **LK543:8Z-K** 30.6.44–25.1.46; **LK553** 31.7.44–FB, RIW 20.9.44, 7.10.44–FA 10.3.45 control column jammed taking off, port uc collapsed, Rivenhall; **LK558** 1.8.44–FB 19.9.44, 1.10.44–19.4.45; **LK567** 13.8.44–FB 21.9.44, 3.10.44–FTR 26/27.4.45 S.O.E. op; **LK589** 9.7.44–28.2.45; **LK591** 1.7.44–EFA 25.7.44 engine trouble, crashed landing Gaydon; **PK226** 15.3.45–4.2.46; **PK228** 13.3.45–FTR 11/12.4.45; **PW255** 16.8.44–10.12.44; **PW425:8Z-N** 3.5.45–25.1.46; **PW439:8E-U** 3.5.45–16.1.46; **PW444** 3.5.45–14.6.46; **PW465** 21.11.45–25.1.46.

---

296 Squadron

LJ503 ?.7.44–FTR 1.9.44; **LK294** 7.6.45–?.

---

299 Squadron

EE966:X9-V 15.8.44–EFA 11.5.45 swung taking off Gardemoen, Norway; **EF237** ?.2.45–FA 5.4.45 undershot Shepherd's Grove; **EF243** 30.4.44–28.6.44; **EF261** 22.1.44–27.4.44; **EF267:X9-C** 22.1.44–FTR 19.9.44 Arnhem; **EF269** 22.1.44–EFA 25.4.44 crashed after dinghy wrapped around rudder, Rowde, Wilts.; **EF272** ?.1.45–FA 13.4.45, swung taking off Keevil; **EF277** 25.1.44–FA, RIW 7.5.44–tyre burst taking off Keevil; **EF293** 30.1.45–1.2.46; **EF305** 24.2.44–FA 7.8.44 overshot; **EF319** 7.1.44–FTR 19.9.44(?); **EF321:X9-A** 7.1.44–20.7.45; **EF322:5G-B** 28.2.45–3.4.45; **EF323:5G-F** 6.5.44–FB 14.2.45 engine fire; **EH950:X9-E** 19.5.44–23.7.45; **LJ572:X9-T** 17.5.44–21.6.45; **LJ583** 11.44–17.6.45; **LJ629:5G-O** 3.9.44–FB 22.4.45 uc collapsed landing; **LJ667** 11.1.46–29.3.46; **LJ668** 31.5.45–EFA 7.10.45 crashed in low cloud 3 miles S. Rennes, France; **LJ669:5G-M** 22.9.44–23.9.45; **LJ811** 18.1.44–RIW 8.8.44; **LJ812:X9-Z** 8.1.44–1.2.45; **LJ813** 13.1.44–29.4.44; **LJ814** 18.1.44–EFB 26.3.44 oil leak, crashed Brize Norton; **LJ815:5G-E** 12.1.44–24.2.45; **LJ817** 18.1.44–FA 2.5.44 Keevil uc collapsed landing; **LJ819** 21.1.44–FTR 6.6.44; **LJ821:5G-G** 24.1.44–FA, RIW 17.4.45, 8.11.45–29.1.46; **LJ835** ?9.44–23.6.45; **LJ836** 10.5.44–12.7.45; **LJ844:5G-E** 9.5.44–23.6.44; **LJ845** 27.9.44–24.5.45; **LJ871** 19.10.44–?.12.44; **LJ874:5G-I** 1.9.44–5.4.45; **LJ876** 15.8.44–1.11.44; **LJ877** 24.2.44–17.11.44; **LJ878** 1.5.44–FTR 6.8.44 S.O.E. op.; **LJ879:5G-W** 25.2.44–23.2.45, 22.10.45–10.3.46; **LJ884** 2.3.44–FB 21.9.44, 21.10.44–1.11.44, 24.1.46–23.2.46; **LJ885:C** 25.2.44–FTR 6.6.44 Op. *Mallard*; **LJ891:5G-D** 25.2.44–FB 24.9.44, RIW, 9.10.44–FA 20.11.44 uc collapsed landing Wethersfield, became 4942M; **LJ893:5G-Y** 9.5.44–FB 22.9.44, 4.10.44–25.5.45; **LJ896:5G-C** 1.5.44–FTR 21.2.45 Rees; **LJ897** 1.3.44–EFA 4.7.44 overshot Tarrant Rushton; **LJ915** 25.2.44–FB 24.9.44; **LJ919:5G-S** 17.5.44–11.1.45; **LJ940** 14.5.44–FTR 14/15.8.44 S.O.E. op.; **LJ942:5G-X** 14.5.44–FTR 2/3.4.45 S.O.E. op.; **LJ948:X9-W** 7.5.44–3.12.44; **LJ955:5G-Z** 14.5.44–FB 21.9.44, 24.10.44–20.7.45; **LJ956:5G-Q** 17.5.44–24.5.45; **LJ971:X9-X** 19.5.44–29.1.46; **LJ996:5G-W** 10.12.44–FTR 2/3.3.45 S.O.E. op.; **LK118:5G-U** 29.8.44–23.9.45; **LK124:X9-B** 25.8.44–12.3.46; **LK130:5G-H** 25.8.44–?9.44; **LK135:5G-N** 3.9.44–09.1.46; **LK148:5G-R** 22.9.44–29.9.45; **LK153:X9-Y** 15.8.44–EFA overshot after engine trouble taking off Shepherd's Grove; **LK156** 9.1.46–19.3.46; **LK226** ?.?.45–25.1.46; **LK232** 5.11.45–18.3.46; **LK239:X9-C** 22.9.44–29.1.46; **LK284:5G-V, X9-U** 28.9.44–29.1.46; **LK294** ?.10.45–11.2.46; **LK296** 14.6.45–29.1.46; **LK298** ?.2.45–FA 15.6.45 uc collapsed landing; **LK301**

19.4.45–18.3.46; **LK304** 31.8.45–29.1.46; **LK328** 21.3.46–25.3.46; **LK331** 15.3.45–FA 3.6.45 swung landing Blackbushe; **LK332** ?.3.45–FTR 30/31.3.45 S.O.E. op.; **LK341** 26.4.45–30.8.45; **LK364** 9.1.46–3.3.46; **LK428:X9-G** ?.12.44–24.5.45; **LK439:5G-J** 30.4.44–20.1.45; **LK509** 1.3.45–29.1.46; **LK542** 13.6.44–28.3.45; **LK544:5G-L** 13.6.44– FB 20.9.44, 10.10.44–0.1.45; **LK545** 13.6.44–FTR 21.9.44 Arnhem; **LK554** 14.6.45– 29.3.46; **PK234** 9.11.43–10.3.46; **PK235** 17.3.45–17.3.46; **PW406** 11.1.46–17.3.46; **PW415** 13.5.45–18.3.46; **PW446** 9.1.46–21.3.46; **PW448** 10.5.45–26.1.46; **PW465** 20.4.45–21.11.45.

513 Squadron

BF529 5.11.43–27.11.43; **EE958** 22.10.43–25.11.43; **EF116** 5.11.43–30.11.43; **EF146** 5.11.43–27.11.43; **EF200** 7.11.43–27.11.43; **EF201** 4.11.43–27.11.43; **EF205** 3.11.43– 27.11.43; **EF206** 4.11.43–27.11.43; **EF211** 3.11.43–27.11.43; **EF465** 26.10.43–28.11.43; **LK390** 8.11.43–27.11.43.

570 Squadron

EF275:E7-Y 10.5.45–20.2.46; **EF292:V8-G** 2.7.44–9.11.44; **EF298:V8-T** 10.8.44–FTR 23.9.44 Arnhem; **EF306:E7-Y** 28.7.44–FB 20.9.44, 23.10.44–4.1.45; **EH897:E7-Z** 28.7.44–FTR 19.9.44 Arnhem; **LJ590** 9.11.44–11.12.44; **LJ594:V8-N** 19.7.44–FTR 18.9.44 crashed nr Breda; **LJ596:V8-K** 28.9.44–20.4.45; **LJ613** 5.7.44–FB, RIW 18.9.44; **LJ615:V8-H** 19.7.44–24.5.45; **LJ616:V8-D** 1.8.44–2.10.45; **LJ620:V8-O** 16.8.44–FB 24.9.44, 20.10.44–19.4.45; **LJ622:V8-M** 9.7.44–FB 24.9.44, 4.11.44–9.11.44; **LJ631** 10.8.44–EFB 25.8.44; **LJ633:E7-R, M** 10.12.44–1.1.46; **LJ636:E7-N** 22.9.44–9.1.46; **LJ638:E7-Y** 21.12.44–FTR 11/12.4.45 S.O.E. op.; **LJ640:V8-B** 10.12.44–20.12.45; **LJ645:E7-M, V** 23.8.44–FB 24.9.44, 14.10.44–FTR 22/23.4.45 S.O.E. op., shot down by flak over Aarhus, crashed Skaering, Denmark; **LJ647:V8-U** 16.8.44–FTR 19.9.44 Arnhem, crashed Grave; **LJ650:E7-W** 23.11.44–9.1.46; **LJ667:V8-U** 22.9.44–29.3.46; **LJ883:V8-K** 9.7.44–FTR 23.9.44 Arnhem; **LJ884** 23.2.46–27.2.46; **LJ890:V8-W** 11.8.44–10.12.44; **LJ913:V8-P** 19.7.44–FTR 18.9.44 Arnhem; **LJ929** 2.7.44–10.12.44; **LJ948** 3.12.44–21.12.44; **LJ975** 28.7.44–3.8.44; **LJ977:V8-B** 18.10.44– 10.12.44; **LJ980** 10.8.44–FB 21.9.44; 2.11.44–14.6.45; **LJ985:V8-S, M** 30.6.44–4.1.45; **LJ991:E7-W** 10.8.44–FTR 23.9.44 Arnhem, crashed Nijmegen; **LJ992:E7-K** 3.9.44– 22.6.45; **LJ994:E7-L** 19.7.44–4.1.45; **LJ996:E7-X** 3.9.44–10.12.44; **LK117:V8-F** 9.7.44– FB 24.9.44; **LK120** 19.7.44–3.8.44; **LK121:V8-F** 9.7.44–FTR 18.9.44 Arnhem; **LK122:V8-R** 23.8.44–10.12.44; **LK126:V8-C** 9.7.44–FB 20.9.44, 8.10.44–3.12.44; **LK133:V8-J** 19.7.44–FTR 28/29.7.44 S.O.E. op.; **LK136:V8-Y** 23.8.44–FB 20.9.44, 30.9.44–10.12.44; **LK138:V8-Q** 28.8.44–FB 21.9.44, 30.9.44–4.1.45; **LK140:V8-E** 28.8.44–10.12.44; **LK150:V8-H** 22.9.44–?.3.46; **LK154:E7-P** 22.9.44–9.1.45; **LK156:V8-I** 22.9.44–9.1.46; **LK190:V8-J** 15.8.44–FB, RIW 20.9.44; **LK191:V8-G** 22.9.44–FTR 23.9.44 Arnhem; **LK119:V8-L** 31.8.44–18.2.46; **LK202:E7-X** 10.12.44– EFA 18.4.45 uc collapsed taking off; **LK203:V8-E** 10.12.44–EFA 9.3.45; **LK240** ?.1.45– 25.1.46; **LK277:V8-O** 26.9.44–19.3.45; **LK286:E7-T** 28.9.44–EFA 2.4.45 swung landing Rivenhall; **LK289:V8-F** 30.9.44–9.1.46; **LK290** ?.12.44–FA 27.10.45 port tyre burst in flight, belly landed Woodbridge; **LK291:V8-A** 30.9.44–25.1.46; **LK292:E7-V** 21.12.44– 25.1.46; **LK328:V8-C** 15.3.45–31.1.46; **LK357** 19.4.45–26.4.45; **LK364:V8-O** 12.3.45– 9.1.46; **LK549:E7-J** 23.9.44–25.1.46; **LK551** 28.9.44–20.4.45; **LK555:V8-S** 31.7.44– 2.10.45; **LK599:V8-X** 21.7.44–16.1.46; **LK560:V8-Z** 19.7.44–EFB 17.9.44 Arnhem;

PK234:V8-E 11.3.45–9.11.45; **PW406:E7-I** 17.3.45–11.1.46; **PW422:E7-M** 3.5.45–EFA 14.11.45 crashed into houses 1 mile S.E. Evere, Belgium; **PW440:E7-O** 10.5.45–EFA 28.12.45 tyre burst landing; **PW446:V8-M** 10.5.45–9.1.46; **PW449:E7-X** 3.5.45–9.1.46; **TS266:V8-K** 15.3.45–18.2.46.

620 Squadron

BF466 19.7.43–EFA 1.8.43 overshot, uc collapsed; **BF502:H** 21.6.43–11.2.44; **BF511** 19.6.43–FTR 26.7.43 Aachen, crashed Hoenderloo, Holland; **BF525:Q** 4.7.43–10.12.43; **BF573** 21.6.43–10.12.43; **BF576:F** 29.6.43–FTR 28.8.43 Nuremberg; **BF580** 21.6.43–10.1.44, 11.6.44–27.11.44; **BK690** 19.6.43–FTR 6/7.8.43 mining, Gironde; **BK713:E** FTR 12/13.8.43 Turin; **BK720** 19.6.43–EFA 25.6.43; **BK724** 19.6.43–EFA 2.7.43 collided when flying in formation with EF394, dived into trees Chedburgh; **BK800** 19.6.43–FTR 24/25.6.43 Wuppertal; **BK801** 19.6.43–FTR 23/24.8.43 Berlin; **BK802:Z** ?.7.43–EFA 20.10.43 icing, baled out White Waltham; **EE875** 21.6.43–FTR 22/23.6.43 Mülheim; **EE905** 3.7.43–FTR 30/31.7.43 Remscheid; **EE906** 3.7.43–FTR 26.7.43(?); **EE946** 5.8.43–FTR 27/28.8.43 Nuremberg; **EE945:S** 26.7.43–30.8.43; **EF117:X** 15.8.43–11.2.44; **EF121:F** 22.8.43–30.3.44; **EF134:G** 30.8.43–11.2.44; **EF136** 30.8.43–EFA 8.9.43 swung taking off Chedburgh; **EF143:C** 3.8.43–9.3.44; **EF189:W** 5.10.43–18.12.43; **EF197:Z** 14.10.43–30.3.44; **EF203:Q** 21.10.43–26.6.44; **EF233** 15.12.43–20.12.43; **EF237** 7.2.44–13.12.44; **EF244** 27.3.44–EFA 19.5.44 hit LJ880 over D.Z., broke up in flight 1 mile W.S.W. Kempsford, Glos.; **EF256** 7.2.44–FTR 10.8.44 S.O.E. op.; **EF268** 30.4.44–FTR 6.6.44; **EF275** 27.2.44–FA 21.8.44; **EF293** 4.2.44–9.7.44; **EF295** 7.2.44–FTR 5/6.6.44; **EF303** 10.2.44–9.7.44; **EF336** 21.6.43–EFA 29.7.43 swung landing Chedburgh; **EF338** 21.6.43–5.7.43; **EF394** 19.6.43–EFA 2.7.43 collided with BK724 Chedburgh; **EF429** 19.6.43–FA, RIW 16.9.43 belly landed Newmarket; **EF433:W** 19.6.43–11.2.44; **EF440:B** 19.7.43–29.5.44; **EF442:O** 30.6.43–10.12.43; **EF451** 19.7.43–FTR 27/28.8.43; **EF456:R** 26.7.43–21.5.44; **EF457:A** 11.7.43–FTR 17/18.8.43 Peene-münde; **EF470:E** 3.8.43–FB, RIW 5.11.43, 11.1.45–8.2.45; **EH886** 19.6.43–FA 5.7.43 heavy landing Chedburgh; **EH891:O** 19.6.43–30.3.44; **EH894:D** 30.6.43–3.2.44; **EH896** 11.7.43–FTR 30/31.7.43 Remscheid; **EH931:O** 8.8.43–FTR 5/6.9.43 Mannheim; **EH946:P** 26.7.43–FTR 31.8.43 Berlin; **EH983** 24.10.43–30.3.44; **EJ116** 13.5.44–FTR 5/6.6.44; **LJ440:V** 10.9.43–30.3.44; **LJ445** 24.9.43–9.3.44; **LJ456:D** 15.10.43–11.2.44; **LJ459:E** 19.10.43–11.2.44; **LJ463** 7.11.43–30.3.44; **LJ475** 27.3.44–EFA 13.4.44 released towrope too steeply, dived in Blackford Farm, Kunsford, Glos.; **LJ566** 18.5.44–FB 20.9.44, 4.10.44–2.6.45; **LJ588** 18.5.44–19.4.45; **LJ627** 10.9.44–EFA 21.4.45 swung into bomb crater Rheine; **LJ668** 18.3.45–31.5.45; **LJ816** 5.10.44–8.10.44; **LJ817** 5.10.44–4.1.45; **LJ828** 15.7.44–16.8.44; **LJ830** 23.6.44–FTR 21.9.44 Arnhem; **LJ847** 7.2.44–20.4.45; **LJ849** 8.2.44–FTR 6.6.44(?); **LJ850** 11.2.44–FTR 17.6.44 S.O.E. op.; **LJ864** 7.2.44–FTR 22.7.44 S.O.E. op.; **LJ865** 10.2.44–9.7.45; **LJ866** 7.2.44–20.4.45; **LJ867** 7.2.44–FTR 11.4.44 S.O.E. op.; **LJ869** 7.2.44–FA, RIW 9.6.44 collided with Horsa LH562, belly landed; **LJ871** 11.6.44–19.10.44, ?–31.3.45; **LJ872** 8.2.44–20.4.45; **LJ873** 10.2.44–FTR 24.9.44(?); **LJ875** 8.2.44–13.3.45; **LJ880** 11.2.44–EFA 19.5.44 hit by AF244 over D.Z., broke up on impact 1 mile W.S.W. Kempsford, Glos.; **LJ886** 24.4.44–FTR 7/8.5.44 S.O.E. op.; **LJ887** 21.5.44–9.7.45; **LJ892** 24.4.44–FB 21.9.44, 17.10.44–7.12.44; **LJ914** 11.5.44–FTR 1.12.44 S.O.E. op.; **LJ917** 2.5.44–FB 21.9.44, 18.10.44–7.12.44; **LJ918** 21.5.44–FB, RIW 21.9.44, 23.10.44–16.11.44; **LJ920** 17.5.44–FTR 4.8.44 S.O.E. op.; **LJ921** 9.5.44–7.6.44; **LJ927** 22.7.44–9.7.45; **LJ930** 21.5.44–FB 24.9.44, 12.10.44–21.12.44; **LJ935** 9.5.44–9.7.44; **LJ948** 8.2.45–9.7.44; **LJ952** 17.5.44–26.4.45; **EF132** 14.9.43–2.12.43; **EF144:R** 15.9.43–1.12.43; **EF145** 21.9.43–1.1.44; **EF150:E** 17.9.43–FTR 22/23.11.43 Berlin; **EF153** 16.9.43–26.9.43; **EF154** 29.9.43–8.10.43;

EF161:Z 22.9.43–27.9.43; **EF186** 8.10.43–18.10.43; **EF208** 22.10.43–8.12.43; **EF217** 24.10.43–9.11.43; **EF351:I** 10.8.43–17.8.43; **EF460** 10.12.43–27.12.43; **EF490** 10.8.43–1.1.44; **EH897:Z** 2.8.43–FA 11.8.43; **EH921:D** 18.8.43–4.12.43; **EH956:F** 16.9.43–27.12.43; **EH991:P** 21.8.43–FTR 27/28.9.43 Hanover; **EH992:O** 28.8.43–4.12.43; **EJ113:Q** 15.9.43–FTR 18.11.43 Mannheim; **EJ114:R** 15.9.43–1.12.43; **LJ444:A** 17.9.43–1.1.44; **LJ451** 13.12.43–1.1.44; **LJ455** 21.10.43–1.1.44; **LJ456** 15.10.43–11.2.44; **LK396** 24.10.43–9.11.43; **LK403** 23.10.43–12.11.43; **MZ264:A** 18.8.43–FTR 31.8.43 Berlin.

622 Squadron

BF521:H 10.8.43–FTR 23/24.8.43 Berlin; **BF562:H** 18.8.43–4.12.43; **BK652:E** 10.8.43–16.10.43; **BK766:G** 10.8.43–8.12.43; **BK816:B** 10.8.43–9.1.44; **EF119:Q** 20.8.43–FTR 31.8.43 Berlin; **EF122:M** 20.8.43–4.12.43; **EF123:A** 30.8.43–EFB 19.11.43 Leverkusen, crashed base on return; **EF126:F, Q** 25.8.43–EFA 21.9.43 swung taking off; **EF127:N** 26.8.43–8.12.43; **EE899:C** 18.8.43–10.2.44; **EE909:H** 13.8.43–FTR 27/28.9.43 Nuremberg; **EE949:G** 10.8.43–FTR 31.8.43 Berlin; **EE966:E** 10.8.43–21.9.43; **EF155:O** 22.9.43–FTR 18/19.11.43 Mannheim; **EF156:E** 22.9.43–FTR 7/8.11.43 mining; **EF157:R** 22.9.43–2.12.43; **EF158:S** 23.9.43–FTR 3/4.10.43 Kassel; **EF194:W** 14.10.43–2.12.43; **EF199:I** 9.10.43–15.12.43; **EF204:E** 22.10.43–2.12.43; **EF241** 2.12.43–13.12.43; **EF246** 29.11.43–13.12.43; **EF252** 7.1.44–9.2.44; **EF262** 5.1.44–14.1.44; **EF271** 23.12.43–30.1.44; **EF461** 14.8.43–4.12.43; **EF489:F** 10.8.43–2.12.43; **EF493** 19.8.43–13.12.43; **EF499:K** 22.8.43–25.9.43; **EH878:I** 13.8.43–FTR 5/6.9.43 Mannheim; **EH925:C** 13.8.43–FTR 23/24.8.43 Berlin; **EH994:P** 27.8.43–FTR 3/4.10.43 Kassel; **EJ121:Q** 22.9.43–2.12.43; **EJ123:A** 22.9.43–2.12.43; **EJ124** 22.9.43–15.12.43; **LJ443:G** 22.9.43–2.12.43; **LJ450:V** 15.10.43–2.12.43; **LJ466** 27.11.43–11.12.43; **LJ477** ?.11.43–14.1.44; **LJ480** 13.12.43–15.12.43; **LJ482** 14.1.44–27.1.44; **LJ509** 4.12.43–15.12.43; **LJ517** 29.12.43–14.1.44; **LJ521** 29.12.43–14.1.44; **LK387:P** 7.10.43–9.11.43.

623 Squadron

BF568:B 13.8.43–15.12.43; **BK727:A** 13.8.43–11.12.43; **BK803:D** 13.6.43–29.11.43; **EE876:T** 18.8.43–29.11.43; **LJ970** 18.5.44–FTR 28.12.44 S.O.E. op.; **LJ973** 11.6.44–9.7.45; **LJ977** 15.8.44–FB 21.9.44, 5.10.44–EFB 20/21.3.45 S.O.E. op., Norway; **LK123** 15.8.44–31.1.46; **LK127** 15.8.44–FTR 20.9.44 Arnhem; **LK134** 11.1.45–31.5.45; **LK298** 21.12.44–?.?.45; **LK303** 18.3.45–14.6.45; **LK304** 4.10.44–31.8.45; **LK391:X** 15.10.43–3.2.44; **LK395** 27.10.43–FTR 4/5.2.44; **LK432** 10.2.44–7.6.45; **LK509** 2.5.44–1.3.45; **LK513** ?.6.44–FB 19.9.44; **LK548** 2.9.44–FTR 20.9.44 Arnhem; **LK554** 28.9.44–14.6.45; **PW395** ?.3.45–20.4.45; **PW410** 22.3.45–31.5.45.

624 Squadron

Aircraft used between June and September 1944: **LJ953**; **LJ969** SOC 31.8.44; **LJ927:S**; **LJ974:Q**; **LJ978** SOC 31.8.44; **LJ984:T** EFB 18.8.44; **LJ987:X**; **LK172**; **LK175:R**; **LK177** SOC 31.8.44; **LK178** SOC 31.8.44; **LK179:M**; **LK180:H**; **LK181**; **LK182** SOC 31.8.44; **LK184:Y**; **LK185**.

Appendix 5

Long Service and Outstanding Stirlings

Records suggest that N3721 flew the highest number of sorties. Initially delivered on 23 February 1942 to 218 Squadron, it was transferred to 1653 Conversion Unit on 1 November 1943 and on the 4th was belly landed. Quickly repaired, it remained active until struck off charge as obsolete on 1 May 1944.

Its operational career began on 26 March 1942. As HA:C it set off for Essen, first of its 61 sorties. Its first mining sortie came on 22 April. After 12 sorties it was overhauled, returning, as HA:S, to attack Bremen on 6 June. Between then and the 29th it flew seven sorties: four to Bremen, three mining. It then came off operations, returning to battle on 23 September as HA:P for the Vegesack raid. Thus identified, it flew 29 bombing and eight mining sorties. Its only visit to Berlin was on 1 March 1942. It once crossed the Alps, to Turin's Fiat works on 28 November 1942. On 13 May 1943 it returned to operations as HA:J. Nine mining sorties were flown before its final operation against Hamburg on 25 July 1943. An incendiary bomb struck the tail unit, ending its front line career.

Runner-up was W7529, with 59 sorties. It joined 7 Squadron on 24 April 1942, passing to 1665 Conversion Unit on 29 September 1943, was transferred to 6 Maintenance Unit on 10 April 1944, and was struck off charge on 14 January 1945. As MG-W it flew 22 Main Force raids in the hands of Flt. Sgt. Runciman, then was piloted by Plt. Off. J. S. Watt. On 20 May 1942 it raided Cologne; its usual load was 192×30 lb. incendiaries. On 1 June 1942 it was damaged by flak, which wounded Sgt. Bryant and the observer. No other sorties flown were abortive.

On 24 August 1942 W7529 began Pathfinder duties. On 10 September 1942 Düsseldorf was the target and the aircraft, carrying flares, was hit by flak. Ten times it went to Italy, aborting once on account of icing. On 21 December 1942, now credited with 41 sorties, MG:W headed for Munich and was holed west of Rheims during a fighter attack. The gunners claimed a Bf 190F; Flt. Lt. C. A. Hughes nursed W7529 home.

Repaired, it resumed operations as MG:E on 4 February 1943 with a Turin raid. It made 16 more sorties bombing and marking and once mined, only once aborting. Berlin was first listed on 27 March 1943. The starboard inner engine gave trouble, the mission ending at Brandenburg. On 29 March port engine trouble brought another abandonment. The final operation came on 11 June 1943, when Flg. Off. J. W. Leitch took the aircraft to Münster.

In third place was N3669. It joined 7 Squadron on 25 August 1941, transferring to 26 Conversion Flight on 31 December. At Waterbeach on 29 January 1942 the tailwheel chassis was damaged by running over a manhole cover. N3669 resumed front line service on 27 February with XV Squadron. Damaged when landing on 13 May after operations, it re-entered battle on the 16th. Finally grounded as 3637M in January 1943, it was displayed outside St. Paul's Cathedral, London, in February, and ended its life as a ground trainer at Manby.

As MG:E N3669 first operated on 28 August 1941 to Duisburg. Berlin was target on 2 September, and Wg. Cdr. Graham took it to Turin on 10 September. After the manhole cover accident, it re-entered operational service as LS:C on 3 March 1942; during mining on the 23rd, flak shot away an elevator tab control. After its eighth sortie as LS:C it was overhauled, returning to operations as LS:H on 28 July 1942 and flying 34 more sorties, five of which were abortive. Three times N3669 went to Italy; its last operation was against Frankfurt on 2 December 1942, when Flt. Sgt. Halkett (19 times captain) headed the crew.

The most successful Mk. III is in fourth place overall: BK687, which between 13 February and 8 October 1943 flew 54 operations as HA:R. From the 55th sortie, to Bremen, it failed to return. Eight of its sorties were mining, three to Berlin and one to Turin.

EJ122 of 149 Squadron flew 51 sorties, many of them mining and S.O.E. operations, ending its active career on 12 August 1944.

Five other Stirlings are known to have made over 40 sorties: EJ109 of 149 Squadron— 46; BK781 of 90 and 149 Squadrons—45; EH993 of 149 Squadron—44; BK784 of 90 Squadron—43, ended when it crashed soon after take-off for the west Frisians on 23 May 1944; and BK619 of 75 Squadron—42.

Appendix 6

Sorties Flown by Stirling Squadrons of 3 Group, 1941–4

1941

Sqn.	7	XV	149	Monthly totals
Feb.	8	—	—	8
Mar.	15	—	—	15
Apr.	30	4	—	34
May	37	17	—	54
June	46	49	—	95
July	35	52	—	87
Aug.	41	40	—	81
Sep.	55	40	—	95
Oct.	63	39	—	102
Nov.	25	47	2	74
Dec.	39	35	9	83
TOTALS	394	323	11	728

1942

Sqn.	7	XV	149	214	75	218	Monthly totals
Jan.	12	31	26	—	—	—	69
Feb.	2	28	13	—	—	8	51
Mar.	52	42	34	—	—	46	174
Apr.	107	93	72	—	—	112	384
May	80	60	81	—	—	79	300
June	93	96	102	92	—	113	496
July	117	98	97	89	—	90	491
Aug.	84	99	78	105	—	94	460
Sep.	65	100	110	85	—	100	470
Oct.	62	82	76	68	—	94	382
Nov.	86	64	61	48	11	80	350
Dec.	49	43	30	50	27	54	253
TOTALS	809	836	780	537	38	870	3880

1943

Sqn.	7	XV	75	90	149	196	199	214	218	620	622	623	Monthly totals
Jan.	19	27	28	33	23	—	—	36	49	—	—	—	215
Feb.	88	62	102	82	113	—	—	102	124	—	—	—	673
Mar.	99	128	90	67	89	—	—	106	122	—	—	—	701
Apr.	84	156	102	108	97	—	—	103	127	—	—	—	777
May	92	187	122	101	121	—	—	129	113	—	—	—	865
June	84	111	106	129	103	—	—	107	110	—	—	—	772
July	42	69	135	111	98	18	6	68	130	52	51	38	1,104
Aug.	10	98	172	186	108	91	94	84	107	65	66	28	995
Sept.	—	90	150	139	94	50	85	67	94	78	46	36	519
Oct.	—	44	56	65	44	3	44	39	49	91	40	35	414
Nov.	—	36	96	57	39	—	38	52	44	46	3	2	198
Dec.	—	4	42	37	35	—	—	50	25	24	—	—	216
TOTALS	518	1,012	1,201	1,115	964	162	267	943	1,094	356	206	139	7,449

1944

M=mining; B=bombing; SD=Special Duty drops; L=leaflet drops

Sqn.	75	90	149	214	218	MONTHLY TOTALS: by type	all sorties
Jan.	69M 65B 6SD	57M 65B —	34M 41B —	11M 17B —	5M 41B —	176M 229B 6SD	411
Feb.	112M —	92M —	18M 44SD	— —	59M —	281M 44SD	325
Mar.	56M 28B 84SD	60M 82B 68SD	41M 43B 56SD	— — —	— — —	157M 153B 208SD	518
Apr.	25M 9B — —	79M 24B 107SD 4L	78M 16B 59SD —	— — — —	51M 62B — —	233M 111B 166SD 4L	514
May	— — —	64M 80SD —	53M 65SD —	— — —	35M — 16B	152M 145SD 16B	313
Jun.	— — —	34M 15B 27SD	— 20B 25SD	— — —	49M — —	83M 35B 52SD	170
Jul.	— — —	— — —	8M 55B 37SD	— — —	38M 35B —	46M 90B 37SD	173
Aug.	— —	— —	31M 26B	— —	— —	31M 26B	57
Sep.	—	—	11B	—	—	11B	11
TOTALS:							
M	262	386	263	11	237	1,159M	
B	102	186	212	17	154	671B	
SD	90	282	286	—	—	658SD	
L	—	4	—	—	—	4L	
ALL TYPES:	454	858	761	28	391	2,492	

Total sorties by 3 Group Stirlings: 14,549

Index

Aachen, 126, 128
Aasfjord, 76
Abbeville, 64, 136
Adams, Group Captain C. D., 88
Aeroplane & Armament Experimental
  Establishment, 33–6, 47, 52, 54, 56
Airborne Forces Experimental
  Establishment, 148, 150
Airfields: Alconbury, 68, 76, 89;
  Bottesford, 108; Bourn, 69, 74, 90, 100,
  105, 108; Chedburgh, 103, 105, 122,
  124, 129, 134, 136; Downham Market,
  103, 107, 124, 128, 129; Fairford, 155,
  156, 158, 163; Feltwell, 118; Gransden,
  118; Graveley, 68; Great Ashfield, 122;
  Great Dunmow, 172; Harwell, 158;
  Keevil, 155, 160; Lakenheath, 76, 106,
  118, 124, 133, 138; Leeming, 37;
  Leicester East, 152, 153; Lossiemouth,
  76, 78, 80; Marham, 76, 103, 104;
  Mepal, 122, 124, 127, 133; Methwold,
  138, 140; Mildenhall, 70, 105, 118, 128;
  Newmarket Heath, 52, 56, 57, 58, 69,
  89, 105, 107, 117, 118, 124, 126, 134;
  North Creake, 138; Oakington, 45, 46,
  47, 48, 50, 51, 52, 54, 56, 60, 65, 67, 68,
  69, 70, 76, 88, 89, 100, 105, 108;
  Peterhead, 77; Polebrook, 183;
  Ridgewell, 108, 122; Rivenhall, 172,
  174; Shepherd's Grove, 172, 174;
  Stradishall, 56, 103, 122, 133, 181;
  Tarrant Rushton, 154, 155; Tilstock,
  158, 163; Warboys, 69; Waterbeach,
  68, 70, 76, 122, 133; Wethersfield, 172;
  Witchford, 133; Woolfox Lodge, 124,
  136, 152; Wyton, 54, 68, 76, 100
Air/Sea Rescue operations, 121, 124, 140
Albemarle, 148, 158
Alps, 69, 104, 106, 129
Amiens, 138
Antwerp, 70
Arnhem, 158, 159–69
Arques, 65
Aulnoye, 138
Austin Motors, 58, 67, 94, 112, 128

B.8/41, 82
B.12/36, 21–6
Baldwin, Air-Vice Marshal J. E. A., 93

Base organisations, 118, 122, 133, 136
B.D.U./Bombing Development Unit, 118,
  128
Beaverbrook, Lord, 48
Berlin, 57, 58, 59, 60, 71, 80, 115, 118,
  131, 132, 135
Billancourt, 87
Boozer, 118, 130
Borkum, 58, 64
Boulogne, 65, 106, 132, 139
Bremen, 68, 70, 95, 96, 100
Bremerhaven, 68, 71
Brest, 52, 66, 69, 70, 72, 74, 75, 76, 78, 80,
  140
Bull, J., 31

Chambley, 138
Chandler, E. F., 160, 161, 164
Chandler, Group Captain M., 19
Chocques, 65
Circus operations, 64–6
Cologne, 68, 78, 88, 92–3, 124
Conversion Flight/Unit, 76, 93, 98, 103;
  No. 26, 70; No. 1651, 70, 76, 78, 94,
  100, 101, 122, 136; No. 1653, 129, 133,
  136; No. 1657, 103, 122; No. 1660,
  136; No. 1665, 122, 124, 136, 153, 158,
  163
Cotton, G., 31
Courtrai, 138
Cuxhaven, 80

Diepholtz, 107
Dornier Do 17z, 38, 52
Dortmund, 121
Downie, I. A., 174, 175
Duisburg, 68, 118, 121, 122
Dunkirk, 64, 65
Düsseldorf, 100, 121, 124

Early production, 36
Elberfeld, 124
Emden, 58, 63, 76, 95
Essen, 87–8, 94, 95, 115, 117, 118, 126,
  127
Exactor throttle, 32, 41, 43, 54, 56, 92,
  105, 110, 154
Exercise *Annex*, 182

Falaise, 140
Fallersleben, 108
First flight, 31–2
Fishpond, 118
Flight: 1575, 171; 1588, 182, 183; 1589, 182
Flight Lieutenant: Baignot, 104; Barr, 98; Bennett, C. E., 52; Best, E. V., 52, 57; Blacklock, G., 48, 52, 57, 63, 64, 66; Campbell, 65, 66, 174; Collins, 63; Crebbin, W. N., 72–4, Crompton, P. R., 70; Cruikshank, 57, 59; Frowde, 180; Gardiner, 158; Gilmour, 64, 78; Gray, 182; Hannah, 154; Heathcote, G. G., 75; Howard-Smith, G., 48; Humphries, 88; Lay, D. J. H., 68, 69; Munro, 166; Parish, C. W., 105, 141–2; Parkin, 94; Parnell, 74; Pike, V. F. B., 52, 57; Raymond, 58, 59; Sanders, D. A. J., 68, 69; Taylor, 156; Thoing, F., 158; Turner, R. T., 165; Weston, 124; Williams, 57; Winch, N. E., 94
Flight Sergeant: Aaron, A. L., 129; Bailey, J. M., 105; Breeze, J. T., 169–70; Corlett, 105; Freeman, 108; Gilbert, T., 156; Halford, W. R., 174; Herger, 162; Macmillan, 94; McMilland, 93; McMonagle, 107; McNamara, 155; Marshall, J. S., 142; Middleton, R. H., V. C., 106–7; Orange, 166; Payne, 174; Roberts, E. J., 127; Rothschild, 121; Shiells, J., 115; Waddicar, 96; Welton, 165; White, O. H., 130–1; Wilkinson, 128; Yardley, 65
Flying accidents, 49, 122, 137
Flying Officer: Allen, 87; Baker, W., 167; Bell, 155; Blunden, K. O., 68; Bunce, G., 75; Carey, 165; Chesterton, G. H., 153, 154, 155, 162, 164; Cox, R. W., 46, 48, 63, 64, 66; Duncan, G., 127; Duro, 106; Ellis-Brown, R., 69, 72–4; Farren, 162, 166; Frazer, 65; Kczvajer, 180; King, 98; Kinnane, J., 64; McKee, J. J., 140; McKewon, 162; Mcleod, 165; Marsh, 64; Mills, J. L. A., 64; Mitchell, 60; Murphy, B. S., 166; Norton, J. A., 166; Owen, 182; Pascoe, 162, 166; Phillips, 93; Rolfe, C. I., 65, 68; Sach, J. F., 57; Sigert, 165; Thompson, 64; Timperly, 169; Torens, D. P. J., 174; Trench, J. P., 101, 118; Turner, G., 127; Vernieux, 75; Walker, 66; Walton, W., 181; Witt, 58, 64, 65, 66, 67, 68

Force: expansion strength, 105, 107, 116, 118, 120, 121, 122, 128, 132, 137, 159, 168, 174
Fôret de Nieppes, 140
Frankfurt, 70, 80, 100, 107, 120, 121, 134
Fromental, 140
Fromontine, 66

Gee, 67, 72, 87, 92, 94, 95, 104
Gee-H, 140
Gelsenkirchen, 124
Gennevilliers, 92, 93
Genoa, 69, 104, 105
Gironde Estuary, 107
Gloster Aircraft/Hucclecote, 40
Gneisenau, 57, 67, 74, 80
Gouge, Arthur, 82
Graf, J., 176, 177, 179
Grevenbroich, 174
Groix, 88

Hamburg, 58, 68, 98, 104, 115, 126, 127, 128
Hamilcar, 148
Hanover, 68, 132
Hardwick, D. H., 157
Harris, Air Chief Marshal Sir Arthur, 92, 94, 116
Hazebrouck, 65
Heinkel He 111, 38
Herrenwyk, 97
Hollinghurst, Air-Vice Marshal, 156
Horsa, 148, 155, 156, 159–68, 175
Hotspur, 148
H2S, 118, 121, 128, 133, 149
Hüls, 68

Junkers Ju 88, 127, 130, 131, 133, 134, 158

Karlsruhe, 80
Kassel, 134
Krefeld, 103
Kristiansund, 80

Lake Bourget, 133
Lancaster: enters 3 Group, 135–7, 138, 150; Mk. II, 116, 128
Laon, 138
La Pallice, 66
Le Creusot, 124
Lens, 65
Les Landes, 139
Les Lanvielles-et-Neuss, 139
Le Trait, 65

Leverkusen, 135
Lille, 64, 65
Lingen, 107
Lista, 80
Lofotens, 76
Long service aircraft, 79–80
Lorient, 115, 116
Lübeck, 88, 103, 127
Ludwigshafen, 135

MacRobert, Lady, 77, 78
'MacRobert's Reply', 75, 77, 78, 79
Magdeburg, 68
Mainz, 89, 100, 135
Mandrel, 139, 171, 172
Mannheim, 59, 71, 78, 80, 89, 92, 93, 120, 132, 135
Massey, Group Captain, 94
Master bomber, 107
May, Bob, 37
Mazingarbe, 65
Meaulte-Albert, 65
Messerschmitt: Bf/Me 109, 63, 64, 65, 66, 72, 96, 124; Bf 110, 57, 59, 68, 93, 95, 96, 107, 122, 134, 141, 165–6
Milan, 104
Mining, 78, 88, 90, 100, 101, 103, 104, 107, 118, 120, 122, 135, 137, 138, 139
Modane, 132, 133
Monica, 118
Mont Candon, 139, 140
Mont Cenis, 133, 134
Montdidier, 139
Montluçon, 124, 132, 133
Mousetrap, 118
Mülheim, 124
München Gladbach, 132
Munich, 100, 118
Munster, 76

Nieuport, 78
Nijkerk, 19
Normandy invasion, 155
Nuremberg, 70, 78, 118, 132

Oboe, 117, 118, 127
Oistreham, 156
Operation: *Amherst*, 177; *Bedlam*, 98; *Fuller*, 80; *Haphazard*, 104; *Mallard*, 157; *Millennium/1,000 Plan*, 92–4; *Oiled*, 76, 80; *Pandemonium*, 98, 102; *Ramrod*, 139, 140; *Scuttle*, 80; *Starkey*, 133; *Tonga*, 155; *Varsity*, 174–7; *Veracity II*, 76
Operations, sorties, 100, 107, 108, 115,
117, 118, 120, 121, 122, 124, 126, 127, 128, 129, 130, 132, 134, 137; *see also* Appendix 6
Operations, loss rates, 94, 98, 101, 103, 104, 105, 108, 115, 116, 117, 118, 119, 120, 122, 124, 126, 127, 130, 132
Osnabruck, 80, 100,
Ostend, 71

Parker, John Lankester, 31
Pathfinder Force, 100, 104, 117, 118, 120, 124, 127, 135
Payne, J., 153
Peenemünde, 130
Phillips, S., 90
Pilot Officer: Barr, 76; Baylie, G. C., 74; Beberfeld, 162, 165; Bennett, R. F., 117; Blunden, K. O., 65; Boylson, 105; Buck, P. J., 121; Campbell, 59, 63, 65, 66; Crebbin, W. N., 68; Gledding, W. N., 102; Gould, 68; Herad, G. T., 74; Hincks, E. D., 163; Jones, 69, 80; Kirkham, W., 167; Macdonald, G. W., 128; Mitchell, G. E., 74; Morley, 65; Needham, 65, 66; Parkins, D. A., 75; Peel, D. M., 165; Pilling, H. G., 74; Robson, D., 158; Runciman, 94; Sellers, 162; Selman, C. L., 102; Shippard, 122; Shoemaker, 98; Steel, J. M., 101; Stokes, 64; Studd, 104; Taylor, N. C., 88; Trott, L. G., 105; Vance, E. R., 142; Wallis, 133; Witt, D. T., 64, 68; Young, G. W., 122
Pilsen, 70, 78, 89
Poissy, 88
Portal, Air Chief Marshal Sir Charles, 48

Rees, 174
Remscheid, 126, 127
Rimeux, 139
Rochester/Short Bros., 30, 36, 38, 40, 72, 133, 148, 150
Rostock, 89, 120
Rotterdam, 48, 49, 56, 59, 80
Rousseauville, 139

Saarbrucken, 100
St. Nazaire, 88, 93, 115, 116, 118
Savona, 104
Scharnhorst, 57, 66, 67, 74, 80
Sebro, 78, 80, 89, 90, 91, 94
Sergeant: Ashton, E. V., 63; Barrett, D. R., 95, 98; Cappell, 66; Carney, W. C., 124; Coeshott, 158, 162; Cotton, H. C., 74; Davine, W., 122;

Davis, 93; Deville, 70; Doig, C., 124;
Edwards, I. J., 101–2; Farley, 142;
Flemming, 98; Franklin, B. A. F., 105,
107; Graham, A. J., 63; Griggs, 96;
Hartstein, 127; Hayward, 74;
Hotchkiss, A. H., 89, 94; Hyder, L. A.,
106; Inman, 74; Irwin, 115; Jones, 66;
Krulicki, L., 142; Lees, 141;
McCarthy, 52; Macree, 68; Madgwick,
B., 64; Mallett, 101; Matkin, S. G., 70,
74, 80; Mitchell, J. R., 122; Needham,
60, 65; Nicholls, T. J., 124; O'Connell,
P., 124; O'Hara, 96; Poole, J., 131;
Prosser, T., 96; Richards, L. T., 104;
Runciman, 89; Sewell, 96; Smith, 166;
Smith, D. V., 141; Smith, J. M., 74, 78;
Spanton, 118; Steel, J. M., 124;
Taunton, 66; Taylor, 72; Templeman,
93; Thorpe, F. A., 102; Todd, E. R.,
121; Tourville, 68–9; Ward, 64;
Watson, 96; Wildey, 96
Serviceability levels, 33, 37, 40, 46, 50, 67,
80, 81, 89, 90, 91, 92
Short & Harland/Belfast, 37, 38, 94, 148,
149
S.O.E. operations, 135, 138, 154, 155,
158, 177
Sorley, Air Chief Marshal Sir Ralph, 83,
86
Squadron Leader: Abecassis, 169; Blake,
W. A., 142; Boggis, P. J. S., 75, 78, 80;
Bribbin, 106; Button, J. J. M., 172;
Cleaver, R. W. F., 165, 167; English,
R., 115; Foulsham, J. F., 68; Freeman,
M. I., 134; Gilliard, 154, 158, 162;
Gilmour, 93, 94; Griffith-Jones, 52;
Hall, J. C., 78–9; Jennens, W. V., 74;
Legh-Smith, 88; Lynch-Blosse, 45, 52,
56, 58, 59, 60; McCleod, D. I., 69;
Menaul, 58, 64; Moreton, E. J., 31;
Morris, 58; Oldroyd, 89; Overton, J.,
139, Pettit, 156; Piper, T. W., 64, 65;
Robertson, A. F., 56; Searle, W. T. C.,
58, 63; Sellick, B. D., 74; Speare,
R. D., 60, 63, 68, 69; Speir, 174;
Swales, 74
Squadrons using Stirling
7: 37, 40, 45, 46, 47, 48, 50, 52, 56, 57,
58, 59, 60, 62, 63, 64, 65, 66, 70, 71,
72, 74, 80, 87, 88, 92, 93, 94, 100,
103, 104, 105, 106, 107, 115, 118,
120, 121, 127, 130–1, 141
XV: 57, 58, 59, 60, 62, 63, 64, 65, 66,
68, 69, 70, 71, 72, 74, 75, 76, 78, 80,
87, 88, 92, 93, 94, 98, 100, 101, 104,
105, 106, 107, 108, 115, 120, 128,
129, 132, 135
46: 180
51: 181, 182
75: 105, 107, 108, 115, 117, 119, 121,
122, 124, 128, 131, 132, 133, 138
90: 20, 108, 115, 122, 124, 130, 132,
134, 136, 138, 139
101: 93
115: 108, 116
138: 135, 169
148: 171
149: 70, 80, 88, 92, 93, 94, 98, 104, 107,
108, 115, 118, 128, 130, 133, 138,
139, 140
158: 181, 182
161: 135, 169
171: 172
190: 152, 154, 155, 156, 158, 159, 160,
161, 162, 163, 165, 166, 172, 175
196: 135, 136, 152, 154, 155, 157, 158,
159, 163, 165, 172, 174, 175, 182
199: 124, 138, 171, 172
214: 93, 94, 95, 96, 98, 100, 103, 104,
106, 107, 115, 118, 124, 128, 129,
132, 136, 140
218: 87, 88, 89, 92, 94, 98, 103, 105,
106, 107, 115, 118, 124, 128, 129,
132, 136, 140
242: 180, 181
295: 158, 159, 160, 161, 163, 165, 172,
175
299: 152, 155, 156, 157, 159, 161, 163,
165, 166, 174, 175, 177
513: 133, 136
570: 158, 159, 160, 161, 165, 166, 172,
174, 175, 177
620: 124, 130, 135, 136, 152, 153, 154,
155, 156, 158, 159, 163, 165, 166,
167, 172, 174, 175
622: 128, 129, 135
623: 129, 136
624: 171
see also Appendices 2 and 4
Stettin, 141
Stirling: armament, 42, 44, 54, 60, 62, 69,
76, 81, 91. 92, 97, 109, 110, 115, 118, 121,
132; bomb loads, 21, 23, 27, 40, 42, 44,
49, 67, 68, 76, 82, 92, 94, 103, 104, 115,
117, 122, 127, 130, 131, 134, 135, 172,
174; half-scale, 25, 27–9; performance,
21, 25, 26, 27, 28, 30, 34, 35, 36, 41, 43,
44, 69, 87, 109, 110, 112; possible new
roles, 128; undercarriage, 37, 42, 44,
49, 50, 52, 53, 54, 95; Mk. II, 110; Mk.

III, 82, 86, 87, 108, 109, 110, 112, 115, 121, 129; Mk. IV performance, conversions, 148, 149, 150, 152–4, 159–69, 172; Mk. V, 148, 149, 179–83
Stuttgart, 104, 118, 120

Tinsel, 130
Tirpitz, 76, 80
Tours, 155
T.R.E., 67
Trinity, 72, 74
Turin, 69, 80, 104, 105, 106, 107, 129

Vegesack, 98, 102
Ventral guns, 118, 128, 133
Volvorde, 138

Walliker, Phyllis, 78, 90
Warnemünde, 92
Warrant Officer: Azouz, M., 165; Cowlrick, 94; Ellis, 156; McGovern, J., 174; Morris, 166; Nicholls, W., 80; Pelater, 162; Taylor, N. L., 74

Wilhelmshaven, 76, 97, 115
Wimeraux Capelle, 140
Window, 126, 127, 130, 135, 138, 139, 171
Wing Commander: Baker, 174; Bangay, R. J. M., 158; Bunker, R. H., 172; Burton, H., 180; Coventry, B. A., 180; Crompton, 136; Dale, H. R., 58, 59, 60; Graham, H. R., 57, 63, 64, 65, 68, 69, 70, 72, 74, 88, 106; Harris, P., 37, 45, 48, 50, 52, 57; Harrison, G. E., 133, 154, 158, 165; Hodder, 93; Hutton, 82; Kerr, B. R., 103; Lay, D. H., 104; Lee, D. H., 124; 166; Macdonald, 89, 93, 94; Mitchell, V., 105, 108; Ogilvie, P. B., 60, 74, 78; Pickford, M. E., 139; Standbury, C. S. G., 171; Strange, 106; Wigfall, C. R. B., 133
Wire throttle control, 110
Wuppertal, 122, 124

Yainville, 65